The Windows 2000 Active Directory Services Infrastructure Cram Sheet

This Cram Sheet contains the distilled, key facts about the Directory Services Infrastructure exam. Review this information last thing before entering the testing center, paying special attention to those areas where you feel you need the most review. You can transfer any of the facts onto a blank piece of paper before beginning the exam.

INSTALLING, CONFIGURING, AND TROUBLESHOOTING ACTIVE DIRECTORY

1. Active Directory can be installed in one of two ways:
   - With the `dcpromo.exe` command
   - By using the Configure Your Server administrative tool
2. Verify Active Directory installation by checking for SRV and A records on the DNS server for the new domain controller.
3. Active Directory initially installs in mixed mode; if you want to change it to native mode, you must do so manually.
4. Once converted to native mode, a domain cannot revert to mixed mode to support NT 4 domain controllers.
5. Perform an authoritative restore by booting the computer in Directory Services Repair Mode and running `ntdsutil.exe`.
6. New sites are configured through Active Directory Sites and Services.
7. After creating a new site, you must complete the following tasks:
   - Add appropriate IP subnets to the site.
   - Install or move a domain controller or controllers into the site. Although a domain controller is not required for a site, it is strongly recommended.
   - Connect the site to other sites with the appropriate site link.
   - Select a server to control and monitor licensing within the site.
8. All site links are bridged by default.
9. Site link bridges can be explicitly defined if a network is not fully routed.
10. Inbound replication can be configured through connection objects.
11. The Knowledge Consistency Checker (KCC) maintains schedules and settings for default site links and bridges. Administrator-configured connection objects require manual configuration and maintenance.
12. Cost is used to determine which path to take between sites when multiple links exist.
13. Global Catalog (GC) servers maintain a read-only subset of information in the complete Active Directory database.
14. To configure a server as a GC server, use Active Directory Sites and Services. Select the desired domain controller and then right-click NTDS Settings and choose Properties. Check the box for Global Catalog.
15. Use the Windows 2000 Backup utility to back up the AD system state data.
16. Use authoritative restore when you want your restored settings to overwrite existing AD settings on other domain controllers, such as if an object (OU, user account, and so on) is accidentally deleted from the database.
17. Use nonauthoritative restore when you are restoring out-of-date information and want the restored data to be overwritten by newer data stored in Active Directory on other domain controllers. For example, you would do this if you were recovering a DC from a failed hard drive and restored the server.

18. All domains in a tree automatically establish two-way trust relationships called *Kerberos trusts*.
19. Trust relationships between Windows 2000 domains and NT 4 domains must be configured manually, just as you would configure a trust relationship between two NT 4 domains.

INSTALLING, CONFIGURING, MANAGING MONITORING, AND TROUBLESHOOTING DNS FOR ACTIVE DIRECTORY

20. Caching servers do not store an editable copy of the zone database.
21. Active Directory integrated zones can reside only on domain controllers, not member servers or non–Windows 2000 servers of any kind (NT 4, Unix, and so on).
22. If a user who is trying to log on gets an error that a domain controller cannot be found, check for the presence of SRV records in the DNS database for domain controllers.
23. Secure dynamic updates allow only computers and users who have been given permission to update their records into the DNS database.
24. Secure dynamic update is supported only for Active Directory integrated zones.
25. DNS replication is accomplished through Active Directory replication for AD integrated zones and zone transfer for standard zones.
26. A reverse lookup zone must be configured in order to perform reverse lookup queries.
27. Installing AD through Configure Your Server does *not* create a reverse lookup zone in DNS.
28. Windows 2000 DHCP can act as a proxy for non–Windows 2000 clients to support dynamic updates into the DNS database.
29. DHCP is required to support dynamic updates.

INSTALLING, CONFIGURING, MANAGING, MONITORING, OPTIMIZING, AND TROUBLESHOOTING CHANGE AND CONFIGURATION MANAGEMENT

30. The No Override setting takes precedence over Block Policy Inheritance.
31. Group Policy settings are applied in the following order:
    - Local
    - Site
    - Domain
    - OU
32. Local policy will always override global policy settings.
33. Unless modified through Block Policy Inheritance or No Override, OU policies overwrite domain policies and domain policies overwrite site policies.
34. Group Policy Objects are linked to sites, domains, and OUs, never directly to security groups.
35. The policies configured in a GPO cannot be selectively applied—it's all or nothing.
36. Create GPOs through Active Directory Users and Computers; edit GPOs with the Group Policy Editor (MMC snap-in).
37. Apply Group Policy and Read are the required permissions to receive the effects of a GPO.
38. Scripts are processed in the following order:
    - Startup
    - Logon
    - Logoff
    - Shutdown
39. Create a RIS boot disk for supported network adapters through the `rbfg.exe` utility.
40. RIPrep is used to create custom installation images. Run it on a Windows 2000 Professional system from a Windows 2000 RIS server (that is, `\\server\riprep.exe` from the Run line on a workstation).
41. An active DHCP server must exist on the same subnet as a RIS client for RIS to work.
42. Running RISetup after installing the RIS service creates a CD-based RIS installation image.
43. If you need to support a few Windows 2000 systems that have hardware not contained by the majority of RIS clients, simply use a CD-based image in the appropriate language.
44. RIS clients must either have a network adapter that supports PXE or be directly supported by the RIS boot disk.
45. Deploy software through the Software Installation extension in the Group Policy Editor.
46. Published applications are available for the user to install through Add/Remove Programs.
47. Published applications, by default, are not configured to auto-install, although they can be configured to auto-install through the package properties.
48. Assigned applications appear in the user's Start menu and/or desktop and automatically install when launched.
49. Assigned applications can be uninstalled by the user but will reinstall themselves after the user logs off and logs back in. Assigned applications are said to be "sticky" applications.
50. Published applications can be uninstalled by the user if so desired.
51. Software deployment problems are almost always attributable to permissions or missing, corrupt, or unavailable source files.

Windows® 2000 Active Directory Services Infrastructure

Peter Bruzzese, David Watts, Will Willis

Windows® 2000 Active Directory Services Infrastructure Exam Cram 2 (Exam 70-217)

International Standard Book Number: 0-7897-2871-0

Library of Congress Catalog Card Number: 2003100806

Printed in the United States of America

First Printing: March 2003

04 03 02 01 4 3 2 1

Trademarks

All terms mentioned in this book that are known to be trademarks or service marks have been appropriately capitalized. Que cannot attest to the accuracy of this information. Use of a term in this book should not be regarded as affecting the validity of any trademark or service mark.

Warning and Disclaimer

Every effort has been made to make this book as complete and as accurate as possible, but no warranty or fitness is implied. The information provided is on an "as is" basis. The author(s) and the publisher shall have neither liability nor responsibility to any person or entity with respect to any loss or damages arising from the information contained in this book or from the use of the CD or programs accompanying it.

Associate Publisher
Paul Boger

Executive Editor
Jeff Riley

Acquisitions Editor
Jeff Riley

Managing Editor
Charlotte Clapp

Project Editor
Tricia Liebig

Copy Editor
Bart Reed

Indexer
Kelly Castell

Proofreader
Jessica McCarty

Team Coordinator
Rosemary Lewis

Multimedia Developer
Dan Scherf

Interior Designer
Gary Adair

Graphics
Tammy Graham

Que Certification • 201 West 103rd Street • Indianapolis, Indiana 46290

A Note from Series Editor Ed Tittel

You know better than to trust your certification preparation to just anybody. That's why you, and more than two million others, have purchased an Exam Cram book. As Series Editor for the new and improved Exam Cram 2 series, I have worked with the staff at Que Certification to ensure you won't be disappointed. That's why we've taken the world's best-selling certification product—a finalist for "Best Study Guide" in a CertCities reader poll in 2002—and made it even better.

As a "Favorite Study Guide Author" finalist in a 2002 poll of CertCities readers, I know the value of good books. You'll be impressed with Que Certification's stringent review process, which ensures the books are high-quality, relevant, and technically accurate. Rest assured that at least a dozen industry experts—including the panel of certification experts at CramSession—have reviewed this material, helping us deliver an excellent solution to your exam preparation needs.

We've also added a preview edition of PrepLogic's powerful, full-featured test engine, which is trusted by certification students throughout the world.

As a 20-year-plus veteran of the computing industry and the original creator and editor of the Exam Cram series, I've brought my IT experience to bear on these books. During my tenure at Novell from 1989 to 1994, I worked with and around its excellent education and certification department. This experience helped push my writing and teaching activities heavily in the certification direction. Since then, I've worked on more than 70 certification-related books, and I write about certification topics for numerous Web sites and for *Certification* magazine.

In 1996, while studying for various MCP exams, I became frustrated with the huge, unwieldy study guides that were the only preparation tools available. As an experienced IT professional and former instructor, I wanted "nothing but the facts" necessary to prepare for the exams. From this impetus, Exam Cram emerged in 1997. It quickly became the best-selling computer book series since "*...For Dummies*," and the best-selling certification book series ever. By maintaining an intense focus on subject matter, tracking errata and updates quickly, and following the certification market closely, Exam Cram was able to establish the dominant position in cert prep books.

You will not be disappointed in your decision to purchase this book. If you are, please contact me at etittel@jump.net. All suggestions, ideas, input, or constructive criticism are welcome!

Ed Tittel

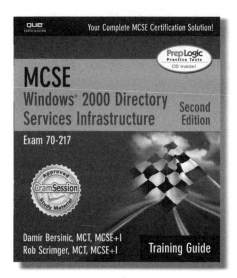

About the Author

David V. Watts (MCSE, MCSD, CNE, Network+) is currently employed by Hilton Computer Strategies in Houston, TX. David is from Basildon, Essex, in England. He has worked in the United States since 1988, as both a consultant and a project lead on enterprise-level deployments of Microsoft technologies.

David has been working with Windows 2000 since the first betas. He has specific expertise in Microsoft BackOffice products, including Systems Management Server, Microsoft SQL Server, and Microsoft Exchange. David is currently a Director for the European Operations of Altiris, a systems-management software vendor. When David is not working on technology, he can be found listening to music. You can reach David at `dwatts@wt.net`.

Will Willis (MCSE, A+ Certified Technician, Network+, B.A.) is an MIS Director/Network Manager responsible for a switched/routed 10/100MB Ethernet and Frame Relay TCP/IP LAN/WAN that connects multiple sites in Texas. Responsibilities include departmental management, vendor relations (negotiating and securing goods and services as needed), and administering/managing the entire network. Administration includes responsibility for documentation, establishing corporate standard operating procedures, maintaining disaster-recovery preparedness, antivirus strategies, firewalls/network security, infrastructure (servers, routers, switches, hubs, and so on) maintenance and upgrades, and ensuring the reliability and availability of network resources.

Will started out as a help desk tech, providing technical support over the phone for PC hardware and software and later moved up to a desktop/LAN support specialist position working on a team of eight to support a 3000+ user multiple-site network. From that position he moved into his current one, where Will also administers Windows 2000 and NT 4.0 servers running BackOffice applications, Exchange Server, IIS, Site Server, SQL Server, and SMS. He can be reached at `WWillis@Inside-Corner.com` and enjoys spending time with his family and writing and recording original music when not busy being a techie. His first album, *Darkness into Light*, was released in late 2002. More information on Will can be found at `www.willwillis.us`.

Peter Bruzzese (MCSE NT/2000, MCSA, MCT, CCNA, CNA, A+, Network+, iNET+, Master CIW) is an Associate Partner with BrainCore.Net. He recently co-authored the book *Windows 2000: Enterprise Storage Solutions*, published by Sybex, Inc., as part of the new *Mark Minasi Series*. He has served on the Storage Network Industry Association Education Committee and has taught classes for New Horizons of Princeton, NJ and CommVault Systems. In addition, Peter writes articles and reviews for *MCP Magazine* and CertCities.com and is a speaker for the biannual MCP TechMentor Conferences.

Acknowledgments

I would like to thank my wife, Siobhan Chamberlin, for our years together. They have been wonderful times. I would like to thank my parents for always being there and for understanding that I am sometimes too busy to get to the telephone. To my family, John and Catherine—and to their families—I miss you all! I want to acknowledge others who have affected me through the years. To Siobhan's mother and brother—Moira and Peter—you are forever on our minds. To Siobhan's father, whom I never got to meet, I know your family thinks of you always.

As well as family, there have been many others who have in so many ways helped me learn, laugh through troubled times, or have had confidence in me. To Zevi Mehlman, who makes me laugh at the end of the day, to Michael Cook, lifelong friend keeping the bar tab at Basildon, Essex. To David Aldridge, who worries about all the things that keep the wheels oiled in Houston.

I would like to thank all those who currently form part of my team, including Bertram Rawe, Ester, Justin, and Lorena. Not forgetting the support team (Younass, Dennis, Scott, John, and Michael). In the U.S. we call upon Ron Porter, Dan Baker, Robert Rose, and Bill Herman. Above all, special mention to Volker Wiora. Volker has been a great colleague and leader.

I would like to thank all the musicians who will never read this book but have helped me during the long hours. To Tim Berne, Jacky Terrasson, Richard Thompson, Tom Verlaine, Karlheinz Stockhausen, Phillip Glass, Steve Reich, Earthworks, Gavin Bryars, Joe Lovano, Paul Bley, Gary Peacock, Gary Thomas, Dave Holland, Greg Osby, Keith Jarrett, Kronos Quartet, Brad Mehldau, to name a few! Music is the purest of escapes. Whenever I find time to simply sit and listen, I am never less than enthralled. To all the musicians who help me through both good times and bad—thank you!

As I get older, I realize that I must take time to cherish all the things I have and all the people that are part of who I am. Sometimes people can touch you in the briefest space of time, but their influence can be lifelong. So many people have helped me along the way that there is no space to thank them all. Some were teachers, some colleagues, but none have been disposable. To my grandparents who are no longer with us, I wish I could have known you better—but I still think of you. To lost family friends, thank you for contributing in any small way to helping me be what I am today. Writing acknowledgments is a humbling experience, because you realize there are so many people to reach out to. Sadly, some are no longer here to thank. But you live on in those you taught, mentored, or touched—and that is the greatest legacy any of us can hope for. Never gone, never forgotten.

—David V. Watts

I'd like to take a moment to acknowledge some of the people who have made an impact on my life and the person I've turned out to be, in no particular order.

Ozzie Smith and Larry Bird, for showing me that excellence on the playing field of life requires countless hours of hard work behind the scenes that no one ever sees or appreciates. Success on "game day" is usually determined by your advance preparation.

Yngwie J. Malmsteen, Fates Warning, and Dream Theater—musical influences that have really lit my creative fire over the years and taught me to bring passion and inspiration to everything I do, and to not always follow the status quo.

Grover Cleveland, the great President who fought the intense resistance to leaving the gold standard, forever changing the U.S. economy and making a huge world impact. To stand by your vision when everyone says you're wrong takes tremendous confidence and determination.

Herb Kelleher, Southwest Airlines CEO, who has recognized that people are his company's greatest asset. Loyalty and commitment from him has bred loyalty and commitment from his employees, an example that more companies should follow and one I hope to foster as a leader in my own company.

Andrew Carnegie, the richest man in the world during his lifetime, for the conviction that the "surplus wealth which a man accumulates in a community is only a sacred trust to be administered for the good of the community in which it was accumulated." An admirable philosophy of using one's own good fortune for the benefit of others.

Jesus Christ, the light in an increasingly darkening world. Through him hope never fades and life is eternal.

"Let's stare the problem right in the eye…racing the clock to please everyone, all but the one who matters the most"—a favorite quote that reminds me not to overcommit myself and lose focus on the person who matters the most to me, Melissa.

—Will Willis

I usually take the time in acknowledgements to thank all those persons who have helped me put this book together and pushed it forward to conclusion. So, with that I'd like to thank David Fugate and the folks at Waterside. I'd like to thank Jeff Riley and the folks at Que: Carol Bowers, Tricia Liebig, Bart Reed, Kelly Castell, Jessica McCarty, and Tim Osborn.

I'd like to thank a great group of guys I've been working with of late: Don Jones, Jeremy Moskowitz, and Derek Melber. These are the founding partners of BrainCore.Net, and I am pleased to serve with them as an Associate Partner. As Don likes to say, "Good things happen to good people," and that may in fact be true.

In addition, I'd like to thank Tim Duggan for his working with me over the years on a variety of projects. Tim, you are well beyond your years in the field, and I've enjoyed working with you. I'd like to thank Chris Wolf for working with me on a bunch of projects, everything from writing to teaching. It was nice to have a kindred spirit to work with, someone as work oriented (more so at times) as me.

This may be my last piece of writing for a while. I may write again, but I have other plans on my agenda currently and so I'd like to take this time to also thank my friends who have always encouraged me toward reaching my goals. I have friends in both my younger years and now as an adult who have stuck close to me and set good examples to follow and learn from. I appreciate all of you and hope to continue to be successful in my true vocation.

Finally, I'd like to thank my wife. I dedicate all my books to her because she really is the key to any success that I have obtained, although I've run out of witty "dedication" sayings to put at the beginning of a book. Without her confidence in me, her support and her love for me, I would, most definitely, be schlepping my way into Manhattan every day, squeaking out a living at the hands of the corporate giants.

—Peter Bruzzese

Contents at a Glance

Table of Contents

We Want to Hear from You!

As the reader of this book, *you* are our most important critic and commentator. We value your opinion and want to know what we're doing right, what we could do better, what areas you'd like to see us publish in, and any other words of wisdom you're willing to pass our way.

As an executive editor for Que Certification, I welcome your comments. You can email or write me directly to let me know what you did or didn't like about this book—as well as what we can do to make our books better.

Please note that I cannot help you with technical problems related to the *topic* of this book. We do have a User Services group, however, where I will forward specific technical questions related to the book.

When you write, please be sure to include this book's title and author as well as your name, email address, and phone number. I will carefully review your comments and share them with the author and editors who worked on the book.

Email: `feedback@quepublishing.com`

Mail: Jeff Riley
Que Publishing
201 West 103rd Street
Indianapolis, IN 46290 USA

For more information about this book or another Que title, visit our Web site at `www.quepublishing.com`. Type the ISBN (excluding hyphens) or the title of a book in the Search field to find the page you're looking for.

Introduction

Welcome to *MCSE Windows 2000 Active Directory Services Infrastructure Exam Cram 2*! Whether this is your first or your fifteenth *Exam Cram 2* book, you'll find information here and in Chapter 1, "Microsoft Certification Exams," that will help ensure your success as you pursue knowledge, experience, and certification. This book aims to help you get ready to take—and pass—Microsoft Certification Exam 70-217, "Implementing and Administering a Microsoft Windows 2000 Directory Services Infrastructure." This Introduction explains Microsoft's certification programs in general and talks about how the *Exam Cram 2* series can help you prepare for Microsoft's Windows 2000 certification exams.

Exam Cram 2 books help you understand and appreciate the subjects and materials you need to pass Microsoft certification exams. *Exam Cram 2* books are aimed strictly at test preparation and review. They do not teach you everything you need to know about a topic. Instead, we (the authors) present and dissect the questions and problems we've found that you're likely to encounter on a test. We've worked to bring together as much information as possible about Microsoft certification exams.

Nevertheless, to completely prepare yourself for any Microsoft test, we recommend that you begin by taking the Self-Assessment included in this book immediately following this Introduction. This tool will help you evaluate your knowledge base against the requirements for an MCSE under both ideal and real circumstances.

Based on what you learn from that exercise, you might decide to begin your studies with some classroom training or some background reading. On the other hand, you might decide to pick up and read one of the many study guides available from Microsoft or third-party vendors on certain topics, including Que's *Training Guide* series. We also recommend that you supplement your study program with visits to ExamCram.com to receive additional practice questions, get advice, and track the Windows 2000 MCSE program.

We also strongly recommend that you install, configure, and fool around with the software you'll be tested on, because nothing beats hands-on experience and familiarity when it comes to understanding the questions you're likely to encounter on a certification test. Book learning is essential, but hands-on experience is the best teacher of all!

The Microsoft Certified Professional (MCP) Program

The MCP Program currently includes the following separate tracks, each of which boasts its own special acronym (as a certification candidate, you need to have a high tolerance for alphabet soup of all kinds):

- **MCP (Microsoft Certified Professional)**—This is the least prestigious of all the certification tracks from Microsoft. Passing one of the major Microsoft exams qualifies an individual for the MCP credential. Individuals can demonstrate proficiency with additional Microsoft products by passing additional certification exams.
- **MCP+SB (Microsoft Certified Professional + Site Building)**—This certification program is designed for individuals who are planning, building, managing, and maintaining Web sites. Individuals with the MCP+SB credential will have demonstrated the ability to develop Web sites that include multimedia and searchable content and Web sites that connect to and communicate with a back-end database. It requires one MCP exam, plus two of these three exams: "70-055: Designing and Implementing Web Sites with Microsoft FrontPage 98," "70-057: Designing and Implementing Commerce Solutions with Microsoft Site Server, 3.0, Commerce Edition," and "70-152: Designing and Implementing Web Solutions with Microsoft Visual InterDev 6.0."
- **MCSE (Microsoft Certified Systems Engineer)**—Anyone who has a current MCSE is warranted to possess a high level of networking expertise with Microsoft operating systems and products. This credential is designed to prepare individuals to plan, implement, maintain, and support information systems, networks, and internetworks built around Microsoft Windows 2000 and its BackOffice Server 2000 family of products.

  To obtain an MCSE, an individual must pass four core operating system exams, one optional core exam, and two elective exams. The operating system exams require individuals to prove their competence with desktop and server operating systems and networking/internetworking components.

For Windows NT 4 MCSEs, the Accelerated Exam, "70-240: Microsoft Windows 2000 Accelerated Exam for MCPs Certified on Microsoft Windows NT 4.0," is an option. This free exam covers all the material tested in the Core Four exams. The hitch in this plan is that you can take the test only once. If you fail, you must take all four core exams to recertify. The Core Four exams are "70-210: Installing, Configuring, and Administering Microsoft Windows 2000 Professional," "70-215: Installing, Configuring, and Administering Microsoft Windows 2000 Server," "70-216: Implementing and Administering a Microsoft Windows 2000 Network Infrastructure," and "70-217: Implementing and Administering a Microsoft Windows 2000 Directory Services Infrastructure."

To fulfill the fifth core exam requirement, you can choose from three design exams: "70-219: Designing a Microsoft Windows 2000 Directory Services Infrastructure," "70-220: Designing Security for a Microsoft Windows 2000 Network," or "70-221: Designing a Microsoft Windows 2000 Network Infrastructure." You are also required to take two elective exams. An elective exam can fall in any number of subject or product areas, primarily BackOffice Server 2000 components. The two design exams that you don't select as your fifth core exam also qualify as electives. If you are on your way to becoming an MCSE and have already taken some exams, visit `www.microsoft.com/trainingandservices/` for information about how to complete your MCSE certification.

New MCSE candidates must pass seven tests to meet the MCSE requirements. It's not uncommon for the entire process to take a year or so, and many individuals find that they must take a test more than once to pass. The primary goal of the *Training Guide* and *Exam Cram 2* test-preparation books is to make it possible, given proper study and preparation, to pass all Microsoft certification tests on the first try.

- **MCSD (Microsoft Certified Solution Developer)**—The MCSD credential reflects the skills required to create multitier, distributed, and COM-based solutions, in addition to desktop and Internet applications, using new technologies. To obtain an MCSD, an individual must demonstrate the ability to analyze and interpret user requirements; select and integrate products, platforms, tools, and technologies; design and implement code as well as customize applications; and perform necessary software tests and quality-assurance operations.

  To become an MCSD, you must pass a total of four exams: three core exams and one elective exam. Each candidate must choose one of these three desktop application exams—"70-016: Designing and Implementing Desktop Applications with Microsoft Visual C++ 6.0," "70-156: Designing and Implementing Desktop Applications with Microsoft Visual FoxPro 6.0," or "70-176: Designing and Implementing Desktop Applications with Microsoft Visual Basic 6.0"—*plus* one of these three distributed application exams: "70-015: Designing and Implementing Distributed Applications with Microsoft Visual C++ 6.0," "70-155: Designing and Implementing Distributed Applications with Microsoft Visual FoxPro 6.0," or "70-175: Designing and Implementing Distributed Applications with Microsoft Visual Basic 6.0." The third core exam is "70-100: Analyzing Requirements and Defining Solution Architectures." Elective exams cover specific Microsoft applications and languages, including Visual Basic, C++, the Microsoft Foundation Classes, Access, SQL Server, Excel, and more.

- **MCDBA (Microsoft Certified Database Administrator)**—The MCDBA credential reflects the skills required to implement and administer Microsoft SQL Server databases. To obtain an MCDBA, an individual must demonstrate the ability to derive physical database designs, develop logical data models, create physical databases, create data services by using Transact-SQL, manage and maintain databases, configure and manage security, monitor and optimize databases, and install and configure Microsoft SQL Server.

  To become an MCDBA, you must pass a total of four exams and one elective exam. The required core exams are "70-028: Administering Microsoft SQL Server 7.0," "70-029: Designing and Implementing Databases with Microsoft SQL Server 7.0," and "70-215: Installing, Configuring and Administering Microsoft Windows 2000 Server."

  The elective exams you can choose from cover specific uses of SQL Server and include "70-015: Designing and Implementing Distributed Applications with Microsoft Visual C++ 6.0," "70-019: Designing and Implementing Data Warehouses with Microsoft SQL Server 7.0," "70-155: Designing and Implementing Distributed Applications with Microsoft Visual FoxPro 6.0," "70-175: Designing and Implementing Distributed Applications with Microsoft Visual Basic 6.0," and two exams relate to Windows 2000: "70-216: Implementing and Administering a Microsoft Windows 2000 Network Infrastructure," and "70-087: Implementing and Supporting Microsoft Internet Information Server 4.0."

If you have taken the three core Windows NT 4 exams on your path to becoming an MCSE, you qualify for the Accelerated exam (it replaces the Network Infrastructure exam requirement). The Accelerated exam covers the objectives of all four of the Windows 2000 core exams. In addition to taking the Accelerated exam, you must take only the two SQL exams—Administering and Database Design.

- **MCT (Microsoft Certified Trainer)**—Microsoft Certified Trainers are deemed able to deliver elements of the official Microsoft curriculum, based on technical knowledge and instructional ability. Thus, it is necessary for an individual seeking MCT credentials (which are granted on a course-by-course basis) to pass the related certification exam for a course and complete the official Microsoft training in the subject area, as well as to demonstrate an ability to teach.

  This teaching skill criterion may be satisfied by proving that one has already attained training certification from Novell, Banyan, Lotus, the Santa Cruz Operation, or Cisco, or by taking a Microsoft-sanctioned workshop on instruction. Microsoft makes it clear that MCTs are important cogs in the Microsoft training channels. Instructors must be MCTs before Microsoft will allow them to teach in any of its official training channels, including Microsoft's affiliated Certified Technical Education Centers (CTECs) and its online training partner network. As of January 1, 2001, MCT candidates must also possess a current MCSE.

Once a Microsoft product becomes obsolete, MCPs typically have to recertify on current versions. (If individuals do not recertify, their certifications become invalid.) Because technology keeps changing and new products continually supplant old ones, this should come as no surprise. This explains why Microsoft has announced that MCSEs have 12 months past the scheduled retirement date for the Windows NT 4 exams to recertify on Windows 2000 topics. (Note that this means taking at least two exams, if not more.)

The best place to keep tabs on the MCP Program and its related certifications is on the Web. The URL for the MCP program is `www.microsoft.com/trainingandservices/`. But Microsoft's Web site changes often, so if this URL doesn't work, try using the Search tool on Microsoft's site with either "MCP" or the quoted phrase "Microsoft Certified Professional" as a search string. This will help you find the latest and most accurate information about Microsoft's certification programs.

Taking a Certification Exam

Once you've prepared for your exam, you need to register with a testing center. Each computer-based MCP exam costs $100, and if you don't pass, you may retest for an additional $100 for each additional try. In the United States and Canada, tests are administered by Prometric and by Virtual University Enterprises (VUE). Here's how you can contact them:

- **Prometric**—You can sign up for a test through the company's Web site at `www.prometric.com`. Or, you can register by phone at 800-755-3926 (within the United States and Canada) or at 410-843-8000 (outside the United States and Canada).
- **Virtual University Enterprises**—You can sign up for a test or get the phone numbers for local testing centers through the Web page at `www.vue.com/ms/`.

To sign up for a test, you must possess a valid credit card, or you can contact either company for mailing instructions to send in a check (in the U.S.). Only when payment is verified, or your check has cleared, can you actually register for a test.

To schedule an exam, call the number or visit either of the Web pages at least one day in advance. To cancel or reschedule an exam, you must call before 7 p.m. pacific standard time the day before the scheduled test time (or you may be charged, even if you don't appear to take the test). When you want to schedule a test, have the following information ready:

- Your name, organization, and mailing address.
- Your Microsoft Test ID. (Inside the United States, this means your Social Security number; citizens of other nations should call ahead to find out what type of identification number is required to register for a test.)
- The name and number of the exam you wish to take.
- A method of payment. (As we've already mentioned, a credit card is the most convenient method, but alternate means can be arranged in advance, if necessary.)

Once you sign up for a test, you'll be informed as to when and where the test is scheduled. Try to arrive at least 15 minutes early. You must supply two forms of identification—one of which must be a photo ID—to be admitted into the testing room.

All exams are completely closed-book. In fact, you will not be permitted to take anything with you into the testing area, but you will be furnished with a blank sheet of paper and a pen or, in some cases, an erasable plastic sheet and an erasable pen. We suggest that you immediately write down on that sheet of paper all the information you've memorized for the test. In *Exam Cram 2* books, this information appears on a tear-out sheet inside the front cover of each book. You will have some time to compose yourself, record this information, and take a sample orientation exam before you begin the real thing. We suggest you take the orientation test before taking your first exam, but because they're all more or less identical in layout, behavior, and controls, you probably won't need to do this more than once.

When you complete a Microsoft certification exam, the software will tell you whether you've passed or failed. If you need to retake an exam, you'll have to schedule a new test with Prometric or VUE and pay another $100.

The first time you fail a test, you can retake it the next day. However, if you fail a second time, you must wait 14 days before retaking that test. The 14-day waiting period remains in effect for all retakes after the second failure.

Tracking MCP Status

As soon as you pass any Microsoft exam (except Networking Essentials), you'll attain Microsoft Certified Professional (MCP) status. Microsoft also generates transcripts that indicate which exams you have passed. You can view a copy of your transcript at any time by going to the MCP secured site and selecting Transcript Tool. This tool will allow you to print a copy of your current transcript and confirm your certification status.

Once you pass the necessary set of exams, you'll be certified. Official certification normally takes anywhere from six to eight weeks, so don't expect to get your credentials overnight. When the package for a qualified certification arrives, it includes a Welcome Kit that contains a number of elements (see Microsoft's Web site for other benefits of specific certifications):

- A certificate suitable for framing, along with a wallet card and lapel pin.
- A license to use the MCP logo, thereby allowing you to use the logo in advertisements, promotions, and documents, and on letterhead, business cards, and so on. Along with the license comes an MCP logo sheet, which includes camera-ready artwork. (Note: Before using any of the artwork, individuals must sign and return a licensing agreement that indicates they'll abide by its terms and conditions.)

- A subscription to *Microsoft Certified Professional Magazine*, which provides ongoing data about testing and certification activities, requirements, and changes to the program.

Many people believe that the benefits of MCP certification go well beyond the perks that Microsoft provides to newly anointed members of this elite group. We're starting to see more job listings that request or require applicants to have an MCP, MCSE, and so on, and many individuals who complete the program can qualify for increases in pay and/or responsibility. As an official recognition of hard work and broad knowledge, one of the MCP credentials is a badge of honor in many IT organizations.

How to Prepare for an Exam

Preparing for any Windows 2000 Server–related test (including "Implementing and Administering a Microsoft Windows 2000 Directory Services Infrastructure") requires that you obtain and study materials designed to provide comprehensive information about the product and its capabilities that will appear on the specific exam for which you are preparing. The following list of materials will help you study and prepare:

- The Windows 2000 Server product CD includes comprehensive online documentation and related materials; it should be a primary resource when you are preparing for the test.
- The exam-preparation materials, practice tests, and self-assessment exams on the Microsoft Training & Services page at `www.microsoft.com/trainingandservices/default.asp?PageID=mcp`. The Testing Innovations link offers examples of the new question types found on the Windows 2000 MCSE exams. Find the materials, download them, and use them!
- The exam-preparation advice, practice tests, questions of the day, and discussion groups on the ExamCram.com e-learning and certification destination Web site (`www.examcram.com`).

In addition, you'll probably find any or all of the following materials useful in your quest for Directory Services Infrastructure expertise:

- **Microsoft training kits**—Microsoft Press offers a training kit that specifically targets Exam 70-217. For more information, visit `http://mspress.microsoft.com/findabook/list/series_ak.htm`. This training kit contains information that you will find useful in preparing for the test.

- **Microsoft TechNet CD**—This monthly CD-based publication delivers numerous electronic titles that include coverage of Directory Services Infrastructure and related topics on the Technical Information (TechNet) CD. Its offerings include product facts, technical notes, tools and utilities, and information on how to access the Seminars Online training materials for Directory Services Infrastructure. A subscription to TechNet costs $299 per year, but it is well worth the price. Visit `www.microsoft.com/technet/` and check out the information under the "TechNet Subscription" menu entry for more details.
- **Study guides**—Several publishers—including Que—offer Windows 2000 titles. Que Certification includes the following:
    - **The *Exam Cram 2* series**—These books give you information about the material you need to know to pass the tests.
    - **The *Training Guide* series**—These books provide a greater level of detail than the *Exam Cram 2* books and are designed to teach you everything you need to know from an exam perspective. Each book comes with a CD that contains interactive practice exams in a variety of testing formats.

Together, the two series make a perfect pair.

- **Multimedia**—The PrepLogic Practice Tests CD that comes with each Exam Cram and Training Guide features a powerful, state-of-the-art test engine that prepares you for the actual exam. PrepLogic Practice Tests are developed by certified IT professionals and are trusted by certification students around the world. For more information, visit `www.preplogic.com`.
- **Classroom training**—CTECs, online partners, and third-party training companies (such as Wave Technologies, Learning Tree, Data-Tech, and others) all offer classroom training on Windows 2000. These companies aim to help you prepare to pass Exam 70-217. Although such training runs upwards of $350 per day in class, most of the individuals lucky enough to partake find it to be quite worthwhile.
- **Other publications**—There's no shortage of materials available about Directory Services Infrastructure. The resource sections at the end of each chapter should give you an idea of where we think you should look for further discussion.

By far, this set of required and recommended materials represents a nonpareil collection of sources and resources for Directory Services

Infrastructure and related topics. We anticipate you'll find that this book belongs in this company.

About This Book

Each topical *Exam Cram 2* chapter follows a regular structure, along with graphical cues about important or useful information. Here's the structure of a typical chapter:

- **Opening hotlists**—Each chapter begins with a list of the terms, tools, and techniques you must learn and understand before you can be fully conversant with that chapter's subject matter. We follow the hotlists with one or two introductory paragraphs to set the stage for the rest of the chapter.
- **Topical coverage**—After the opening hotlists, each chapter covers a series of topics related to the chapter's subject title. Throughout this section, we highlight topics or concepts likely to appear on a test using a special Exam Alert layout, like this:

This is what an Exam Alert looks like. Normally, an Exam Alert stresses concepts, terms, software, or activities that are likely to relate to one or more certification test questions. For that reason, we think any information found offset in Exam Alert format is worthy of unusual attentiveness on your part. Indeed, most of the information that appears on The Cram Sheet appears as Exam Alerts within the text.

Pay close attention to material flagged as an Exam Alert; although all the information in this book pertains to what you need to know to pass the exam, we flag certain items that are really important. You'll find what appears in the meat of each chapter to be worth knowing, too, when preparing for the test. Because this book's material is very condensed, we recommend that you use this book along with other resources to achieve the maximum benefit.

In addition to the Exam Alerts, we have provided tips that will help you build a better foundation for Directory Services Infrastructure knowledge. Although the information may not be on the exam, it is certainly related and will help you become a better test-taker.

This is how tips are formatted. Keep your eyes open for these, and you'll become a Directory Services Infrastructure guru in no time!

- **Practice questions**—Although we talk about test questions and topics throughout the book, a section at the end of each chapter presents a series of mock test questions and explanations of both correct and incorrect answers.
- **Details and resources**—Every chapter ends with a section titled "Need to Know More?". This section provides direct pointers to Microsoft and third-party resources offering more details on the chapter's subject. In addition, this section tries to rank or at least rate the quality and thoroughness of the topic's coverage by each resource. If you find a resource you like in this collection, use it, but don't feel compelled to use all the resources. On the other hand, we recommend only resources we use on a regular basis, so none of our recommendations will be a waste of your time or money (but purchasing them all at once probably represents an expense that many network administrators and would-be MCPs and MCSEs might find hard to justify).

The bulk of the book follows this chapter structure slavishly, but there are a few other elements we'd like to point out. Chapter 16, "Sample Test," includes a sample test that provides a good review of the material presented throughout the book to ensure you're ready for the exam. Chapter 17, "Answer Key," is an answer key to these questions.

Finally, the tear-out Cram Sheet attached next to the inside front cover of this *Exam Cram 2* book represents a condensed and compiled collection of facts and tips we think you should memorize before taking the test. Because you can dump this information out of your head onto a piece of paper before taking the exam, you can master this information by brute force—you need to remember it only long enough to write it down when you walk into the test room. You might even want to look at it in the car or in the lobby of the testing center just before you walk in to take the test.

How to Use This Book

We've structured the topics in this book to build on one another. Therefore, some topics in later chapters make more sense after you've read earlier chapters. That's why we suggest you read this book from front to back for your initial test preparation. If you need to brush up on a topic or you have to bone up for a second try, use the index or table of contents to go straight to the topics and questions you need to study. Beyond helping you prepare for the test, we think you'll find this book useful as a tightly focused reference to some of the most important aspects of Directory Services Infrastructure.

Given all the book's elements and its specialized focus, we've tried to create a tool that will help you prepare for—and pass—Microsoft Exam 70-217. Please share your feedback on the book with us, especially if you have ideas about how we can improve it for future test-takers.

Send your questions or comments to us at `learn@examcram.com`. Please remember to include the title of the book in your message; otherwise, we'll be forced to guess which book you're writing about. And we don't like to guess—we want to *know*! Also, be sure to check out the Web pages at `www.examcram.com`, where you'll find information updates, commentary, and certification information.

Thanks, and enjoy the book!

Self-Assessment

The reason we included a Self-Assessment in this *Exam Cram 2* book is to help you evaluate your readiness to tackle MCSE certification. It should also help you understand what you need to know to master the topic of this book—namely, Exam 70-217, "Implementing and Administering a Microsoft Windows 2000 Directory Services Infrastructure." But before you tackle this Self-Assessment, let's talk about concerns you may face when pursuing an MCSE for Windows 2000, and what an ideal MCSE candidate might look like.

MCSEs in the Real World

In the next section, we describe an ideal MCSE candidate, knowing full well that only a few real candidates will meet this ideal. In fact, our description of that ideal candidate might seem downright scary, especially with the changes that have been made to the program over the years. But take heart: Although the requirements to obtain an MCSE may seem formidable, they are by no means impossible to meet. However, be keenly aware that it does take time, involves some expense, and requires real effort to get through the process.

Increasing numbers of people are attaining Microsoft certifications, so the goal is within reach. You can get all the real-world motivation you need from knowing that many others have gone before, so you will be able to follow in their footsteps. If you're willing to tackle the process seriously and do what it takes to obtain the necessary experience and knowledge, you can take—and pass—all the certification tests involved in obtaining an MCSE. In fact, we've designed *Training Guides*, the companion to the *Exam Cram 2* series, to make it as easy on you as possible to prepare for these exams. We've also greatly expanded our Web site, `www.examcram.com`, to provide a host of resources to help you prepare for the complexities of Windows 2000.

Besides MCSE, other Microsoft certifications include the following:

- MCSD, which is aimed at software developers and requires one specific exam, two more exams on client and distributed topics, plus a fourth elective exam drawn from a different, but limited, pool of options.
- Other Microsoft certifications, whose requirements range from one test (MCP) to several tests (MCP+SB, MCDBA).

The Ideal Windows 2000 MCSE Candidate

Just to give you some idea of what an ideal MCSE candidate is like, here are some relevant statistics about the background and experience such an individual might have. Don't worry if you don't meet these qualifications or don't even come that close—this is a far-from-ideal world, and where you fall short is simply where you'll have more work to do:

- Academic or professional training in network theory, concepts, and operations. This includes everything from networking media and transmission techniques through network operating systems, services, and applications.
- Three-plus years of professional networking experience, including experience with Ethernet, token ring, modems, and other networking media. This must include installation, configuration, upgrade, and troubleshooting experience.

The Windows 2000 MCSE program is rigorous; therefore, you'll really need some hands-on experience. Some of the exams require you to solve real-world case studies and network design issues, so the more hands-on experience you have, the better.

- Two-plus years in a networked environment that includes hands-on experience with Windows 2000 Server, Windows 2000 Professional, Windows NT Server, Windows NT Workstation, and Windows 95 or Windows 98. A solid understanding of each system's architecture, installation, configuration, maintenance, and troubleshooting is also essential.
- Knowledge of the various methods for installing Windows 2000, including manual and unattended installations.
- A thorough understanding of key networking protocols, addressing, and name resolution, including TCP/IP, IPX/SPX, and NetBEUI.

- A thorough understanding of NetBIOS naming, browsing, and file and print services.
- Familiarity with key Windows 2000–based TCP/IP-based services, including HTTP (Web servers), DHCP, WINS, and DNS, plus familiarity with one or more of the following: Internet Information Services (IIS), Index Server, and Internet Security and Acceleration Server.
- An understanding of how to implement security for key network data in a Windows 2000 environment.
- Working knowledge of NetWare 3.*x* and 4.*x*, including IPX/SPX frame formats, NetWare file, print, and directory services, and both Novell and Microsoft client software. Working knowledge of Microsoft's Client Service for NetWare (CSNW), Gateway Service for NetWare (GSNW), the NetWare Migration Tool (NWCONV), and the NetWare Client for Windows (NT, 95, and 98) is essential.
- A good working understanding of Active Directory. The more you work with Windows 2000, the more you'll realize that this operating system is quite different from Windows NT. Newer technologies such as Active Directory have really changed the way that Windows is configured and used. We recommend that you find out as much as you can about Active Directory and acquire as much experience using this technology as possible. The time you take learning about Active Directory will be time very well spent!

Fundamentally, this boils down to a bachelor's degree in computer science, plus three years' experience working in a position involving network design, installation, configuration, and maintenance. We believe that well under half of all certification candidates meet these requirements, and that, in fact, most meet less than half of these requirements—at least when they begin the certification process. But because all the people who already have been certified have survived this ordeal, you can survive it, too, especially if you heed what our Self-Assessment can tell you about what you already know and what you need to learn.

Put Yourself to the Test

The following series of questions and observations is designed to help you figure out how much work you must do to pursue Microsoft certification and what kinds of resources you may consult on your quest. Be absolutely honest in your answers; otherwise, you'll end up wasting money on exams you're not yet ready to take. There are no right or wrong answers, only steps along the path to certification. Only you can decide where you really belong in the broad spectrum of aspiring candidates.

Two things should be clear from the outset, however:

- Even a modest background in computer science will be helpful.
- Hands-on experience with Microsoft products and technologies is an essential ingredient to certification success.

Educational Background

1. Have you ever taken any computer-related classes? [Yes or No]

   If Yes, proceed to question 2; if No, proceed to question 4.

2. Have you taken any classes on computer operating systems? [Yes or No]

   If Yes, you will probably be able to handle Microsoft's architecture and system component discussions. If you're rusty, brush up on basic operating system concepts, especially virtual memory, multitasking regimes, user mode versus kernel mode operation, and general computer security topics.

   If No, consider some basic reading in this area. We strongly recommend a good general operating systems book, such as *Operating System Concepts, 5th Edition*, by Abraham Silberschatz and Peter Baer Galvin (John Wiley & Sons, 1998, ISBN 0-471-36414-2). If this title doesn't appeal to you, check out reviews for other, similar titles at your favorite online bookstore.

3. Have you taken any networking concepts or technologies classes? [Yes or No]

   If Yes, you will probably be able to handle Microsoft's networking terminology, concepts, and technologies (brace yourself for frequent departures from normal usage). If you're rusty, brush up on basic networking concepts and terminology, especially networking media, transmission types, the OSI Reference Model, and networking technologies such as Ethernet, token ring, FDDI, and WAN links.

   If No, you might want to read one or two books in this topic area. The two best books that we know of are *Computer Networks, 3rd Edition*, by Andrew S. Tanenbaum (Prentice-Hall, 1996, ISBN 0-13-349945-6) and

Computer Networks and Internets, 2nd Edition, by Douglas E. Comer (Prentice-Hall, 1998, ISBN 0-130-83617-6).

Skip to the next section, "Hands-on Experience."

4. Have you done any reading on operating systems or networks? [Yes or No]

   If Yes, review the requirements stated in the first paragraphs after questions 2 and 3. If you meet those requirements, move on to the next section. If No, consult the recommended reading for both topics. A strong background will help you prepare for the Microsoft exams better than just about anything else.

Hands-on Experience

The most important key to success on all the Microsoft tests is hands-on experience, especially with Windows 2000 Server and Professional, plus the many add-on services and BackOffice components around which so many of the Microsoft certification exams revolve. If we leave you with only one realization after taking this Self-Assessment, it should be that there's no substitute for time spent installing, configuring, and using the various Microsoft products upon which you'll be tested repeatedly and in depth.

5. Have you installed, configured, and worked with:

   - Windows 2000 Server? [Yes or No]

   If Yes, make sure you understand basic concepts as covered in Exam 70-215. You should also study the TCP/IP interfaces, utilities, and services for Exam 70-216, plus implementing security features for Exam 70-220.

   You can download objectives, practice exams, and other data about Microsoft exams from the Training and Certification page at `http://www.Microsoft.com/trainingandservices/default.asp?PageID=mcp/`. Use the "Exams" link to obtain specific exam information.

   If you haven't worked with Windows 2000 Server, you must obtain one or two machines and a copy of Windows 2000 Server. Then, learn the operating system and whatever other software components on which you'll also be tested.

   In fact, we recommend that you obtain two computers, each with a network interface, and set up a two-node network on which to practice. With decent Windows 2000–capable computers selling for about $500 to $600 apiece these days, this shouldn't be too much of a financial hardship. You may have to scrounge to come up with the necessary software, but if you scour the Microsoft Web site you can usually find low-cost options to obtain evaluation copies of most of the software you'll need.

- Windows 2000 Professional? [Yes or No]

  If Yes, make sure you understand the concepts covered in Exam 70-210.

  If No, you will want to obtain a copy of Windows 2000 Professional and learn how to install, configure, and maintain it. You can use *MCSE Windows 2000 Professional Exam Cram 2* (ISBN 0-7897-2872-9) to guide your activities and studies, or you can work straight from Microsoft's test objectives if you prefer.

  For any and all of these Microsoft exams, the Resource Kits for the topics involved are a good study resource. You can purchase soft cover Resource Kits from Microsoft Press (search for them at `http://mspress.microsoft.com/`), but they also appear on the TechNet CDs (`www.microsoft.com/technet`). Along with the *Exam Cram 2* and *Training Guide* series, we believe that Resource Kits are among the best tools you can use to prepare for Microsoft exams.

6. For any specific Microsoft product that is not itself an operating system (for example, SQL Server), have you installed, configured, used, and upgraded this software? [Yes or No]

   If the answer is Yes, skip to the next section. If it's No, you must get some experience. Read on for suggestions on how to do this.

   Experience is a must with any Microsoft product exam, be it something as simple as FrontPage 2000 or as challenging as SQL Server 7.0. For trial copies of other software, search Microsoft's Web site using the name of the product as your search term. Also, search for bundles such as "BackOffice" or "Small Business Server."

If you have the funds, or your employer will pay your way, consider taking a class at a Certified Training and Education Center (CTEC) or at an Authorized Academic Training Partner (AATP). In addition to classroom exposure to the topic of your choice, you get a copy of the software that is the focus of your course, along with a trial version of whatever operating system it needs, with the training materials for that class.

Before you even think about taking any Microsoft exam, make sure you've spent enough time with the related software to understand how it may be installed and configured, how to maintain such an installation, and how to troubleshoot that software when things go wrong. This will help you in the exam, and in real life!

Testing Your Exam-Readiness

Whether you attend a formal class on a specific topic to get ready for an exam or use written materials to study on your own, some preparation for the Microsoft certification exams is essential. At $100 a try, pass or fail, you want to do everything you can to pass on your first try. That's where studying comes in.

We have included a practice exam in this book, so if you don't score that well on the test, you can study more and then tackle the test again. We also have exams that you can take online through the ExamCram.com Web site at `www.examcram.com`. If you still don't hit a score of at least 70 percent after these tests, you'll want to investigate the other practice test resources we mention in this section.

For any given subject, consider taking a class if you've tackled self-study materials, taken the test, and failed anyway. The opportunity to interact with an instructor and fellow students can make all the difference in the world, if you can afford that privilege. For information about Microsoft classes, visit the Training and Certification page at `http://www.microsoft.com/education/partners/ctec.asp` for Microsoft Certified Education Centers or `http://www.microsoft.com/aatp/default.htm` for Microsoft Authorized Training Providers.

If you can't afford to take a class, visit the Training and Certification page anyway, because it also includes pointers to free practice exams and to Microsoft Certified Professional Approved Study Guides and other self-study tools. And even if you can't afford to spend much at all, you should still invest in some low-cost practice exams from commercial vendors.

7. Have you taken a practice exam on your chosen test subject? [Yes or No]

   If Yes, and you scored 70 percent or better, you're probably ready to tackle the real thing. If your score isn't above that threshold, keep at it until you break that barrier.

   If No, obtain all the free and low-budget practice tests you can find and get to work. Keep at it until you can break the passing threshold comfortably.

When it comes to assessing your test readiness, there is no better way than to take a good-quality practice exam and pass with a score of 70 percent or better. When we're preparing ourselves, we shoot for 80-plus percent, just to leave room for the "weirdness factor" that sometimes shows up on Microsoft exams.

Assessing Readiness for Exam 70-217

In addition to the general exam-readiness information in the previous section, you can do several things to prepare for the Implementing and Administering a Microsoft Windows 2000 Directory Services Infrastructure exam. As you're getting ready for Exam 70-217, visit `www.examcram.com` for the latest information on this exam, and be sure to sign up for the Question of the Day. You'll also find `www.cramsession.com` to be an excellent resource for your exam preparation.W We also suggest that you join an active MCSE mailing list. One of the better ones is managed by Sunbelt Software. Sign up at `www.sunbelt-software.com` (look for the "Subscribe to..." button).

Microsoft exam mavens also recommend checking the Microsoft Knowledge Base (available on its own CD as part of the TechNet collection, or on the Microsoft Web site at `http://support.microsoft.com/support/`) for "meaningful technical support issues" that relate to your exam's topics. Although we're not sure exactly what the quoted phrase means, we have also noticed some overlap between technical support questions on particular products and troubleshooting questions on the exams for those products.

Onward, Through the Fog!

Once you've assessed your readiness, undertaken the right background studies, obtained the hands-on experience that will help you understand the products and technologies at work, and reviewed the many sources of information to help you prepare for a test, you'll be ready to take a round of practice tests. When your scores come back positive enough to get you through the exam, you're ready to go after the real thing. If you follow our assessment regime, you'll not only know what you need to study, but when you're ready to make a test date at Prometric or VUE. Good luck!

Microsoft Certification Exams

Terms you'll need to understand:

- ✓ Case study
- ✓ Multiple-choice question formats
- ✓ Build-list-and-reorder question format
- ✓ Create-a-tree question format
- ✓ Drag-and-connect question format
- ✓ Select-and-place question format
- ✓ Fixed-length tests
- ✓ Simulations
- ✓ Adaptive tests
- ✓ Short-form tests

Techniques you'll need to master:

- ✓ Assessing your exam-readiness
- ✓ Answering Microsoft's varying question types
- ✓ Altering your test strategy depending on the exam format
- ✓ Practicing (to make perfect)
- ✓ Making the best use of the testing software
- ✓ Budgeting your time
- ✓ Guessing (as a last resort)

Exam taking is not something that most people anticipate eagerly, no matter how well prepared they may be. In most cases, familiarity helps offset test anxiety. In plain English, this means you probably won't be as nervous when you take your fourth or fifth Microsoft certification exam as you'll be when you take your first one.

Whether it's your first exam or your tenth, understanding the details of taking the new exams (how much time to spend on questions, the environment you'll be in, and so on) and the new exam software will help you concentrate on the material rather than on the setting. Likewise, mastering a few basic exam-taking skills should help you recognize—and perhaps even outfox—some of the tricks and snares you're bound to find in some exam questions.

This chapter, besides explaining the exam environment and software, describes some proven exam-taking strategies that you should be able to use to your advantage.

Assessing Exam-Readiness

We strongly recommend that you read through and take the Self-Assessment included with this book (it appears just before this chapter, in fact). This will help you compare your knowledge base to the requirements for obtaining an MCSE, and it will also help you identify parts of your background or experience that may be in need of improvement, enhancement, or further learning. If you get the right set of basics under your belt, obtaining Microsoft certification will be that much easier.

Once you've gone through the Self-Assessment, you can remedy those topical areas where your background or experience may not measure up to an ideal certification candidate. But you can also tackle subject matter for individual tests at the same time, so you can continue making progress while you're catching up in some areas.

Once you've worked through an *Exam Cram 2*, have read the supplementary materials, and have taken the practice test, you'll have a pretty clear idea of when you should be ready to take the real exam. Although we strongly recommend that you keep practicing until your scores top the 75 percent mark, 80 percent would be a good goal to give yourself some margin for error in a real exam situation (where stress will play more of a role than when you practice). Once you hit that point, you should be ready to go. But if you get through the practice exam in this book without attaining that score, you should keep taking practice tests and studying the materials until you get there. You'll find more pointers on how to study and prepare in the Self-Assessment. But now, on to the exam itself!

The Exam Situation

When you arrive at the testing center where you scheduled your exam, you'll need to sign in with an exam coordinator. He or she will ask you to show two forms of identification, one of which must be a photo ID. After you've signed in and your time slot arrives, you'll be asked to deposit any books, bags, or other items you brought with you. Then, you'll be escorted into a closed room.

All exams are completely closed book. In fact, you will not be permitted to take anything with you into the testing area, but you will be furnished with a blank sheet of paper and a pen or, in some cases, an erasable plastic sheet and an erasable pen. Before the exam, you should memorize as much of the important material as you can, so you can write that information on the blank sheet as soon as you are seated in front of the computer. You can refer to this piece of paper anytime you like during the test, but you'll have to surrender the sheet when you leave the room.

You will have some time to compose yourself, to record this information, and to take a sample orientation exam before you begin the real thing. We suggest you take the orientation test before taking your first exam, but because they're all more or less identical in layout, behavior, and controls, you probably won't need to do this more than once.

Typically, the room will be furnished with anywhere from one to half a dozen computers, and each workstation will be separated from the others by dividers designed to keep you from seeing what's happening on someone else's computer. Most test rooms feature a wall with a large picture window. This permits the exam coordinator to monitor the room, to prevent exam-takers from talking to one another, and to observe anything out of the ordinary that might go on. The exam coordinator will have preloaded the appropriate Microsoft certification exam—for this book, that's Exam 70-217—and you'll be permitted to start as soon as you're seated in front of the computer.

All Microsoft certification exams allow a certain maximum amount of time in which to complete your work (this time is indicated on the exam by an onscreen counter/clock, so you can check the time remaining whenever you like). All Microsoft certification exams are computer generated. In addition to multiple choice, you'll encounter select and place (drag and drop), create a tree (categorization and prioritization), drag and connect, and build list and reorder (list prioritization) on most exams. Although this may sound quite simple, the questions are constructed not only to check your mastery of basic facts and figures about Directory Services Infrastructure, but they also require you to evaluate one or more sets of circumstances or requirements.

Often, you'll be asked to give more than one answer to a question. Likewise, you might be asked to select the best or most effective solution to a problem from a range of choices, all of which technically are correct. Taking the exam is quite an adventure, and it involves real thinking. This book shows you what to expect and how to deal with the potential problems, puzzles, and predicaments.

In the next section, you'll learn more about how Microsoft test questions look and how they must be answered.

Exam Layout and Design

The format of Microsoft's Windows 2000 exams is different from that of its previous exams. For the design exams (70-219, 70-220, 70-221), each exam consists entirely of a series of case studies, and the questions can be of six types. For the Core Four exams (70-210, 70-215, 70-216, 70-217), the same six types of questions can appear, but you are not likely to encounter complex multiquestion case studies.

For design exams, each case study or "testlet" presents a detailed problem that you must read and analyze. Figure 1.1 shows an example of what a case study looks like. You must select the different tabs in the case study to view the entire case.

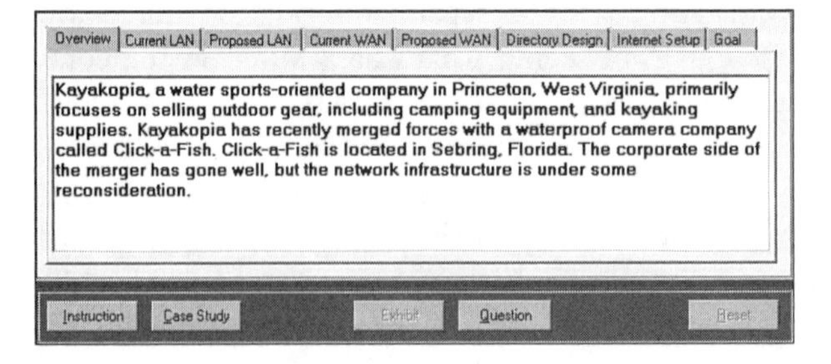

Figure 1.1 This is how case studies appear.

Following each case study is a set of questions related to the case study; these questions can be one of six types (which are discussed next). Careful attention to the details provided in the case study is the key to success. Be prepared to toggle frequently between the case study and the questions as you work. Some of the case studies also include diagrams (called *exhibits*) that you'll need to examine closely to understand how to answer the questions.

Once you complete a case study, you can review all the questions and your answers. However, once you move on to the next case study, you may not be able to return to the previous case study and make any changes.

The six types of question formats are as follows:

- Multiple choice, single answer
- Multiple choice, multiple answers
- Build list and reorder (list prioritization)
- Create a tree
- Drag and connect
- Select and place (drag and drop)

Exam formats may vary by test center location. You may want to call the test center or visit ExamCram.com to see if you can find out which type of test you'll encounter.

Multiple-Choice Question Format

Some exam questions require you to select a single answer, whereas others ask you to select multiple correct answers. The following multiple-choice question requires you to select a single correct answer. Following the question is a brief summary of each potential answer and why it is either right or wrong.

Question 1

Which of the following elements is required to successfully install and configure DNS? [Choose the best answer]

❍ a. DHCP

❍ b. Static IP address

❍ c. Active Directory

❍ d. Windows 2000 clients

Answer b is correct. To install and configure a working DNS server, the server running DNS must have a static IP address. Answer a is incorrect because DHCP is not required to use DNS, although it is necessary if you want to enable dynamic update. Answer c is incorrect because Active Directory is not required. Answer d is incorrect because DNS works with legacy clients as well as Windows 2000 clients.

This sample question format corresponds closely to the Microsoft certification exam format—the only difference on the exam is that questions are not followed by answer keys. To select an answer, you would position the cursor over the radio button next to the answer. Then, you would click the mouse button to select the answer.

Let's examine a question where one or more answers are possible. This type of question provides check boxes rather than radio buttons for marking all appropriate selections.

Question 2

Kayla is a domain administrator who has placed permissions on a parent OU, and through inheritance, those permissions have flowed down toward the child OUs beneath. What can Kayla do to prevent the flow of inheritance while retaining the permissions that already exist on the objects? [Check all correct answers]

- ❑ a. Go into the properties of the OU and deselect the Allow Inheritable Permissions from Parent to Propagate to This Object check box.
- ❑ b. Go into the properties of the OU and select the Allow Inheritable Permissions from Parent to Propagate to This Object check box.
- ❑ c. Select Copy at the Security screen.
- ❑ d. Select Remove at the Security screen.

Answers a and c are correct. To remove inheritance, you must deselect the check box on the OU that allows inheritance. To retain the preexisting permissions, you must select Copy from the corresponding warning box that appears. Answer b is incorrect because it would apply inheritance from above to the object. Answer d is incorrect because it would remove all permissions that existed prior to the change.

For this particular question, two answers are required. Microsoft sometimes gives partial credit for partially correct answers. For Question 2, you have to check the boxes next to items a and c to obtain credit for a correct answer. Notice that picking the right answers also means knowing why the other answers are wrong!

Build-List-and-Reorder Question Format

Questions in the build-list-and-reorder format present two lists of items—one on the left and one on the right. To answer the question, you must move items from the list on the right to the list on the left. The final list must then be reordered into a specific order.

These questions can best be characterized as "From the following list of choices, pick the choices that answer the question and then arrange the list in a certain order." To give you practice with this type of question, some questions of this type are included in this study guide. Here's an example of how they appear in this book; for an example of how they appear on the test, see Figure 1.2.

Question 3

From the following list of famous people, pick those that have been elected President of the United States. Arrange the list in the order that they served.

Thomas Jefferson

Ben Franklin

Abe Lincoln

George Washington

Andrew Jackson

Paul Revere

The correct answer is:

George Washington

Thomas Jefferson

Andrew Jackson

Abe Lincoln

On an actual exam, the entire list of famous people would initially appear in the list on the right. You would move the four correct answers to the list on the left and then reorder the list on the left. Notice that the answer to the question did not include all items from the initial list. However, this may not always be the case.

To move an item from the right list to the left list, first select the item by clicking it and then click the Add button (left arrow). Once you move an item from one list to the other, you can move the item back by first selecting the item and then clicking the appropriate button (either the Add button or the Remove button). Once items have been moved to the left list, you can reorder an item by selecting the item and clicking the up or down button.

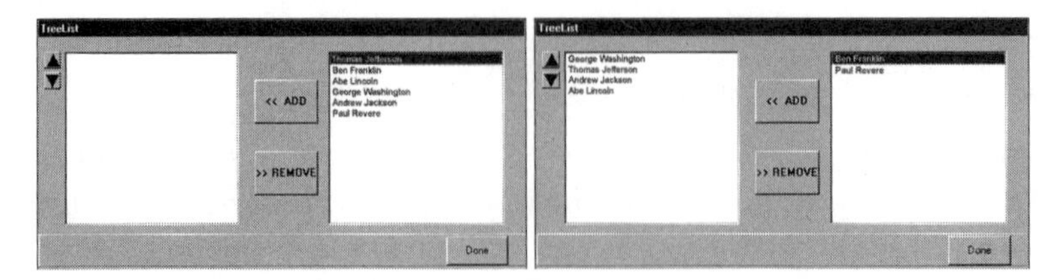

Figure 1.2 This is how build-list-and-reorder questions appear.

Create-a-Tree Question Format

Questions in the create-a-tree format also present two lists—one on the left side of the screen and one on the right side of the screen. The list on the right consists of individual items, and the list on the left consists of nodes in a tree. To answer the question, you must move items from the list on the right to the appropriate node in the tree.

These questions can best be characterized as simply a matching exercise. Items from the list on the right are placed under the appropriate category in the list on the left. Here's an example of how they appear in this book; for an example of how they appear on the test, see Figure 1.3.

Question 4

The calendar year is divided into four seasons:

Winter

Spring

Summer

Fall

Identify the season when each of the following holidays occur:

Christmas

Fourth of July

Labor Day

Flag Day

Memorial Day

Washington's Birthday

Thanksgiving

Easter

The correct answer is:

Winter

Christmas

Washington's Birthday

Spring

Flag Day

Memorial Day

Easter

Summer

Fourth of July

Labor Day

Fall

Thanksgiving

In this case, all the items in the list were used. However, this may not always be the case.

To move an item from the right list to its appropriate location in the tree, you must first select the appropriate tree node by clicking it. Then, you select the item to be moved and click the Add button. If one or more items have been added to a tree node, the node will be displayed with a plus sign (+) icon to the left of the node name. You can click this icon to expand the node and view the item(s) that have been added. If any item has been added to the wrong tree node, you can remove it by selecting it and clicking the Remove button.

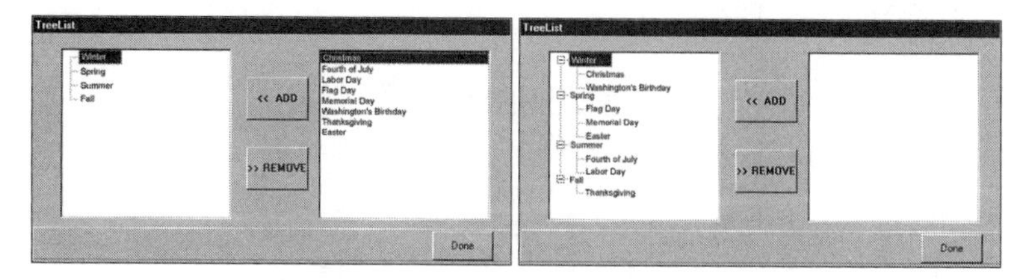

Figure 1.3 This is how create-a-tree questions appear.

Drag-and-Connect Question Format

Questions in the drag-and-connect format present a group of objects and a list of "connections." To answer the question, you must move the appropriate connections between the objects.

This type of question is best described using graphics. Here's an example.

Question 5

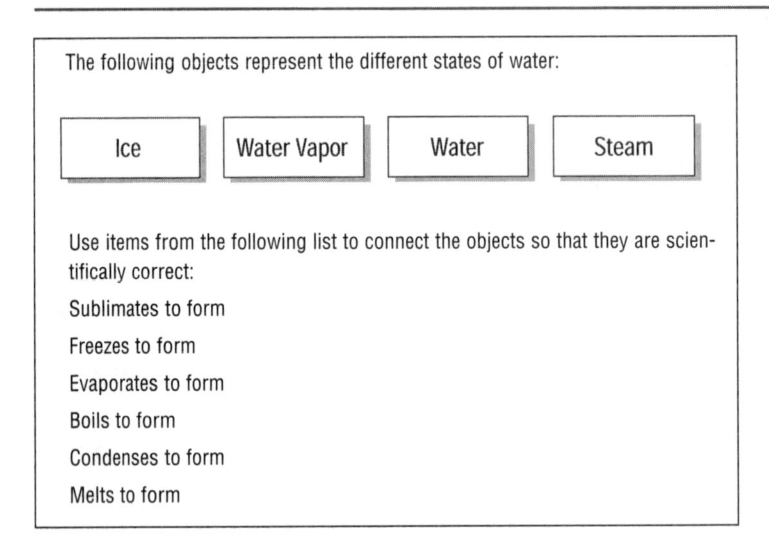

The correct answer is:

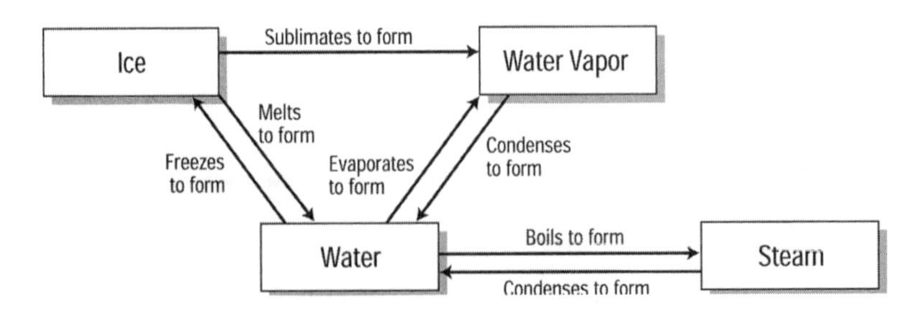

For this type of question, it's not necessary to use every object, and each connection can be used multiple times.

Select-and-Place Question Format

Questions in the select-and-place (drag-and-drop) format present a diagram with blank boxes as well as a list of labels that need to be dragged to correctly fill in the blank boxes. To answer the question, you must move the labels to their appropriate positions on the diagram.

This type of question is best described using graphics. Here's an example.

Question 6

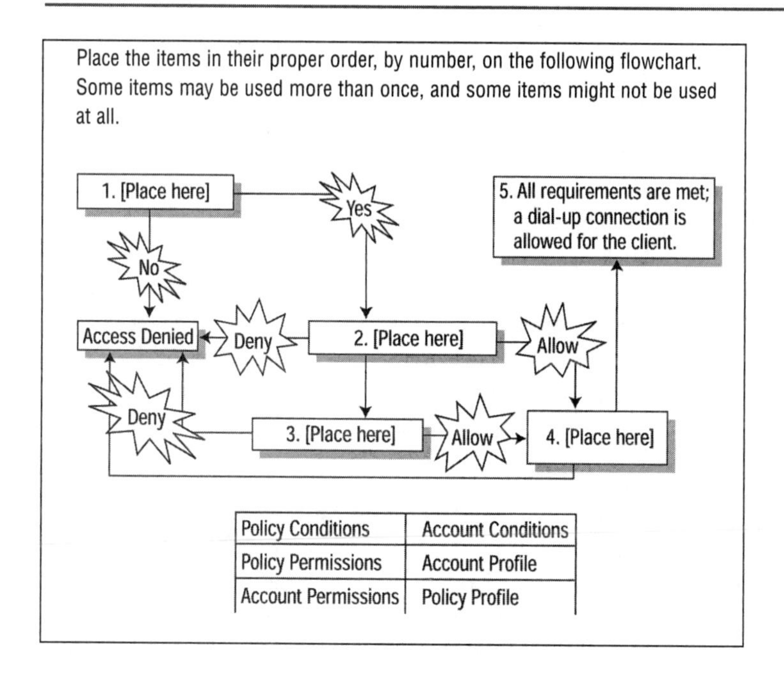

Here's the correct answer:

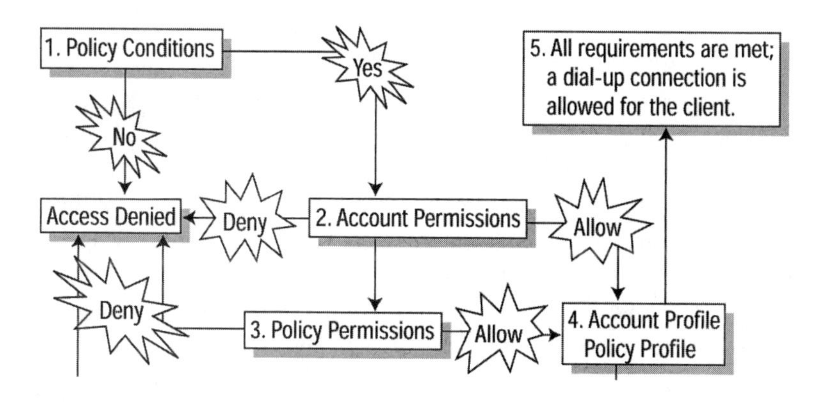

Microsoft's Testing Formats

Currently, Microsoft uses four different testing formats:

- Case study
- Fixed length
- Adaptive
- Short form

As we mentioned earlier, the case study approach is used with Microsoft's design exams. These exams consist of a set of case studies that you must analyze to enable you to answer questions related to the case studies. Such exams include one or more case studies (tabbed topic areas), each of which is followed by 4 to 10 questions. The question types for design exams and for Core Four Windows 2000 exams are multiple choice, build list and reorder, create a tree, drag and connect, and select and place. Depending on the test topic, some exams are totally case based, whereas others are not.

Other Microsoft exams employ advanced testing capabilities that might not be immediately apparent. Although the questions that appear are primarily multiple choice, the logic that drives them is more complex than older Microsoft tests, which use a fixed sequence of questions, called a *fixed-length test*. Some questions employ a sophisticated user interface, which Microsoft calls a *simulation*, to test your knowledge of the software and systems under consideration in a more or less "live" environment that behaves just like the original. The Testing Innovations linkat `www.microsoft.com/trainingandservices/default.asp?PageID=mcp` includes a downloadable practice simulation.

For some exams, Microsoft has turned to a well-known technique, called *adaptive testing*, to establish a test-taker's level of knowledge and product competence. Adaptive exams look the same as fixed-length exams, but they discover the level of difficulty at which an individual test-taker can correctly answer questions. Test-takers with differing levels of knowledge or ability therefore see different sets of questions; individuals with high levels of knowledge or ability are presented with a smaller set of more difficult questions, whereas individuals with lower levels of knowledge are presented with a larger set of easier questions. Two individuals may answer the same percentage of questions correctly, but the test-taker with a higher knowledge or ability level will score higher because his or her questions are worth more.

Also, the lower-level test-taker will probably answer more questions than his or her more-knowledgeable colleague. This explains why adaptive tests use ranges of values to define the number of questions and the amount of time it takes to complete the test.

Adaptive tests work by evaluating the test-taker's most recent answer. A correct answer leads to a more difficult question (and the test software's estimate of the test-taker's knowledge and ability level is raised). An incorrect answer leads to a less difficult question (and the test software's estimate of the test-taker's knowledge and ability level is lowered). This process continues until the test targets the test-taker's true ability level. The exam ends when the test-taker's level of accuracy meets a statistically acceptable value (in other words, when his or her performance demonstrates an acceptable level of knowledge and ability), or when the maximum number of items has been presented (in which case, the test-taker is almost certain to fail) .

Microsoft also introduced a short-form test for its most popular tests. This test delivers 25 to 30 questions to its takers, giving them exactly 60 minutes to complete the exam. This type of exam is similar to a fixed-length test, in that it allows readers to jump ahead or return to earlier questions, and to cycle through the questions until the test is done. Microsoft does not use adaptive logic in this test but claims that statistical analysis of the question pool is such that the 25 to 30 questions delivered during a short-form exam conclusively measure a test-taker's knowledge of the subject matter in much the same way as an adaptive test. You can think of the short-form test as a kind of "greatest hits exam" (that is, the most important questions are covered) version of an adaptive exam on the same topic.

Some of the Microsoft exams can appear as a combination of adaptive and fixed-length questions.

Microsoft tests can come in any one of these forms. Whatever you encounter, you must take the test in the form it appears; you can't choose one form over another. If anything, it pays more to prepare thoroughly for an adaptive exam than for a fixed-length or a short-form exam: The penalties for answering incorrectly are built in to the test itself on an adaptive exam, whereas the layout remains the same for a fixed-length or short-form test, no matter how many questions you answer incorrectly.

The biggest difference between an adaptive test and a fixed-length or short-form test is that on a fixed-length or short-form test, you can revisit questions after you've read them over one or more times. On an adaptive test, you must answer the question when it's presented and will have no opportunities to revisit that question thereafter.

Strategies for Different Testing Formats

Before you choose a test-taking strategy, you must know whether your test is case study based, fixed length, short form, or adaptive. When you begin your exam, you'll know right away if the test is based on case studies. The interface will consist of a tabbed Window that allows you to easily navigate through the sections of the case.

If you are taking a test that is not based on case studies, the software will tell you that the test is adaptive, if in fact the version you're taking is an adaptive test. If your introductory materials fail to mention this, you're probably taking a fixed-length test (50 to 70 questions). If the total number of questions involved is 25 to 30, you're taking a short-form test. Some tests announce themselves by indicating that they will start with a set of adaptive questions, followed by fixed-length questions.

You'll be able to tell for sure whether you are taking an adaptive, fixed-length, or short-form test by the first question. If it includes a check box that lets you mark the question for later review, you're taking a fixed-length or short-form test. If the total number of questions is 25 to 30, it's a short-form test; if more than 30, it's a fixed-length test. Adaptive test questions can be visited (and answered) only once, and they include no such check box.

The Case Study Exam Strategy

Most test-takers find that the case study type of test used for the design exams (70-219, 70-220, and 70-221) is the most difficult to master. When it comes to studying for a case study test, your best bet is to approach each case study as a standalone test. The biggest challenge you'll encounter is that you'll feel that you won't have enough time to get through all the cases that are presented.

Each case provides a lot of material you'll need to read and study before you can effectively answer the questions that follow. The trick to taking a case study exam is to first scan the case study to get the highlights. Make sure you read the overview section of the case so that you understand the context of the problem at hand. Then, quickly move on and scan the questions.

As you are scanning the questions, make mental notes to yourself so that you'll remember which sections of the case study you should focus on. Some case studies may provide a fair amount of extra information that you don't really need to answer the questions. The goal with this scanning approach is to avoid having to study and analyze material that is not completely relevant.

When studying a case, carefully read the tabbed information. It is important to answer each and every question. You will be able to toggle back and forth from case to questions, and from question to question within a case testlet. However, once you leave the case and move on, you may not be able to return to it. You may want to take notes while reading useful information so you can refer to them when you tackle the test questions. It's hard to go wrong with this strategy when taking any kind of Microsoft certification test.

The Fixed-Length and Short-Form Exam Strategy

A well-known principle when taking fixed-length or short-form exams is to first read over the entire exam from start to finish while answering only those questions you feel absolutely sure of. On subsequent passes, you can dive into more complex questions more deeply, knowing how many such questions you have left.

Fortunately, the Microsoft exam software for fixed-length and short-form tests makes the multiple-visit approach easy to implement. At the top-left corner of each question is a check box that permits you to mark that question for a later visit.

Marking questions makes review easier, but you can return to any question by clicking the Forward or Back button repeatedly.

As you read each question, if you answer only those you're sure of and mark for review those you're not sure of, you can keep working through a decreasing list of questions as you answer the trickier ones in order.

There's at least one potential benefit to reading the exam over completely before answering the trickier questions: Sometimes, information supplied in later questions sheds more light on earlier questions. At other times, information you read in later questions might jog your memory about Directory Services Infrastructure facts, figures, or behavior that helps you answer earlier questions. Either way, you'll come out ahead if you defer those questions about which you're not absolutely sure.

Here are some question-handling strategies that apply to fixed-length and short-form tests. Use them if you have the chance:

- When returning to a question after your initial read-through, read every word again. Otherwise, your mind can fall quickly into a rut. Sometimes, revisiting a question after turning your attention elsewhere lets you see something you missed, but the strong tendency is to see what you've seen before. Try to avoid that tendency at all costs.
- If you return to a question more than twice, try to articulate to yourself what you don't understand about the question, why answers don't appear to make sense, or what appears to be missing. If you chew on the subject awhile, your subconscious might provide the details you lack, or you might notice a "trick" that points to the right answer.

As you work your way through the exam, another counter that Microsoft provides will come in handy—the number of questions completed and questions outstanding. For fixed-length and short-form tests, it's wise to budget your time by making sure you've completed one-quarter of the questions one-quarter of the way through the exam period, and three-quarters of the questions three-quarters of the way through.

If you're not finished when only five minutes remain, use that time to guess your way through any remaining questions. Remember, guessing is potentially more valuable than not answering, because blank answers are always wrong, but a guess may turn out to be right. If you don't have a clue about any of the remaining questions, pick answers at random or choose all a's, b's, and so on. The important thing is to submit an exam for scoring that has an answer for every question.

At the very end of your exam period, you're better off guessing than leaving questions unanswered.

The Adaptive Exam Strategy

If there's one principle that applies to taking an adaptive test, it could be summed up as "Get it right the first time." You cannot elect to skip a question and move on to the next one when taking an adaptive test, because the testing software uses your answer to the current question to select whatever question it plans to present next. Nor can you return to a question once you've moved on, because the software gives you only one chance to answer the question. You can, however, take notes, because sometimes information supplied in earlier questions will shed more light on later questions.

Also, when you answer a question correctly, you are presented with a more difficult question next, to help the software gauge your level of skill and ability. When you answer a question incorrectly, you are presented with a less difficult question, and the software lowers its current estimate of your skill and ability. This continues until the program settles into a reasonably accurate estimate of what you know and can do, and it takes you on average through somewhere between 15 and 30 questions as you complete the test.

The good news is that if you know your stuff, you'll probably finish most adaptive tests in 30 minutes or so. The bad news is that you must really, really know your stuff to do your best on an adaptive test. That's because some questions are so convoluted, complex, or hard to follow that you're bound to miss one or two, at a minimum, even if you do know your stuff. So the more you know, the better you'll do on an adaptive test, even accounting for the occasionally weird or unfathomable questions that appear on these exams.

Because you can't always tell in advance whether a test is fixed length, short form, or adaptive, you will be best served by preparing for the exam as if it were adaptive. That way, you should be prepared to pass no matter what kind of test you take. But if you do take a fixed-length or short-form test, remember the tips from the preceding section. They should help you improve on what you could do on an adaptive test.

If you encounter a question on an adaptive test that you can't answer, you must guess an answer immediately. Because of how the software works, you may suffer for your guess on the next question if you guess right, because you'll get a more difficult question next!

Question-Handling Strategies

For those questions that take only a single answer, usually two or three of the answers will be obviously incorrect, and two of the answers will be plausible—of course, only one can be correct. Unless the answer leaps out at you (if it does, reread the question to look for a trick; sometimes those are the ones you're most likely to get wrong), begin the process of answering by eliminating those answers that are most obviously wrong.

Almost always, at least one answer out of the possible choices for a question can be eliminated immediately because it matches one of these conditions:

- The answer does not apply to the situation.
- The answer describes a nonexistent issue, an invalid option, or an imaginary state.

After you eliminate all answers that are obviously wrong, you can apply your retained knowledge to eliminate further answers. Look for items that sound correct but refer to actions, commands, or features that are not present or not available in the situation that the question describes.

If you're still faced with a blind guess among two or more potentially correct answers, reread the question. Try to picture how each of the possible remaining answers would alter the situation. Be especially sensitive to terminology; sometimes the choice of words ("remove" instead of "disable") can make the difference between a right answer and a wrong one.

Only when you've exhausted your ability to eliminate answers, but remain unclear about which of the remaining possibilities is correct, should you guess at an answer. An unanswered question offers you no points, but guessing gives you at least some chance of getting a question right; just don't be too hasty when making a blind guess.

If you're taking a fixed-length or a short-form test, you can wait until the last round of reviewing marked questions (just as you're about to run out of time, or out of unanswered questions) before you start making guesses. You will have the same option within each case study testlet (but once you leave a testlet, you might not be allowed to return to it). If you're taking an adaptive test, you'll have to guess to move on to the next question if you can't figure out an answer some other way. Either way, guessing should be your technique of last resort!

Numerous questions assume that the default behavior of a particular utility is in effect. If you know the defaults and understand what they mean, this knowledge will help you cut through many Gordian knots.

Mastering the Inner Game

In the final analysis, knowledge breeds confidence, and confidence breeds success. If you study the materials in this book carefully and review all the practice questions at the end of each chapter, you should become aware of those areas where additional learning and study are required.

After you've worked your way through the book, take the practice exam in the back of the book. Taking this test will provide a reality check and help you identify areas to study further. Make sure you follow up and review materials related to the questions you miss on the practice exam before scheduling a real exam. Only when you've covered that ground and feel comfortable with the whole scope of the practice exam should you set an exam appointment. Only if you score 80 percent or better should you proceed to the real thing (otherwise, obtain some additional practice tests so you can keep trying until you hit this magic number).

If you take a practice exam and don't score at least 80 to 85 percent correct, you'll want to practice further. Microsoft provides links to practice exam providers and also offers self-assessment exams at **www.microsoft.com/trainingandservices/**). You should also check out ExamCram.com for downloadable practice questions.

Armed with the information in this book and with the determination to augment your knowledge, you should be able to pass the certification exam. However, you need to work at it or else you'll spend the exam fee more than once before you finally pass. If you prepare seriously, you should do well. We are confident that you can do it!

The next section covers other sources you can use to prepare for the Microsoft certification exams.

Additional Resources

A good source of information about Microsoft certification exams comes from Microsoft itself. Because its products and technologies—and the exams that go with them—change frequently, the best place to go for exam-related information is online.

If you haven't already visited the Microsoft Certified Professional site, do so right now. The MCP home page resides at `www.microsoft.com/trainingandservices` (see Figure 1.4).

This page might not be there by the time you read this, or it may be replaced by something new and different, because things change regularly on the Microsoft site. Should this happen, be sure to read the sidebar titled "Coping with Change on the Web."

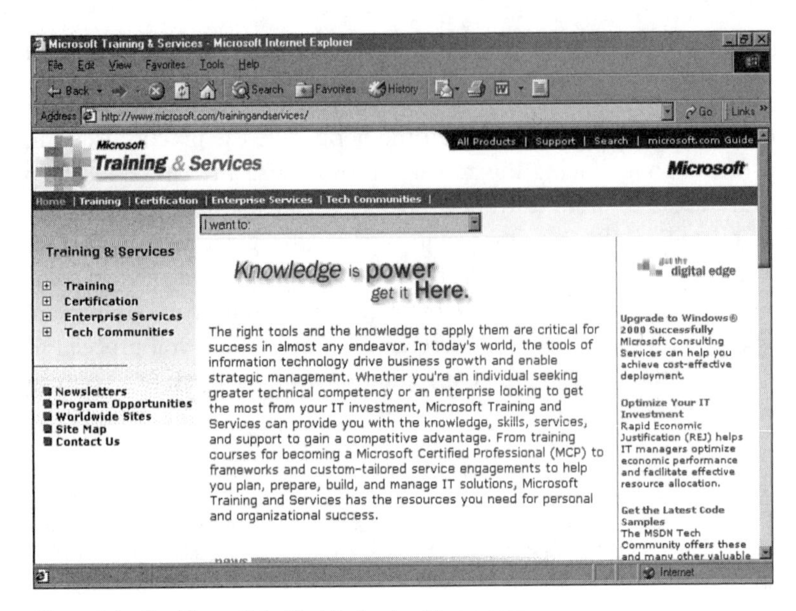

Figure 1.4 The Microsoft Certified Professional home page.

Coping with Change on the Web

Sooner or later, all the information we've shared with you about the Microsoft Certified Professional pages and the other Web-based resources mentioned throughout the rest of this book will go stale or be replaced by newer information. In some cases, the URLs you find here might lead you to their replacements; in other cases, the URLs will go nowhere, leaving you with the dreaded "404 File not found" error message. When that happens, don't give up.

There's always a way to find what you want on the Web if you're willing to invest some time and energy. Most large or complex Web sites—and Microsoft's qualifies on both counts—offer a search engine. On all of Microsoft's Web pages, a Search button appears along the top edge of the page. As long as you can get to Microsoft's site (it should stay at **www.microsoft.com** for a long time), use this tool to help you find what you need.

The more focused you can make a search request, the more likely the results will include information you can use. For example, you can search for the string

```
"training and certification"
```

to produce a lot of data about the subject in general, but if you're looking for the preparation guide for Exam 70-217, "Implementing and Administering a Microsoft Windows 2000 Directory Services Infrastructure," you'll be more likely to get there quickly if you use a search string similar to the following:

```
"Exam 70-217" AND "preparation guide"
```

Likewise, if you want to find the Training and Certification downloads, try a search string such as this:

```
"training and certification" AND "download page"
```

Finally, feel free to use general search tools—such as **www.search.com**, **www.altavista.com**, and **www.excite.com**—to look for related information. Although Microsoft offers great information about its certification exams online, there are plenty of third-party sources of information and assistance that need not follow Microsoft's party line. Therefore, if you can't find something where the book says it lives, intensify your search.

Introduction to Windows 2000 Active Directory

Terms you'll need to understand:

- ✓ Active Directory (AD)
- ✓ Delegation of control
- ✓ Object class
- ✓ Attributes
- ✓ Domain
- ✓ Site
- ✓ Organizational Unit (OU)
- ✓ LDAP
- ✓ Tree
- ✓ Forest

Techniques you'll need to master:

- ✓ Explaining the difference between the logical and physical aspects of AD
- ✓ Defining trees and forests
- ✓ Describing how the centralized nature of AD aids in system administration

Windows 2000 is a major step forward for enterprise computing using Microsoft software. It has been designed to achieve improved performance and scalability. Scalability is the ability to support organizations that range from smaller companies with a few hundred users to enterprises with hundreds of thousands of users.

At the heart of Windows 2000 is Active Directory (AD). AD is a directory service that stores data about users and groups, shared folders, and other network resources. This book discusses many facets of AD and how you use it to simplify system administration.

AD lets you centrally manage your network. This means that administrative tasks can be performed from a single location. When necessary, administrators can use the "delegation of control" tools to assign specific tasks to individuals outside of this central location. Because AD provides a fine level of granularity, you can assign administrative tasks safely, without giving too much power to your users.

This chapter briefly discusses topics that will be important to you when using AD, as well as for Microsoft's MCSE Exam 70-217, "Implementing and Administering a Microsoft Windows 2000 Directory Services Infrastructure." This introductory chapter also lays the foundation for your comprehension of upcoming chapters. The topics discussed here are covered in more detail later in the book.

Introduction to AD

AD is the single component that enables many of the new features of Windows 2000. AD is a directory service, which means that it both stores data about your network resources and provides methods for accessing and distributing that data. It does this by adopting several key industry standards. This provides AD with interoperability out of the box.

Although your users need fast and efficient access to the resources on your network, they should not have to know the specifics of where the resources physically reside or how the data is being retrieved. One of the primary functions of AD is to hide the physical elements of your network from your users. This includes all protocols and hardware, such as servers, routers, and hubs. From a user perspective, these are invisible.

AD is the central repository for many different types of data. Some of this data might detail the existence of a particular user object; other data might detail the look and feel of the user's workstation environment. AD can then make sure that this look and feel is applied to all workstations on the network. This is achieved through Group Policy. When Group Policy is applied, AD makes sure that copies of the policies are stored as close to the user as possible, making the application efficient and fast.

AD also allows for a centralized method of authentication. This means that a user can log on to a Windows 2000 network and be authenticated a single time. This feature simplifies the user's ability to access resources no matter where they reside on the network.

Objects in AD

AD must store a great deal of data. Each piece of data stored within AD is an *object*. Each object has a set of attributes associated with it. These attributes are used to describe the object and make it unique.

Objects within AD include users, groups, computers, servers, domains, and sites, among others. As you can see, the list is extensive and far-reaching. Because data is stored as objects, users can search through the directory for objects they wish to access based on object names. Because objects have attributes, objects can also be searched for based on their attributes. For a user object, the attributes might include the user's telephone number, job title, and first and last names. This provides a flexible environment where users are empowered in ways we have not seen before.

The Schema

To understand how data is defined within AD, you must be aware of the schema. The *schema* is a definition of all object types and their attributes. Because there is a single schema for an entire Windows 2000 forest, you can achieve consistency no matter how large your enterprise grows.

Two types of definitions are stored in the schema: object classes and attributes. Object classes define the types of objects that can be stored within AD. Each class consists of a class name and a set of attributes that are associated with the object. Attributes are stored separately within the schema. This allows for further consistency within the database, because a single definition for the "last name" attribute can be used over and over again.

The schema can be searched by user applications and modified to allow custom object classes and attributes. To prevent it from being modified without permissions, each object is secured using discretionary access control lists (DACLs). These DACLs ensure that only authorized users are able to access the schema.

Directory Service Protocol

We mentioned that Microsoft had adopted some key industry standards to ensure interoperability. One of the key standards that enables AD is the Lightweight Directory Access Protocol (LDAP). This protocol is used to query and update data within the directory. Active Directory supports LDAP versions 2 and 3.

Part of the LDAP standard defines naming standards. It states that objects must be represented by a series of components, such as domain and Organizational Unit (OU), and that these components be represented as a unique path to the object. There are two LDAP naming paths: distinguished names and relative distinguished names.

Distinguished Names

You can think of the *distinguished name* as the complete path from the root domain all the way down to the object. Every object in AD must have a unique distinguished name. Here is an example:

```
CN=Donna George,OU=Sales,DC=HCSNET,DC=COM
```

Table 2.1 defines each of the components of the distinguished name.

Table 2.1 Distinguished Name Elements

Key	Attribute	Meaning
CN	Common Name	Any object stored within the directory, with the exception of domain components and Organizational Units
OU	Organizational Unit	An Organizational Unit that can contain other objects
DC	Domain Component	Defines the DNS name, such as COM

Relative Distinguished Name

A *relative distinguished name* is a truncated distinguished name. It identifies the part of the distinguished name that uniquely identifies the object within its container. For instance, in the example given previously, the relative distinguished name would be `CN=Donna George`, because Donna George is the unique name within the Sales OU.

Depending on the details you know about an object, the relative distinguished name may be different. For instance, in this example, we do not know the name of a user object:

```
OU=Sales,DC=HCSNET,DC=COM
```

In this case, the relative distinguished name would simply be `OU=Sales`, because Sales is the name that uniquely identifies the OU within the domain.

The Structure of AD

AD is made up of two distinct structures: the logical structure and the physical structure. When designing your AD implementation, you are dealing with the logical aspects of what AD offers. When deciding precisely where each component will be on your network, you are dealing with the physical limitations of your infrastructure.

Let's take a brief look at the major elements that make up both the logical and physical pieces of a Windows 2000 network. From a design perspective, you need to know what each element is and how the elements work together to build an enterprise-level system.

The Logical Structure

When designing your Windows 2000 network, you will be using the various logical components. These components are useful for both administrators and users. For administrators, they allow for the logical design of your AD infrastructure. From a user's perspective, they allow for efficient searching of the AD database.

There are five logical components in AD:

- Domains
- Organization Units
- Trees
- Forests
- Global Catalogs (GCs)

Understanding what each of these components does helps you understand how to design and administer AD. They also provide the foundation for your comprehension of the material that follows.

Domains

The *domain* is one of the core elements that make up a Windows 2000 network. A domain is a *security boundary*. This means that each domain has its own administrators that can be assigned full control over the domain—and only the domain (unless specified otherwise).

A domain is an entity with its own users and groups. These users can be granted permissions in other domains if necessary. Some group types can be assigned permissions outside of the domain in which they were created, whereas others cannot.

Domains are also used for replication purposes. Although AD is a single database containing data about all elements of your network, it does not replicate all data across the entire network. Domain data is replicated only within a single domain. A subset of data from a domain can be replicated; this is the function of a GC server, which we will define in a moment.

Domain controllers (DCs) within a domain replicate with each other and share domain information. Controlling this replication is a key part of the design process. A domain can also run in one of two modes: native or mixed. Full functionality cannot be achieved until a domain is running in native mode.

Organizational Units

Organizational Units are container objects that are used to organize objects within the directory. Remember that we are talking about the logical layer. Objects are not physically stored within this structure, even if Windows 2000 represents them this way. OUs commonly contain user and group objects. They can also contain computers and other OUs.

OUs are used to simplify administration. Permissions can be assigned at the OU level both to grant container objects access to other network resources (or to deny them) and to assign specific users administrative privileges.

Commonly, the OU structure is built around the administrative model for your organization. Because administrative tasks such as adding user objects or applying policies is done at the OU level, it makes sense to organize network resources and other objects within them. Objects that will be administered by a single administrator or administrative group, or objects that will have policies and permissions assigned to them in a uniform fashion should be grouped within OUs.

Less commonly, OUs are designed around the organizational structure, such as by department or geographic location. A geographic hierarchy of OUs allows you to organize users by country or region.

Administration of objects within an OU can be delegated. This means that once objects have been stored within the OU container, you can assign permissions to manage these objects to groups other than domain administrators. This can reduce the amount of day-to-day administrative tasks that are performed by domain administrators.

Trees

Domains are combined to produce a *tree*, which is a hierarchical representation of your Windows 2000 network. The first domain that is installed in a Windows 2000 network is known as the *root domain*. All subsequent domains are installed beneath this root domain. All domains in a tree share a common schema and a common GC.

You cannot uninstall the root domain. Doing so would effectively force you to uninstall all domains in your environment.

If you have more than one domain, each domain forms part of a tree. When you have several domains forming a tree, it is said that they share a *contiguous namespace*. As domains are added to the tree, they become child domains to the domain above them in the hierarchy. For instance, the second domain you install becomes a child of the root domain. It derives part of its name from its position within the hierarchy.

An example of this hierarchical structure can be illustrated in the following way. An AD designer installs a root domain called `chamberlin.local`. Once this is complete, she installs a second domain, which becomes a child domain to the root domain. This domain's name is "Houston." Therefore, the full name in Windows 2000 is `houston.chamberlin.local`. As you can see, the domain inherited part of its name from the root domain. This maintains the hierarchical nature of AD.

This naming scheme echoes the DNS (Domain Name System) naming scheme from which it is derived. DNS is a key part of a Windows 2000 network. Domain names are based on DNS standards.

You might be familiar with trusts from previous versions of Windows NT. Trusts allow objects in one domain to gain access to objects in another domain. In previous versions, these trusts were created manually as needed. In Windows 2000, they are created automatically. In addition, they are *transitive*, which means that a trust between two domains can be used by every other domain. These trusts are always two-way.

Forests

A *forest* is a collection of trees. Trees in a forest do not have to share a contiguous namespace. However, they *must* share a common schema and GC. For instance, say you have two trees—one called `chamberlin.local` and another with a root domain of `watts.local`. These trees can be joined together to join a forest via a two-way trust relationship.

Forests allow users in two different trees to access resources in a different namespace, thereby easing administration. Because trees in a forest must share a common schema, they share all object and attribute types.

Global Catalogs

Because DCs within a domain only store data about objects contained within the domain, another mechanism must be in place to allow users to gain transparent access to resources outside of the domain in which they are contained. This is the job of a Global Catalog (GC).

A GC server is also a DC. It contains data about all objects within a forest. Because this data is stored locally on a DC, a user can quickly search for network resources stored anywhere in the forest. In addition, because the Global Catalog contains the permission list for all objects, it can also grant access. This prevents the user from having to contact a DC in the remote domain, thereby reducing network traffic.

The GC does not contain every attribute for an object. Instead, it contains a subset of attributes defined as those that are most commonly searched. For the user object, this might be the first name or last name. The attributes that are replicated to the GC server are controlled by an attribute of the object. By editing the schema, you can force or prevent attributes from appearing in the GC.

One of the key benefits of the GC is that it makes the logical structure of your Windows 2000 network invisible to your users. Along with a reduction of network traffic, GCs are an essential part of your Windows 2000 implementation.

The Physical Structure

The physical structure of AD is used to manage network traffic on your network. The two elements that make up the physical structure are DCs and sites.

These elements are involved in the underlying infrastructure that makes up your network. You should consider issues such as the amount of network bandwidth you have available and how your TCP/IP (Transmission Control Protocol/Internet Protocol) network has been segmented.

The physical design of your network is distinct and separate from the logical layer. When designing either one, you do not have to take the other into account. Whichever logical design you come up with, the physical implications will never force you to change it.

Let's look briefly at each of these components. By combining both the logical and physical elements of your network, you can optimize your Windows 2000 network.

DCs

A *domain controller* (DC) is a server on a Windows 2000 network that stores a replica of the AD database. Its job is to manage access to this data via searches and also to accept and make changes to the data as necessary. The DC must then replicate any changes it has accepted to all other DCs in the domain. A small network might require only two controllers (but for fault-tolerance reasons, never less than two), whereas a large network could require hundreds of DCs.

Along with these tasks, the DC also manages the authentication of users as they log on to the network. This authentication includes assigning a security token that contains a list of group memberships and permissions to each user.

Each replica of AD is read/write enabled. This means that any DC has the ability to accept changes. The process of AD replication ensures that all DCs receive copies of these changes. Because this cannot happen in real time, there will be short periods when one replica may hold slightly different information than other replicas.

AD replication works well for most network operations. However, there are times when the latency involved with moving changes to AD can cause problems. To resolve this issue, some operations on the network do not strictly follow the peer nature of DCs and AD replication. These special servers are called *operations masters*. Operation masters have other functions, as well, which are discussed in Chapter 13.

Operations masters ensure that security remains intact on your network and that changes made to the schema of your network do not conflict. Operations masters exist at both the domain and forest level.

Sites

A site can be defined as a group of one or more IP subnets connected by high-speed access links. Sites are used on your network to optimize AD replication traffic and user authentication.

IP subnets within a site are considered to have fast connectivity. By creating a site that contains a group of subnets, you are telling Windows 2000 that communication between these subnets is both fast and efficient. The inverse is also true: By putting two IP subnets into different sites, you are telling Windows 2000 that the IP subnets are separated by a slow or inefficient link.

AD uses this information to build its replication topology. Replication among sites can be scheduled to occur during certain times of day. Replication traffic among sites is also compressed (however, replication traffic within a site is not).

Sites are also used for several other Windows 2000 features, including allowing users to find a DC that is local to them (in the same IP subnet) during the logon process. This minimizes logon traffic across the WAN.

Administering Windows 2000

Windows 2000 leverages AD to provide several methods to administer the network. These methods work together to provide an efficient and safe networking environment. The three methods are as follows:

- Centralized management
- Group Policy
- Delegation of control

Let's briefly look at each method.

Centralized Management

AD centrally stores data. This eases administration, because having all data about the domain stored in a central location (on each DC) allows administrators to manage objects easily. It also allows users to locate any object in a single search.

The structure of AD allows objects to be grouped logically into OUs. This structure allows for multiple levels and inheritance. Through the use of Group Policy, you can apply a group of settings at one level of the hierarchy and have it flow down and affect all objects—or a subset of objects—within the domain.

Because all site, domain, and OU data is stored centrally, Group Policies can be applied at any of these levels. Being able to affect as much or as little of your network as you want further simplifies management.

Group Policy

Group Policy allows you to centrally manage your user environment through the creation and application of policies throughout your domain or domains. When you apply a Group Policy a single time, you can rely on Windows 2000 to continually apply it, even if the user's attributes and permissions change.

Group Policy leverages containers, including sites, domains, and OUs, within AD. Using this information is efficient, because it has already been defined within AD.

Group Policies are applied when a user logs on. If applied to user objects, Group Policies follow the user around the network, regardless of which computer the user logs in to. The ability of Group Policies to follow the user means your user community will enjoy a consistent interface and experience, thus reducing help desk calls and total cost of ownership (TCO) .

Delegation of Control

When combined with the granular nature of the AD security model, the delegation of control allows administrators of a Windows 2000 network to give unprecedented freedom to groups of users. By delegating control, administrators can allow users to administer their own environment.

You can delegate control at several different levels. For a wide range of control, you can delegate at the OU level. For instance, if you assigned Full Control permission to a user at the OU level, that user would be able to create new user objects within that OU and also delete them. This offloads day-to-day tasks from the central administrative team.

Control can also be delegated at the attribute level. It is entirely possible to assign a group of users the ability to edit a subset of attributes at the OU level. For instance, you might decide that personal information such as first name, last name, or telephone number should be controlled by the user community. You could do this by delegating control of these attributes to the users.

Delegating control relies on the creation of an effective logical structure. You should always design your logical structure before concerning yourself with the physical aspects of your network.

Practice Questions

Question 1

Jeannie Griswold has been asked to give a brief presentation to describe the new features of Windows 2000. One of the most significant new features is the inclusion of Active Directory. Which of the following statements best describes Active Directory?

- ❍ a. Active Directory is a database that contains a list of all users and their passwords.
- ❍ b. Each domain has its own Active Directory. By you creating trusts between domains, each Active Directory can communicate with another. Because trusts are transitive, once you have connected all the domains with trusts, a user can go anywhere on the network.
- ❍ c. Active Directory is a database of information regarding users, groups, and computers on a Windows 2000 network.
- ❍ d. Active Directory is a directory service. Not only does it contain data about all network resources, it also provides mechanisms for searching for data.

Answer d is correct. Active Directory is a set of data and services that allows you to manipulate and access information from any location on the network. Answers a and c are incorrect because Active Directory is much more than simply a database. Answer b is incorrect because each domain does not have its own Active Directory.

Question 2

Brad Finch is a system administrator for a video company. The network is widely dispersed. Brad's manager told him that he wants all their video equipment data to be stored within Active Directory. Brad has looked through all the property sheets but cannot find any way to enter data about these devices. Brad tells his boss that this cannot be done. However, his boss tells him that it can be done and that Brad should do more research. What should Brad do to store this data?

- ❍ a. Brad should store the data as a user object. Because he doesn't have to fill out all the attributes of an object, he should use just enough attributes to describe each piece of equipment.
- ❍ b. Brad must create a new object class within the schema of Active Directory.
- ❍ c. An object class for video equipment already exists within Active Directory. Brad should use it to store data about his equipment.
- ❍ d. Brad should tell his boss that despite what he may have heard, this is not possible. Active Directory does not allow for the storage of objects that represent items such as video equipment.

Answer b is correct. Although it is not often necessary to alter the schema for Active Directory, it would be necessary in this situation. By creating a new object type, Brad would be able to create entries for the equipment. Answer a is incorrect because user objects would not have the properties Brad will need to store data about the video equipment. Answer c is incorrect because Microsoft has not provided an object class for video equipment. Answer d is incorrect because Active Directory can be extended to include information about any kind of device or piece of equipment.

Question 3

Siobhan has suggested to the members of her management team that they migrate their old network to a Windows 2000–based system. However, she is meeting resistance because her bosses do not want to support a proprietary system. What should Siobhan tell her management team?

- ❍ a. That Active Directory supports many industry standards. Three key standards are TCP/IP, DNS, and LDAP. These standards allow for interoperability out of the box.
- ❍ b. That although Windows 2000 is a proprietary system, Microsoft has a large market share. Therefore, using Windows 2000 is a good idea.
- ❍ c. That she will come up with an alternative network operating system.
- ❍ d. That although Windows 2000 is proprietary, it does provide access to APIs that allow one to write integration tools.

Answer a is correct. Active Directory supports many industry standards. Answer b is incorrect because, although some aspects of Windows 2000 are indeed proprietary, it does support all key Internet standards. Answer c is incorrect because an alternative operating system would not be necessary. Answer d is incorrect because Active Directory is based on standards and therefore is not a proprietary directory service.

Question 4

Gene Simmons is a system administrator who has hired a consultant to help him integrate two trees and make them a forest. Gene knows that this involves creating a trust and thinks it will only be a short period of time before they are done. However, the consultant tells him that the consolidation cannot happen because one company has customized the schema to include data about video equipment. Gene doesn't see why this is a problem. Who is correct and why?

- ❑ a. Gene is correct. Because he effectively is only setting up a trust between two trees, it does not matter that one tree has a different schema.
- ❑ b. Gene is correct. When the trust is created, the schemas will merge.
- ❑ c. The consultant is correct. Because the schemas are currently different, creating a forest is not possible.
- ❑ d. The consultant is correct. When the trust is created, the schemas will merge. However, before they can proceed, they need to determine which schema will be adopted for the forest.

Answer c is correct. Before the merge can take place, the two schemas must be identical. Answer a is incorrect because trees in a forest must share a common schema. Answers b and d are incorrect because there is no mechanism built in to the trust process to merge schemas. All trees in a forest share both a schema and a Global Catalog.

Question 5

Which of the following is a distinguished name?

- ❍ a. **CN=Donna George,OU=Sales,DC=HCSNET,DC=COM**
- ❍ b. **CN=Donna George**
- ❍ c. **OU=Donna George,CN=Sales,DC=HCSNET,DC=COM**
- ❍ d. **DC=Donna George,DC=Sales,OU=HCSNET,CN=COM**

Answer a is correct. Distinguished names are read from right to left, becoming increasingly more unique. A distinguished name uniquely identifies an object within the directory. Answer b is incorrect because a distinguished name must list the entire path to the object. Answer c is incorrect the container (CN) must always be listed first. Answer d is incorrect because DCs must not be listed first.

Question 6

John Watts is in the process of designing his Windows 2000 network. He has two sets of users—one in London and another in Houston. Although they share many items, they do have different security requirements, help desks, and administrative teams. John decides to incorporate two domains in his network design. However, the review committee in his organization tells him that it wants a single domain. It tells John that he should use OUs to create the security requirements. John considers this request and then resolves to attend the next committee meeting to justify his position and to insist that he be allowed to create two domains. Why did John decide to do this?

❍ a. John does not understand the scalability of Windows 2000. Because Windows 2000 scales better than previous versions of Windows NT, it is a good idea to make things as simple as possible. One domain is simpler than two.

❍ b. John knows that domains are security boundaries. He knows that in the case of two regions that must have their own security settings and control, creating two domains is far easier.

❍ c. John does not understand OUs. John should create a single domain and use OUs to create the security model he wants.

❍ d. John understands that multiple domains are a good idea when data needs to cross slow links. Active Directory works well when there are fast connections, but slow connections cause problems.

Answer b is correct. There are times when you are forced into creating multiple domains. A domain acts as a security boundary. By giving each geographic area its own domain, you make them totally autonomous. John can be a member of the Enterprise Admins group to maintain control over both domains. Answer a is incorrect because it addresses scalability without meeting the security requirements. Answer c is incorrect because OUs allow for control over objects contained within them but will not help with dividing Domain Admins on John's network. Answer d is incorrect because Active Directory traffic can be controlled with sites; it is not necessary to create multiple domains to deal with slow links.

Question 7

Peter Chamberlin is designing a Windows 2000 network with two domains—one in London and the other in Houston. His design calls for 50 DCs in each domain. He then decides to add another DC in each domain. The additional DC in London will be placed in Houston, and vice versa, to enable users in each domain to search for data in the other's network. When Peter presents this idea to a consultant, the consultant tells him that he does not need these additional DCs. Peter concludes that the consultant probably has never worked in an enterprisewide network before, and he forges ahead with his plan. Who is right?

❍ a. Peter is right. If users will be performing searches across domains, they need access to a DC in all domains.

❍ b. Peter is right. Because each domain will contain a DC from the other domain, they will be able to replicate data between them.

❍ c. The consultant is right. Even if the DCs are moved, it will not solve the problem. Peter needs to set up a directory connector between the domains.

❍ d. The consultant is right. It is not the job of a DC to allow searches across domains. To achieve this, the DC must be designated as a Global Catalog server.

Answer d is correct. A Global Catalog server allows searches to be performed across domains. Although a Global Catalog server is indeed a DC, it is not necessary that the DC belong to a specific domain. No additional DCs are needed in this instance. Answer a is incorrect because DCs cannot perform searches across domains. Answer b is incorrect because the issue at hand is not replication but rather searches across domains. Answer c is incorrect because it is not necessary to create a directory connector between the domains; directory connectors are used to connect different types of directory services, such as Active Directory and Novell Directory Services.

Question 8

Jason inherited a Windows 2000 network. When the network was installed, the root domain was misnamed. Instead of reading **Basildon.local**, it was named **Absildon.local**. Jason's manager has told him that this must be corrected as soon as possible because it is confusing users. Jason's network is made up of several child domains. All user accounts exist in these child domains (there are a few accounts in the root domain). Because the root domain has been created incorrectly, the names of the other domains have inherited the problem. Jason assures his manager that he will uninstall the root domain the next weekend. Once this is done, he will reinstall it with the correct spelling. He will then go ahead and rename the child domains. What will happen if Jason uninstalls the root domain?

❍ a. Jason will lose his entire network. If the root domain goes away, all other domains will be orphaned and fail.

❍ b. Jason will lose all user accounts. Although the user accounts appear to exist in the child domains, they are, in fact, first created in the root domain. Jason will need to re-create the user accounts.

❍ c. Jason will finish more quickly than he thought. Because the domain names are inherited, once he reinstalls the root domain, the corrected name will flow down through the domain hierarchy.

❍ d. Jason can simply rename the child domains. There is no need to uninstall the root domain.

Answer a is correct. The root domain should not be uninstalled. If you uninstall a root domain, you have essentially destroyed the tree. Jason would have to start again and re-create all objects and network resources. Answer b is incorrect because accounts are not created in the root domain first. Also, Jason will lose his tree once he has uninstalled the root domain. Answer c is incorrect because uninstalling the root domain means Jason will have to re-create all domains, and this will not save him time. Answer d is incorrect because child domains cannot simply be renamed.

Question 9

Natasha is a system designer who is new to Windows 2000. She has just finished her first Windows 2000 network design for a pharmaceutical company. This company will have three domains. Natasha is just putting the finishing touches on a list of tasks that must be done. One of the items reads, "Create two-way trusts between each of the domains." When Natasha shows this plan to a friend, he tells her that this step is not necessary. Natasha, who has worked extensively with Windows NT 4, does not believe him. Who is correct?

❍ a. Natasha is correct. Without specific trusts, users won't be able to access resources in other domains.

❍ b. Natasha is correct. Although trusts are set up automatically in Windows 2000, they are one-way trusts, and they only travel up the hierarchy.

❍ c. The friend is correct. This step is not necessary. Windows 2000 creates two-way transitive trusts.

❍ d. The friend is correct. However, because the trusts automatically created are not transitive, Natasha will have to create some trusts manually. They will be far fewer in number than anticipated, though.

Answer c is correct. Although it is possible to create trusts between domains in Windows 2000, this is not generally necessary. All trusts created by Windows 2000 are two-way transitive. Answer a is incorrect because Windows 2000 automatically creates two-way transitive trusts. Answer b is incorrect because the trusts automatically created by Windows 2000 are not one-way trusts—they are two-way. Answer d is incorrect because trusts are indeed transitive.

Question 10

Zevi Mehlman is working with a single Windows 2000 domain. Zevi's company has offices around the country with 128Kbps links between them. They have their own DCs and IP subnets. No office has more than 500 users. Zevi has a problem with the slow links on his network. During the day, these links are getting swamped with traffic. When he analyzes the traffic, he finds it is all related to Active Directory. Zevi decides to fix this problem. Fortunately, it did not take long. What did Zevi do to resolve this issue?

- ❍ a. Zevi created multiple domains, one for each office. This reduced the amount of Active Directory traffic.
- ❍ b. Zevi ordered faster connections between each office. The extra bandwidth will solve the problem.
- ❍ c. Zevi changed his work hours. Because he will now only be in the office in the evenings, the amount of traffic generated by his administrative tasks should not inconvenience anyone.
- ❍ d. Zevi created sites within his domain. Each remote office was given its own site. Zevi then planned for replication to occur on a schedule in the evening.

Answer d is correct. Sites are used to facilitate management of replication traffic. By creating sites, Zevi will enjoy the benefits of compressed replication data, and he'll be able to schedule when replication occurs. Answer a is incorrect because creating multiple domains would increase the administrative burden on his network. Answer b is incorrect because, although faster connections would help with the problem, a more reasonable alternative is available. Keep in mind that faster connections do not always solve bandwidth issues. Answer c is incorrect because Zevi is doing nothing to control when replication takes place on his network.

Need to Know More?

Blum, Daniel J. *Understanding Active Directory Services.* Microsoft Press. Redmond, WA, 1999. ISBN 1572317213.

This book includes details of Active Directory design.

Iseminger, David. *Active Directory Services for Microsoft Windows 2000.* Microsoft Press. Redmond, WA, 2000. ISBN 0735606242.

This book includes design tips for Active Directory and introduces you to new terminology.

Minasi, Mark. *Mastering Windows 2000 Server, Second Edition.* Sybex Computer Books. Berkeley, CA, 2000. ISBN 0782127746.

This book does a good job of aiming content at all levels of readers.

Northrup, Anthony. *Introducing Microsoft Windows 2000 Server.* Microsoft Press. Redmond, WA, 1999. ISBN 1572318759.

This book acts as a high-level introduction to Active Directory and its features.

Willis, Will, David Watts, and Tillman Strahan. *Windows 2000 System Administration Handbook.* Prentice Hall. Upper Saddle River, NJ, 2000. ISBN 0130270105.

This book examines a day in the life of an administrator and gives examples of day-to-day tasks you will need to perform.

Implementing and Administering DNS

Terms you'll need to understand:

- ✓ Domain Name System (DNS)
- ✓ Fully qualified domain name (FQDN)
- ✓ Relative distinguished name
- ✓ Zone
- ✓ Dynamic update
- ✓ Active Directory (AD) integrated zone
- ✓ Primary zone
- ✓ Secondary zone
- ✓ WINS
- ✓ HOSTS
- ✓ Forward lookup
- ✓ Reverse lookup
- ✓ Root server
- ✓ Resource records (RR)
- ✓ NSLOOKUP

Techniques you'll need to master:

- ✓ Installing and configuring DNS for AD
- ✓ Integrating AD DNS zones with non-AD DNS zones
- ✓ Configuring zones for dynamic update
- ✓ Managing replication of DNS data
- ✓ Troubleshooting DNS

The Domain Name System (DNS) is a name-resolution database most commonly associated with the Internet. It was first defined as a way to replace the aging HOSTS file system, which is explained in the next section. With Windows 2000, Microsoft has made DNS the primary method of name resolution for Active Directory (AD) networks. In fact, DNS is a required element for installing AD—so much so that the process of upgrading a member or standalone server to an AD domain controller (DC) automatically installs the DNS server service if you do not have a valid DNS server for AD to use.

We'll briefly touch on how and why DNS was created, because without that background, troubleshooting DNS by testing with alternative name-resolution methods won't fully make sense.

You will need to know how to install, configure, and troubleshoot the DNS server service.

Brief History of DNS

As mentioned previously, DNS has its origins in the Internet. When the Internet was small, every single TCP/IP (Transmission Control Protocol/Internet Protocol) host on the Internet had a file called HOSTS that contained mappings of every other host on the Internet and its IP address (hence, the name). Whenever a new host (such as a workstation or server) was added to the Internet, a new master HOSTS file was created and posted, and everyone on the Internet would download the updated file. This was fine when the Internet was small and changes were infrequent. However, as the Internet grew, the process of updating HOSTS files on every system became increasingly unmanageable. Enter DNS. DNS was conceived as a hierarchical namespace that allows the management of the Internet namespace to be partitioned and distributed. As such, not every system needs to know the name and IP address of every other system on the Internet. Conceptually, the DNS hierarchy looks like a tree. At the very top is what is known as the *root domain*, which is represented by a period (.). Below the root domain are the *top-level domains*, which are the `.com`, `.net`, `.edu`, `.org`, and so on that we are all familiar with.

Below the top-level domains are the *second-level domains*, which are what we work with every day when sending email or visiting a Web site. `Microsoft.com` is a second-level domain, as is `Army.mil` and `Harvard.edu`. When you visit www.`Inside-Corner.com`, you are accessing a host computer called www in the `Inside-Corner.com` second-level domain.

Fully Qualified Domain Names (FQDNs)

With DNS, another important term to understand is the *fully qualified domain name* (FQDN). This refers to the complete, unambiguous name of a host. The FQDN contains everything from the host name through the root domain. An example is the `www.microsoft.com.` FQDN. In this example, `www` is the host, `microsoft.com` is the second-level domain, `com` is the top-level domain, and the trailing period represents the root domain. This FQDN is said to be "unambiguous" because it uniquely defines a single host on the Internet.

Relative Distinguished Names (RDNs)

Unlike an FQDN, a *relative distinguished name* (RDN) is just the part of the host name that represents the host system. In the previous example, `www` would be the RDN. These types of names are not used on the Internet because of the likelihood the name would be ambiguous and unable to be resolved to an IP address. However, RDNs are common on internal networks, because corporate DNS servers check their local zones first to resolve a name (more on zones later).

Now that we have explored some background information, let's examine DNS as it relates to Windows 2000 and AD.

Dynamic DNS and AD in Windows 2000

Windows 2000 runs on TCP/IP, and to utilize AD, you must forsake the older Windows Internet Naming Service (WINS) technology in favor of DNS. WINS can still be useful on Windows 2000 networks, especially if you have non-Windows 2000 or XP clients. However, Active Directory will not use WINS for name resolution.The biggest downside to DNS has been that although distributed, it was still designed as a system that requires manual updates. Whenever a new host is added to a domain, an administrator needs to manually update the zone database on the primary DNS server to reference the new host. If there are secondary name servers on the network, the changes are replicated in a zone transfer.

However, a dynamic updating feature proposed in RFC 2136 provides the means for updating a zone's primary server automatically. Windows 2000 supports this new dynamic DNS, or simply *DDNS*. The caveat is that it works only with Windows 2000 clients, and older Windows NT, Windows 9*X*, and non-Windows clients still require manual updates, or at minimum, a Windows 2000 Dynamic Host Configuration Protocol (DHCP) proxy to act on their behalf during the dynamic registration process. When DDNS is enabled and Windows 2000 boots up and contacts a DHCP proxy for IP addressing information, it automatically sends an update to the name server it has been configured to use, adding its Address (A) resource record. This greatly simplifies the administration of DNS on a Windows 2000 network. In addition, DDNS simplifies the administration of AD by allowing domain controllers (DCs) to automatically register their Service (SRV) resource records into DNS without administrator intervention. It is important to note that, by default, DHCP will not automatically update DNS; you have to configure DHCP explicitly to update DNS by editing its properties and checking the box labeled Enable Updates for Clients That Do Not Support Dynamic Updates.

WINS is a proprietary Microsoft name-resolution scheme for resolving NetBIOS names to IP addresses on Microsoft networks. It's a dynamic database that allows clients to register themselves automatically and, as with DNS, is a replacement for an older, manually updated system. On Microsoft networks, LMHOSTS was the equivalent of the HOSTS files used on the Internet.

Throughout this chapter, we discuss many of the terms used in this section, including zones, zone transfers, and resource records. Also, before installing DNS, you'll need to take into account some planning considerations. We'll examine those next.

DNS Planning Considerations

Before you actually install DNS, you must first analyze your current network and determine your name-resolution requirements. The areas of planning include the following:

- Site structure
- Types of name servers
- Types of network clients
- Naming hosts and domains
- Static IP addresses

Site Structure

The structure of your physical network plays an important role in the design of your DNS infrastructure. How you choose to implement DNS will be different depending on your setup. For example, you wouldn't have the same configuration for a single site with a couple of DCs as you would where you had multiple sites connected by WAN links with multiple DCs in each location.

The concept of sites is discussed in Chapter 12, "Active Directory Replication," but for our purposes here, we will define a site to be an IP subnet that is well connected (all hosts in the site have at least a 10Mbps Ethernet connection between them). A common problem with enterprise network environments with many sites connected by WAN links is bandwidth utilization. The DNS name-resolution process involves queries against a DNS database, and at times of high network utilization, this traffic can place an extra burden across the WAN links. In this type of situation, it is recommended that you place DNS servers at each site so that name-resolution traffic does not have to cross the lower-bandwidth links.

When presented with exhibits of existing networks, you need to be able to determine how to set up DNS for those various environments.

Types of Name Servers

Different types of name servers need to be considered. In this section, we cover the following:

- Primary DNS servers
- Secondary DNS servers
- Caching-only DNS servers
- Forwarding DNS servers
- AD integrated servers

Primary DNS Servers

There are really two main types of non-AD DNS servers: primary servers and secondary servers. As briefly mentioned earlier, the DNS namespace is partitioned into what are known as *zones*. We discuss zones in detail in the "DNS Zones" section later in this chapter, but for now just understand that a zone is the part of the overall DNS namespace that is controlled by a primary server. There can only be one primary server in a zone, and that primary server is said to be *authoritative* for the zone. It is the master, and any changes to the DNS domain must be made on the primary server.

Secondary DNS Servers

A secondary server is essentially a backup server for the primary server. Note that during the name-resolution process, if a primary server cannot resolve a host name, the query is *not* submitted to a secondary server (if one exists in the zone). The secondary server is used as a failover if the primary server fails. If a client is unable to contact the primary DNS server, it attempts to use the secondary server if one has been configured. Another potential use of a secondary server is load-balancing. If you have 1,000 network clients, for example, you could configure half of them to use the primary server first and half of them to use the secondary server first. This would reduce the load on the primary server.

Changes are never made directly to a secondary server, which receives a copy of the master zone file from the primary name server in a zone. This process is called *zone transfer* and is covered in more detail in the "Zone Transfer" section, later in this chapter. Unlike with primary servers, a zone can have multiple secondary servers.

Caching-Only Name Servers

This type of name server does pretty much what the name implies—it functions only to cache queries. The caching-only name server does not maintain a zone database file, nor does it receive updates from a primary server. It simply performs queries, caches the results, and returns results to querying clients. You can use caching-only name servers to deploy DNS services to sites that you do not wish to have an editable copy of the DNS zone.

The advantage to using a caching-only name server is the reduction in network traffic. The reduction is twofold. First, there is no replication traffic being generated between the primary name server and the caching-only server as there is between a primary and secondary server. Second, a caching-only server reduces name-resolution traffic by reducing the need for subsequent queries to go through the entire name-resolution process.

The disadvantage of caching-only servers, however, is that if a server is rebooted, the cache is flushed; the server must build its cache back up again from scratch.

Caching-only servers can also perform what is called *negative caching*, which caches failed results. This reduces the timeout process when a client queries for a site that does not exist or is unavailable.

Forwarding DNS Servers

Forwarding DNS servers exist solely to communicate with DNS servers outside the local zone. By default, any DNS server that receives a query it cannot resolve will contact an outside DNS server to resolve the name for the client making the query. A DNS forwarder functions like a proxy, becoming the only DNS server in a zone that can communicate outside the zone. This is similar in concept to a bridgehead server, which improves the utilization of network bandwidth by designating a single server as the contact point to other sites. If the primary name server, for example, cannot resolve a name, it sends the query to the forwarding DNS server for resolution. Figures 3.1 and 3.2 show a DNS infrastructure not using a forwarder and using a forwarder, respectively.

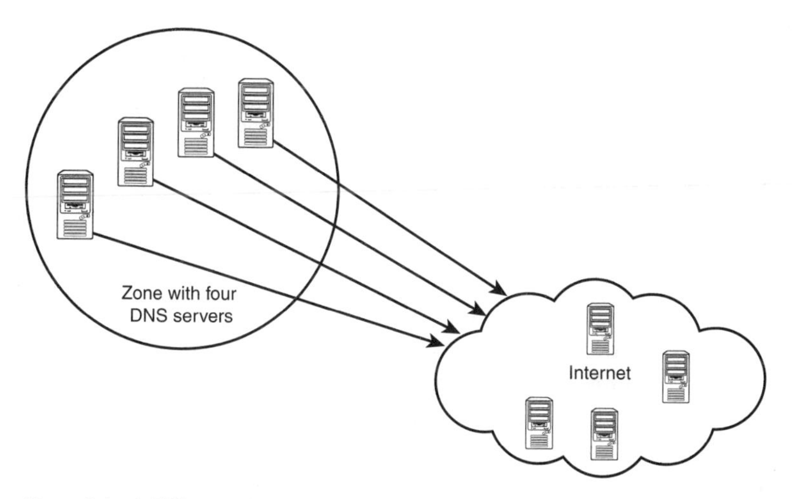

Figure 3.1 A DNS zone where all name servers communicate outside of the local zone.

Forwarding servers can be configured to use either nonexclusive or exclusive mode. In nonexclusive mode, a name server can attempt to resolve a query through its own zone database files if a forwarder cannot resolve the query. In exclusive mode, if a forwarder cannot resolve a query, the server that sent the query to the forwarder does not attempt to resolve the name itself and simply returns a failure notice to the client that originated the request.

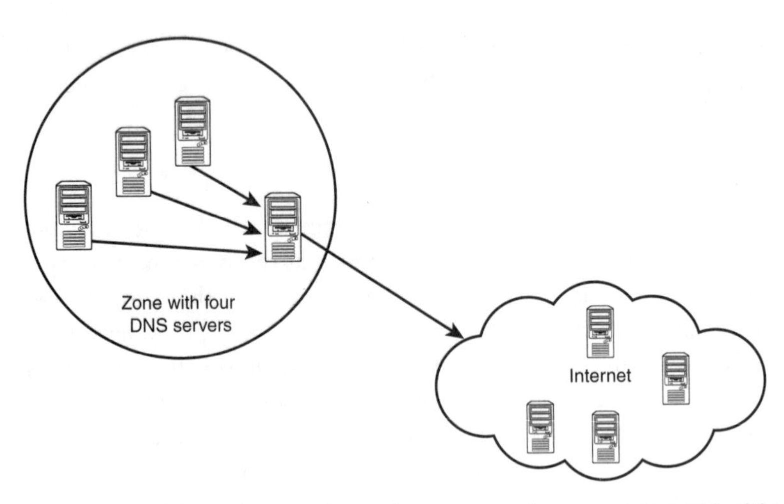

Figure 3.2 A DNS zone that uses a forwarding name server to communicate outside of the local zone.

AD Integrated Servers

Although the previous types of name servers are what are known as "standard" name server types, Windows 2000 introduces the ability to integrate DNS zones into AD. With AD integrated zones, each DC functions as a primary server and contains an editable copy of the zone. Through multimaster replication, discussed in Chapter 12, AD ensures that each copy of the zone is kept current across all DCs.

AD integrated zones provide the following benefits:

- **Fault tolerance**—Standard zones rely on zone transfers for replication, a process that requires the primary server to send updates to the secondary servers. If a primary server goes offline, there is no way to promote a secondary server to become a primary, and updates do not occur again until the primary server is brought online. With AD integrated zones, there isn't the same single point of failure.
- **Security**—AD integrated zones do not store zone information in a text file as standard primary and secondary zones do, and in addition, zone updates can be set so that only secure updates are allowed.
- **Integrated replication**—Because the DNS zone is integrated into AD, it is replicated through the normal AD replication process. Standard zones would require creating an additional replication topology for DNS.

Types of Network Clients

The types of network clients that you have on your network impact your DNS strategy. If you have all Windows 2000 clients, for example, you can utilize all the features of Windows 2000 DNS, such as dynamic updates and secure updates. Legacy Windows NT and Windows 9*X* clients can't register their resource records automatically through the dynamic update process. However, Windows 2000 can accommodate these clients if they are Dynamic Host Configuration Protocol (DHCP) clients.

A Windows 2000 DHCP server can register legacy clients on their behalf in DNS by you enabling the Enable Updates for DNS Clients That Do Not Support Dynamic Updates option in the DHCP management console.

Naming Hosts and Domains

It is easy to get spoiled by the ability to create DNS domain names that are lengthy. However, if legacy clients exist or you are operating in mixed mode with NT 4 DCs, you must be aware of the limitations on NetBIOS-created names. Windows 2000 attempts to create a default NetBIOS name at the time you create the DNS domain name; however, you might run into problems with existing domains. NetBIOS names are limited to 14 characters, so if you have an existing NT 4 domain called `WINDOWSNETWORK` and you attempt to create a new domain called `windowsnetwork1.com`, the default NetBIOS name will be the same as the aforementioned Windows NT domain, and creation will fail.

You should be comfortable with situations where you have to manage both NetBIOS and DNS domain names.

Static IP Addresses

For obvious reasons, DNS servers must have static IP addresses. If the server you are planning to use for DNS is currently configured as a DHCP client, be sure to assign it a unique static IP address for its subnet before installing the DNS server service. IP addresses are configured through TCP/IP properties within the properties of My Network Places.

Before we get to installing and configuring DNS for AD, we first need to take a moment to expand on the concept of DNS zones.

DNS Zones

Zones were mentioned previously in this chapter, but we haven't really taken the time to talk about them in much depth. As stated earlier, a zone is a partitioned portion of the overall DNS namespace. Zones make the manageability of the namespace much easier than the flat namespace of HOSTS files did. A zone must encompass a contiguous namespace, however. For example, a single zone could not be authoritative for both `Inside-Corner.com` and `quepublishing.com`, because those two domains are not part of the same namespace. A *contiguous namespace* encompasses a single second-level domain name. For example, the domains `Inside-Corner.com`, `Studio.Inside-Corner.com`, `GuitarShop.Studio.Inside-Corner.com`, and `Production.Inside-Corner.com` are all part of the same namespace.

Multiple zones within a contiguous namespace are used primarily to distribute administrative responsibilities. In many corporations, there are political boundaries that must be managed, with different divisions/departments having their own administrators. Multiple zones allow multiple administrators to be responsible for their individual pieces of the namespace.

Another reason to partition the namespace into zones is to reduce the load on a DNS infrastructure. Consider a megacorporation such as Microsoft, with more than 100,000 nodes on the network spread out across the globe. A single zone would place a tremendous burden on the primary DNS server (remember, there can be only one primary server in a zone), and the replication traffic to secondary DNS servers would make a significant impact on network performance. Dividing the Microsoft.com namespace into multiple zones distributes the load, thus increasing performance and easing administration. Even using AD integrated zones would require that updates with the zone be replicated to every other DNS server in the zone. Again, the bandwidth usage for this type of traffic would potentially have a detrimental effect on network performance, particularly if changes were being made frequently.

Windows 2000 supports two types of zones: forward lookup and reverse lookup. These zones are associated with the types of name-resolution queries they enable. We discuss these zones in greater detail when we look at installing and configuring Windows 2000 DNS later in this chapter.

Zone Transfer

Zone transfer is the process by which changes made on the primary server are replicated to all the secondary servers in the zone. There are three types of zone transfer to consider:

- Full zone transfer
- Incremental zone transfer
- AD replication

Full Zone Transfer

Originally, the only method of replication between primary and secondary servers was the *full zone transfer*. With this method, the entire zone database file is transferred whenever an update is made. The zone transfer is performed through a "pull" mechanism rather than a "push." This means that the secondary servers initiate the zone transfer. The process is as follows:

1. The secondary server waits a predetermined amount of time before contacting the primary server. When it does establish contact, it requests the primary server's Start of Authority (SOA) record. (Record types are discussed in depth in the "Resource Records" section later in this chapter.)
2. The primary server responds to the secondary server with its SOA record.
3. Whenever a change is made to the primary name server, the serial number held in the SOA record is incremented. When the secondary server receives the SOA record from the primary server, it compares the serial number to its own. If the serial number in the SOA record sent by the primary server is higher than the serial number in the SOA record currently on the secondary server, the secondary server knows its zone database is out of date. It then sends a request back to the primary server for a full zone transfer. This full transfer is done through an AXFR request.
4. The primary server then sends its full zone database file back to the secondary server. After the update is complete, the process begins again with the waiting period.

Incremental Zone Transfer

As you can probably imagine, performing a full zone transfer every time a single change is made to the primary server is inefficient. It also can generate a lot of network traffic if the primary server receives frequent updates and there are multiple secondary servers. To get around this problem, RFC 1995 allows for *incremental zone transfers*. As the name implies, with an incremental transfer, only the portion of the database that has been changed is replicated.

The process with an incremental transfer is the same as a full transfer, except with an incremental transfer, the secondary server sends an IXFR request, signifying an incremental transfer, rather than the AXFR request, which signifies a full zone transfer.

If you think of AXFR as A (all) XFR (transfer), it is easy to remember that AXFR is a full transfer. Likewise, you can think of IXFR as I (incremental) XFR (transfer).

For an incremental transfer to work, a version history must be kept so that name servers will know what changes have already been applied. The primary server maintains a version history, which keeps tracks of all changes that have been made since the last version update was transferred to a secondary server. When a secondary server requests an IXFR transfer, the primary server starts sending the recent updates, beginning with the oldest updates and progressing to the most recent updates.

When the secondary server begins receiving the updates, it creates a new version of the zone and begins applying the updates to that copy. When all the updates are committed to the copy of the zone database, the original database is replaced with the copy.

If the primary server does not support incremental transfers, it simply ignores the incremental request of the secondary server and performs a full zone transfer.

AD Replication

AD integrated zones are able to piggyback off of the standard AD replication scheme already in place on the network. Therefore, you do not have to manage a separate replication scheme for DNS data as you would if you used standard primary and secondary servers. AD replication is covered in Chapter 12.

Installing DNS

Installing DNS is quite easy. With Windows 2000 already installed, follow these steps:

1. Select Control Panel, Add/Remove Programs, Add/Remove Windows Components.
2. When the Windows Components Wizard launches, navigate to Networking Services.
3. Highlight Networking Services and click Details.
4. Select the Domain Name System (DNS) check box and click OK.

After you've installed DNS, the real work comes in configuring it for use on your Windows 2000 network.

Configuring DNS

Several configuration issues need to be considered when setting up DNS. These include the following:

- Root servers
- Forward lookup zones
- Reverse lookup zones
- Resource records
- Dynamic DNS

Root Servers

When you initially launch the DNS Microsoft Management Console (MMC) snap-in after installing the DNS service, a configuration wizard opens. You initially have the option of configuring your server as a root server. Root servers on the Internet are authoritative for the entire DNS namespace. Obviously, you would not be able to create a root server that is authoritative for the entire Internet, so you should only create a root server if your network is not connected to the Internet. If your LAN is not connected to the Internet and you create a root server, the root server is authoritative for any namespace you create in the AD forest.

Forward Lookup Zones

For DNS services to work, at least one forward lookup zone must be configured on your server. The reason is that forward lookup zones are what enable forward lookup queries, the standard method of name resolution in DNS, to work. Forward lookup zones allow computers to resolve host names to IP addresses.

To create a forward lookup zone, right-click Forward Lookup Zones in the DNS MMC console and click New Zone. A configuration wizard launches.

The first choice you have to make when configuring a new zone is what type of zone it will be. The choices are as follows:

- Active Directory integrated
- Standard primary
- Standard secondary

The zones correspond with the types of name servers discussed previously in this chapter. If you have not installed AD yet (which isn't required for DNS), the AD integrated option will be grayed out. In many cases, it is easier to configure DNS before installing AD, then create the zones as primary and secondary zones, and finally convert them to AD integrated zones after installing AD. The reason is that installing both at the same time requires configuring two major services and significant network changes simultaneously. Instead, you should take on one task at a time, which makes troubleshooting much easier in the event of problems.

Unless you have a need to communicate with non-Windows 2000 DNS servers, you should use AD integrated zones whenever possible.

You need to know when to use one type of AD integrated zone versus another.

Reverse Lookup Zones

A reverse lookup zone is not required for DNS services to function; however, you will want to create a reverse lookup zone to allow reverse lookup queries to function. Without a reverse lookup zone, troubleshooting tools such as NSLOOKUP that can resolve host names from IP addresses cannot work. Whereas forward lookup zones allow computers to resolve host names to IP addresses, reverse lookup zones allow computers to resolve IP addresses to host names. As with forward lookup zones, you have the option of creating AD integrated, standard primary, or standard secondary zones.

Unlike naming a forward lookup zone, you name a reverse lookup zone by its IP address. You can either type your network ID into the first field and watch the reverse lookup zone name automatically be created for you, or you can choose to type in the reverse lookup zone name into the second field following RFC conventions. The information text between the network ID and reverse lookup zone name fields describes how to name a reverse lookup zone.

As with forward lookup zones, if you are creating an AD integrated zone, you are done after supplying the zone name. With standard primary and standard secondary zones, you have to also supply the zone filename, which defaults to adding a `.dns` extension onto the end of your zone name. With a standard secondary zone, you have to list the IP addresses of the primary DNS servers with which the secondary zone should communicate.

With your zones configured and DNS services functioning, let's look at the entries, known as *resource records*, you'll find within the server.

Resource Records

Resource records (RRs) are the basic units of information within DNS used to resolve all DNS queries. When the Windows 2000 DNS service starts up, a number of records are registered at the server.

Several common RRs are used with Windows 2000 DNS:

- Start of Authority (SOA)
- Name Server (NS)
- Address (A)
- Pointer (PTR)
- Mail Exchanger (MX)
- Service (SRV)
- Canonical Name (CNAME)

Start of Authority Record (SOA)

The SOA record is contained at the beginning of every zone, both forward lookup and reverse lookup zones. It defines a number of details for the zone, including the following:

- **Time-to-live (TTL)**—The amount of time a record is considered valid in the DNS database. Higher values reduce network bandwidth utilization but increase the possibility of outdated information existing.
- **Authoritative server**—Shows the primary DNS server that is authoritative for the zone.
- **Responsible person**—Shows the e-mail address of the person who administers the zone.
- **Serial number**—Shows the serial number of the zone. Remember that the serial number is incremented whenever an update is made and that secondary servers use serial numbers to determine whether their copy of the zone database is out of date.
- **Refresh**—Shows how often secondary servers check to see whether their zone database files need updating.
- **Retry**—Shows how long a secondary server will wait after sending an AXFR (full zone transfer for standard zones) or IXFR (incremental zone transfer for standard zones) request before resending the request.
- **Expire**—Shows how long after a zone transfer that a secondary server will respond to zone queries before discarding the zone as invalid because of no communication with the primary server.
- **Minimum TTL**—Shows the minimum TTL a resource record will use if it does not explicitly state a TTL value.

Name Server (NS) Records

NS records show all servers that are authoritative for a zone, both primary and secondary servers for the zone specified in the SOA record, and primary name servers for any delegated zones.

Address (A) Records

The most basic entry in DNS, the A record maps the FQDN of a host to its IP address. When a client sends a standard forward lookup name-resolution query, the server uses A records to resolve the name.

Pointer (PTR) Records

The opposite of A records, PTR records provide reverse lookup services for DNS. That is, a PTR record maps an IP address to an FQDN. When a reverse lookup query is sent to a DNS server, such as through the NSLOOKUP utility, PTR records are consulted to resolve the address. PTR records are mapped in reverse lookup zones, which are in the `in-addr.arpa` zone.

Mail Exchanger (MX) Records

MX records designate a mail exchanging server for a DNS zone, which is a host that processes or forwards e-mail. In addition to the standard Owner, Class, and Type fields, MX records also support a fourth field: Mail Server Priority. This field is used when you have multiple mail servers in your domain, and mail exchangers with lower values are "preferred" over mail exchangers with higher values when determining which server to use to process an email message.

Service (SRV) Records

SRV records allow you to specify the location of servers providing a particular service, such as Web servers. You can create SRV records to identify hosts in the zone that provide a service, and then a resolver can find the A record of a service to resolve the name.

If you are having trouble with name-resolution services, where clients cannot successfully contact DCs, ensure that the appropriate SRV records exist for the DCs on the network.

Canonical Name (CNAME) Records

A CNAME record creates an alias for a specified host. This type of record is used most commonly to hide implementation details of your network. For example, say you have a Web server running at `www.mycorp.com`. The server that the Web site is running on might really be `server1.mycorp.com`. You don't want users to have to use the real server name, and you want the flexibility of being able to move the Web site to a newer, faster server in the future as traffic grows, without having to change the address of your Web site from `server1.mycorp.com` to `server2.mycorp.com`. CNAME provides the ability to alias the host name so that problems like this do not occur.

DDNS

DDNS, defined in RFC 2136, is used in Windows 2000 in conjunction with DHCP. When a Windows 2000 client boots up and receives addressing information from DHCP, it can register itself with DNS, automatically adding the requisite resource records.

Dynamic Updates

DDNS is enabled/disabled through zone properties. To do so, open the DNS MMC console from the Start menu, right-click your forward or reverse lookup zone, and then click Properties. On the General property sheet is the Allow Dynamic Updates? option. The choices are Yes, No, and Only Secure Updates. When DDNS is enabled, DHCP manages the resource records for DHCP clients. When a DHCP lease expires, the DHCP service cleans up the A and PTR records from DNS. By default, a dynamic update is performed from Windows 2000 clients every 24 hours, or immediately when one of the following occurs:

- A DHCP-obtained IP address is renewed or a new lease is obtained.
- A static IP address is added or removed from a computer.
- The TCP/IP configuration of a client changes.
- A Plug and Play event occurs on a client, such as the installation of a new network adapter.

Secure Updates

In addition to enabling dynamic updates, you can configure Windows 2000 DNS to perform only secure updates. As just mentioned, this is enabled by selecting Only Secure Updates on the General property sheet of the desired zone. So what do secure updates do?

Once you have enabled secure updates, you can control which users and computers can register themselves into DNS. By default, all members of the Authenticated Users security group are granted permission, although this can be changed as necessary through access control lists (ACLs) by clicking the Security tab on a zone's property sheet.

A dynamic update in general requires that the client computers be capable of registering an FQDN. Windows 2000 clients are capable of this; Windows NT and 9*X* clients are not. As we've previously discussed, Windows 2000 DHCP can act as a proxy for these legacy clients, because DHCP can register them in DNS on their behalf. The reason the FQDN consideration is important is that once you've enabled secure updates, you can reserve FQDNs in DNS so that only certain users can use them. To do this, create a new host record in the DNS console with the desired FQDN. Then, on the Security tab, configure the ACL so that only the desired user can update the resource records associated with the particular FQDN.

Note that all resource records for a single FQDN share a single ACL. In other words, if you create an A record for `workstation1.inside-corner.com` and then create an MX record for the same host, there is only one ACL for the two records. This would be true even if you added additional records for the same host.

Monitoring and Troubleshooting DNS for AD

As with any network service, most likely there will be times when some sort of problem occurs. Windows 2000 provides some tools to monitor and troubleshoot DNS, so there are steps you can take when the DNS service is not behaving as expected.

Figure 3.3 shows the monitoring options in Windows 2000. To reach this window, follow these steps:

1. Right-click the DNS server you want to monitor in the DNS MMC snap-in and then click Properties.
2. Once there, click the Monitoring tab. The options and their descriptions are as follows:

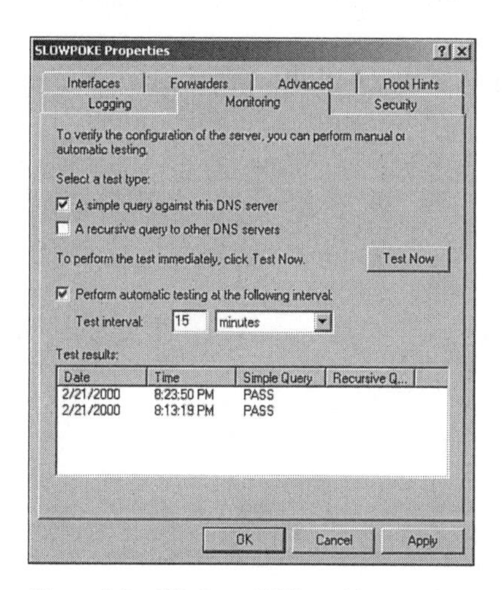

Figure 3.3 Windows 2000 enables an administrator to monitor the DNS service.

- **Simple query**—As the name implies, a simple forward lookup query is passed to the server for resolution. The results are either pass or fail, and the time and date are stamped in the Test Results box at the bottom of the window.
- **Recursive query**—This is a more complex query where the server queries other servers until it can resolve the query or until it runs out of options and fails. With a recursive query, the name server cannot simply refer the client query to another name server.
- **Perform automatic testing**—This option tells the server to run the tests you chose at the interval you've specified. This is helpful in troubleshooting intermittent server problems.

DNS Logging

In addition to monitoring, you can also enable logging of selected DNS events. When you install the DNS server service, Windows 2000 adds a log for DNS into the Event Viewer. If you enable logging, you can view the results there.

You configure logging through the Logging property sheet in the DNS server's properties, which is right next to the Monitoring tab previously discussed. Enable logging only for debugging/troubleshooting purposes, because the act of logging will have a negative impact on server performance and hard disk space. The Logging property sheet is shown in Figure 3.4. DNS log files are stored as `dns.log` in the `\winnt\system32\dns` folder.

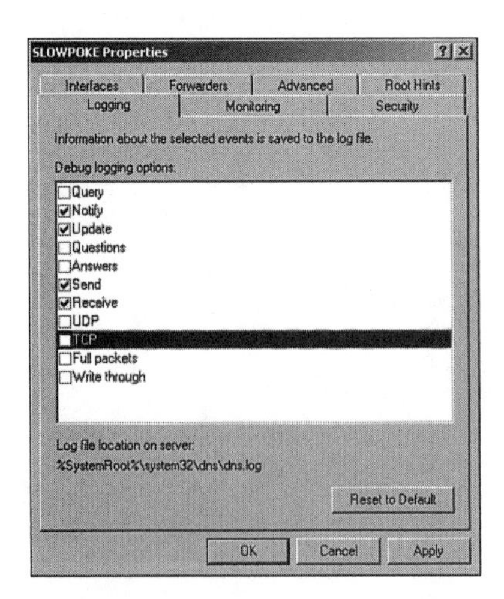

Figure 3.4 Logging is a useful troubleshooting tool when a DNS server is not responding as expected.

NSLOOKUP

NSLOOKUP is the primary command-line tool for troubleshooting DNS. In addition, it makes a handy security tool for tracing hackers back to their source. If you have the TCP/IP protocol installed, this basic TCP/IP tool is already on your system.

Resolving Host Names from IP Addresses

Remember that if you want NSLOOKUP to be able to resolve host names from IP addresses, you must have already configured a reverse lookup zone. NSLOOKUP has two modes: noninteractive and interactive. In noninteractive mode, you simply enter a command such as this:

```
C:\> nslookup 192.168.0.1 <enter>
```

If NSLOOKUP is successful, it returns the host name associated with the IP address in question. There are a number of options for NSLOOKUP in noninteractive mode, accessible by typing **nslookup /?** at a command prompt. One of the more common options is `-server`, which allows you to specify a name server to test other than the current primary DNS server configured on the client.

You enter interactive mode just by typing **nslookup** at a command prompt and pressing Enter. To leave interactive mode, type **exit** at a prompt. Typically, you'll use interactive mode when you want more than a single piece of information returned or are running multiple queries, one after another.

Verifying Resource Records

You can also use NSLOOKUP to verify the existence of resource records for troubleshooting purposes. For instance, if when workstations log in to a domain you get errors saying that a DC cannot be found, you could use NSLOOKUP to verify that the SRV and A records exist in DNS for the domain controllers. Figure 3.5 shows an example of using NSLOOKUP for this purpose.

To view the registered SRV records for the `inside-corner.com` domain, enter NSLOOKUP interactive mode by typing **nslookup** from a command prompt and pressing Enter. Then type the following:

```
ls -t SRV inside-corner.com
```

Figure 3.5 You can troubleshoot DNS by verifying resource records with NSLOOKUP.

The syntax for this command is found on the NSLOOKUP help screen, which is accessed by typing **?** and pressing Enter from the NSLOOKUP console.

This command, as written, lists all records (`ls`) of type (`-t`) SRV (service) for `inside-corner.com` (the domain in question). The output shows you whether the domain controllers are properly registered.

You should understand how to troubleshoot name-resolution scenarios.

Practice Questions

Question 1

Reorder the following events in setting up an AD network into their proper order:

Run **dcpromo.exe**.

Configure a static IP address on the DNS server.

Install DNS.

Configure a forward lookup zone.

The correct answer is:

Configure a static IP address on the DNS server.

Install DNS.

Configure a forward lookup zone.

Run `dcpromo.exe`.

Question 2

Which of the following is *not* a reason to use AD integrated zones rather than standard zones?

❍ a. Fault tolerance.

❍ b. Security.

❍ c. Simplicity of management.

❍ d. The database is stored in easy-to-edit text files.

Answer d is correct. AD integrated zones store zone information within the AD database. Answer d refers to standard zones, which store the DNS database in text files that carry a `.dns` extension. Answers a, b, and c are incorrect because fault tolerance, security, and simplicity of management are all legitimate reasons to use AD integrated zones.

Question 3

Which of the following DC resource record types would you look for if trying to troubleshoot workstations not being able to log on to a domain? [Check all correct answers]

- ❑ a. A
- ❑ b. CNAME
- ❑ c. SRV
- ❑ d. MX

Answers a and c are correct. You would check for the proper registration of Address and Service records. Answer b is incorrect because CNAME records are aliases. Answer d is incorrect because MX records are for mail servers.

Question 4

The following are types of name servers:

Active Directory integrated

Standard primary and secondary

Match the following features with the name server type they are most associated with:

Single point of failure

Zone transfer

Fault tolerant

Replication

Text database

Secure

The correct answer is:

Active Directory integrated

Fault tolerant

Replication

Secure

Standard primary and secondary

Single point of failure

Zone transfer

Text database

Question 5

Under which of the following circumstances could you use Windows 98 clients in a dynamic update situation? [Choose the best answer]

- ❍ a. When the Only Secure Updates option is enabled on the DNS server.
- ❍ b. When the Allow Dynamic Updates? option is set to Yes on the DNS server.
- ❍ c. When the Enable Updates For DNS Clients That Do Not Support Dynamic Updates option is enabled on the DHCP server.
- ❍ d. Legacy clients cannot be supported by dynamic update.

Answer c is correct. By default, dynamic update is not supported by legacy clients; however, DHCP can be configured to act as a proxy on their behalf. Answers a and b are incorrect because simply enabling dynamic updating or secure updates will not allow Windows 98 clients to register with DNS. Answer d is incorrect because they can be supported.

Question 6

Which of the following types of name servers store copies of a zone database? [Check all correct answers]

- ❑ a. AD integrated
- ❑ b. Caching
- ❑ c. Primary
- ❑ d. Secondary

Answers a, c, and d are correct. AD integrated, primary, and secondary name servers all store copies of a zone database. Answer b is incorrect because caching is the only type in the list that does not store an editable copy of a zone database.

Question 7

Which of the following name-resolution methods use manually updated text files to record name mappings? [Check all correct answers]

- ❑ a. DNS
- ❑ b. HOSTS
- ❑ c. WINS
- ❑ d. LMHOSTS

Answers b and d are correct. HOSTS was a name-to–IP address mapping system used prior to the advent of DNS on the Internet. LMHOSTS resolved NetBIOS names on Windows networks before WINS and later DNS. Answers a and c are incorrect because DNS and WINS are both dynamically updated databases, whereas HOSTS and LMHOSTS use text files to store their mappings.

Question 8

Which of the following elements is required to successfully install and configure DNS? [Choose the best answer]

- ❍ a. DHCP
- ❍ b. Static IP address
- ❍ c. Active Directory
- ❍ d. Windows 2000 clients

Answer b is correct. To install and configure a working DNS server, the server running DNS must have a static IP address. Answer a is incorrect because DHCP is not required to use DNS, although it is necessary if you want to enable dynamic update. Answer c is incorrect because Active Directory is not required. Answer d is incorrect because DNS works with legacy clients as well as Windows 2000 clients.

Question 9

When monitoring a DNS server, which type of test sends a query to other name servers for resolution? [Choose the best answer]

❍ a. Simple query

❍ b. Recursive query

❍ c. Forward lookup query

❍ d. Iterative query

Answer b is correct. A recursive query sends a resolution query to other servers when monitoring the server. Answer a is incorrect because a simple query resolves the name against only the server being tested. Answers c and d are incorrect because these are not valid choices for DNS monitoring.

Question 10

In a standard primary zone, what name server(s) can an administrator update the zone database on? [Choose the best answer]

❍ a. Secondary

❍ b. Active Directory integrated

❍ c. Primary

❍ d. Any server

Answer c is correct. In a standard primary zone, only the primary server can be updated directly. Answer a is incorrect because secondary servers receive updates through zone transfer. Answer b is incorrect because Active Directory integrated servers don't exist in a standard primary zone. Answer d is incorrect because only the primary server can be updated in this way.

Need to Know More?

Iseminger, David. *Active Directory Services for Windows 2000 Technical Reference*. Microsoft Press. Redmond, WA, 2000. ISBN 0735606242.

A solid reference for planning and deploying Active Directory networks, this book has good coverage of DNS as it relates to Active Directory.

Microsoft Corporation. *Microsoft Windows 2000 Server Resource Kit*. Microsoft Press. Redmond, WA, 2000. ISBN 1572318058.

The quintessential resource for Windows 2000 Server and Active Directory, this kit has extensive coverage of Active Directory and DNS in particular.

Norris-Lowe, Alistair. *Windows 2000 Active Directory Service*. O'Reilly & Associates. Sebastopol, CA, 2000. ISBN 1565926382.

Another good AD resource, this book contains good information on DNS planning and infrastructure issues.

Willis, Will, David Watts, and Tillman Strahan. *Windows 2000 System Administration Handbook*. Prentice-Hall Computer Books. Upper Saddle River, NJ, 2000. ISBN 0130270105.

This handbook explains Windows 2000 systems administration concepts in detail, including building an Active Directory network on a DNS foundation. This is a solid all-around Windows 2000 reference with good coverage of Active Directory.

Windows 2000 Domains: Planning and Installation

Terms you'll need to understand:

- ✓ Workgroup
- ✓ Domain
- ✓ Member server
- ✓ Scalability
- ✓ Forest root
- ✓ Domain controller
- ✓ **SYSVOL**
- ✓ **dcpromo**
- ✓ Organizational Unit (OU)
- ✓ Active Directory integrated domains

Techniques you'll need to master:

- ✓ Planning for your Active Directory install
- ✓ Installing your first Active Directory domain
- ✓ Making installation decisions based on your corporate needs
- ✓ Verifying and troubleshooting your Active Directory installation
- ✓ Performing an unattended installation of Active Directory
- ✓ Performing post-installation procedures

After the installation of Windows 2000 Server, Advanced Server, or Datacenter Server, the system will exist in one of two settings. The server will be a member server (or standalone server) of a workgroup, or it will be a member server of an existing domain. In either state, the server will have the capability of holding several roles. For example, a standalone server would be able to handle the sharing of folders and files, Web services through IIS, media services, database services, print services—the list of functional uses is long. However, directory services are not part of a member server's functionality. For that reason, you may need to consider implementing a "domain" environment.

What are some of the immediate advantages of a domain environment? Perhaps your company requires a single point of logon, centralized management of resources, scalability, or your network and directory infrastructure to be able to grow with your company over time. Making that first move toward a domain begins with establishing your first domain controller (DC). To accomplish this with Windows 2000, you need to install the Windows 2000 Active Directory (AD) service and configure it properly to suit your company's needs. This endeavor requires some forethought and planning to allow for a smooth domain deployment.

The Windows 2000 Domain

The term *domain* is not new to the networking vernacular. The way Windows 2000 utilizes the concept, however, is quite advanced. The Windows 2000 domain is defined as being a boundary for security that provides an organized means of structuring users, resources, and directory information. It also provides a method for replicating that information, and it provides the core administrative services in a Windows 2000 network. In Windows 2000, only one directory database, called the *AD*, stores all the user accounts and other resources for the domain. This centralized structure means that users need only have one account that will provide access to all resources for which they are given permission.

In the actual creation of a domain, you identify a Domain Name System (DNS) name for the domain. This requires some planning, in harmony with the material in Chapter 3, "Implementing and Administering DNS," to choose a name that is appropriate from both a corporate and legal standpoint. Windows 2000 domains utilize the DNS naming convention to maintain an organized structure. Because the first domain created will be the top-level domain in your directories' infrastructure, this domain is the most crucial, especially if you will be implementing additional domains in the network. Another term for the first domain is the *root domain*, so named because it is the root of the entire domain tree and, by extension, the entire forest.

Even though it is small, a single domain without child domains is still considered its own domain tree. In addition, this single domain is called the *forest root* because it becomes the first tree of a possible new forest. The forest root can be likened to the foundation of a building, which holds up the rest of the structure. The foundation of a domain must be solid, and it begins by the promotion of a member server to be a domain controller. You accomplish this promotion by installing AD. Before installation can proceed, however, you must ensure that certain requirements have been met on the server that will be your DC.

Requirements for AD

Whenever you implement a new feature within a Windows product, minimum hardware and software requirements must be met so that the feature will work adequately. The first requirement is fairly obvious: You must have a computer running Windows 2000 Server, Advanced Server, or Datacenter Server. Meeting this AD requirement ensures that your system meets the minimum hardware for your operating system.

The following list identifies the requirements for the installation of Windows 2000 Server:

- **CPU**—Pentium 133 MHz or higher
- **Memory**—256MB recommended (128MB supported)
- **Hard disk space**—2GB with 1GB of free space
- **Display**—VGA resolution or higher
- **CD-ROM or network installation**—Supported

Windows 2000 Server will install with 64MB of RAM, but it won't perform well with less than 128MB, so the preceding requirements have been provided by Microsoft.

Once the operating system is installed, the following requirements are necessary to install AD:

- Depending on the partition of the hard disk where you plan to install your AD database and transaction log files, you will need 200MB for the database and 50MB for the transaction log. The files can reside on a partition that is formatted with the FAT (file allocation table), FAT32, or NTFS (NT File System) file system. These files will grow over time as more objects are added, so you need to ensure the space is sufficient. Additional space is required if your DC is also configured to be a Global Catalog server.
- Along with the database and transaction logs, a special folder structure is installed during the installation, and the root folder is called SYSVOL. This folder must reside on an NTFS partition. If your system doesn't have an NTFS partition, the AD installation will fail.

If you would like to install your **SYSVOL** folder on a partition that you already have allocated as FAT and you cannot reformat the partition without losing critical data (as in the case of your boot and system partition), you need to use the **convert** command. Go to a command prompt and type **convert.exe c: /fs:ntfs**, where **c:** should be replaced with the drive letter you require.

- Another requirement is that your system is functioning under TCP/IP and utilizing a Domain Name System (DNS) server. If you've forgotten to establish a DNS server, this will be provided as an option during AD installation.

Once you've established that your server meets the requirements to install AD and you have invested the necessary time in planning your first DC, it's time to kick off the installation.

The AD Installation Wizard

The actual creation of the first domain of your network is not a difficult task. You are simply promoting a Windows 2000 Server to be a domain controller by using the AD Installation Wizard. You are creating your forest root as the first DC of your new domain.

The AD Installation Wizard, unlike some wizards, does not have an icon or shortcut to execute. It requires that you select Start, Run. In the box, type **dcpromo.exe** (or just **dcpromo** for short) and hit Enter.

This wizard offers the following directory service installation options:

➤ Create a domain controller for a new domain.

➤ Create a new domain tree or join an existing domain as a child domain.

➤ Create a new forest of domain trees or join an existing forest.

Let's consider the different areas of the wizard.

Installing Your First Domain

To install the first DC by promoting a member server, follow these steps:

If you install Windows 2000 on a server that is a primary or backup domain controller for an NT 4 domain, upgrading the server will automatically make it a Windows 2000 DC that includes the user and group accounts and configurations, unless you specify that the install is not an upgrade of the NT 4 domain controller.

1. Begin the promotion by selecting Start, Run and typing **`dcpromo.exe`**. Press Enter.

2. Once your AD Installation Wizard has initialized, you will see a screen that welcomes you to the wizard. Select Next.

3. As shown in Figure 4.1, you are presented with two options: creating a DC of a new domain (either a child domain, new domain tree, or new forest), and creating an additional DC for an existing domain (which will take on the account information of the domain joined). Because this is the first domain of a new forest, select the first radio button and click the Next button.

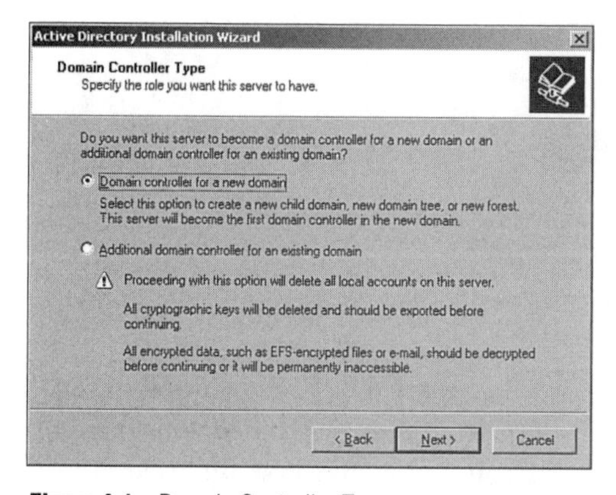

Figure 4.1 Domain Controller Type screen.

4. You are now asked whether you want to create a new domain tree or a new child domain in an existing domain tree, as shown in Figure 4.2. In the case of creating a new tree, you select the first radio button and click the Next button.

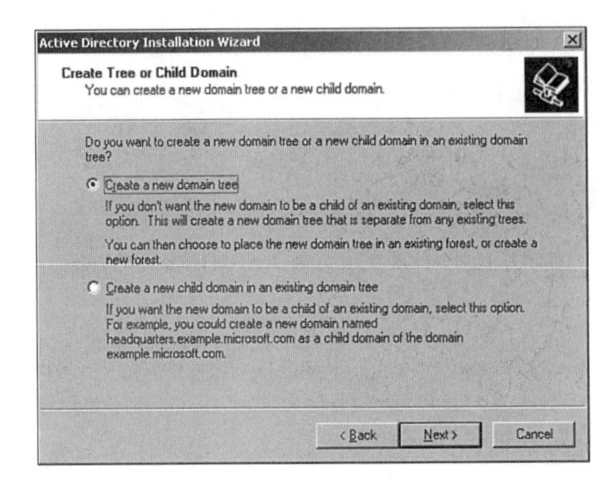

Figure 4.2 Create a new tree or a child domain.

5. The next screen in the wizard asks whether you want to create a new forest of domain trees or place the new domain tree in an existing forest, as shown in Figure 4.3. Again, to create the first domain (also considered the forest root domain), select the first radio button and click the Next button.

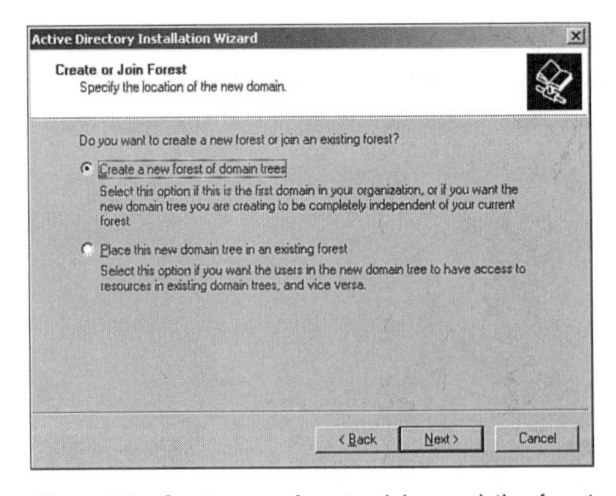

Figure 4.3 Create a new forest or join an existing forest.

6. The next screen is short, as shown in Figure 4.4. You are asked to supply the full DNS name of your domain. If you've planned your naming strategy and registered a name for your company's domain, use that name. If you are implementing your directory structure in a test

environment without a registered domain name, use a fictitious DNS name. Click the Next button.

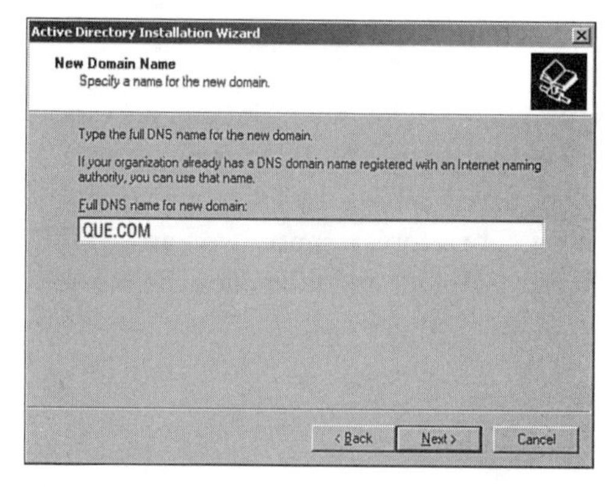

Figure 4.4 Your forest root domain name.

7. The next screen requests your NetBIOS name. This name is used for clients running earlier versions of Windows or NT that utilize NetBIOS for the location of their DCs. It is usually the same as the first part of your domain name. Enter the name and click the Next button.

8. The next screen, shown in Figure 4.5, specifies the location of the AD database and log files. These files can exist on any of the supported files systems for Windows 2000. Remember, the minimum requirement for AD is 200MB for the database and 50MB for the log files. Also, remember that minimum requirements should usually be exceeded to allow for flexibility and growth. Choose your location and then click the Next button.

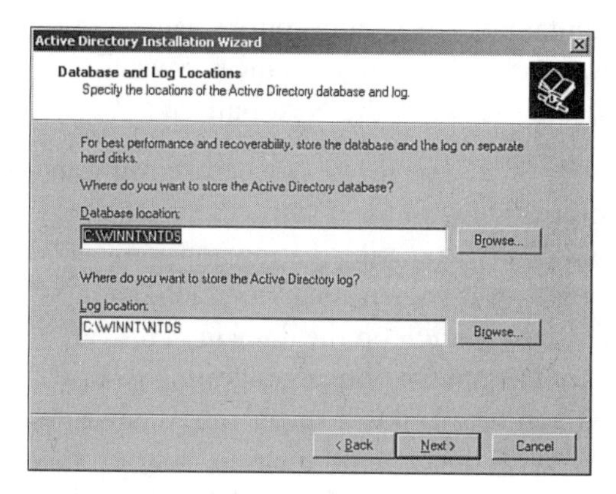

Figure 4.5 Database and log files.

Placing your database files and your log files on separate hard drives is recommended. Your database holds your directory, whereas your log file holds your temporary database changes before they are written to the actual database. This creates a conflict of interest for your hard drive as information is written back and forth. Placing the files on different drives (not partitions) will ensure equal time to both files.

9. The next screen, shown in Figure 4.6, is quite important and necessary to your AD installation. Here you specify the location for the SYSVOL folder. This folder, which will be shared, allows the DCs to receive replicas of the information within. Therefore, it must be on an NTFS partition. Indicate the location of this folder and then click the Next button.

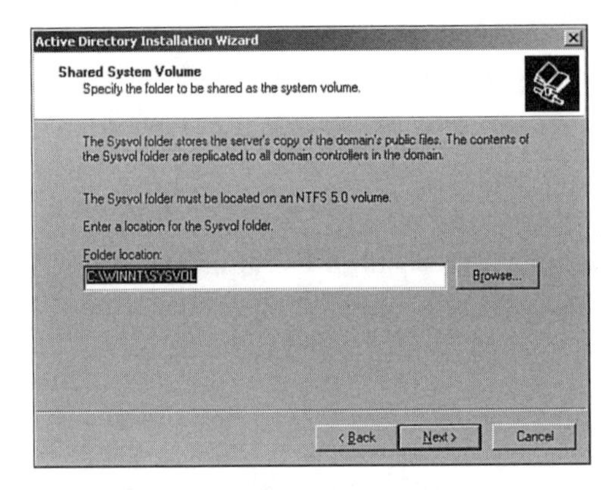

Figure 4.6 The placement of the **SYSVOL** folder.

10. The next screen allows you to specify the password for the administrative account that is used during Directory Services Restore Mode. Because the AD service is not started when entering this mode, it will be necessary for you to be authenticated by the server through another means. A non-AD database containing the administrator's name and password allows authentication under these circumstances. Specify your administrative password and then click the Next button.

11. The final question screen, shown in Figure 4.7, asks whether you want to allow permissions to be compatible with pre–Windows 2000 servers or you want to allow Windows 2000–compatible permissions only. The first selection comes with a warning. If you enable this option, anonymous users will be able to read information on the domain. This can be beneficial in some cases—for example, if you are migrating toward Windows 2000 from an NT 4 platform and will have a mixed environment of remote access servers. With this type of situation, your users dialing in from home will have difficulty logging in to the domain if

they contact a Windows 2000 DC, unless the permissions are oriented toward a pre–Windows 2000 system. Select your choice and then click the Next button.

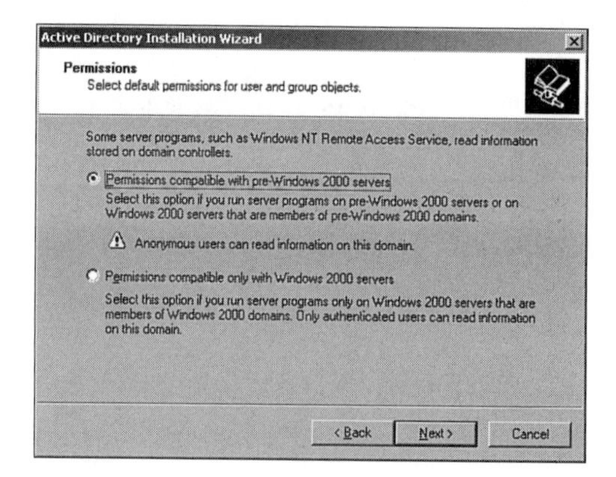

Figure 4.7 Permission compatibility screen.

12. When all your information is complete, you get the final screen, shown in Figure 4.8, which is customized to your choices. Look them over before clicking the Next button. After you do, the installation will follow through until you see a final screen of completion, where you should click Finish.

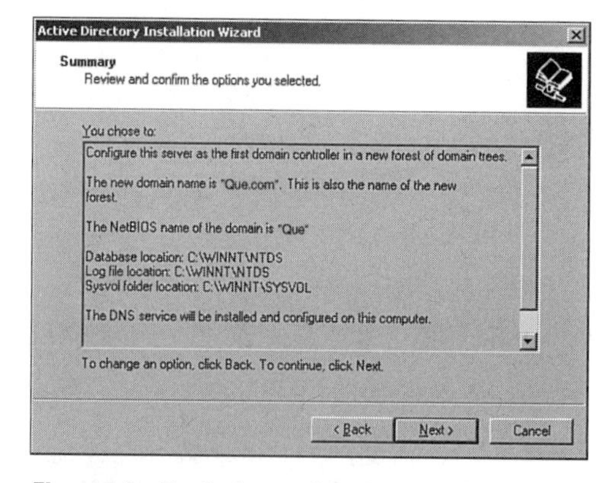

Figure 4.8 The final promotion screen.

Your installation will now proceed by establishing your system as the first DC for your new domain tree under a new forest root.

Deciding Which Type of DNS to Use

As already mentioned, having a DNS server for your AD installation is a prerequisite. However, you may determine which type of DNS server you will use. Although your choices are limited, they do exist, as discussed in Chapter 3. Let's assume that you haven't made your decision by the time you install AD. Not a problem—Windows 2000 will make the decision for you.

After you've indicated the location of the SYSVOL folder, the wizard will begin a search for the DNS in the IP stack to see whether it exists and whether it supports dynamic updates. In our scenario, a DNS server doesn't exist, and you will therefore receive an informative prompt that it will be created for you. Click OK at this point.

The screen that follows asks whether you want the DNS configured and installed on this computer or you want to install it yourself, as shown in Figure 4.9.

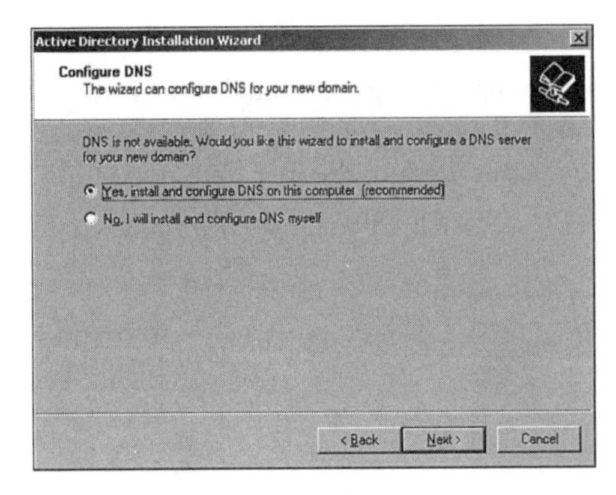

Figure 4.9 The Configure DNS screen.

Once the DNS is configured and it supports dynamic updates (which would be automatically done during the installation), the rest of your installation proceeds.

Active Directory installation does not automatically set the DNS to allow automatic updates unless you tell the wizard to do so. Microsoft recommends that you set this or allow the AD Installation Wizard to set it for you if the wizard is also installing DNS as part of AD installation. However, AD will work without enabling dynamic updates. If you do not allow dynamic updates, you have to manually synchronize the SRV resource records when you add or remove additional domain controllers.

The Lesser-Known Roles of the Wizard

On the surface, the AD Installation Wizard appears merely to handle the various screens that require user input. However, this understates its full role. Prior to an installation, the wizard performs the following checks:

1. Before the wizard even opens, it makes sure the user is a member of the local Administrators group and is on a Windows 2000 Server. It also checks that the server is ready to move forward without needing to reboot or complete some previously begun procedure. If the User Interface portion clears, the wizard moves on.
2. The wizard verifies that the NetBIOS and server names are unique.
3. The wizard checks the TCP/IP configuration to ensure that the system is fully functional and capable of reaching the DNS server. That DNS server must be able to provide dynamic updates or have manually provided an SRV resource record within your DNS; otherwise, the AD Installation Wizard will prompt you later to create a DNS server.
4. The wizard checks to ensure uniqueness and then validates DNS and NetBIOS domain names.
5. The final stages of verification involve checking the user's credentials to ensure that the user has the correct security permissions, and finally, that the files can be located where the user has specified.

In configuring the directory service, the AD Installation Wizard handles the following tasks:

- Making Registry changes for the AD
- Setting up Kerberos
- Setting the Local Security Authority (LSA) policy
- Placing the new tools into Administrative Tools (accessed through Start, Programs, Administrative Tools)
- Establishing performance counters for AD
- Setting up X.509 certificate acceptance

In addition, depending on the installation, the wizard might create the schema directory partition, the configuration directory partition, and the domain directory partition, which are portions of the directory that are held in a hierarchical fashion and replicated out to other DCs.

Fault-Tolerant Replicas

The concept of fault-tolerant replicas is simple: It refers to creating additional DCs within a single domain tree. Additional DCs in a domain help share the load and improve performance. They also provide fault tolerance, because if one DC goes down, the other DCs can authenticate the users and provide normal operations while the damaged DC is repaired.

When adding more DCs to a domain, keep the following factors in mind:

- The more DCs you have in a domain, the greater the logon authenticity, because when users log on to the domain, they can gain authentication from any one of the DCs.
- Each of the DCs will replicate or share its copy of the AD database with the other DCs in the domain. Adding more DCs to a domain also increases the following, thereby degrading network performance:
    - The amount of replication that takes place within the domain
    - The amount of bandwidth that is used on the network

When deciding how many DCs are going to be on the domain, you must consider both of these factors. You need to balance increased speed of logon authenticity against bandwidth usage due to directory replication.

Adding DCs to a domain is not a difficult task. Starting with a Windows 2000 server, you promote it using the `dcpromo.exe` command, which executes the AD Installation Wizard. Instead of selecting the option Domain Controller for a New Domain, you select Additional Domain Controller for an Existing Domain (refer back to Figure 4.1).

Once you have created the first domain, you are in a position to create Organizational Units (OUs) within the domain. But how do you know that your installation was a successful one? This topic is discussed in the next section.

Troubleshooting Your AD Installation

Any number of things can cause your AD installation to fail. Here are a few scenarios:

- *You get an Access Denied error message when creating or adding DCs.* These types of error messages usually indicate an incorrect user account. Perhaps you have logged on with an account that doesn't have permissions in the Local Administrators group of the server on which you are trying to create a new domain. Or, as in the case of adding a DC to a preexisting domain, it's possible that you are not a member of the Domain Administrators group.

Be conscious of situations where you are not a member of the Domain Administrators group, especially if you are asked about the accounts needed to install AD on a system.

- *Your DNS and NetBIOS names are not unique.* Not much of a choice here; you must have unique names, so you need to change them to names that are unique. The only exception to this rule would be in the case of a testing/training situation, where you are testing the various options for the domain structure in a lab environment (not a production environment, we hope), and you've added systems to the domain and then failed to remove them correctly, perhaps by merely formatting the drive. Now your AD domain tree might still see these nonexistent names as being present. To resolve this problem, you need to edit AD with some additional tools that Microsoft provides, such as ADSI Edit, a snap-in for the Microsoft Management Console (MMC) that acts as a low-level AD Editor.
- *The DC cannot be contacted, and you are sure that there is a DC up and running.* This situation might indicate that DNS is not set up correctly. Several areas of concern with DNS have already been discussed, but you should ensure that SRV resource records are present for the domain being contacted. Check your DNS server first to make certain these records exist. If they do exist, use the NSLOOKUP tool to determine whether you can resolve DNS names on the computer where you are installing AD.
- *You have an insufficient amount of disk space or you don't have an NTFS partition.* You must have a minimum disk space of 250MB for the database and transaction logs. You must also have an NTFS partition for the SYSVOL folder. If you can't free enough space, consider using another volume or partition to store these files. If you do not have an NTFS partition and cannot create one, you need to convert your existing partition. If you are running Windows 2000 Server in a dual-boot situation with Windows 98 on a FAT32 partition, you will not be able to make

the move toward a DC and retain your Windows 98 operating system under FAT32; you must convert your partition or remain a member server with FAT32.

Microsoft does not recommend having a Windows 2000 Server in a dual-boot configuration.

Verifying Your AD Installation

Once your installation is complete and the system has rebooted, you may want to verify your installation. Verification can be accomplished in a number of ways, the easiest being a check of your newly acquired Administrative Tools. However, you have a few other options to ensure a valid install.

File Verification

One way to verify that your installation is complete is to ensure that the AD files are located where you've specified. The following is a list of files that are necessary for AD:

- **NTDS.DIT**—The directory database file.
- **EDB.LOG and EDB.CHK**—The EDB files are the transaction logs and the checkpoint files. Transaction logs temporarily hold transactions before they are written to the directory. The checkpoint file is a pointer file that tracks transaction logs once they have been committed to the database. These files work in harmony to ensure an accurate database with multiple points of strength.
- **EDB.LOG**—The transaction log file temporarily holds transactions before they are written to the directory. It works in harmony with the EDB.CHK file to ensure an accurate database with multiple points of strength.
- **RES1.LOG and RES2.LOG**—RES files are reserved files that are used for low-disk-space situations. These two files are 10MB in size, as are all transaction logs. Because these are permanent, there is always a way to write to a file, even when disk space is low.

SYSVOL

Another way to make sure you've had a successful install is to ensure the SYSVOL folder structure is on an NTFS partition and contains a server copy of all shared files, including Group Policy and scripts. The `SYSVOL` folder should include several subfolders, including:

- `Domain`
- `Staging`
- `Staging Areas`
- `Sysvol`

The `Sysvol` folder within should be shared out as, you guessed it, `SYSVOL`. Another necessary folder that should be shared is the `Scripts` folder under the `Domain` folder, which is under the `SYSVOL` folder. The `Scripts` folder is shared out as `NETLOGON` and is used for backward compatibility with NT systems that search for scripts during logon in the `NETLOGON` share.

Final Checkpoints

You can investigate many avenues to ensure your AD install was successful, but the most direct method is to check within the event logs. Event logs retain several different types of logs that help you quickly pinpoint a failure, whether on the system itself or with one of the services, such as DNS.

If DNS doesn't seem to be functioning properly, refer to Chapter 3, which focuses on several tools to troubleshoot your DNS installation (such as verifying records with the NSLOOKUP tool and monitoring your DNS forward and recursive queries within the DNS properties on the Monitoring tab).

AD Removal

At times, you might want to remove your AD, especially if you've done some restructuring of your accounts and find that some domains require unnecessary administrative overhead or if certain DCs are simply not required and are creating a strain on the network because of an overabundance of replication. You remove AD with the same tool you used to install it—the AD Installation Wizard. Logically, not just any user can remove AD from the DC. If you are removing the last DC in the forest, you must be logged on as a member of the Domain Administrators group. If you are not removing the last DC in the forest, you must be a member of either the Domain Administrators group or the Enterprise Administrators group.

What Removing AD Entails

When you remove AD, the following actions occur (which are reversals of what took place when you installed AD):

- Group Policy security settings are removed, and Local Security is reenabled for local security settings.
- Any Flexible Single Master Operations (FSMO) roles are transferred over to other DCs, if any exist.
- The `SYSVOL` folder hierarchy is removed, along with any related items within, including the `NetLogon` share.
- The DNS is updated to remove DC Locator service records.
- The local Security Accounts Manager (SAM) is now used for user authentication.
- Services that related to AD are stopped and configured not to start automatically.
- If there is another DC, final changes are replicated to that controller before AD is shut down. The system that is removing AD will notify the remaining DCs to remove it from the DC's OU.

Troubleshooting AD Removal

Follow these hints if you run into problems during AD removal:

- If your DC cannot verify that no child domains exist and you believe there aren't any, you probably had these child domains at one time and failed to remove them the correct way from the domain. Your AD database still holds records for these domains, although they have been physically taken offline. Now your DC won't allow you to uninstall without cleaning these out with some effort and searching.
- If you cannot connect to a DC in the parent domain to replicate changes, your removal may not proceed smoothly or any final changes may not replicate. In either case, your parent DC would not be notified properly of the removal, and a similar dilemma to the preceding one would exist.

Now that we've covered the usual procedures for the installation and removal of AD, let's go back and explore some other types of installation, such as an unattended installation of AD.

Unattended Installation of AD

An unattended installation is not a new idea, although the AD portion of it is completely new. The concept is simple: Instead of manually answering the questions posed in dialog boxes during installation, an unattended installation of Windows 2000 provides all the answers to the installation questions automatically. These questions are answered through the use of an answer file and usually a uniqueness database file (UDF file) so that both the standard questions and the unique ones are given responses without human intervention.

Because the installation of Windows 2000 Server only completes to the point where the server is assigned as either a member server of a workgroup or a member server of a domain, the final portion of the installation, the promotion, is still manually handled. Microsoft, however, has established a method of directory services installation that can be either completely automated from start to finish or at least automated for the promotion to AD.

The installation of Windows 2000 Server is not our primary concern at this point, although you should have a thorough understanding of the two executable programs that begin the installation (namely, `winnt.exe` and `winnt32.exe`) and the various switches that allow for the selection of an answer file and a UDF file for an unattended installation. You should also know that the Setup Manager program (which can be found in the Windows 2000 Resource Kit, officially titled `setupmgr.exe`) is used to create these important files. Finally, you should be aware that you can automate the installation of AD in one of these ways:

- You can provide additional information within the answer file that is used to automate the installation of Windows 2000.
- You can create a separate answer file to be run in conjunction with the `dcpromo.exe` program.

Regardless of the option you choose, the command executed is the same:

```
dcpromo/answer:<answer file>"
```

The GuiRunOnce Section

To automate a complete installation of both the operating system and AD, you will need to make some configuration changes to the answer file under a section called `[GuiRunOnce]`. This section contains a list of commands to be executed the first time a user logs on to the computer after GUI (graphical user interface) mode Setup has completed. Each line specifies a command to be executed by the GuiRunOnce entry. One of those entries could include the command to begin the AD Installation Wizard with dcpromo.exe. In addition, the command could include the request to reach out for another answer file (named by the administrator who created it) so that the installation creates a complete DC under Windows 2000.

A side point to keep in mind when running commands using the GuiRunOnce key is that they will run in the context of the user who is currently logged in. Therefore, the user must have the permissions to run such a command. However, this is usually not an issue in establishing a complete unattended installation of Windows 2000 Server with AD.

Here is an example of an unattended installation file that uses the GuiRunOnce key to search for the AD answer file:

```
[Unattended]
  OemSkipEula = Yes

[GuiUnattended]
  AutoLogon = Yes
  AdminPassword = *
  OEMSkipRegional = 1
  OemSkipWelcome = 1
  TimeZone = 33

[UserData]
  FullName = "Polo DC Servers"
  OrgName = "Polo Fuzzball Suppliers, Inc."
  ComputerName = DC-Polo1

[LicenseFilePrintData]
  AutoMode = PerSeat

[GuiRunOnce]
  Command0 = "dcpromo /answer:dcanswer.txt"

[Identification]
  DomainAdmin = "CORPDOM\InstallAcct"
  DomainAdminPassword = 12345678A
  JoinDomain = "POLODOM"
```

Logically, if the unattended file can contain a line that utilizes dcpromo with an answer file for AD, two things must be true. First, you must create that AD answer file; otherwise, the command won't work. Second, you can utilize that answer file at any time by typing in the command and path from the Run option in the Start menu.

The DCInstall Section

This section of the answer file is necessary for the AD Installation Wizard to have its questions answered automatically. Below this section are many keys that hold values that allow for the questions to be answered without human intervention. If a key doesn't have a value specified, a default value will be used. Here are descriptions of a few of the keys; their values and defaults are listed in Table 4.1.

The keys are listed alphabetically, not according to the order in which they are used in the answer file. This is an abbreviated list of important keys. To learn a great deal more about unattended installation files and the keys involved, refer to the **\Support\Tools** folder on the Windows 2000 installation CD. When executed, the **deploy.cab** file allows you to view a document called **unattend.doc**. This document contains about 150 pages of information on unattended installs.

- **`AutoConfigDNS`**—Answers the question as to whether or not DNS should be configured automatically, if dynamic DNS updates aren't available.
- **`ChildName`**—Indicates the name of the child domain. This name would be added to the portion of the domain name that is the parent domain. For example, if the domain you are joining is `que.com` and the name specified here is `sales`, then the total domain would be `sales.que.com`.
- **`CreateOrJoin`**—Indicates whether the new domain that is created is part of an existing forest or would become a separate forest of domains.
- **`DatabasePath`**—Specifies the location of the database files. Logically, enough disk space should be available on the disk that you specify. As mentioned in the "Deciding Which Type of DNS to Use" section earlier in this chapter, for performance purposes, placing the database files on a separate disk from the log files is best.
- **`DomainNetBiosName`**—Indicates the NetBIOS name within the domain. This must be a unique name.
- **`LogPath`**—Specifies the location of the log files. Logically, enough disk space should be available on the disk you specify. As mentioned in the "Deciding Which Type of DNS to Use" section earlier in this chapter, for performance purposes, placing the database files on a separate disk from the database files is best.
- **`NewDomainDNSName`**—Specifies the full name of a new tree within a preexisting domain. This could also specify the full name when a new forest is being created.
- **`ReplicaDomainDNSName`**—Indicates the DNS name of the domain that will be replicated from. This name must be accurate because the installation will search for the DC that is considered its replication point of contact. That DC must be up and running to handle the request for the replication.

- **`ReplicaOrNewDomain`**—Indicates whether a new DC will be the first DC of a new domain or will be a replica of a preexisting domain.
- **`SysVolPath`**—Provides the path for the `Sysvol` folder structure. By extension, the path must lead toward an NTFS version 5 partition for the install to be functional.
- **`TreeOrChild`**—Indicates whether the new domain will be a root domain of a new tree or will become a child domain beneath a preexisting parent domain.

Table 4.1 Values and Defaults of Keys

Key	Value	Default
AutoConfigDNS	Yes | No	Yes
ChildName	Value: *<child domain name>*	—
CreateOrJoin	Create | Join	Join
DatabasePath	*<path to database files>*	"%*systemroot*%\NTDS"
DomainNetBiosName	*<domain NetBIOS name>*	—
LogPath	*<path to log files>*	"%*systemroot*%\NTDS"
NewDomainDNSName	*<DNS name of domain>*	—
ReplicaDomainDNSName	*<DNS name of domain>*	—
ReplicaOrNewDomain	Replica | Domain	Replica
SysVolPath	*<path to database file>*	"*%systemroot%*\sysvol"
TreeOrChild	Tree | Child	Child

You may be wondering whether remembering all these options is absolutely necessary. That is not the reason they are listed. These only comprise a portion of the entire list of options you can research when and if you plan on creating your unattended installation file for AD. They are provided to help you realize the amount of work that can go into setting up the file correctly so that it deploys smoothly.

Post-AD Installation Options

Once AD is installed and running correctly, there are several different options that you might want to investigate.

Integrated Zones

Now that AD is installed, perhaps you would like to implement AD integrated zones within your DNS structure. Integrated zones allow the DNS zone files to be replicated by the AD replication engine, as opposed to being replicated through DNS zone transfers, because the zone database files will be included within AD rather than stored in their usual `systemroot/System32/DNS` folder.

Once your server is supporting AD integrated zones, you will be able to configure your zones for secure dynamic updates with the DNS Secure Update Protocol. This will allow a greater level of security on your DNS updates.

Domain Mode Options

Windows 2000 supports two different types of domain modes: mixed mode and native mode. Upon first installing or upgrading your domain to Windows 2000, you will be running in mixed mode. You may decide to change over to native mode, however, to take advantage of added functionality that becomes available. The differences between the two modes are described in the following sections.

Mixed Mode

Mixed mode is used for supporting DCs that are NT 4 controllers. While moving your current structure toward Windows 2000, there may be a period of time during which you will continue to use NT 4 backup domain controllers (BDCs), and by running in mixed mode, the Windows 2000 DCs will be able to synchronize information. Although there is no timetable for how long you must run in mixed mode, Microsoft recommends that you switch to native mode when you no longer have NT 4 DCs in your domain so that you can take advantage of native mode's additional functionality.

You can continue to run in mixed mode even if there are no NT 4 DCs in the domain. Also, you can make the move toward native mode even if you still have remaining NT 4 member servers present in your domain because they do not require the synchronization between the servers.

Native Mode

If you are installing Windows 2000 in a fresh environment with no preexisting NT 4 DCs, you should consider native mode. Native mode provides several enhancements, including the following:

- **Group nesting**—Allows you to place groups within other groups to allow permissions to flow through.
- **Universal groups**—Enables another level of group possibilities, allowing for forest-wide group implementations.
- **Security ID (SID) history**—Used during migrations to retain the original SID of the objects that are moved.

Keep in mind that although you can change from mixed mode to native mode, you cannot change back. So, if you are going to make the move, ensure your readiness. You can change modes in one of two ways:

- Through AD Users and Computers
- Through AD Domains and Trusts

In either tool the options will be the same. Open either AD Users and Computers or AD Domains and Trusts, select the domain, and then go into the properties of the domain. On the General tab, you should see a button toward the bottom called Change Mode, as shown in Figure 4.10. Once you click this button, you are eternally committed.

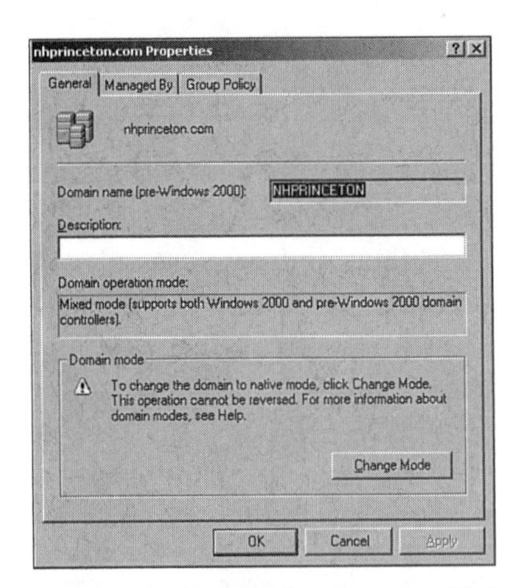

Figure 4.10 Changing domain modes with the click of a button.

You are still in the early stages of the installation at this point. Now you can move on to thinking about the next stage: Organizational Units.

Organizational Units

Within the domain in Windows 2000, you can implement OUs that will further segment the domain for organization of the objects in the network.

Also, OUs have the ability to contain other OUs. This feature enables you to create a hierarchy within a single domain, as opposed to creating additional domains to establish delegation of network authority.

When planning the structure of OUs within a domain, you must first understand the purpose of OUs. To dispel a common misconception: Organizational Units are *not* primarily used to help the end user find resources in the AD database. In fact, the end users will probably not even have to know that OUs exist within the domain. OUs are, however, used for the following reasons:

- To help administrators manage network resources in an orderly fashion and enable them to keep track of all the objects within a domain. This is accomplished by forming a hierarchy of containers within the domain and assigning permissions directly to the OU at various levels to users or groups of users.
- To provide identical security requirements to network resources that require the same levels.
- To control Group Policy implementation, which is covered in Chapter 7, "Understanding Group Policy Implementation," through Chapter 9, "Using Group Policy in Software Deployment and Management."

You can create OUs if you've been delegated permissions to do so by your administrators. By default, members of the Domain Admins and Enterprise Admins groups have permissions to create OUs. If you are not a member of either of these groups, you will have to be assigned the following permissions on a parent OU:

- Read
- List Contents
- Create Child (OU)

Creating OUs is done through the AD Users and Computers tool by selecting the domain or OU that you wish to create the OU in. Then you right-click and choose New, Organizational Unit. Finally, you type the name of the OU and click OK.

You're ready now to understand the next facet of implementing a directory service infrastructure—administration of users and groups, which is covered in Chapter 5, "User and Group Administration."

Practice Questions

Question 1

You install Active Directory on a server and you want it to be a separate domain that is part of an existing tree structure with a forest root containing a contiguous namespace. What is this type of domain called?

- ❍ a. A replica
- ❍ b. A backup domain controller
- ❍ c. A child domain
- ❍ d. A forest root

Answer c is correct. A child domain is one that exists below a parent domain and continues to use a contiguous namespace. Answer a is incorrect because a secondary domain controller, as a replica, would not be a "separate domain." Answer b is incorrect because Active Directory doesn't have primary and backup domain controllers. Answer d is incorrect because the forest root would have been established first in order to add a child domain.

Question 2

You want to begin an installation of Active Directory and would like for this installation to be handled automatically and run by an administrator with no background knowledge of Active Directory installation. Which of the following would assist you in this goal? [Check all correct answers]

- ❑ a. **dcpromo.exe**
- ❑ b. **udf.txt**
- ❑ c. **adpromo.txt**
- ❑ d. **ntdsutil.exe**

Answers a and c are correct. You need `dcpromo` to begin the Active Directory Installation Wizard, and you need `adpromo.txt` to be your answer file. The correct syntax for the command used by the administrator running the installation would be `dcpromo /answer:adpromo.txt`. Answer b is incorrect because `udf.txt` is a UDF that is used for unattended installations of the operating system itself. Answer d is incorrect because `ntdsutil.exe` is a tool that handles the seizing of FSMO roles and can handle movement of the directory database and log files.

Question 3

You're attempting to install Active Directory within a network infrastructure that already has an NT 4.0 DNS server in place. The DNS server has functioned very well up until this point. During the installation of Active Directory you get a request for DNS installation. What could be causing a problem that pushes the installation to request that an additional DNS server be established on the new domain controller?

❍ a. NT 4.0 DNS is not compatible with Active Directory.

❍ b. The BIND version needs to be updated.

❍ c. Active Directory requires only Windows 2000 DNS.

❍ d. NT 4.0 uses a different protocol suite than Windows 2000.

Answer a is correct. NT 4.0 DNS is not compatible with Active Directory, so your system will attempt to install its own DNS server on the Windows 2000 Server. Answer b is incorrect because NT 4.0 doesn't use BIND. BIND is used on Unix systems. Answer c is incorrect because Windows 2000 works with DNS servers that support RFCs (SRV records) and (dynamic updates). Answer d is incorrect because both NT 4.0 and Windows 2000 use TCP/IP as their protocol suite of choice.

Question 4

Your installation of Active Directory halts because the **SYSVOL** folder cannot seem to be placed where you've specified. What is the most likely cause of the problem?

❍ a. You've requested that it go on a partition that doesn't have enough space.

❍ b. You've formatted the partition with NTFS.

❍ c. The drive letter you've specified doesn't exist.

❍ d. The partition you are specifying is FAT or FAT32.

Answer d is correct. The SYSVOL folder structure must be on an NTFS partition. Answers a and c are incorrect because, although they are possible causes, the question asks for the "most likely" cause. Answer b is incorrect because putting the SYSVOL folder on an NTFS partition would have actually been the correct thing to do.

Question 5

In selecting the locations of your database and log files, which two of the following options would enhance the performance of these files?

- ❑ a. Placing them on the same NTFS partition.
- ❑ b. Ensuring plenty of hard disk space for these files to expand.
- ❑ c. Placing them on separate physical disks.
- ❑ d. Restricting them to small-sized partitions for additional control over their size.

Answers b and c are correct. Plenty of room and separate physical disks will make for a healthy database and log file configuration. Answer a is incorrect because, although placing the files on an NTFS partition isn't a bad idea, it doesn't enhance performance. Answer d is incorrect because you don't want to prevent your database and log files from growing. This is a normal part of the directory service.

Question 6

To allow for backward compatibility with NT 4 domain controllers, what mode should your domains be running in?

- ❍ a. Mixed mode
- ❍ b. Native mode
- ❍ c. RIS mode
- ❍ d. FLIP mode

Answer a is correct. Mixed mode allows for backward compatibility and synchronization with the accounts manager. Answer b is incorrect because native mode would ensure incompatibility with NT 4 domain controllers. Answers c and d are invalid modes.

Question 7

Handles Corp. creates handles for various products, from broomsticks to briefcases. The network administration team is planning its AD directory services infrastructure and would like to delegate administrative control over various locations and departments throughout the organization. What should this team use in Active Directory to delegate administrative control over users, groups, and computers within the organization?

- ❍ a. Organizational Units
- ❍ b. Global Catalog servers
- ❍ c. Additional domain controllers
- ❍ d. Additional domains as child domains

Answer a is correct. OUs are used in Windows 2000 to allow for delegation of authority. Answer b is incorrect because Global Catalog servers provide additional searching functionality and logon authentication features within the domain. Answer c is incorrect because, although additional domain controllers will add fault tolerance, they will not delegate authority. Answer d is also incorrect. Although under NT 4 resource domains would be established, this is no longer necessary under Windows 2000.

Question 8

What utilities would you use to change domain modes from mixed to native mode? [Check all correct answers]

- ❑ a. Group Policy Editor
- ❑ b. Active Directory Users and Computers
- ❑ c. Delegation of Control Wizard
- ❑ d. Active Directory Domains and Trusts

Answers b and d are correct. AD Users and Computers and AD Domains and Trusts allow for changes in the domain mode. Answer a is incorrect because Group Policy Editor allows you to specify the settings for a user or computer that relate to desktop views or software and security policy. Answer c is incorrect because the Delegation of Control Wizard provides a graphical way to assign Active Directory access permissions to individuals with trusted administrative control.

Question 9

If you want to provide secure DNS updates for Active Directory, what should you implement?

❍ a. A Kerberos server

❍ b. A certificate server

❍ c. Active Directory integrated zones

❍ d. Native mode

Answer c is correct. Active Directory integrated zones allow for the DNS zone files to be replicated with the directory information and also allow for secure updates to be configured. Answers a and b are incorrect because they have nothing to do with secure zones; a Kerberos server is one that issues and verifies tickets for validation, and a certificate server is used in software security systems that employ public key technologies. Answer d is incorrect because you can have secure updates with mixed or native mode domains.

Question 10

Under which part of the answer file for an unattended installation of both Windows 2000 and Active Directory would you specify the command to install Active Directory?

❍ a. **GuiRunPromo**

❍ b. **GuiRunOnce**

❍ c. **DCInstall**

❍ d. **ADInstall**

Answer b is correct. The `GuiRunOnce` section within the answer file would specify the command `dcpromo` and then specify an additional answer file that is specific to the Active Directory install. Answer c is incorrect because, although `DCInstall` is a section of the Active Directory answer file, it is not the section that installs the operating system. Answers a and d are invalid answers.

Need to Know More?

Bersinic, Damir and Rob Scrimger. *MCSE Training Guide (70-217): Installing and Administering a Windows 2000 Directory Services Infrastructure*. Que Publishing. Indianapolis, IN, 2002. ISBN 0735709769.

Chapter 3, "Building Your Active Directory Structures," covers many of the same concepts we've discussed here in this chapter but with extended information on Active Directory design and implementation.

Boswell, William. *Inside Windows 2000 Server*. New Riders. Indianapolis, IN, 2000. ISBN 1562059297.

This is a great resource for clear and in-depth information that strengthens your knowledge of Windows 2000 technology.

Hudson, James and Sean Fullerton. *Special Edition Using Active Directory*. Que Publishing, Indianapolis, IN, 2001. ISBN 0789724340.

Covers installation of Active Directory in Chapter 2. This book is an excellent resource that includes the real-world experiences of the authors and brings the reader up to speed on the challenges of an AD implementation.

Kouti, Sakari and Mike Seitsonen. *Inside Active Directory: A System Administrator's Guide*. Addison Wesley Professional. Boston, MA, 2002. ISBN 0201616211.

Chapter 1, "Active Directory: The Big Picture," gives a good overview of the concepts of Active Directory and the need for a good design before your installation.

Search the TechNet CD (or its online version through `www.microsoft.com`) using the keywords "DCPROMO" and "Active Directory," along with related query items.

User and Group Administration

Terms you'll need to understand:

- ✓ Single sign-on
- ✓ Domain user account
- ✓ Local user account
- ✓ Built-in account
- ✓ User logon name
- ✓ User principal name
- ✓ User principal suffix
- ✓ Csvde
- ✓ Ldifde
- ✓ Attribute line
- ✓ Universal groups
- ✓ AGDLP

Techniques you'll need to master:

- ✓ Bulk-importing user accounts
- ✓ Using groups to organize user accounts
- ✓ Deciding on a user logon name strategy
- ✓ Performing a search of Active Directory

Active Directory (AD) is essentially a database that stores data about network resources and other objects. Two of the most common types of objects stored within AD are users and groups. Having these objects stored within AD allows people to log on to the network and gain access to a range of network resources. Because all objects are stored within AD along with access permissions, you can achieve a *single sign-on*, which is a feature in Windows 2000 that allows users to log in to the network with a single username and password and receive access to a host of network resources. The user does not need to enter any additional usernames or passwords to gain access to network shares, printers, or other network resources.

Generally, *groups* are collections of user accounts (although they can also include computers) that are used to ease administration. Because you can create a group and assign permissions for a resource to this single entity, using groups is far easier than assigning permissions to individual user accounts. In Windows 2000, you can also nest groups, which allows groups themselves to contain other groups, further simplifying network administration. In this chapter, we examine users and groups and how they can be used in a Windows 2000 environment.

Introducing Users and Groups

Obviously, if a user cannot log on to a Windows 2000 network, he or she cannot gain access to the data and resources—such as files and folders, email accounts, and printers—that are stored there. User accounts are the fundamental building blocks of your network. Because they are so important, you will likely spend a lot of time working with user accounts in your environment.

A Windows 2000 network has three different types of user accounts:

- **Domain user account**—This account is used to gain access to a Windows 2000 domain and all its associated resources. This is the most common type of logon you will experience on a Windows 2000 network. A logon that exists on one domain can be given permissions in other Windows 2000 domains.

- **Local user account**—This account exists on a standalone server or a Windows 2000 Professional system. It enables a user to log on to a specific computer and gain access to the local resources that it offers. By definition, a standalone computer is not acting as part of a Windows 2000 network. Therefore, a local user account cannot grant access to resources in a domain.

- **Built-in user accounts**—These accounts have been created for specific administrative tasks to ease the burden of administration. They define special accounts up front that have permissions to both resources and AD itself.

Because your enterprise network might have a few hundred user accounts—perhaps even hundreds of thousands—creating accounts can be an arduous process. To ease this burden, you can bulk-import accounts using tools provided with Windows 2000. In this chapter, we take a closer look at these tools. Creating user accounts in bulk fashion saves the administrator a great deal of time.

The most commonly used network resources include files, folders, and printers. Given that you might have to deal with several hundred or thousand user accounts, granting access to resources based solely on user accounts would be time-consuming and hugely repetitive. So, instead, we use groups. The concept of *groups* is very simple: You create a single object within AD and grant access permissions (or deny access) to this single entity. User accounts are then added as members of the group. By being members of a group, the user accounts inherit the permissions assigned to the group. If these permissions must be changed, you can then simply modify them on the group object a single time. Any changes to the group permissions are applied to the user accounts that are members of the group.

In addition, Windows 2000 allows you to build a hierarchy of groups and assign different permissions to each level of the hierarchy. This is achieved through the nesting of groups. Nesting groups further simplifies your security model.

User Logon Names

User logon names are also known as *user account names*. However, be careful with your use of terminology in Windows 2000; a user can have more than one type of account, because Microsoft has provided the ability to use older-style usernames in a Windows 2000 network along with a new type of logon name.

Types of Logon Names

When logging in to a Windows 2000 network, users can use either one of the two types of names they have been assigned: their user principal name or their user logon name. The end result will be the same, although the older-style logon names should slowly be phased out. Domain controllers (DCs) are able to authenticate the users regardless of what method they use. Let's look at these two types of usernames.

User Principal Name

The *user principal name* is the new-style logon name on Windows 2000 networks. A user principal name is made up of two parts. One part uniquely identifies the user object in AD; the second part identifies the domain where the user object was created. A user principal name looks like this:

```
kit@basildon.local
```

As you can see, the two parts of the user principal name are divided by the "at" sign (`@`). This tells Windows 2000 which part of the name is the user object name and which is the domain name. These two parts can further be defined as the following:

- **User principal name prefix**—In the preceding example, this is `kit`.
- **User principal name suffix**—By default, the suffix is derived from the root domain name on your Windows 2000 network. You can also create additional user principal names by using other domains on your network, although doing so increases the administrative overhead of your network. Windows 2000 administrators who have deployed Exchange 2000 commonly use the email address as the user principal name. In the preceding example, the user principal name suffix would be `basildon.local`.

Because user principal names are by default tied to the root domain's name, moving a user object from one domain to another on a Windows 2000 network does not require a username change. This effectively makes the change invisible for the users. They need not be concerned that their user account has been moved from one domain to another. Also, because a user principal name can be the same as a user's email account, the name is easy to remember.

User Logon Name

The *user logon name* is used to describe backward-compatible usernames. It is used by clients logging on to a Windows 2000 network from an older operating system, such as Windows 9*x* or Microsoft Windows NT 4.0.

Logging on to a Windows 2000 domain using the user logon name means that users must provide two distinct pieces of information. First, they must enter their username; second, they must enter the name of the domain where their account exists. This can be confusing to users who sometimes have trouble remembering all the details of the logon process. In addition, because the user account is unique within a domain only (see the next section on rules for logon names), gaining access to resources outside of that domain can also be unnecessarily difficult. In this case, the user may have to enter an additional username and password. In our example, the user logon name would simply be `kit`.

Rules for Logon Names

Because user accounts are used to gain access to a Windows 2000 network, a username must be unique. The scope of this uniqueness varies depending on the type of logon name you intend to use. This enables single sign-on. The administrator must ensure that user accounts follow a set of rules so that they are unique within a Windows 2000 forest.

User principal names must be unique within a forest. This can make coming up with a naming strategy more difficult, especially when you have tens of thousands of users. The benefits outweigh the difficulties; however, you should come up with a naming strategy that allows for usernames that are easy to remember yet at the same time are easily distinguishable.

User logon names must be unique within the domain in which they are created. If you think you will use these account types exclusively, you have a little more flexibility in naming conventions, because in effect, you can share a single username across multiple domains. However, using a single name exclusively is discouraged. Over time, this will undoubtedly cause additional administrative overhead.

The username suffix (in our case, `basildon.local`) is derived from the root domain by default. However, this can be changed. By adding additional suffixes, you ensure that users have a standard and easy-to-understand user principal name. Before an additional suffix can be used, it must be added to AD. This is done through the AD Domains and Trusts tool. The dialog box for adding additional suffixes is shown in Figure 5.1.

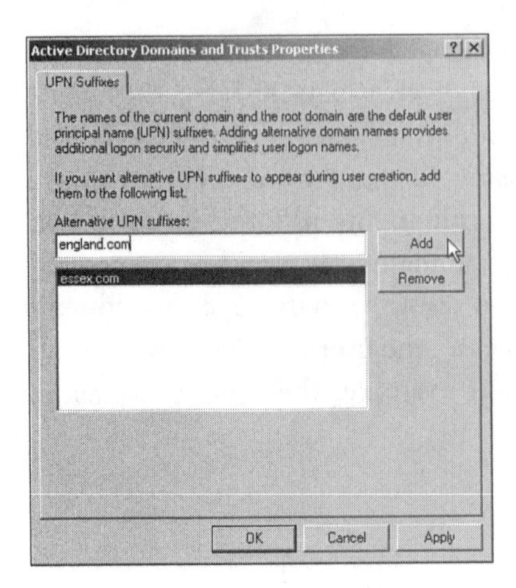

Figure 5.1 Adding additional suffixes.

Creating User Accounts

Creating user accounts in an enterprise environment can be time-consuming. In addition, if you are creating the accounts one at a time, you will find that a lot of repetitive information needs to be entered. To alleviate this, Microsoft has provided two utilities that can be used to import user account information in bulk.

These utilities work by using a text file as the source for new account information. This text file can be in one of two formats—comma-delimited and line-separated—supported by the tools that ship with Windows 2000. The format of the source file dictates which utility you use. You can create these files in any database application that supports exporting to either of these formats (almost all database applications on the market today are able to do this) or with a spreadsheet such as Microsoft Excel.

These files can be used to bulk-import user accounts, groups, and even attributes. The two utilities are as follows:

- **Csvde**—The Comma-Separated Value Directory Exchange utility can perform a bulk import based on comma-delimited source files.
- **Ldifde**—The Lightweight Directory Access Protocol Interchange Format Directory Exchange utility allows you perform a bulk import based on line-separated values.

Keep the following in mind when you are considering using these bulk import tools:

- You must ensure that the user object you are about to create is unique. You achieve this by giving the full path for the user object within the directory, including the Organizational Unit (OU) that will contain the object. You must also specify the object type and the user logon name.
- You should set a value to define whether the user accounts you are creating are enabled or disabled. By default, any user accounts you create are disabled. This helps ensure security when objects are created in bulk.
- The user principal name is optional; however, because this is the recommended method of logging on to a Windows 2000 domain from a native Windows 2000 system, it is strongly suggested that you provide a user principal name.
- You cannot include passwords with the bulk import. When user objects are created with this process, the passwords are blank. The users will be prompted the first time they log on to change their password. Because this could be a significant security breach, it is suggested that you allow the default option of having the new accounts disabled to take effect.
- You can also include other properties or attributes, such a telephone number, of the object to be imported at the same time. The more data you can enter automatically, the less data you have to worry about later. Also, the more data that is included as part of the user object, the more data users will have to search against when they are looking for a particular user in AD.

The Csvde Utility

If you plan to use a source file that is in comma-delimited format, you must use the Csvde command-line utility. For help with this utility, type **`csvde /?`** at the command prompt. Some of the switches are shown in Figure 5.2.

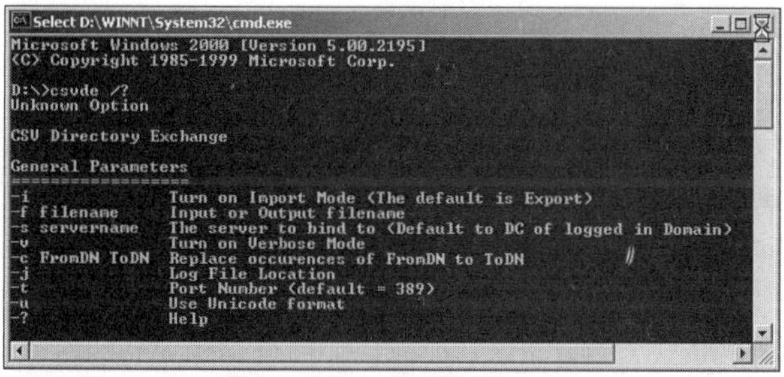

```
Select D:\WINNT\System32\cmd.exe
Microsoft Windows 2000 [Version 5.00.2195]
(C) Copyright 1985-1999 Microsoft Corp.

D:\>csvde /?
Unknown Option

CSV Directory Exchange

General Parameters
==================
-i               Turn on Import Mode (The default is Export)
-f filename      Input or Output filename
-s servername    The server to bind to (Default to DC of logged in Domain)
-v               Turn on Verbose Mode
-c FromDN ToDN   Replace occurences of FromDN to ToDN
-j               Log File Location
-t               Port Number (default = 389)
-u               Use Unicode format
-?               Help
```

Figure 5.2 Getting help with the Csvde utility.

The Csvde utility can be used to import data into AD; it cannot be used to delete or modify data. Whenever using command-line bulk import tools, you must make sure your source file is correctly formatted. An incorrectly formatted file will cause the process to fail. Because the format for this utility is a comma-delimited file, you can use just about any text-editing program to create the source, including all major word processors and spreadsheet applications, such as Notepad.

The format of the source file is fairly simple and is briefly discussed here with the some points highlighted. It's not possible to include every parameter that can be added for a user object using this utility. Don't forget that in the real world, you should add as much data as possible to help identify the new user object.

The first line of the source file should contain the *attribute line*. This line defines the format of the data lines to follow. Fields are included on this line separated by commas. Each field entered must be subsequently included in each user record. Windows 2000 does not care what order these fields are in as long as the lines in the file that contain the user data follow the same order. Here's an example of an attribute line:

```
DN, objectClass,sAMAccountname,userPrincipalName,displayName
```

Once you have defined which fields exist in your source file, you can enter the user data you want to include in your bulk import. This data must comply with the following set of rules:

- The sequence of the source values must be in the same order as those specified in the attribute line.
- If a value contains commas, you must contain the value in quotation marks.
- If you have a user object that will not have entries for all the values specified in the attribute line, you can leave the field blank; however, you must include the commas.

Here's an example of a code line that conforms to these rules:

```
"cn=michael cook, ou=art department,
dc=england,dc=basildon,dc=local"user,mikec,mikec@london.local,Michael Cook
```

In this case, the following attributes have been defined:

- **DN (distinguished name)**—`cn=michael cook, ou=art department, dc=england, dc=basildon, dc=local`
- **objectClass**—`user`

- **sAMAccountName**—`mikec`
- **userPrincipalName**—`mikec@london.local`
- **displayName**—`Michael Cook`

To include more parameters, simply add them to the attribute line. Make sure you follow the rules outlined in this chapter, paying particular attention to the rules when a particular field is going to be skipped.

Once you have a text file that has been correctly formatted, you can run Csvde to perform a bulk import. Two switches you should pay particular attention to are `-i` and `-f` (refer back to Figure 5.2). The `-i` switch indicates that an import is being performed. The `-f` switch specifies the name of the source file.

The Csvde utility can only be used to add users to AD; it cannot be used to delete objects.

You should always use AD Users and Computers to check the user accounts you have imported. The Csvde utility also provides you with a status message and log file, but regardless, you should double-check to make sure that the accounts were created and that the optional parameters you have specified have been entered correctly.

The Ldifde Utility

The Ldifde utility is in some ways similar to Csvde. However, it offers additional functionality. Unlike Csvde, the Ldifde utility can be used to add objects, delete objects, and modify objects in the directory.

To import, delete, or modify data with this utility, you must create a source file. This source file is a text file, but its format differs from that of the Csvde utility. The Ldifde utility uses a line-separated format, which is a list of records, with each separated by a blank line. A *record* is a distinct collection of data that will either be added to AD or will be used to modify data within the directory. Each entry is considered a record.

The format of the file required by this utility is also known as the Lightweight Directory Access Protocol Interchange Format (LDIF). The format of the file is the attribute name followed by a colon and the attribute value. The names of the attributes are defined within the Schema partition of AD. In the following example of the LDIF format, we have used the text from the comma-delimited file data you saw earlier in this chapter. This should make it easier for you to compare the two formats:

```
# create Michael Cook
DN:  cn=michael cook, ou=art department,dc=local
ObjectClass:  user
SAMAccountName:  mikec
UserPrincipalName:  mikec@london.local
DisplayName:  Michael Cook
```

Note that any line that starts with the pound sign (#) is a comment line and is ignored when the file is being used to import data into AD. Some significant command-line switches for this utility are shown in Figure 5.3 (you can view this on your own computer by typing **ldifde /?** at the command prompt.) Note again the `-i` and `-f` switches. These offer the same functionality as mentioned for the Csvde utility.

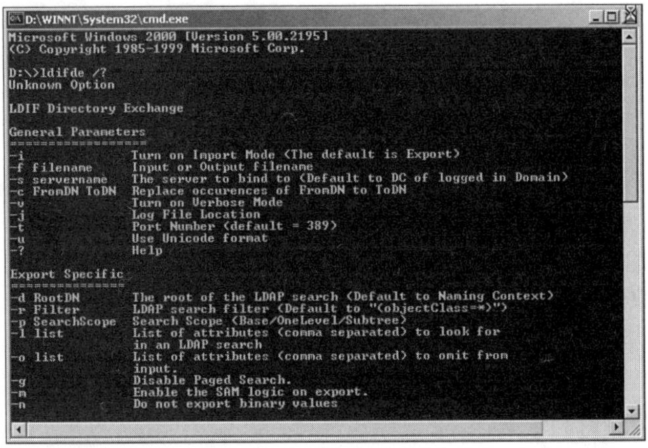

```
D:\WINNT\System32\cmd.exe
Microsoft Windows 2000 [Version 5.00.2195]
(C) Copyright 1985-1999 Microsoft Corp.

D:\>ldifde /?
Unknown Option

LDIF Directory Exchange

General Parameters
==================
-i              Turn on Import Mode (The default is Export)
-f filename     Input or Output filename
-s servername   The server to bind to (Default to DC of logged in Domain)
-c FromDN ToDN  Replace occurences of FromDN to ToDN
-v              Turn on Verbose Mode
-j              Log File Location
-t              Port Number (default = 389)
-u              Use Unicode format
-?              Help

Export Specific
===============
-d RootDN       The root of the LDAP search (Default to Naming Context)
-r Filter       LDAP search filter (Default to "(objectClass=*)")
-p SearchScope  Search Scope (Base/OneLevel/Subtree)
-l list         List of attributes (comma separated) to look for
                in an LDAP search
-o list         List of attributes (comma separated) to omit from
                input.
-g              Disable Paged Search.
-m              Enable the SAM logic on export.
-n              Do not export binary values
```

Figure 5.3 Getting help with the Ldifde utility.

User Accounts

Many of the ongoing administrative tasks performed on a Windows 2000 network are based around user accounts. This includes the creation and maintenance of these accounts. In this section, we look at the common administrative tools you will use as well as how to search AD for specific data.

The most common administrative tool, shown in Figure 5.4, is AD Users and Computers. To access this utility, select Start, Programs, Administrative Tools, Active Directory Users and Computers.

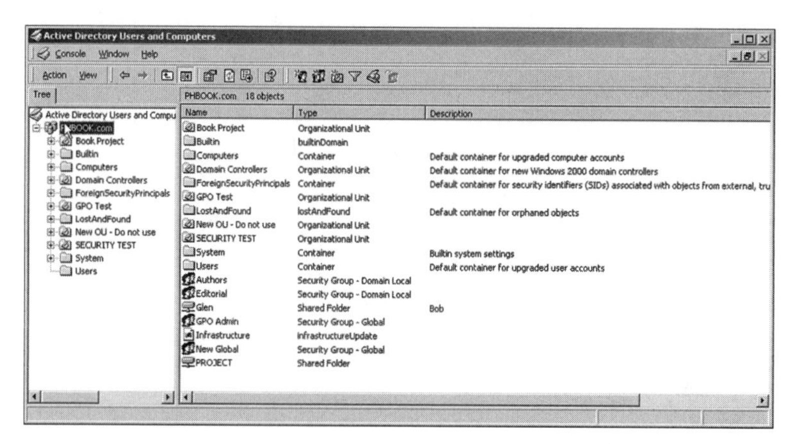

Figure 5.4 AD Users and Computers.

AD Users and Computers provides you with all the day-to-day functionality you need. In this section, we look at some of the most common functions you are likely to perform. Being familiar with the interface of AD Users and Computers helps you be more efficient at administering user accounts in your environment. The common administrative tasks we will look at include the following:

- Resetting passwords
- Unlocking user accounts
- Deleting user accounts
- Renaming user accounts
- Copying user accounts
- Disabling and enabling user accounts

Because these are common tasks, Microsoft has provided an easy method to access them. To access each of these tasks, simply select the Users container in the left panel of AD Users and Computers and then right-click the user object you want to change in the panel on the right. When you do this, you are presented with the context-sensitive menu shown in Figure 5.5.

As you can see, this menu offers you a wealth of functionality. Note that it is possible to perform some tasks on multiple user accounts. For instance, if you highlight five user accounts and then right-click them, you will see a context-sensitive menu with a subset of functions. One of these functions is the ability to disable an account, which in this case lets you disable several accounts simultaneously.

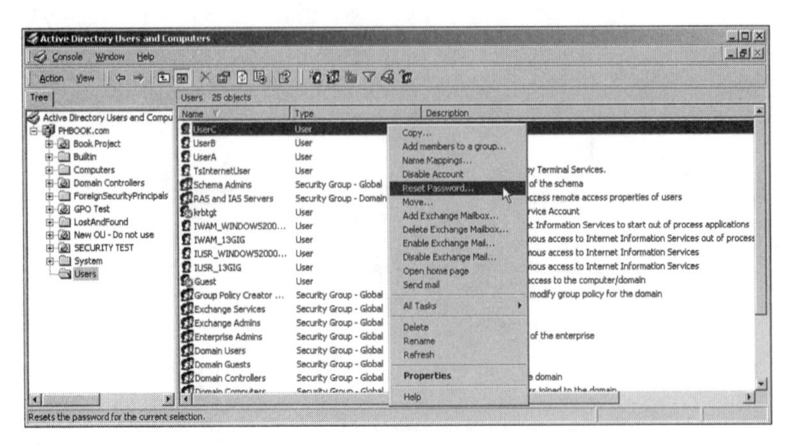

Figure 5.5 AD Users and Computers context-sensitive menu.

Resetting Passwords

Passwords are at the heart of the security of your network. They should be secure, changed often, and hard to crack (for instance, you should not use the name of your spouse or family pet).

You may also find that users sometimes forget their password and request that you change it for them. As an administrator, you do not need to know the user's old password to change it. If you do make a change to a user's password, don't forget to check the User Must Change Password at Next Logon check box.

You access this function by selecting Reset Password from the context-sensitive menu.

Unlocking User Accounts

User accounts are subject to the security settings that have been defined in Group Policy. One of the most common settings is for an account to be locked out after three failed login attempts. This occurs when a user has forgotten his or her password and makes several consecutive attempts, guessing wrong each time.

To unlock an account, select Properties on the context-sensitive menu. You are then presented with the User Properties dialog box. Click the Account tab and uncheck the Account Is Locked Out check box, as shown in Figure 5.6.

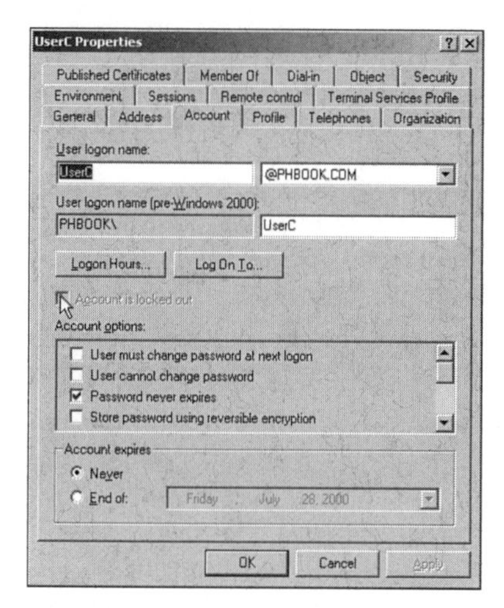

Figure 5.6 The User Properties dialog box.

Deleting User Accounts

If a user leaves your organization, you have two choices. If the user is being replaced, you can simply rename the account for use by someone else, or you can delete it. The choice here should be based on security, not just convenience. If the user is being replaced immediately, it is easier to rename the account. Otherwise, you should delete the account to maintain the integrity of security on your network.

To delete a user account, select Delete from the context-sensitive menu. When prompted with the message "Are you sure you want to delete this object?", click Yes to delete the object or No to abort the deletion.

Renaming User Accounts

Renaming a user account is convenient when a user's function is being taken over by someone else. A user account is not simply a name and password; it is also a set of permissions and group memberships. Sometimes it is easier to rename a user account so that this data is maintained rather than re-creating it from scratch.

When renaming a user account, remember to take every object property into account. As a minimum, you should change the first name, last name, and logon name fields. However, several optional attributes will likely need to be changed, such as telephone number and description.

To rename an account, select Rename from the context-sensitive menu. Simply type the new name and press Enter when you are done.

Copying User Accounts

You can also create an account and use it as a template for other accounts. For instance, you might have a standard set of permissions and group memberships that all users are assigned upon creation of the account. Say, for example, you have a member of the Finance group who has already been configured with all necessary group memberships. When a new employee joins the finance department, you can just copy a current account rather than create one from scratch.

When copying an account, you are prompted to enter a new first name, last name, and user logon name. You are also prompted to assign a new password. To copy a user account, simply select Copy from the context-sensitive menu. You are then presented with the Copy Object-User Wizard.

Disabling and Enabling User Accounts

A variation on locking out an account, disabling an account temporarily prevents a user from logging in to the network. This is commonly performed when the user is going on an extended absence. For the account to become active again, you must then enable the account.

To disable an account, select Disable Account from the context-sensitive menu. The account is immediately disabled, and the username is displayed with a red X through it. To enable the account, select Enable Account from the context-sensitive menu (the Disable Account option will be grayed out).

Finding User Accounts

Finding the user accounts you want to administer is a simple task on a relatively small network. However, Windows 2000 is designed to scale to large enterprises, and locating user accounts in AD Users and Computers can take quite some time.

Because AD is a database, it stands to reason that searching for the specific data you want is easily done. In this case, we are interested in user accounts, but you can also search for any AD object, such as a computer or group. Once you have found the user account you are looking for, you can administer the account from within the Search dialog box.

To access the Find option within AD Users and Computers, right-click the domain name in the left panel and select Find. The Find Users, Contacts, and Groups dialog box appears, as shown in Figure 5.7.

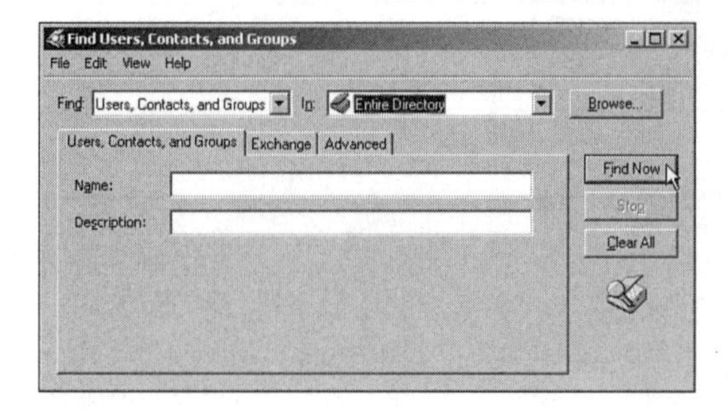

Figure 5.7 The Find Users, Contacts, and Groups dialog box.

Note the Find and In drop-down boxes in the dialog box. These options allow you to narrow your search to a particular object type and to restrict the search to a particular domain (as opposed to searching the entire directory, which can be time-consuming and resource-intensive).

If you choose to perform a search against the entire directory, you must contact a Global Catalog server. This can cause heavy network traffic.

The options available on the Find drop-down box include the following:

- Users, Contacts, and Groups
- Computers
- Printers
- Shared Folders
- Organizational Units
- Custom Search

Most of these options are self-explanatory. They allow you to search for a particular object type and help decrease the amount of time it takes for a search to complete. The Custom Search option is used when you want to make complex searches using additional attributes. You can also access these options when searching for any of the other object types by clicking the Advanced tab, which is shown in Figure 5.8.

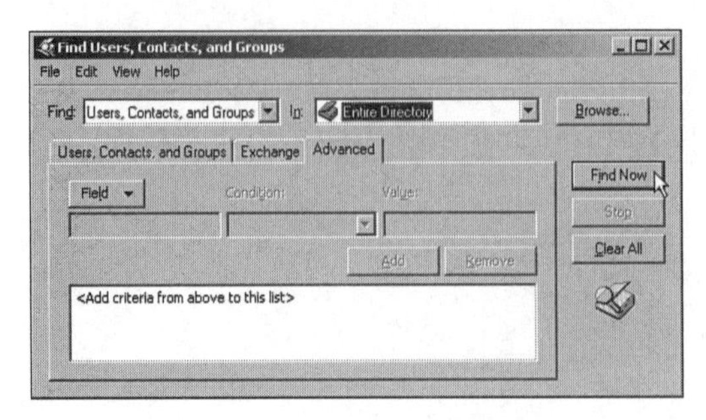

Figure 5.8 The Advanced tab.

The Field drop-down box in the Advanced tab allows you to search for a specific attribute of an object. The options you see in this drop-down menu vary depending on the object type you are searching for.

Using the Find Users, Contacts, and Groups Dialog Box to Administer User Accounts

Once you have performed a search for an object, you are presented with an additional pane of information—the Results pane—in the Find Users, Contacts, and Groups dialog box. The Results pane displays all the objects that have been returned based on your search criteria. By right-clicking the objects listed in the pane, you can access the same context-sensitive menu you saw displayed in AD Users and Computers (refer to Figure 5.5). This enables you to administer the accounts directly without switching between tools.

The Use of Groups

Groups exist to ease the administrative burden of the system administrator. Groups are used to collect users together, either to assign them permissions to a set of files, folders, or network resources or for the purposes of distribution in email applications. There are two types of groups:

- Security groups
- Distribution groups

In addition, three different scopes define where the groups can be used on the network; groups can be one of the following types:

- Local groups
- Global groups
- Universal groups

Combining the group type and scope determines how a group can be used (in a single domain or in multiple domains within a forest).

Microsoft has published some conflicting documents regarding universal groups. A Windows 2000 domain can be in two modes: mixed mode or native mode. Mixed mode generally means you are still using Windows NT 4 computers as DCs alongside your Windows 2000 DCs. You might read that universal groups are only available if the domain is in native mode. This is only partially correct. In fact, you *can* create universal groups in mixed mode—but only for distribution lists. *Distribution lists cannot be used for security purposes.*

Security groups differ from distribution groups in that they can be used to assign security rights—that is, if you want to collect a group of user accounts together so that you can more easily assign them access to a shared folder, you must create a security group. You cannot use distribution groups for this purpose.

A new feature of Windows 2000 is the ability to *nest* groups. Nesting groups is used to further simplify the management of users when assigning security permissions. When a group is nested within another group, it inherits all the security permissions from its parent.

Group nesting is not available in mixed-mode domains.

A user can be a member of many different groups, thereby inheriting all the security permissions that have been assigned to them. This is far simpler than assigning permissions on a user-by-user basis.

Defining Group Types

All group types are used to gather together a set of users who are going to share a particular set of permissions to a file, folder, or network resource. However, the scope of each group and the possible membership list differs. Table 5.1 lists the differences among the three group types.

Table 5.1 Group Comparison

	Global	Local	Universal
Member list	Mixed mode: accounts from same domain. Native mode: accounts and other global groups.	Mixed mode: User accounts and global groups from any domain in the forest. Native mode: user accounts, local groups from the same domain, global groups, and universal groups from any domain in the forest.	Mixed mode: distribution lists only. Native mode: user accounts, global groups, and other universal groups in any domain in the forest.
Nesting	Mixed mode: local groups. Native mode: universal and local groups in any domain and global groups in the same domain.	Mixed mode: cannot be a member of another group. Native mode: local groups in the same domain.	Mixed mode: none. Native mode: local and universal groups in any domain.
Scope	Can be used in its own domain and any trusted domains.	Can be used only in its own domain.	Can be used in any domain in the forest.
Permissions to	All domains in a forest.	Resources in the domain in which the local group exists only.	Resources in any domain in the forest.

How to Use Groups

For groups to be effective, you must use them in a structured way. This helps ensure that you get the maximum benefit from using them. The group scope determines when the best time to use a particular group type is. For instance, if you have a resource that will be available across an entire forest, you will likely start by adding users to global groups and then nesting them within a universal group.

The mere mention of universal groups implies that you are in native mode (because you cannot use universal groups for security purposes in mixed mode). Be sure to remember what can and cannot be achieved in both modes. If a scenario mentions a single domain, there is no use for universal groups.

The method of assigning permissions within a single domain has been used for a long time, and it still holds true for a Windows 2000 network. Let's now look at using groups in both a single domain and in a forest.

Groups in a Single Domain

As mentioned previously, in a single domain there is no need to be concerned about universal groups. With a single domain, you can achieve all the simplification you need using only local and global groups. In this section, we'll use Microsoft's acronym AGDLP to describe the use of both local and global groups. This acronym stands for the following:

- **A**—Accounts (user)
- **G**—Global group
- **DL**—Domain local group
- **P**—Permissions

By using this acronym, you can easily recall the order in which permissions should be granted. Although this is only a suggested method, it's designed to make sure you enjoy maximum flexibility and ease of use when assigning permissions to resources.

In the following example, we use this strategy to organize access to a network resource (in this case, a folder share). This illustrates how the AGDLP strategy can work for you. This example assumes a single domain.

A publishing company has an author team. Members of this team need access to files in a folder on the network that contains the text of a book the authors are writing. To achieve this, the system administrator creates a global group called Author Team. The names of the authors are added as members to this global group.

The practical limit on the number of users a group can contain in a Windows 2000 network is 5,000 members.

Next, the administrator creates a local group called Windows 2000 Cram. The Author Team global group is then nested within the Windows 2000 Cram local group. Permissions to the file share are granted to the local group. This offers the flexibility and manageability we are looking for. If additional authors need access to the folder, the administrator simply has to add them to the global group.

Let's take this example one step further. Once the book is halfway complete, the publishing company needs to give access to the editorial team. The system administrator simply creates a second global group called Editors and adds the editorial team as members of the group. This group is then nested within the Windows 2000 Cram local group. This task is now complete. As you can see, because we used our AGDLP strategy, it was very simple to grant permissions to an additional set of users. If the Windows 2000 network had included multiple domains, the method of applying permissions would have changed slightly. In this case, the administrator would use the acronym AGUDLP (where *U* stands for *universal*), creating global groups first and then nesting them within universal groups. The universal group is then nested within the local group.

Universal groups are unique because AD treats them slightly differently. Although all group names are listed in a Global Catalog server, their membership list is generally not. The exception to this rule is the universal group. Both the universal group name and the membership list is replicated to every Global Catalog server. If you add a single user to a universal group, the *entire* membership list must be replicated. Therefore, it is a good idea to keep your universal group usage to a minimum, and when you do use this type of group, keep the membership lists fairly static. Nesting universal groups is far better than adding members to a single group.

User and Group Recommendations

Users can log on to a Windows 2000 domain using either their principal names or their down-level logon names. From a user perspective, this might not seem to make any difference. However, from an administrative point of view, it is better for users to use principal names. Because using a principal name means users don't have to enter domain names for their accounts, using this type of name exclusively gives administrators the ability to move user objects from one domain to another without any user education. It is always best to use the principal name.

Because you can create a suffix for the principal name, you should consider making it as easy on the user community as possible by making the suffix match the users' email accounts. This will make remembering their logon names easier.

You will likely be creating a lot of global groups in your domains. It is best to come up with a naming scheme for your groups so they are easily recognizable. In addition, you should create them based on job function. Doing this makes it easy to add users based on their responsibilities within the organization.

Universal groups cause additional replication on your network. Because the group name and the group membership have to be replicated to each Global Catalog server, be careful when using universal groups. Try to make them static. It is far better to nest universal groups than to create a lot of them.

When performing bulk import of user accounts, don't forget two very important defaults:

- The password is blank.
- The account is disabled.

Do not enable accounts until they are ready to be used. Doing so prematurely can open your network to hackers.

Practice Questions

Question 1

Active Directory offers Windows 2000 users many advantages, including the ability to search for users, groups, and other network resources. Along with this, the logon process has been simplified. What is the term used to describe the feature of Windows 2000 that simplifies access to resources for the users?

- ❍ a. Single-access
- ❍ b. Single sign-on
- ❍ c. Domain sign-on
- ❍ d. Forest sign-on

Answer b is correct. Single sign-on is a feature that allows users to log on a single time and to be granted access to many different resources on the network. When users want to use a network resource, they do not have to log on additional times. Answers a, c, and d are incorrect because they are invalid answers.

Question 2

Samantha is in the process of putting together a network security plan. Because she will be granting users access to shared folders and printers, she wants to use groups extensively. Samantha's company also has several kiosks in the foyer of company headquarters that visitors can use to browse the Web and access email. Samantha is not sure how she is going to limit the access of users. What method would be the easiest from an administrative standpoint? [Choose the best answer]

- ❍ a. Because groups can only contain user accounts, Samantha should create groups for her user community and put a firewall between the kiosk machines and her network.
- ❍ b. Samantha should create groups for the employees of her company. For the kiosk machines, Samantha can create a single logon and apply permissions to this group so users can access the resources they need. Because this can be a single group, this task would not involve a lot of work.
- ❍ c. Because groups can contain both user accounts and computer accounts, Samantha can go ahead and create a single group that includes both users from her company and the computers that operate as kiosks.
- ❍ d. Samantha should create a single logon for the kiosk machines. She should create a group for her employees and assign them permissions, and she should grant the user who is going to be used in the kiosks specific permissions to network resources.

Answer c is correct. Groups can contain both user accounts and computer accounts. Although answers a, b, and d are all feasible, they increase the administrative burden for the administrator. Specifically, answer a is incorrect because a firewall can be difficult to administer. Answers b and d are incorrect because adding specific user accounts to permission lists is also administratively intensive.

Question 3

Samantha has been called to troubleshoot a problem on a member server in her domain. A user called BradMehldau says he is logging in to the domain, and although he is being granted access (he is able to get to the desktop of the server), he is not able to access any network resources. Samantha checks BradMehldau's account and finds everything is normal. He has been granted access to resources and is a member of several groups that should enable him to access file shares. No one else has reported a problem with the network. Samantha goes to visit BradMehldau's office. What is a possible cause for this problem?

- ❍ a. The user is typing the wrong password. He is being granted access to the network, but because he used the wrong password, he is being denied access to network resources.
- ❍ b. The user is logging in to the member server using a local user account. This means he has not yet been validated by the domain and is therefore not allowed access to network resources.
- ❍ c. The user's password must be changed. The system is giving him sufficient access to do this, but it will not let him access network resources until the change is confirmed.
- ❍ d. The user has to wait for the logon process to complete. AD is complex, and it can take a long time for the security token to be created for a user the first time he or she logs on.

Answer b is correct. There are three types of user accounts: domain user accounts, local user accounts, and built-in accounts. Domain accounts are designed to allow users to log in to a network and gain access to resources. Local user accounts are used on member server and Windows 2000 Professional systems to allow users to log on to the local computer without network access (as in this instance). Built-in accounts are created by default for administrative purposes. Answer a is incorrect because typing in a bad password would result in the user being unable to see the desktop. Answer c is incorrect because the user would have had to have typed the correct password in order to access the system. Answer d is incorrect because there should be no lag when the user logs on. When a user logs on, the security token for the user is created. If there is a delay in the creation of the token, the entire logon process is delayed.

Question 4

What are the names given to the types of logon names that will be accepted by a Windows 2000 network? [Check all correct answers]

- ❑ a. User logon name
- ❑ b. User account name
- ❑ c. Principal name
- ❑ d. Domain username

Answers a and c are correct. The user logon name requires the user to enter the name of the domain that contains his or her account. The principal name resembles an email address. The user does not have to specify the domain name when using principal names. Answers b and d are other names commonly used to describe the user logon name. However, you should not use these terms because they can have more than one meaning on a Windows 2000 network.

Question 5

Keith Jarrett is a system administrator for a Windows 2000 network. He is trying to make a decision about which method users should use to log on to his network. There are four domains in his forest, and he wants to make the logon method as simple for the users as possible. The company is owned by the Smith family. Three generations of Smiths work in his organization, and he has 25 members of the Smith family working in one context or another. Family members include David Smith, David Smith II, Darrell Smith, John Smith, John Smith II, and John Smith III. After careful consideration, Keith decides to stick with using the logon method that requires users to know which domains they belong to. Why did Keith make this decision?

- ❍ a. Keith knows that he has some duplicate names on his network. Because a principal name must be unique in a forest, he cannot guarantee he won't run into problems. To avoid this, he is stuck with forcing the users to enter their domain name.
- ❍ b. Keith has decided that user education is going to be a problem. His user community has been migrated from a Windows NT 4 environment and is used to entering the domain name. Also, the benefits of using principal names is not great.
- ❍ c. Keith eventually wants to collapse two of his domains. By forcing the users to use a domain name, he can more easily identify those who are going to be affected by such a move and perform a smoother transition.
- ❍ d. It really doesn't make much difference to Keith which method is used. Because, administratively, it does not gain him anything, he decides to make sure users enter the domain name.

Answer a is correct. Because Keith has a lot of duplicate names, using principal names won't work. Keith would need to come up with a new user-naming strategy to use principal names. Therefore, answers b, c, and d are all incorrect.

Question 6

Meredith Brittain has been asked to deploy a Windows 2000 network. One of the largest tasks is going to be creating 10,000 user accounts. Her customer has provided her with a text file containing the usernames from its previous network system, along with information such as telephone numbers and first and last names. This file was exported from Microsoft Excel in a comma-delimited format. What is the best way for Meredith to enter these names into AD?

- ❍ a. To make sure these accounts are accurate, Meredith should type each account in manually.
- ❍ b. Meredith should use the Ldifde command-line utility.
- ❍ c. Meredith should use the Csvde command-line utility.
- ❍ d. Meredith should use the Import function on AD Users and Computers.

Answer c is correct. Only Csvde will work. Answer b is incorrect because Ldifde uses a line-separated format and will not work. Answer d is incorrect because Active Directory User and Computers does not have a bulk-import function. Answer a would work, but it is much more likely that Meredith will make a typo when entering 10,000 user accounts, not to mention it would take a lot more time.

Question 7

Peter Chamberlin has been asked to secure some shared folders. He knows he should not grant access to network resources at the user level, because this increases the amount of system administration the network requires. He decides to use groups. Rather than having to manage different kinds of groups and worry about their scope, he decides to use universal groups extensively. He creates a lot of groups early Monday morning, but before he can finish, users call in and complain that the network is slow. What would cause this?

- ❍ a. Adding large amounts of data to AD causes a lot of network traffic, and this traffic has caused the network to be slow. Administration of AD should be performed after hours.
- ❍ b. Creating groups is processor-intensive because the DC has to gather data about all user accounts in the domain. This should be done after hours.
- ❍ c. As Peter is adding users to groups, the users are being informed by their local DCs of their new permissions. This is causing the traffic.
- ❍ d. Universal groups cause more network traffic than other group types because both the group name and membership list are replicated to all Global Catalog servers. If Peter had used another group type, he would not have had this problem.

Answer d is correct. Because the membership of a universal group is replicated to Global Catalog servers, more network traffic is generated. Peter should be careful about creating a large number of universal groups. Answers a, b, and c are all incorrect choices.

Question 8

Jeff Hilton has been migrating his Windows NT 4 network to Windows 2000. He is currently running in mixed mode. Because Jeff has multiple domains, he wants to use local groups, global groups, and universal groups. A consultant tells Jeff that he must be running Windows 2000 in native mode to create universal groups. However, Jeff has already created a universal group, and he doubts the consultant knows what he is doing. Who is right?

- ❍ a. Jeff is correct. Universal groups can be used in either mixed mode or native mode.
- ❍ b. Both are correct. Universal groups can be created in either mode, but they can only be used as distribution groups in mixed mode.
- ❍ c. Both are correct. Universal groups can be created in either mode, but they can only be used as security groups in mixed mode.
- ❍ d. The consultant is correct. Universal groups can only be used in native mode.

Answer b is correct. Although universal groups can be used in mixed mode, their function is limited to distribution groups. You must be in native mode to use them to grant access to network resources. Therefore, answers a, c, and d are incorrect.

Question 9

Gus is a system administrator of a Windows 2000 network that has a single domain. Gus needs to come up with a group strategy. He decides to use domain local groups and global groups. His manager asks him to go back to the drawing board and come up with a strategy that uses universal groups, unless Gus has good reason not to. Why did Gus choose not to use universal groups?

- ❍ a. Gus wants to minimize the replication traffic on his network.
- ❍ b. Universal groups simply add another layer of global groups. Gus has a "keep it simple" philosophy.
- ❍ c. Universal groups cannot be used for security purposes. They are used for distribution groups. Using universal groups would not help in assigning permissions to network resources.
- ❍ d. Universal groups could be used, but in a single-domain environment, they simply add an extra level of complexity. Universal groups are really only useful in multidomain environments.

Answer d is correct. Don't forget, in a single domain, there is no need to use universal groups. They cause additional replication, and in a single-domain environment, you gain nothing by using them. Therefore, answers a, b, and c are incorrect.

Question 10

Zevi Mehlman has been asked to change the password for a user account. Zevi is a domain administrator. However, he has tried to contact the user to get her current password but has been unable to. His boss is worried that someone might have the password for this account. What is the best course of action for Zevi to take?

❍ a. Zevi should delete the user account and re-create it with the new password. The user will call as soon as she is unable to log on.

❍ b. Because Zevi is a domain administrator, he does not need the user's current password to make the change.

❍ c. Zevi should disable the account. This will force the user to call in with the information Zevi needs.

❍ d. Zevi should lock the account out. This will force the user to call in with the information Zevi needs.

Answer b is correct. Zevi does not need the user's password. It is not advisable to change users' passwords without them knowing, but there might be times when it is necessary. Therefore, answers a, c, and d are all incorrect.

Need to Know More?

Boswell, William. *Inside Windows 2000 Server*. New Riders. Indianapolis, IN, 1999. ISBN 1-56205-929-7.

This book is a highly technical read that explains the details of all facets of a Windows 2000 Server, including replication.

Iseminger, David. *Active Directory Services for Microsoft Windows 2000*. Microsoft Press. Redmond, WA, 2000. ISBN 0-7356-0624-2.

This book introduces you to all aspects of working with a Windows 2000 domain, specifically dealing with AD administration.

Minasi, Mark. *Mastering Windows 2000 Server, Second Edition*. Sybex Computer Books. Alameda, CA, 2000. ISBN 0-7821-2774-6.

Active Directory Delegation of Administrative Control

Terms you'll need to understand:

- ✓ Security principal
- ✓ Security ID (SID)
- ✓ Discretionary access control list (DACL)
- ✓ System access control list (SACL)
- ✓ Access control entry (ACE)
- ✓ Access tokens
- ✓ Permissions
- ✓ Child objects
- ✓ Inheritance
- ✓ Ownership
- ✓ Microsoft Management Console (MMC)
- ✓ Taskpads

Techniques you'll need to master:

- ✓ Viewing Active Directory object permissions
- ✓ Assigning delegation of authority with the wizard
- ✓ Designing administrative control with inheritance and blocking in mind
- ✓ Viewing and taking ownership of objects
- ✓ Creating specialized management consoles and taskpads

If you understand that placing permissions on various objects determines who has access to objects such as printers, folders, files, and so on, you will easily understand the concept of the delegation of administrative authority. Delegating administrative control defines which trusted individuals will have access to Active Directory (AD) objects (either to create, delete, or modify) for distributing the administrative workload and maintaining control in the process. There are several other ways to maintain control, such as the use of customized Microsoft Management Consoles (MMCs) and taskpads. The implementation of these functions is discussed in the sections "Creating MMC Consoles" and "Taskpads," toward the end of the chapter.

Object Security

AD security involves many abstract technical terms that are often used without being properly defined. Let's look at the terminology behind the security components.

Terminology for AD Security

Often, words are misused in the computer field. Here is a list of important security terms and a description of how each relates to the authentication process:

- **Security principal**—This is an account to which permissions can be assigned—for example, a user, a group, or a computer account. If you are Bob, a member of the Accounting group on a computer with a domain computer account named System01, there are several security principals involved that permissions could be applied toward—namely, the user "Bob," the group "Accounting," or the computer account "System01."
- **Security ID (SID)**—Every security principal is issued a unique SID that is assigned once to an account and is never reused, even if the object is removed. The SID is a numeric value that is assigned automatically when an object is added to the directory.
- **Security descriptor**—This becomes part of created objects and defines access control information for those objects. When a user attempts to access an object, the descriptor checks its information against the user's SID and then compares the SID against its access control list (ACL). The two types of ACLs are discretionary access control lists (DACLs) and system access control lists (SACLs).

- **Discretionary access control list (DACL)**—This is a list of access control entries (ACEs) that indicates security levels of Allow Access and Deny Access permissions as well as to what degree these permissions apply. One key point in a DACL is that the Deny Access entries are placed first in the ACE. A user could have plenty of access permissions for an object but may belong to one group that has Deny Access for all permissions. The Deny Access will prove stronger than all the other options. By placing the Deny Access entries first in the list, you save a lot of time because the user may not have the permissions for the object he or she was hoping to access.
- **System access control list (SACL)**—This is a list used for auditing object access based on ACEs that indicates to the object when an account has accessed an object or has attempted to access an object. In the event that access is attempted or achieved, a record of the access is placed in the object security list.
- **Access control entries (ACEs)**—ACEs are used by DACLs and SACLs. When used with a DACL, the ACE determines the level of security access on an object by breaking it down into four types: Access Denied, Access Allowed, Access Denied Object Specify, and Access Allowed Object Specify. When used with an SACL, the ACE determines the level of security access based on two remaining types of ACEs: System Audit and System Audit Object Specific. These six different entry types assist in determining the permissions to be applied.
- **Access tokens**—All the items in this list would be ineffective without an access token. When a user logs on, an access token is created and sent by the DC to the user's machine. This token is necessary for a user to access any network resource. The access token is attached to that user and is needed to access any object, to run any application, and to use system resources. The access token is what literally holds the SID and the group IDs, which indicate what groups the user belongs to. These group IDs are really SIDs that are given to the groups upon their creation. If a user belongs to a group, that group's SID is added to the user's access token.

Only global and domain local groups are added to the token from the DC to which the user logs on. The DC will contact a Global Catalog (GC) for SIDs of universal group membership.

User rights are also included in the access token—for example, the right to log on locally to a computer or a domain controller (DC), if that right is assigned to a specific user.

From Logon to Object Access

To fully understand all the terms in the preceding list, we need to put them in a context that brings them to life. Say a domain administrator sits down at a DC and creates a user account named "Lamar." This is a security principal that can now be assigned permissions. Lamar's account is automatically assigned a unique SID, never again to be used. This identifies the Lamar object. Lamar may be assigned to the Sales and Managers groups during creation as well. The account may also be given certain user rights specific to the account.

At the same time, in another part of the building, a physical print device is attached to a print server. The printer object is shared out on the network. Certain permissions are applied to the object, and as a result, the object has a security description. Auditing is also enabled on this printer.

When user Lamar logs on, he receives his access token (a token provided by the DC that contains the SID, group SIDs, and user rights) and then attempts to access the printer object. The object checks its security description for permissions. Specifically, it checks its DACL for ACEs for which the user has either Allow or Deny permissions, and it checks Allow or Deny permissions for any groups to which the user belongs. Then, because auditing is enabled, the object checks its SACL for ACEs that determine whether an entry should be made in the log for this attempt at access.

As you can see, accessing a resource requires a rather involved process. This concept is also the key to understanding how AD objects such as Organizational Units (OUs) can be structured to allow access from selected individuals.

Access Permissions on AD Objects

Although file/folder permissions and AD object permissions are similar in access theoretics, their purposes are dissimilar. You apply permissions on AD objects (for example, an OU, a hierarchical group of OUs, or even an individual object such as a user, group, or computer account) for the purpose of delegating authority, whereas you apply file/folder permissions to control access to those specific resources for the users and groups within your organization.

The actual permissions that you can apply to objects are also different from those of files and folders. Here are the five standard permissions that can be applied to an object:

- **Full Control**—Allows the user the ability to view an object and its attributes, the owner of the object, and the AD permissions, along with the ability to change any of those settings. In addition, a user with Full Control can literally change permissions on the object and take ownership of an object.
- **Write**—Enables the user to view an object and its attributes, the owner of the object, and the AD permissions. Write also allows the user to change any of those settings.
- **Read**—Enables the user to view an object and its attributes, the owner of the object, and the AD permissions.
- **Create All Child Objects**—Enables the user to create and add child objects to an OU.
- **Delete All Child Objects**—Enables the user to delete existing objects from an OU.

All objects within the AD have an owner. Similar to the owners that exist in files and folders, the owner of an object can change permissions on the object and how those permissions are handed out. Logically, the initial owner of any object is the one who created it. Therefore, if Tim creates an OU named "Sales," Tim's account would be registered as the owner—unless he provides permissions for another individual to have Full Control, in which case that person would be able to take ownership of the object.

Viewing AD Permissions

To view the permissions that exist on an AD object (an OU is the embodiment of a perfect-example AD object, so we will consider that as the standard object for this section), you must perform the following tasks:

1. Open AD Users and Computers by selecting Start, Programs, Administrative Tools, Active Directory Users and Computers.
2. On the View menu, make sure that Advanced Features is selected.
3. Expand your domain structure and select an OU that you can use as an example.
4. Right-click the OU and select Properties.

5. Select the Security tab. From here, you can see the standard permissions for your OU, as shown in Figure 6.1 and mentioned in the previous section.

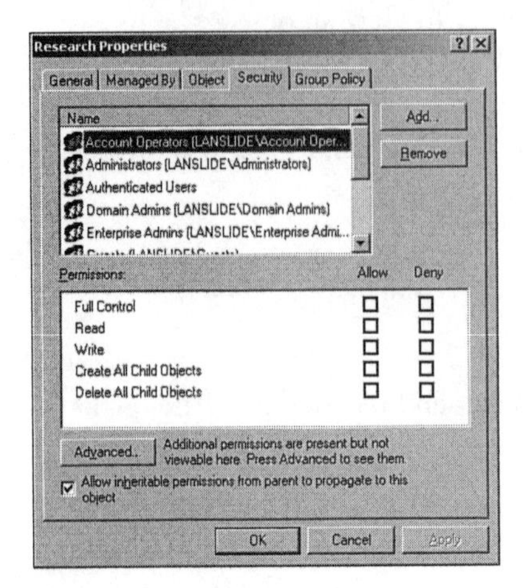

Figure 6.1 Viewing object permissions through the Security tab.

To see additional permission options called *special permissions*, select the Advanced button. In the resulting dialog box, you can select one of three tabs: Permissions, Auditing, and Owner. On the Permissions tab, shown in Figure 6.2, you can see all the permission entries that have already been applied. From here, you can add or remove user or group permissions, or you can select View/Edit to see the special permission options shown in Figure 6.3.

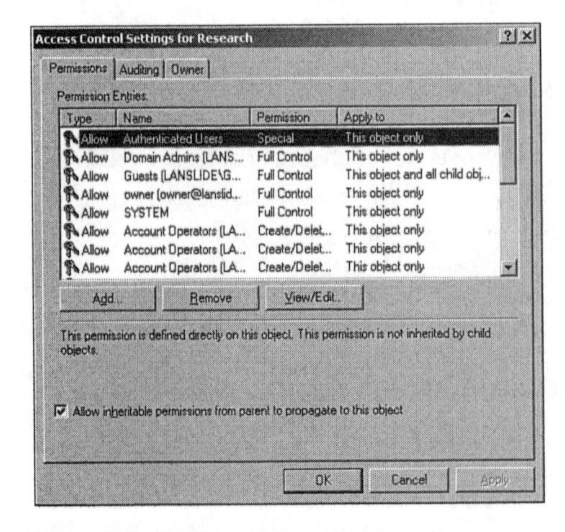

Figure 6.2 The advanced permissions options.

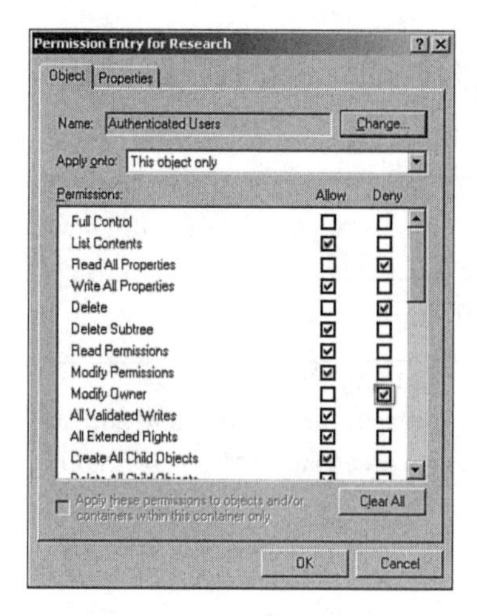

Figure 6.3 The special permissions options.

Notice the Allow Inheritable Permissions from Parent to Propagate to This Object check box at the bottom of Figures 6.1 and 6.2. This option is part of the inheritance concepts we will discuss shortly.

To Allow or to Deny

Permissions under Windows 2000 are considered "granular" because of the miniscule ways they can be applied to objects. Allow permissions are always easy to conceptualize, but with AD object permissions, Deny permissions are also available. These Deny permissions have a stronger effect on an individual who attempts certain functions.

For example, if Jeremy is a member of the Research Admins security group and that group has Full Control Allow permissions over the Research OU, then logically Jeremy also has Allow permissions by extension. However, if it has been determined that Jeremy, as a new employee, should not be given Delete All Child Objects permission, rather than pulling Jeremy out of his security group or changing the permissions for the entire group, you can place specific Deny permissions on Jeremy's user account that will deny him access to the Delete All Child Objects permission. When the DACL for the Research OU sees a Deny setting for the Delete All Child Objects permission in its ACE for Jeremy, that permission applies above and beyond the Full Control permissions of his group.

Theoretical Delegation of Authority

After the deployment of a domain, there is still quite a bit of administrative work that needs to be performed. In a small environment, the work would be easy—just put all your administrators in the Domain Admins group and leave it at that. However, in an enterprise network infrastructure, you need to *delegate* your administration and mold it in your company's best interests.

So, where do you begin? As with many tasks, you begin by documenting your existing structure. A planning team should be put together to examine the current infrastructure of the administrative team, along with the responsibilities that the administrators hold. Keep in mind that the changes made to the network structure in the future will greatly alter some of those administrative responsibilities.

The planning team can take this knowledge and start posing the following types of questions:

- Can we combine some of the current administrative teams into a more decisive administrative structure?
- Are there employees who might assist to some degree in administration without having the technical background to do so (or the request for a tech's salary)?
- What should each administrative group or individual be allowed to control and to what degree?

Once the planning team has a basic understanding of the task at hand, the members can use the following points to help delegate administrative control properly:

- *Assign control at the OU level for easier administration.* This allows you to track permissions in a simpler manner. Try to assign administrative control at the highest OU levels as well, and allow inheritance to control the flow of administration. This will be an easier and more efficient way of managing permissions. Remember, the domain and OU levels of the hierarchy are designed to meet the administrative needs of the organization. Design and build it in such a way that it simplifies delegating administrative authority.
- *Try to avoid assigning control at the property or task level as much as possible.* To handle permissions more efficiently, try to place objects in OUs based on management rather than have OUs with multiple objects inside and different access permissions for each object. You can see how this

would become messy if you needed to track down a permissions problem. This will also make it difficult for your administrators to know what objects they have control over. On the one hand, they've been told they can control permissions under a certain OU, but perhaps the objects within have permissions all their own.

- *Utilize a small Domain Administrators group*. The Domain Admins group contains the all-powerful rulers of the network. They can take ownership of any object, define policies, change passwords at the senior management level, and so on. That makes any member of the Domain Admins group a highly trusted individual. Limit the membership to this group, and allow other administrators to handle administrative tasks throughout the domain at the OU level. Members of the Domain Admins group should also be under strict instruction not to give out their network authentication method, whether it's a password or a smart card (a smart card is a good idea if you need high levels of security).
- *Finally, document everything*. Tracking down problems with administrative delegation will be much easier if you've documented your procedures.

Setting AD Permissions

You can establish permissions on AD objects in two ways. The first is by directly adding users and their corresponding permissions. You simply follow the same procedure for the viewing of permissions, noted earlier in the "Viewing AD Permissions" section, and add new users or groups with permissions that will ease your administrative concerns. Microsoft's preferred method is through the Delegation of Control Wizard because it involves a simpler sequence of steps.

The Delegation of Control Wizard

You can use the Delegation of Control Wizard to delegate common tasks, or you can create a customized task to delegate. This section explains how to do both.

Delegating Common Tasks

The standard procedural steps for using the Delegation of Control Wizard are as follows:

1. In the AD Users and Computers administrative tool, find the OU to which you wish to delegate control.

2. To start the wizard, you can select Action, Delegate Control, or you can right-click the OU and select Delegate Control.
3. The wizard presents an opening screen and dialog box. Click the Next button.
4. On the Users and Groups page, you are prompted to select a user, several users, a group, or several groups (the choice depends on your needs). After highlighting your selections, click Add and then click OK.
5. The Tasks to Delegate screen, shown in Figure 6.4, appears. From the list of common tasks, select the tasks you want and then click Next.
6. Click Finish.

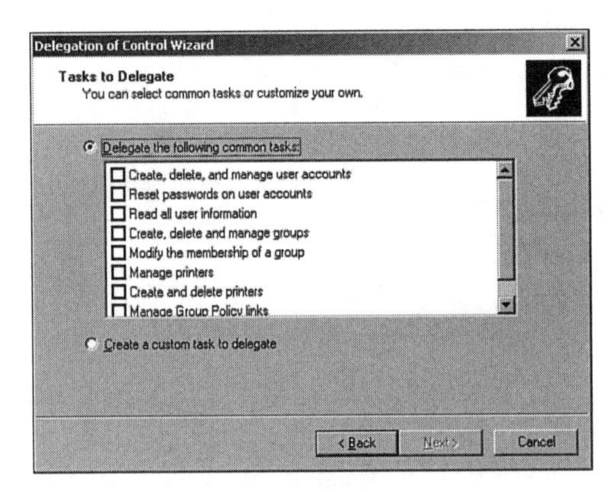

Figure 6.4 Delegating common tasks over an object.

Creating a Custom Task

The steps for creating a customized task in the Delegation of Control Wizard are as follows:

1. Follow the first five steps in the previous section, with the following change: In Step 5, select Create a Custom Task to Delegate instead of choosing from the list of common tasks. Click Next.
2. The screen in Figure 6.5 appears. Notice that you can use the option This Folder, Existing Objects in This Folder, and Creation of New Objects in This Folder to set permissions on these respective items. You can also select the Only the Following Objects in the Folder option, which displays a long list of different types of objects to choose from. Notice the granularity of control that can be implemented on an OU. Make your selections and then click Next.

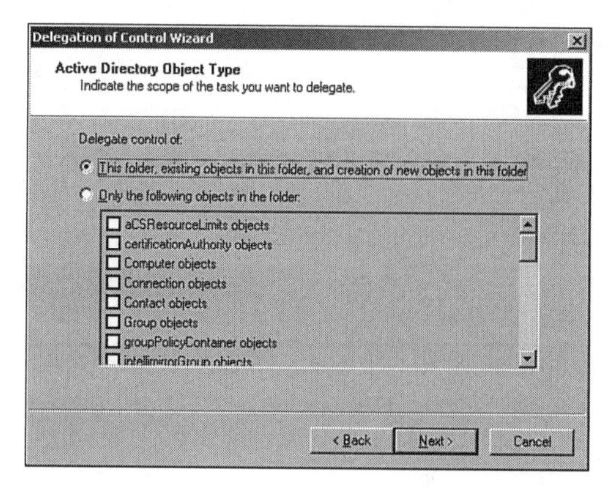

Figure 6.5 Setting customized permission options.

3. The next screen shows three options of permission detail: General, Property-Specific, and Creation/Deletion of Specific Child Objects, as shown in Figure 6.6. Each selection provides additional check box options. By selecting the type of permissions and their corresponding check boxes, you complete your creation of a customized set of delegation options. Click Next to move to the final screen.

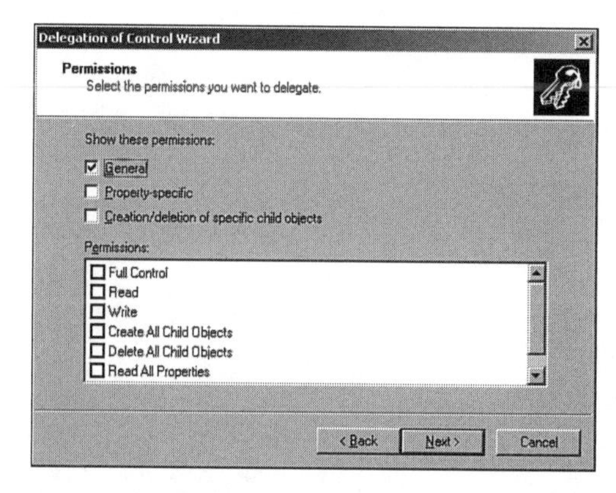

Figure 6.6 The specific permissions you choose to delegate.

4. The final screen displays a listing of your choices. Review your selections and click Finish.

Once you've used the wizard to delegate authority, your next concern is how permissions should flow between parent and child objects.

The Flow of Permissions

To simplify the setting of permissions, the implementation of inheritance is utilized by Windows 2000. Inheritance is automatic for child objects within parent containers. Put simply, if a parent object—an OU, for example—has permissions implemented on it, the child objects beneath will automatically inherit the permissions from above. The benefit of inheritance is that permissions need to be applied only at high-level containers, and they will flow down throughout child containers that are already in existence. This makes the administrative task of delegating authority much easier for the following reasons:

- When you create a child object within a parent container that holds certain permissions, the child object automatically contains the permissions of its parent, as shown in Figure 6.7.
- When you set permissions at higher levels, those permissions are applied consistently through the lower child objects.
- Any changes made to permissions above automatically apply to the child objects below.

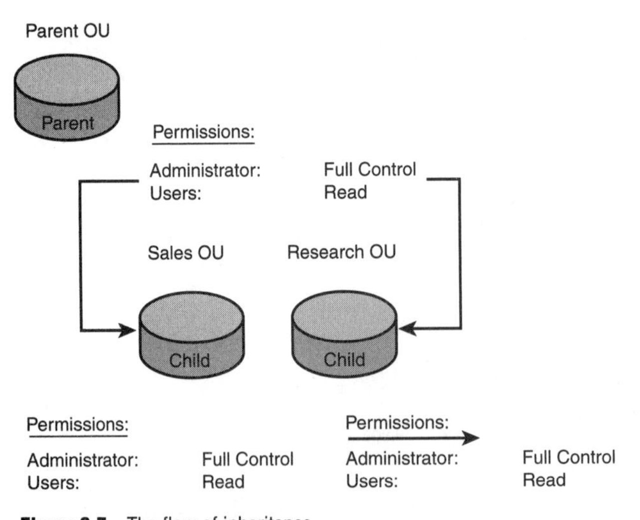

Figure 6.7 The flow of inheritance.

Redirecting the Flow of Permissions

There are times when the flow from above will not logically work for your lower containers. For example, say you have an OU called "Ontario" for your branch location in Ontario. Most tasks and OUs within the Ontario parent container are cared for through the Ontario Admins security group. You would like to create a new OU inside of the Ontario OU. The new OU will be called “Research” and will be completely managed by a separate team of admins. To prevent AD permissions from the parent OU from taking precedence, here’s what can you do:

1. Note the Allow Inheritable Permissions from Parent to Propagate to This Object check box at the bottom of Figure 6.2. When this box is selected, permissions are inherited. Remove the check in this box to remove the permission inheritance.

2. As shown in Figure 6.8, prior to the removal of all permissions from above, you’ll see a Security dialog box that presents two options: Copy and Remove. Choose Copy to retain permissions that were already in place on the OU. With this option, you can then make revisions. Choose Remove to remove all preexisting permissions. With this option, you must assign permissions from scratch.

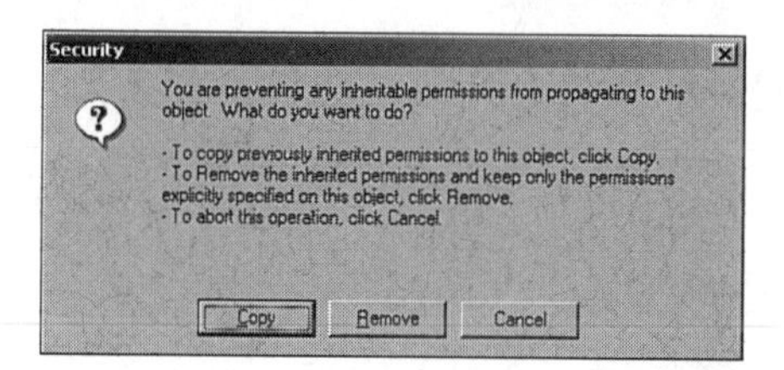

Figure 6.8 The options for removal of inheritance from above.

This ability to remove inheritance from above is an important exam topic that often surfaces when considering a design decision that will allow you to create and control your Active Directory.

Ownership of AD Objects

Just as all print jobs, files, and folders have owners, each object within the AD has an owner who is responsible for the existence of the object. The owner is usually the one who created the object and the one who holds Full Control over that object.

At times, the ownership of an object needs to change hands. If an individual with permissions creates several objects within the AD and that individual is no longer with the company or has changed departments, it may be necessary for another assigned individual to take ownership of those objects. Note the word *take*. Ownership cannot be given away; users with the correct permissions must take it.

Viewing Ownership

As with an OU, to view who owns a particular object, follow these steps:

1. Go into the properties of the object by right-clicking the object itself.
2. At the top of the object's properties page, select the Security tab.
3. Select the Advanced button.
4. This takes you to a familiar place—the Access Control Settings page. At the top, select the Owner tab, as shown in Figure 6.9. The current owner is displayed.

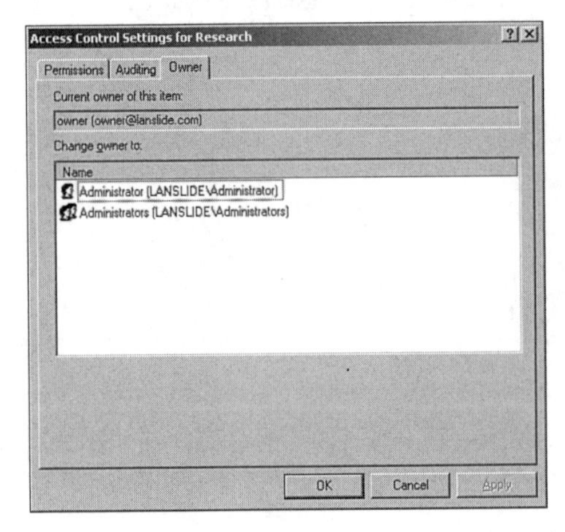

Figure 6.9 The Owner tab shows the current owner of the object you are viewing.

Taking Ownership

Ownership changes hands in one of two ways. First, the current owner or a user with Full Control over an object specifies that another user can take ownership. That user, then, officially takes ownership of the object. Second, an administrator or a domain administrator takes ownership of an object, regardless of who the owner currently is or whether the admin was given specific permissions for an object.

If an administrator takes ownership of an object, the Domain Admins group is also listed as an owner for an object. The logic is that if one administrator needs to have ownership control over an object, the entire Domain Admins group should hold ownership.

To take ownership of an object, follow the same steps as for viewing an object's owner:

1. Go into the properties of the object by right-clicking the object itself.
2. At the top of the object's properties page, select the Security tab.
3. Select the Advanced button.
4. This takes you to the Access Control Settings page. At the top, find and select the Owner tab. The current owner is displayed.
5. If you have permissions to be owner, your name will appear in the options below (or if you are an administrator, your name and the Domain Admins group will appear). Select your name and click Apply. You have taken ownership of the object.

Delegation of Administrative Tools

Although delegating authority is a great way to distribute administrative responsibilities, another way to delegate is to allow individuals to use certain administrative tools that are necessary.

Windows 2000 uses the Microsoft Management Console (MMC) as a one-stop tool for all the administrative tools within the suite. Although various predefined consoles are already in place when you install Windows 2000, it is important that ordinary users not have access to such tools. However, you may need to allow users access to some of the tools so that they can use the authority you've delegated. For example, if you've delegated authority over an OU to a user, it is a good idea to provide the user with an MMC that holds the AD Users and Computers tool.

Another benefit of customizable MMC consoles is that they allow you, as an administrator, to create your own consoles with tools that you use most frequently.

Creating MMC Consoles

Before creating a specialized console, you must determine which mode to use to create your console. Two modes are available: author mode and user mode. Author mode is for administrative consoles that are specially designed for easy control by other administrators who receive these consoles. Author mode is used to create new consoles and modify existing consoles. User mode is more tailored toward limiting the user from customizing the console any further than what you've already determined. User mode is for working with existing consoles. There are three levels of user mode:

- Full access
- Limited access, multiple windows
- Limited access, single window

Once the mode is determined, you can proceed with the creation. To create a console, follow these steps:

1. Select Start, Run. Type **`mmc`** in the text box and hit Enter. An empty console appears.
2. At the top, select Console and choose Add/Remove Snap-In. This takes you to an empty list of snap-ins. (Notice under Console that the Options selection is also available. This is where you would specify the mode.)
3. Select Add. A list of the many available tools appears. Select a few snap-ins, click Add for each snap-in selected, and select whether it will manage a local computer or another computer. Then click Finish. Select Close when you are finished adding snap-ins. Click OK, and you are brought to your newly created MMC console.
4. Once the console is created, you must save it. Select Console and then Save As. Give the console a name and location, and the console will be saved with an `.msc` extension.

After creating the console, your next concern is distributing it.

Distributing MMC Consoles

There are a few recommended ways to send consoles:

- If small enough, they can be distributed via floppy or e-mail.
- They can be placed in a shared folder for administrators to access. This would allow for NTFS (NT File System) permissions to provide a lock-down of Write permissions, preventing changes to your consoles. (Make sure your administrators have Read permissions, though.)
- You can package them and distribute them through Group Policy.

How you distribute your saved console is up to you; however, one key point to remember is that any administrator who receives the console also needs to install the tools on his or her system. These tools are not installed on the Windows 2000 Professional workstations. You must install them manually.

Installing Administrative Tools

Microsoft provides these tools on the Windows 2000 Advanced Server CD or off of a server running Windows 2000 Advanced Server in the `systemroot/system32` folder. The file is an MSI file called `adminpak`. Because it is an MSI file, it is part of the Windows Installer team and can be distributed through Group Policy or installed manually. On the system running Windows 2000 Professional, you need to execute and install the `adminpak.msi` file. Now the consoles you've created will have tools to draw upon.

Taskpads

After you assign permissions to an AD object and create specific MMC consoles, taskpads are the next level of administrative delegation. A *taskpad* is a simplified version of an MMC. They are used when administrators want to delegate administrative control to people who are not yet comfortable using these types of tools.

Creating a Taskpad

Once you've created your customized MMC console, the steps to create a taskpad are simple. You use the Taskpad Creation Wizard as follows:

1. Select Snap-In from within the console you've created.
2. To start the wizard, highlight the snap-in and select Action, New Taskpad View.
3. The first screen requires you to determine the taskpad display, as shown in Figure 6.10. From here, you can determine the look of your taskpad and the amount of detail.

The wizard takes you through the steps of configuration. The end result is a simplified presentation to users who are not as comfortable with the true console. The options that users select actually point toward shortcuts of the real MMC console. All the same rules apply for taskpad distribution that applied for MMC console distribution.

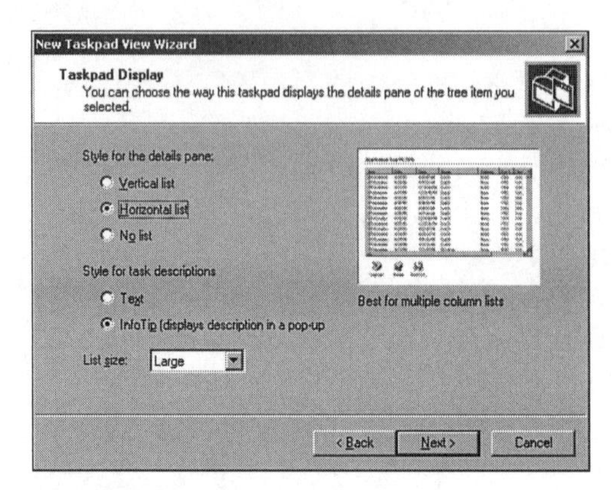

Figure 6.10 The Taskpad Display screen.

Customizing a Taskpad

Once your taskpad is officially created, you can customize it for your users and simplify it even further. You can establish large buttons that correlate with actual tasks that an individual might perform. For example, Figure 6.11 shows a taskpad view of the AD Users and Computers tool. From there, a specific taskpad was created of the Users folder of the snap-in. Finally, a large shortcut button was added to the taskpad to allow for the creation of a new user. Using this taskpad, the user can create users easily; all he or she has to do is click the shortcut button. By making these types of customizations and distributing the taskpad to others, you will make administration very easy for those to whom you've delegated control.

Instead of using shortcut buttons, you can customize your taskpads even further by specifying batch files or scripts to be run off of a simple button selection.

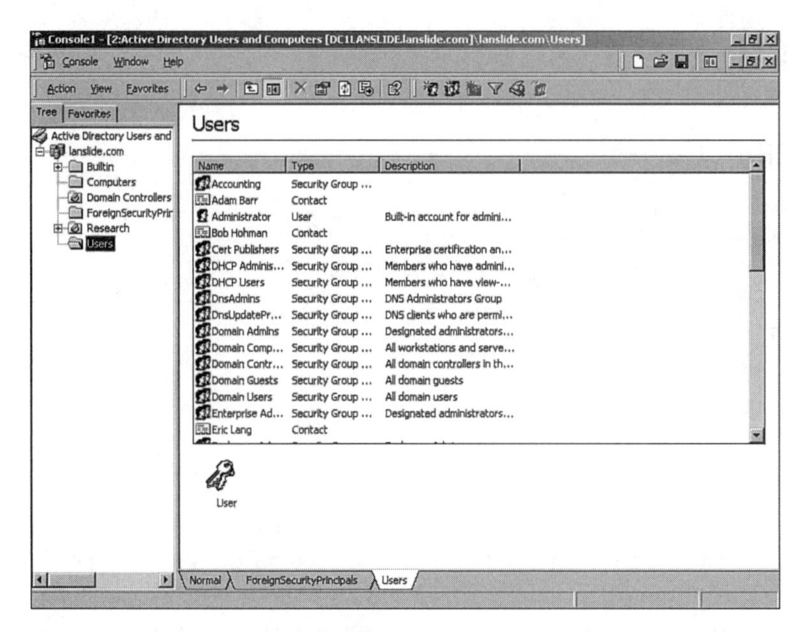

Figure 6.11 A customized taskpad for the creation of users.

Practice Questions

Question 1

To simplify administrative tasks, you've decided to apply permissions of object control to your Active Directory. Where should you assign control to qualified users in your organization?

❍ a. Folders.

❍ b. Files.

❍ c. OUs.

❍ d. You should add the users to the Domain Admins group.

Answer c is correct. Assigning control at the OU level is the best way to administer control over objects within Active Directory, although it is possible to assign permissions directly to objects, such as a user or a printer. Answers a and b are incorrect because they relate to file/folder access permissions and not to Active Directory objects. Answer d is incorrect because, although this will give control over Active Directory objects, it is not a recommended way of delegating responsibility; rather, it is a way of sharing responsibility with peers, not users.

Question 2

In establishing a more granular control over permissions, Windows 2000 provides what permissions options over Active Directory objects? [Check two of the following answers]

❑ a. Allow

❑ b. Permission

❑ c. Access

❑ d. Deny

Answers a and d are correct. Through the use of Allow and Deny permissions, administrators can provide more granular control over the depth of permissions an individual user might have. Answer b is incorrect because it is not a permissions option. Answer c is incorrect because it, too, is not a permissions option; rather, it is more of a diversion from the correct answer.

Question 3

You are the administrator for one of the branch offices of the company Braincore. The branch you currently oversee is located in Edinburgh, Scotland. You manage several child OUs under the Edinburgh OU and have just recently hired an assistant who will co-manage these child OUs under your charge. Which of the following permissions would your assistant need in order to perform all tasks, with the exception of the ability to remove an OU from the Edinburgh OU? [Check all correct answers]

- ❑ a. Full Control
- ❑ b. Modify
- ❑ c. Delete OUs
- ❑ d. Change
- ❑ e. Read
- ❑ f. Create All Child Objects
- ❑ g. Delete All Child Objects
- ❑ h. Write

Answers e, f, and h are correct. The goal here is to provide just enough permission to accomplish the task. Being able to read, write, and create all child objects will accomplish this. In this situation your assistant doesn't require Full Control because his or her abilities are limited. Therefore, answer a is incorrect. Your assistant cannot have Delete All Child Objects permission. Therefore, answer g is incorrect. Answers b and d are for file/folder permissions and are therefore inapplicable.

Question 4

Which of the following tools would you use to view Active Directory object permissions?

- ❍ a. AD Domains and Trusts
- ❍ b. AD Users and Computers
- ❍ c. AD Sites and Services
- ❍ d. AD Object Permissions

Answer b is correct. You go to AD Users and Computers to view object permissions. Remember to select View and then Advanced Features before going into the properties of an OU to see the permissions on the Security tab. Answers a and c are incorrect because these tools handle site and domain issues, not Active Directory object creation or permissions. Answer d is incorrect because it is not valid.

Question 5

Kayla is a domain administrator who has placed permissions on a parent OU, and through inheritance, those permissions have flowed down toward the child OUs beneath. What can Kayla do to prevent the flow of inheritance while retaining the permissions that already exist on the objects? [Check all correct answers]

- ❑ a. Go into the properties of the OU and deselect the Allow Inheritable Permissions from Parent to Propagate to This Object check box.
- ❑ b. Go into the properties of the OU and select the Allow Inheritable Permissions from Parent to Propagate to This Object check box.
- ❑ c. Select Copy at the Security screen.
- ❑ d. Select Remove at the Security screen.

Answers a and c are correct. To remove inheritance, Kayla must deselect the check box on the OU that allows inheritance. To retain the preexisting permissions, Kayla must select Copy from the corresponding warning box that appears. Answer b is incorrect because it would apply inheritance from above to the object. Answer d is incorrect because it would remove all permissions that existed prior to the change.

Question 6

If an administrator takes ownership of an object, who else is listed as an owner of that object?

- ❍ a. The object's creator
- ❍ b. Previous owners
- ❍ c. The Domain Admins group
- ❍ d. The Enterprise Admins group

Answer c is correct. The Domain Admins group is also listed as an owner for an object. The logic is that if one administrator needs to have ownership control over an object, the entire Domain Admins group should hold ownership. Answer a is incorrect because the creator isn't always listed under the ownership section, although the creator is always the original owner of an object. Answer b is incorrect because the ownership is tracked from one person to the next. Answer d is incorrect for obvious reasons.

Question 7

You are the network administrator for a company called Lan-Slide Technologies. You are looking to design an AD structure to accommodate the following situation: You have five branch offices located all over the world and a headquarters located in San Diego, California. At each location you have small administrative teams that would like to handle the resources and administrative needs for their location. You would like to provide this but continue to maintain ultimate control if necessary. How would you accomplish this design?

❍ a. Create a parent domain and have each branch location be a separate child domain, with the administrative teams being domain admins for their domains and you retaining the Enterprise admin position.

❍ b. Create a single domain and have OUs for each branch location. Create administrative security groups for each location and place those in their respective OUs. Delegate authority over the OU to the administrative team in each location.

❍ c. Create a single domain and have OUs for each branch location. Place all the administrators in the Domain Admins group for the domain. Then delegate authority over the OUs to the Domain Admins group.

❍ d. Create a parent domain and have one OU for the headquarters. Beneath the headquarter OU place five other OUs for your organization. Place all your administrators in the Enterprise Admins group and delegate authority to the top OU. Inheritance will flow down to the other OUs.

Answer b is correct. A single domain structure is all you need for this scenario. Using OUs will help to restructure the OU into its physical layout and will allow you to delegate authority to the teams you create, without giving up the power you need to administer the entire organization. Answer a is incorrect because you do not need multiple domains in this situation. Answers c and d are incorrect because they are more complicated and give away more authority than necessary.

Question 8

After you create a specialized console and save it in a place for distribution, what will the extension be on that saved console?

❍ a. **.doc**

❍ b. **.mmc**

❍ c. **.msi**

❍ d. **.msc**

Answer d is correct. The console will be saved with an `.msc` extension. Answer a is incorrect because this is a Word document extension. Answer b is incorrect because "mmc" is typed in the Run box to open an empty console. Answer c is incorrect because an `.msi` extension indicates a file for the Windows Installer.

Question 9

Quinn has created a console for certain users who are new to their departments. He has assigned them correct permissions and has emailed them the console. They attempt to use the console from their Windows 2000 Professional desktops and yet are having difficulty. What is a logical cause of such a problem?

❍ a. They are missing the correct permissions.

❍ b. They are not in the Domain Admins group.

❍ c. They do not have the Administrative Tools installed on their stations.

❍ d. They are too new to the company and need more time before all utilities will work.

Answer c is correct. Individuals who attempt to use consoles off their workstations need to install those tools, either from the server or from the server CD. Answer a is incorrect because permissions were already mentioned as being provided. Answer b is incorrect because the whole point of delegating control is so these users don't have to be in a specific group with total control. Answer d is incorrect because utilities aren't judgmental based on time with the company.

Question 10

Individuals who have been assigned delegation of control are in need of a simpler console because they do not yet understand how to use the customized consoles you've provided. What can you do to provide the shortest learning curve for those individuals? [Choose the best answer]

❍ a. Create taskpads.

❍ b. Delegate less authority.

❍ c. Give them a class on using consoles.

❍ d. Allow them time to learn.

Answer a is correct. A taskpad makes performing their jobs much easier until these individuals become more comfortable with their tasks. Answer b is incorrect because it defeats the purpose of delegation. Answer c is incorrect, although it's a good idea for any new administrators. Answer d is incorrect, although it is a good idea to be patient with people in new positions.

Need to Know More?

Bersinic, Damir and Rob Scrimger. *MCSE Training Guide (70-217): Installing and Administering a Windows 2000 Directory Services Infrastructure*. Que Publishing. Indianapolis, IN, 2002. ISBN 0735709769.

Chapter 4, "Administering Active Directory Services," discusses the creation of OUs and the delegation of AD permissions within Windows 2000.

Boswell, William. *Inside Windows 2000 Server*. New Riders. Indianapolis, IN, 2000. ISBN 1562059297.

Delegation of authority is an integral part of Windows 2000, and the functional implementation is logically presented within this necessary resource for Windows 2000 administrators.

Hudson, James and Sean Fullerton. *Special Edition Using Active Directory*. Que Publishing. Indianapolis, IN, 2001. ISBN 0789724340.

Covers the Delegation of Control Wizard in Chapter 19, "Authorization." The conclusion of this chapter includes a discussion of troubleshooting delegated permissions that can really prove helpful when things should work, but don't.

Kouti, Sakari and Mike Seitsonen. *Inside Active Directory: A System Administrator's Guide*. Addison Wesley Professional. Boston, MA, 2002. ISBN 0201616211.

Another resource to try for further AD delegation wisdom.

Search the TechNet CD (or its online version through `www.microsoft.com`) using the keywords "Delegation Wizard" and "OU Inheritance," along with related query items.

Understanding Group Policy Implementation

Terms you'll need to understand:

- ✓ Profiles
- ✓ Security groups
- ✓ Policy
- ✓ Group Policy Object (GPO)
- ✓ Site
- ✓ Domain
- ✓ Organizational Unit (OU)
- ✓ Linking
- ✓ Storage domain
- ✓ Inheritance
- ✓ No Override
- ✓ Change and configuration management
- ✓ IntelliMirror
- ✓ Filtering
- ✓ Delegation of control

Techniques you'll need to master:

- ✓ Creating a Group Policy Object (GPO)
- ✓ Linking an existing GPO
- ✓ Modifying Group Policy
- ✓ Delegating administrative control of Group Policy

✓ Modifying Group Policy inheritance

✓ Filtering Group Policy settings by associating security groups to GPOs

Change and configuration management is a strong area of emphasis for Microsoft with Windows 2000, as the company seeks to enable IT professionals and corporations to reduce the total cost of ownership (TCO) of IT resources. Likewise, change and configuration management topics are emphasized on the exam. In this chapter, we will examine Group Policy as it fits into a change and configuration management strategy. Then we will cover the implementation details you should know.

Change and Configuration Basics

Understanding Microsoft's underlying philosophies with Windows 2000 is important, because these basic philosophies permeate everything Microsoft has done with the operating system and will play a role in how well you do on the exam. Primarily, Windows 2000 and Active Directory (AD) seek to reduce the TCO and increase the return on investment (ROI) for business systems. IT professionals must become increasingly familiar with business terms such as TCO and ROI in today's changing economy, where IT is expected to function more as a business unit than as a traditional cost center.

Change and configuration management concerns the developing of processes within an organization to manage ongoing day-to-day issues that typically arise with computers and information technology. The goal is to maximize a user's ability to be productive while reducing the costs associated with support and downtime. Microsoft includes several technologies in Windows 2000 that are dependent on AD and make up Microsoft's change and configuration management initiative. This collection of technologies is commonly referred to as *IntelliMirror*. Here is a quick summary of IntelliMirror's benefits:

- Enables administrators to define environment settings for users, groups, and computers. Windows 2000 then enforces the settings.
- Allows the Windows 2000 Professional operating system to be installed remotely onto compatible computers.
- Enables users' local folders to be redirected to a shared server location and enables files to be synchronized automatically between the server and local hard drive for working offline. This is a boon for laptop users.
- Enables users' desktop settings and applications to roam with them no matter what computer users log on from.

- Enables administrators to centrally manage software installation, updating, and removal. Self-healing applications replace missing or corrupted files automatically, without user intervention.
- Makes the computer a commodity. A system can simply be replaced with a new one, and settings, applications, and policies are quickly regenerated on the new system with a minimum amount of downtime.

One of the key features of a Windows 2000 change and configuration management strategy involves Group Policy, which is the focus of this chapter and the following two chapters. After a quick overview of Group Policy, we will show you the skills you need to be successful on the exam.

Group Policy Overview

Group Policy is one cog in the Windows 2000 change and configuration management wheel, but it is arguably one of the most critical features of an AD-based network. In fact, Group Policy relies on AD and its dependencies to function.

The goals of Group Policy are for an administrator to have to define settings only once for a user, group, or computer, and to ensure that those settings are enforced by Windows 2000 until the administrator specifies otherwise. It is extremely important to understand that Group Policy is not the same as system profiles, which were used in Windows NT 4 to specify desktop settings. System policies still exist for backward compatibility; however, in Windows 2000–only environments, using only Group Policy is recommended.

Group Policy is also used to enhance the end-user computing experience by providing customized environments to meet the user's work requirements. That might involve something like putting specialized application icons on the desktop or Start menu, or redirecting the `My Documents` folder to a network drive so the user's files are available no matter what computer he or she has logged on to. In addition, an administrator can execute tasks such as startup, logon, logoff, or shutdown to meet the user's needs. Group Policy can therefore create a positive working environment for users.

Group Policy supports only Windows 2000 and Windows XP clients, so Windows 9*X* and NT 4 and earlier systems cannot realize the benefits of a Group Policy implementation. As we've mentioned, system policies are available to use with these legacy clients.

Group Policy Objects

The basic unit of Group Policy is the Group Policy Object (GPO). A GPO is a collection of policies that can be applied at the site, domain, Organizational Unit (OU), or local level. Additionally, GPO settings are passed along from a parent object to all child objects, a process known as *inheritance*.

Group Policy is processed by Windows 2000 and Windows XP clients in the following order:

- Local
- Site
- Domain
- OU

The first level—local—is covered in the "Local GPOs" section later in this chapter. The last three levels are known as *global* GPOs and are stored within the AD database. These policies are applied based on user, group, or computer membership. In the "Filtering Group Policy" section later in this chapter, we will look at filtering the effects of Group Policy through security groups, but for now, we will consider a GPO that has not been filtered. The following is true of unfiltered GPOs:

- A GPO that is linked to a site will apply to all objects in the site.
- A GPO that is linked to a domain will apply to all objects in the domain.
- A GPO that is linked to an OU will apply to all objects in the OU.

Although the preceding points sound fairly obvious, they are essential in understanding the scope that Group Policy has. As an organizational structure becomes more complex and the number of GPOs grows, keeping track of the effects of individual GPOs and the combined effects multiple GPOs might have becomes more difficult. By default, GPO settings applied later will override settings applied earlier. Therefore, a domain GPO will override settings made by a site GPO. This provides an administrator with highly granular control over the policy behavior on a network. As you will see in the "Group Policy Inheritance" section later in this chapter, this default behavior can be modified if so desired.

Nonlocal GPOs

Nonlocal GPOs are stored ithin AD. Two locations within the AD database are used to store nonlocal GPOs: a Group Policy container and a Group

Policy template. A globally unique identifier (GUID) is used in naming the GPOs to keep the two locations synchronized.

A *Group Policy container* is an AD storage area for GPO settings for both computer and user Group Policy information. In addition to the Group Policy container, AD stores information in a Group Policy template, which is contained in a folder structure in the System Volume (`SYSVOL`) folder of domain controllers, located under `\winnt\SYSVOL\sysvol\`*`domain_name`*`\Policies`.

When a GPO is created, the Group Policy template is created, and the folder name given to the Group Policy template is the GUID of the GPO. Supplied by the manufacturer of a product, a *GUID* is a hexadecimal number that uniquely identifies the hardware or software. The GUID includes the braces that surround the number and takes the following form:

{*8 characters-4 characters-4 characters-4 characters-12 characters*}

For example, {15DEF489-AE24-10BF-C11A-00BB844CE637} is a valid format for a GUID.

Data that is small in size and changes infrequently is stored in Group Policy containers, whereas data that is either large in size or changes frequently is stored in Group Policy templates.

Local GPOs

So far, we've mentioned local GPOs but have not defined them. A local GPO applies only to the local Windows 2000 computer and is *not* a global object, because the GPO is not stored within the AD database. Local GPOs are stored on the local hard drive of the Windows 2000 system, in the `\winnt\system32\GroupPolicy` directory. Local GPO settings take precedence over any nonlocal GPO settings applied from the site, domain, or OU level and are only recommended for use on standalone Windows 2000 Professional systems that are not part of an AD domain.

Because the local GPO does not utilize AD, some AD features that are normally configurable in the Group Policy Editor, such as Folder Redirection and Software Installation, are unavailable. Also keep in mind that a Windows 2000 computer can have only one local GPO.

Group Policy Versus System Policies

As previously mentioned, Group Policy is not the same as NT 4's system policies. The following is a summary of the differences. Keep in mind that for the exam you will need to know under which circumstances you would use one or the other.

Windows NT 4 and Windows 9*X* System Policies

The following points apply to system policies:

- They are applied only to domains.
- They are limited to Registry-based settings an administrator configures.
- They are not written to a secure location of the Registry; hence, any user with the ability to edit the Registry can disable the policy settings.
- They often last beyond their useful life spans. A system policy remains in effect until another policy explicitly reverses the existing policy or a user edits the Registry to remove the policy.
- They can be applied through NT domain security groups.

Windows 2000 Group Policy

The following points apply to Group Policy:

- It can be applied to sites, domains, or OUs.
- It can be applied through domain security groups and can apply to all or some of the computers and users in a site, domain, or OU.
- It is written to a secure section of the Registry, thereby preventing users from being able to remove the policy through the `regedit.exe` or `regedt32.exe` utilities.
- It is removed and rewritten whenever a policy change takes place. Administrators can set the length of time between policy refreshes, ensuring that only the current policies are in place.
- It provides a more granular level of administrative control over a user's environment.

This overview of Group Policy theory sets the stage for the rest of this chapter. Although you may not think that the theory will be directly applicable to the exam, without the understanding of what Group Policy is and what it is used for, answering scenario questions involving Group Policy implementation would be very difficult. However, because you do need to know how to perform Group Policy tasks, let's end our theory discussion and examine the hands-on skills you will need to have for the Directory Services exam.

Creating a Group Policy Object

The first step when implementing Group Policy is to create a GPO. In fact, without any GPOs created, you cannot even access the Group Policy Editor. Fortunately, Windows 2000 creates a GPO—the Default Domain Policy—by default when you install AD.

Creating a GPO is done primarily through the Active Directory Users and Computers Management Console. To create a GPO, follow these steps:

1. Select Start, Programs, Administrative Tools to access the Active Directory Users and Computers Management Console.
2. From within the console, right-click the domain name and click Properties. Next, click the Group Policy tab, which will bring up the property sheet shown in Figure 7.1. You will notice the options Add, New, Edit, and Delete. These are the major commands, and they perform the following functions:
   - **Add**—Used to add a Group Policy Object link
   - **New**—Used to create a new GPO
   - **Edit**—Used to modify an existing GPO
   - **Delete**—Used to remove a GPO, a GPO link, or both

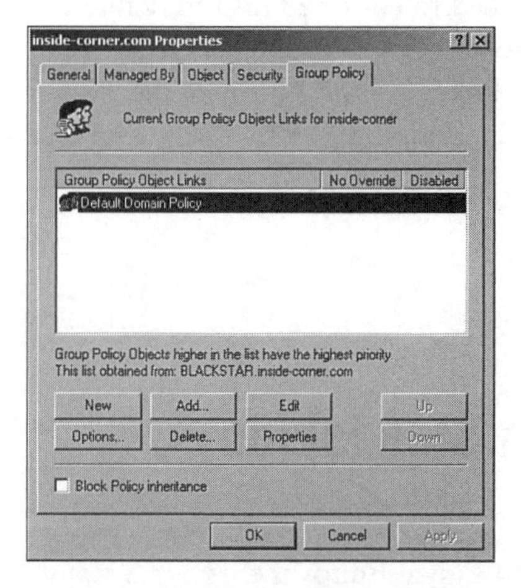

Figure 7.1 The Group Policy tab of a site, domain, or OU's properties dialog box supplies the options for creating, linking, and modifying GPOs.

3. To create a new GPO, simply click the New button. As shown in Figure 7.2, clicking New will create a new GPO with a generic name,

New Group Policy Object. You will probably want to rename it something more descriptive.

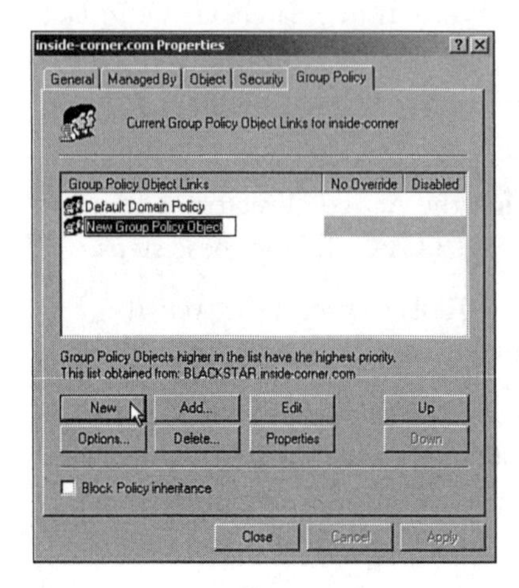

Figure 7.2 Creating a new GPO is as simple as clicking the New button.

Modifying a Group Policy Object

When you create a GPO, the default settings that are automatically created do not really accomplish anything. You need to edit the GPO to define the settings that will affect the behavior of objects linked to the GPO. To edit a Group Policy Object, you use the Group Policy Editor. Although there is no administrative utility for the Group Policy Editor, it can be invoked in one of two ways:

- Via a standalone console
- By editing a GPO

Group Policy Editor as a Standalone Console

The first method of accessing the Group Policy Editor is through a standalone console. Follow these steps:

1. To open a new, empty Microsoft Management Console (MMC), select Start, Run and type the following:

```
MMC /A
```

2. From the Console menu at the top left, select Add/Remove Snap-in. The dialog shown in Figure 7.3 appears.

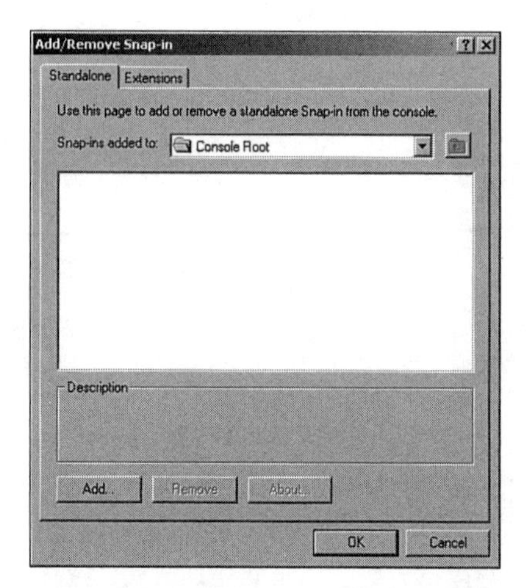

Figure 7.3 The first step in adding a snap-in is to select the Add/Remove Snap-in Console menu option.

3. Select Group Policy from the list of available snap-ins, as shown in Figure 7.4. Click Add.

Figure 7.4 The list of snap-ins shows the available standalone snap-ins that can be added to the console.

4. Now, you must define the scope of the Group Policy Editor, which equates to what GPO you will be editing. Figure 7.5 illustrates that the Group Policy Editor defaults to the Local Computer GPO. Most likely you will want to edit a nonlocal GPO, so click Browse to look for the desired GPO.

Step 4 is the most important and the reason we are stepping through this process in the first place.

Figure 7.5 You must determine the focus of the Group Policy Editor when you add the snap-in to the console.

As you can see in Figure 7.6, you have a number of browsing options. You can browse by domains/OUs, sites, or computers, or you can browse all GPOs. Windows 2000 defaults to the current storage domain that you are logged in to, but that could be changed by dropping down the list next to Look In.

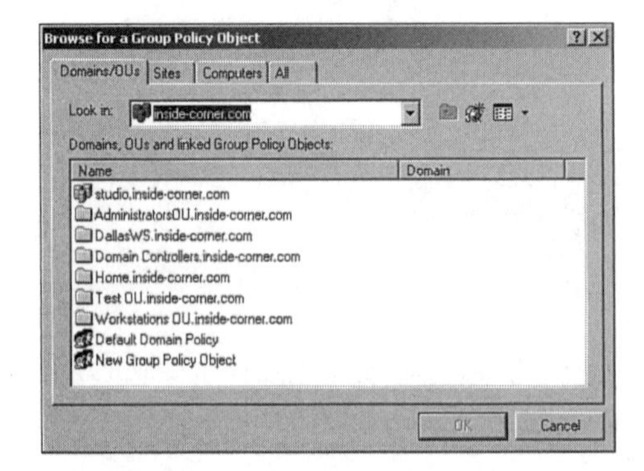

Figure 7.6 You can browse for nonlocal GPOs in the current storage domain, as well as other available domains.

5. Click OK. The screen shown previously in Figure 7.5 appears.

6. By default, a check box appears that reads "Allow the Focus of the Group Policy Snap-in to Be Changed When Launched from the Command Line. This Applies Only If You Save the Console" is not selected; however, if you plan on saving your console, you might choose to enable this option. The option simply allows you to specify a different GPO to be the focus of the console when entering the command line.

7. If you plan on editing a particular GPO frequently, saving the console after you have opened the snap-in and returned to the console screen makes sense. Windows 2000 will prompt you for a filename, and it will save the file with an `.msc` extension to your `Administrative Tools` folder, located in the `\Documents and Settings\`*`username`*`\Start Menu\Programs` folder. The name you assign to the console will be what appears as the console name when you browse the `Administrative Tools` folder in the Start menu, so you should choose something descriptive.

Accessing the Group Policy Editor Through Editing a Group Policy Object

The other method of accessing the Group Policy Editor is to simply edit the GPO from the Group Policy tab of a site, domain, or OU's property sheet. This can be accessed from the Active Directory Users and Computers administrative utility. For example, if you want to edit the Default Domain Policy GPO, follow these steps:

1. From Active Directory Users and Computers, right-click the desired domain (if you have more than one domain) and then click Properties.

2. Select the Group Policy tab.

3. Click the Edit button, which will launch the Group Policy Editor with the Default Domain Policy GPO as the focus. This is illustrated in Figure 7.7.

In the following two chapters, we will work with the Group Policy Editor to manage the user environment and to manage and deploy software. For now, let's just briefly discuss the Group Policy Editor environment.

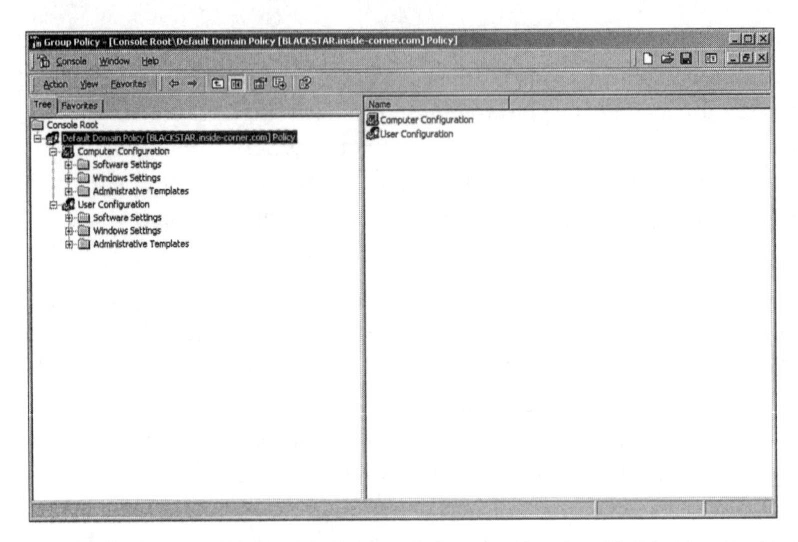

Figure 7.7 Editing a GPO through the Group Policy properties of an AD object launches the Group Policy Editor with the selected GPO as the focus.

Working Inside the Group Policy Editor

Regardless of whether you open the Group Policy Editor as a standalone console or by editing a GPO in Active Directory Users and Computers, the appearance of the console will be the same. The sample console in Figure 7.7 shows the following structure:

- **Root Container**—Defines the focus of the Group Policy Editor by showing the GPO that is being edited as well as the fully qualified domain name (FQDN) of the domain controller from which you are editing the GPO. In the figure, the GPO New Group Policy Object is being edited by `blackstar.inside-corner.com`. If you were to open the GPO for editing on a domain controller named `pulsar.inside-corner.com`, the root of the Group Policy Editor would reflect that.
- **Computer Configuration**—A container for settings specifically covering computer policies. Computer policies are processed before user policies by default.
- **User Configuration**—A container for settings specifically covering user policies. User policies are processed after computer policies by default.
- **Software Settings**—Subcontainer under both Computer Configuration and User Configuration containers that contains Software Installation settings for computers and users.

- **Windows Settings**—Subcontainer under both Computer Configuration and User Configuration containers that contains script and security settings, as well as other policy settings that affect the behavior of the Windows environment.
- **Administrative Templates**—Subcontainer under both Computer Configuration and User Configuration containers that provides the majority of settings for controlling the desktop environment and restricting access to applications, applets, and the appearance of the desktop. Administrative templates are discussed at length in the next chapter.

Linking a GPO

Because nonlocal GPOs are stored within the AD database, they must be linked to an object to apply the desired settings. As you have learned, the object of a GPO link can be a site, domain, or OU. The effects of a GPO are applied to the object(s) that it is linked to.

As previously mentioned, by default, the effects of GPOs are inherited by all child objects of a parent object. Put another way, a GPO linked to a site will apply to all domains and all OUs within the site. A GPO linked to a domain will apply to all OUs within the domain. A GPO applied to an OU will apply to all users, computers, groups, printers, shared folders, contacts, and other Organizational Units within the OU. Because of the effects of inheritance and the overriding effects of policies applied later in the processing order, you should be careful with GPO links. Failure to account for the interaction between different sets of polices can have an adverse impact on your network by introducing undesired behavior of policy recipients.

Before you can link a GPO, you must have at least the permissions necessary to edit it—that is, Read/Write or Full Control permissions. By default, administrators have this capability. As you will see later in this chapter, administrators can delegate the authority to perform certain Group Policy functions such as linking GPOs to non-administrators.

To link a GPO, follow these steps:

1. Open Active Directory Users and Computers (or Active Directory Sites and Services if you wish to link a GPO at the site level) and right-click the domain or OU to which you want to link a GPO.
2. Choose Properties and then choose the Group Policy tab.

3. Click the Add button and navigate to select the GPO that you want to link to the particular domain or OU. In Figure 7.8, we have selected an OU called *Test OU*. As you can see, there are currently no linked GPOs within `Test OU.inside-corner.com`. However, if we click the All tab, as shown in Figure 7.9, we see all the GPOs that have been created.

4. Click OK when you are done selecting a GPO to link to. The GPO is now successfully linked to this domain or OU.

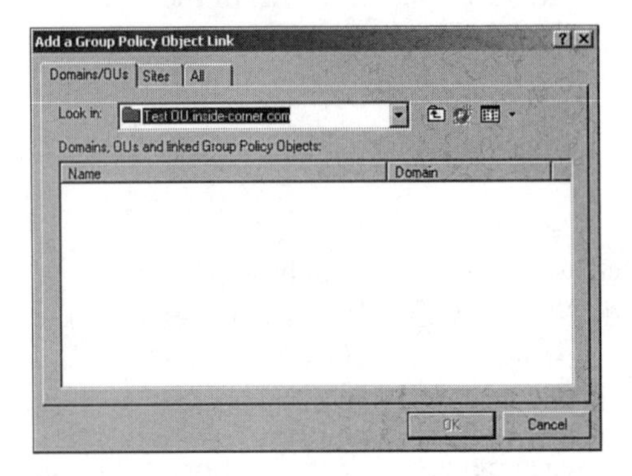

Figure 7.8 When adding a GPO link, you first see the domains, OUs, and linked GPOs within the object selected.

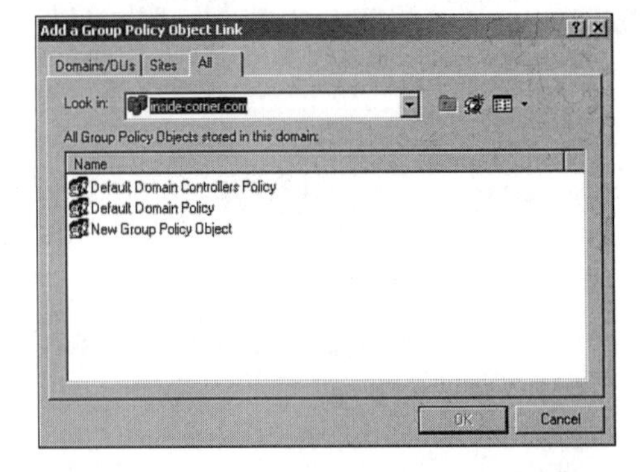

Figure 7.9 Clicking the All tab brings up the entire list of GPOs stored in the AD database.

Note that GPOs *cannot* be linked to the generic AD containers, which are as follows:

- Builtin
- Computers
- ForeignSecurityPrinciples

- LostAndFound
- System
- Users

Linking Multiple GPOs

Nonlocal GPOs are stored in the AD database and are in theory available to all members of an AD forest. We say "in theory" because in reality there are some limitations on GPO linking. First, let's look at how GPOs can and can't be linked.

Multiple GPOs can be linked to a single site, domain, or OU. As you saw in Figure 7.1, a second GPO was added to the `inside-corner.com` domain. The converse is also true—that is, multiple sites, domains, and OUs can be linked to a single GPO. Every GPO is stored within AD in the domain in which it was created, which is called its *storage domain*. The storage domain is not necessarily the domain in which the GPO is linked, although that is usually the case. The reason is that linking GPOs across domains causes a significant performance hit; therefore, Microsoft recommends that you avoid linking a GPO to an object in a different domain.

A GPO does not have to be linked to its storage domain, although it usually would be. Linking across domains brings up a security condition as well as the performance issue. To edit a GPO in another domain, you have to be logged in to the storage domain of the GPO or to a domain that is trusted by the storage domain.

One last note on linking: It is *not* possible to link to only a subset of a GPO's settings. The Group Policy Object is the most basic unit of Group Policy, so you can link to only an entire GPO.

Cross-Domain GPO Links

Creating GPOs in one domain and having them apply to users and computers in another domain is possible. However, as stated in the previous section, this is not recommended in most cases because computer startup and user logon is slowed, sometimes dramatically, if authentication must be processed by a domain controller (DC) from another domain. To apply a GPO, the target of the policy must be able to read the GPO and have the permission to apply Group Policy for the GPO.

There are additional authentication mechanisms to validate the computer or user account in the remote domain, so processing is not as fast as when reading a GPO in the same domain. Because of this, normally it is better to create duplicate GPOs in multiple domains rather than attempting to cross-link GPOs to other domains.

Other than the performance issue, there's no real reason not to cross-link domain GPOs rather than create multiple duplicate GPOs. In fact, cross-linking a single GPO is actually easier to manage, because if you make a modification to the GPO, the change automatically applies to all users and computers in the sites and domains that link to the GPO. Otherwise, you would have to make the same change on every GPO that you had created to perform the same functions in other domains.

Delegating Administrative Control of Group Policy

In larger enterprises, network administration is usually distributed among multiple individuals, often at multiple locations in multiple cities. It becomes necessary for more than one person to be able to complete a given task, and in some instances, you might need to allow a non-administrator to have a subset of administrative authority to complete a task. Such would be the case at a small, remote branch office that does not have enough staff to warrant having a full-time systems administrator on site to manage the servers. To accommodate this, Windows 2000 provides the ability for administrators to delegate authority of certain Group Policy tasks.

Three Group Policy tasks can be delegated individually:

- Managing Group Policy links for a site, domain, or OU
- Creating GPOs
- Editing GPOs

Keep in mind that the delegation applies to only nonlocal GPOs. Local Group Policy applies to standalone computers only, whereas nonlocal Group Policy requires a Windows domain controller.

Managing Group Policy Links

The Delegation of Control Wizard is used to delegate control to users or groups that will manage GPO links. To use the wizard, follow these steps:

1. Right-click the desired domain or OU in Active Directory Users and Computers and select Delegate Control.
2. When the wizard starts, select the users or groups to which you want to delegate control. Once the appropriate users and/or groups are selected, click Next.
3. The screen shown in Figure 7.10 appears, displaying a list of tasks to be delegated. As you can see, the Delegation of Control Wizard can delegate tasks other than Manage Group Policy Links. For Group Policy, though, only the last task is applicable. Select your settings and click Next.
4. Click Finish; the wizard requires no other settings.

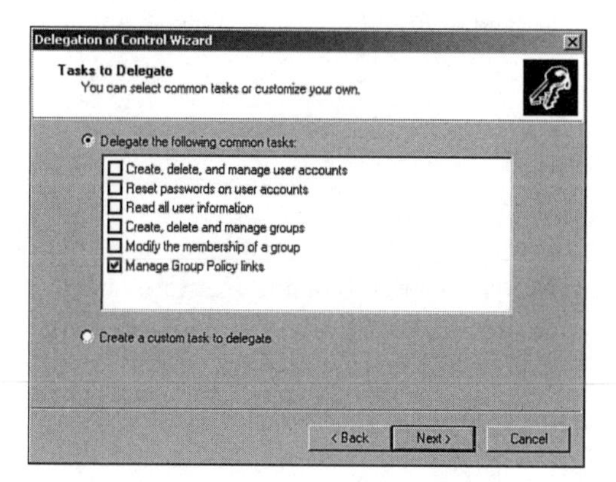

Figure 7.10 The Delegation of Control Wizard is used to delegate control of managing Group Policy links to users and groups.

When you delegate control, you are allowing the individuals or groups to perform those functions as if they were an administrator. Therefore, you must be careful not to delegate control wantonly.

Creating GPOs

Delegating the ability to create GPOs is accomplished through Active Directory Users and Computers as well. To create a GPO, a user account must belong to the Group Policy Creator Owners administrators group. Double-click the Group Policy Creator Owners group in the Users container and click the Members tab, as shown in Figure 7.11. Add the users who should be able to create GPOs.

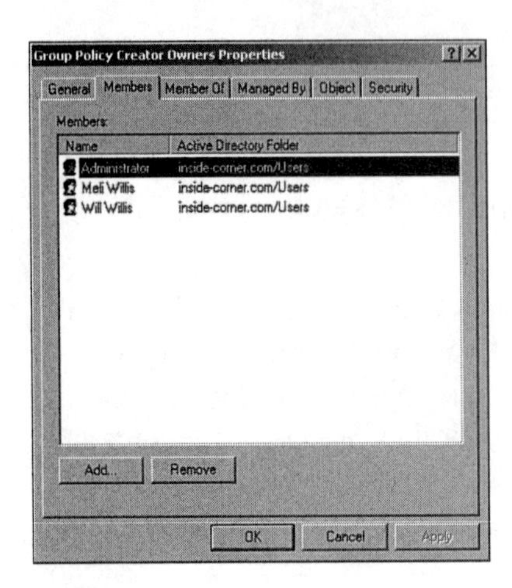

Figure 7.11 To create a GPO, a user or group must belong to the Group Policy Creator Owners group.

Editing GPOs

You might also want a non-administrator to be able to edit a specific GPO in the domain. The ability to edit a GPO comes from an administrator having delegated administrative control of a specific GPO. Here's how to delegate this control:

1. Open the GPO in the Group Policy Editor.
2. Right-click the GPO name and choose Properties.
3. Click the Security tab.
4. Add the user(s) you want to have administrative control and then set the appropriate permission levels. At minimum, a user or group would need Read/Write permissions to edit a GPO, although you could go so far as to grant Full Control if necessary.

You need to know how the following Group Policy tasks are delegated:

- **Managing Group Policy links**—Delegated through the Delegation of Control Wizard
- **Creating GPOs**—Delegated through the Group Policy Creator Owners membership
- **Editing GPOs**—Delegated through the security properties of the specific GPO (Group Policy Editor)

Group Policy Inheritance

As mentioned previously in this chapter, Group Policy is processed in the following order:

- Local
- Site
- Domain
- Organizational Unit

Inheritance is enabled by default and is the process where a policy applied at one level is passed down to lower levels. Objects have parent/child relationships, and parent objects pass their settings down to child objects. The child objects can override parent settings by different policy settings being explicitly defined (with the exception that local policy is not overridden). However, in the absence of a specifically defined setting, the settings from the parent object apply.

To look at it from the perspective of the preceding list, an OU would automatically inherit all the settings from the domain it belongs to, which automatically inherit settings from the site.

In many cases, it is not desirable for inheritance to take effect. An administrator might want a setting to remain unconfigured if it isn't specifically defined. Because of this, Windows 2000 allows for two methods of changing the default behavior of setting inheritance:

- Block Policy Inheritance
- No Override

Block Policy Inheritance

Block Policy Inheritance prevents policies from higher up in the AD structure from being automatically applied at lower levels. This setting cannot be applied to the site level, because it is the top level and does not inherit policies from anywhere else. However, it can be applied at the domain, OU, and local levels.

You would use Block Policy Inheritance to protect settings from higher-level objects from applying later in the processing order. For example, you can block a domain policy from applying settings to an OU Group Policy Object by selecting the Block Policy Inheritance check box.

To enable Block Policy Inheritance, open the Group Policy tab of an object's properties, as discussed earlier, and select the check box in the lower-left corner of the Group Policy property sheet.

No Override

Like Block Policy Inheritance, *No Override* is a method of altering the default behavior of policy inheritance in Windows 2000. Unlike Block Policy Inheritance, which is applied at the domain, OU, or local level, No Override is applied to a GPO link. Table 7.1 summarizes these differences.

Table 7.1 Block Policy Inheritance Versus No Override

Method	Applied To	Conflict Resolution
Block Policy Inheritance	Domains, OUs, local computers	Defers to No Override
No Override	GPO links	Takes precedence

No Override is used to prevent policies at lower levels in the AD tree from overwriting policies applied from a higher level. For example, say you had linked a GPO to a domain and set the GPO link to No Override, and then you configured Group Policy settings within the GPO to apply to OUs within the domain. GPOs linked to OUs would not be able to override the domain-linked GPO. This is a way to minimize the effects of multiple GPOs interacting and creating undesirable policy settings. If you want to ensure that a default domain policy is applied regardless of OU polices, use No Override.

If you want to view what objects a GPO is linked to in order to determine the effects of setting No Override, follow these steps:

1. Open the Group Policy property sheet for an object in Active Directory Users and Computers.
2. Select the desired GPO and click Properties.
3. Click the Links tab.
4. Click Find Now to search the default domain, or you can select a different domain from the drop-down list.

Make sure you know that No Override will take precedence over Block Policy Inheritance when the two are in conflict.

Here's how to configure No Override:

1. Open the Group Policy property sheet for an object in Active Directory Users and Computers.
2. Select the GPO in question and click the Options button. The dialog box shown in Figure 7.12 appears.

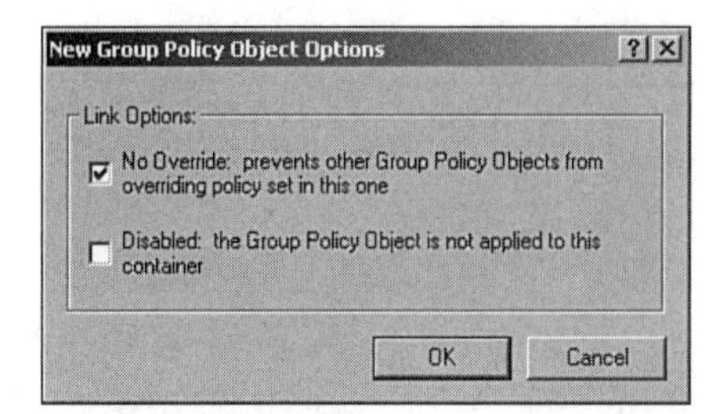

Figure 7.12 You can configure No Override through the Group Policy Object's options.

Block Policy Inheritance and No Override can make troubleshooting policy-related problems on a network extremely complex, especially as the size of the network and the number of GPOs grows. For that reason, avoiding these options whenever possible is recommended.

Disabling a GPO

Although not exactly the same as the previous methods of preventing policy inheritance, Figure 7.12 shows another option that prevents the effects of a GPO from being applied to an object. By selecting the Disabled check box, an administrator can prevent this from happening within the selected container, such as a domain or an OU.

Filtering Group Policy

We previously mentioned security groups when we delegated control over editing Group Policy Objects. The other time you use security groups in relation to Group Policy is for the purpose of filtering the scope of a GPO. For example, you might have a GPO that applies to an entire OU, yet there are specific objects within the OU that you do not want to be affected by the policies. Through security groups, you can filter out the desired object from the OU so that the policy won't be applied to it.

When filtering the effects of a GPO by security group, you are essentially editing the discretionary access control list (DACL) on that GPO. Using the

DACL, you allow or deny access for users and computers to the GPO based on their memberships in security groups. In addition to DACLs, you also have access control entries (ACEs), which are the permission entries within a DACL. ACEs are permissions such as Full Control, Read, Write, and Apply Group Policy.

All authenticated users have two required default permissions that enable objects to receive policy settings from a GPO. These permissions are as follows:

- Read
- Apply Group Policy

The easiest way to prevent Group Policy from applying to an object is to remove that object's Read permission. If the Read permission is taken away, an object cannot access the GPO, and therefore policy settings will not be applied. Microsoft strongly recommends removing the Apply Group Policy permission as well, however, because it will speed up the time it takes to process Group Policy for an object if unused permissions are not having to be processed.

To reiterate, the security settings for a GPO are selected by going into the property sheet for a specific GPO and choosing the Security tab.

Filtering affects the entire Group Policy Object. You cannot filter only specific settings within a GPO from applying to a security group. However, if you are not using a portion of a GPO, you can disable it so that it won't apply.

Disabling Unused Portions of a GPO

Windows 2000 Group Policy gives you the option of disabling either the Computer Configuration or User Configuration container (or both, but that would be pointless) within a GPO if you are not using it. Doing so will speed up Group Policy processing and can be beneficial if you have targeted GPOs that apply only to computers or only to users.

To disable an unused portion, open the Group Policy property sheet for an object such as a domain, as was done in the "Creating a Group Policy Object" section earlier in this chapter. Select the desired GPO and click Properties. As shown in Figure 7.13, at the bottom of the page are options to disable Computer Configuration and User Configuration settings to speed up performance.

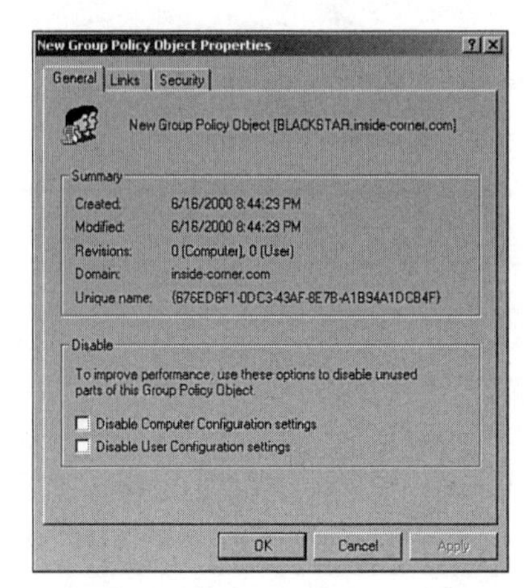

Figure 7.13 Disabling the Computer Configuration or User Configuration settings for a GPO can speed up processing if you have GPOs that apply only to computers or only to users.

Practice Questions

Question 1

Which of the following levels of GPO processing are nonlocal? [Check all correct answers]

- ❑ a. Local Computer
- ❑ b. Site
- ❑ c. Domain
- ❑ d. User

Answers b and c are correct. GPOs applied at the site, domain, or OU level are considered nonlocal, because they are stored in the Active Directory database. By its name, you can tell that Local Computer is obviously a local policy and not a nonlocal one, so answer a is incorrect. User is not a level in which GPOs can be applied, so answer d is incorrect.

Question 2

The following are containers or nodes within a Group Policy Object:

Windows Settings

Computer Configuration

Software Settings

Root

User Configuration

Administrative Templates

Reorder them into their hierarchical structure as would appear in the Group Policy Editor.

The correct answer is:

Root

- Computer Configuration
- User Configuration
  - Software Settings
  - Windows Settings
  - Administrative Templates

In the Group Policy Editor, the Software Settings, Windows Settings, and Administrative Templates nodes exist under both the Computer Configuration and User Configuration containers, which are under the Root container.

Question 3

Which permissions are required for an object so that the effects of a GPO can be applied? [Check all correct answers]

- ❑ a. Read
- ❑ b. Write
- ❑ c. Full Control
- ❑ d. Apply Group Policy

Answers a and d are correct. Read and Apply Group Policy are the required permissions to accomplish this objective. Answer b is incorrect because Write permission is not required in order for a GPO's settings to be applied. Although Full Control would accomplish the task of allowing Group Policy settings to be applied, it is not required, so answer c is incorrect.

Question 4

Put the following items in order to show the correct processing sequence for Group Policy.

Domain

Local

OU

Site

The correct answer is:

Local

Site

Domain

OU

Local policies are applied first and, by default, can override any global settings. Nonlocal GPOs are processed last, starting at the highest level in the Active Directory tree.

Question 5

Which of the following methods are used to change the default behavior for policy inheritance? [Check all correct answers]

- ❑ a. Disabled
- ❑ b. Block Policy Inheritance
- ❑ c. Override
- ❑ d. No Override

Answers a, b, and d are correct. Block Policy Inheritance and No Override are different means to change inheritance, and Disabled prevents any of the GPO's settings from being applied to the selected container. Answer c is incorrect because Override is actually the default behavior; by default, policy settings are inherited from parent objects to child objects.

Question 6

Choose all the generic Active Directory containers in the list that Group Policy Objects *cannot* be linked to. [Check all correct answers]

- ❑ a. Computers
- ❑ b. Users
- ❑ c. ForeignSecurityPrinciples
- ❑ d. LostAndFound
- ❑ e. Domain Controllers
- ❑ f. System
- ❑ g. Builtin
- ❑ h. Domain

Answers a, b, c, d, f, and g are correct. Computers, Users, ForeignSecurityPrinciples, LostAndFound, System, and Builtin cannot be linked to Group Policy Objects. Answer e is incorrect because Domain Controllers is an OU created when Active Directory is installed and can have GPOs linked to it. Likewise, answer h is incorrect because each domain has a Default Domain Policy GPO created for it when Active Directory is installed.

Question 7

If you want to disable unused portions of a GPO to improve processing times, which portions could you disable? [Check all correct answers]

- ❑ a. Specific settings within a GPO
- ❑ b. Windows Settings subcontainer
- ❑ c. Computer Configuration container
- ❑ d. User Configuration container
- ❑ e. Software Settings subcontainer
- ❑ f. Administrative Templates subcontainer

Answers c and d are correct. Windows 2000 Group Policy allows an administrator to disable the Computer Configuration and User Configuration containers from being processed. Answer a is incorrect because you cannot filter specific settings within a GPO. Answers b, e, and f are incorrect because if either the Computer Configuration or User Configuration container is disabled, the Windows Settings, Software Settings, and Administrative Templates subcontainers for that container would be disabled along with it.

Question 8

What utility would you use to create a new Group Policy Object?

- ❍ a. Group Policy Editor
- ❍ b. Active Directory Users and Computers
- ❍ c. Delegation of Control Wizard
- ❍ d. Group Policy MMC Console

Answer b is correct. Active Directory Users and Computers is used to create new GPOs. Answer a is incorrect because the Group Policy Editor cannot be invoked for a GPO that does not exist yet. Answer c is incorrect because the Delegation of Control Wizard only gives permission to manage Group Policy links. Answer d is incorrect because the Group Policy MMC Console is the same thing as the Group Policy Editor.

Question 9

Which of the following Group Policy tasks can be delegated through the Delegation of Control Wizard?

- ❍ a. Managing Group Policy links
- ❍ b. Creating GPOs
- ❍ c. Modifying/editing GPOs
- ❍ d. Filtering GPOs

Answer a is correct. The Delegation of Control Wizard is used to delegate control of managing Group Policy links. Answers b and c are incorrect because the Active Directory Users and Computers administrative utility is used to delegate control of creating GPOs by editing membership of the Group Policy Creator Owners security group, and the permission to edit a GPO is granted through the GPO's security sheet within its properties, accessible through the Group Policy Editor. Answer d is incorrect because filtering GPOs is not a task that can be delegated; rather, it falls under the category of editing GPOs.

Question 10

When would you use system policies rather than Group Policy? [Choose the best answer]

- ❍ a. When you have only Windows 2000 systems on your network.
- ❍ b. When you have a mix of Windows 2000, Windows NT, and Windows 98 systems on your network.
- ❍ c. When you want to have policy settings refresh periodically.
- ❍ d. You would never use system policies above Group Policy.

Answer b is correct. Group Policy is supported only on Windows 2000, so you would need to use system policies if you had to support legacy Windows NT and 98 clients. Answer a is incorrect because it refers to Windows 2000 systems. Answer c is incorrect because system policies do not support periodic refresh as Group Policy does. System policies also do not support a host of other features that Group Policy supports; however, they do provide the ability to manage the user environment for legacy systems. Answer d is incorrect because answer b presents a scenario in which you would use system policies above Group Policy.

Need to Know More?

Iseminger, David. *Active Directory Services for Windows 2000 Technical Reference*. Microsoft Press. Redmond, WA, 2000. ISBN 0-7356-0624-2.

A solid reference book for planning and deploying Active Directory networks. Although coverage of Group Policy is minor, there is an extensive change and configuration management section.

Microsoft Corporation. *Microsoft Windows 2000 Server Resource Kit*. Microsoft Press. Redmond, WA, 2000. ISBN 1-57231-805-8.

The quintessential resource for Windows 2000 Server and Active Directory, this kit has extensive coverage of Active Directory and Group Policy in particular. If you can have only one Windows 2000 reference, this is the one to have.

Nielsen, Morton Strunge. *Windows 2000 Server Architecture and Planning*. The Coriolis Group. Scottsdale, AZ, 1999. ISBN 1-57610-436-2.

Although it was written during the Windows 2000 beta period, this book is an excellent resource for Active Directory planning and deployment.

Norris-Lowe, Alistair. *Windows 2000 Active Directory Service*. O'Reilly & Associates. Sebastopol, CA, 2000. ISBN 1-56592-638-2.

A great complement to the *Windows 2000 System Administration Handbook*, this book is another good Active Directory resource. This reference is more of a high-level technical book rather than a hands-on "how to" type of book, and it's an excellent way to learn the theory behind the technology.

Watts, David V., Will Willis, and Tillman Strahan. *MCSE Windows 2000 Directory Services Exam Prep*. The Coriolis Group. Scottsdale, AZ, 2000. ISBN 1-57610-624-1.

This book provides more extensive coverage of the exam objectives and related topics covered in this book. Good complementary material to go along with this book.

Willis, Will, David Watts, and Tillman Strahan. *Windows 2000 System Administration Handbook.* Prentice-Hall Computer Books. Upper Saddle River, NJ, 2000. ISBN 0-1302-7010-5.

This book explains Windows 2000 systems administration concepts in detail and is a solid all-around Windows 2000 reference with good coverage of Active Directory.

Using Group Policy in Security and Environment Control

Terms you'll need to understand:

✓ Scripts
✓ Windows Script Host
✓ Folder redirection
✓ Offline Folders
✓ Templates
✓ User profiles
✓ Roaming profiles
✓ Mandatory profiles

Techniques you'll need to master:

✓ Controlling user environments by using administrative templates
✓ Managing security configurations
✓ Assigning script policies to users and computers
✓ Using Folder Redirection

Arguably the most common use of Group Policy is to manipulate the user environment in order to meet the specific needs of an organization. Some companies seek to have a consistent desktop appearance across all desktop systems, with the same set of applications. Environments such as these often have users who float among multiple systems or seek to reduce customization as a way of keeping down information technology (IT) support costs for desktop systems.

In environments where security is an issue, or where nonemployees are accessing company computers (such as in a mall kiosk or an applicant entry terminal), Group Policy can be used to lock down specific configurations that cannot be modified by the user. These scenarios might use highly restrictive policies that prevent access to certain operating system functions and throw out any configuration changes at system shutdown.

In this chapter, we examine using Group Policy as both a security device for the purpose of locking down system configurations and as a means of supplying consistent user computing environments that are available no matter what computer a user logs in to on your network.

It is important to note that Group Policy works with Windows 2000 and later clients; so, Windows XP is supported as well.

Controlling User Environments with Administrative Templates

Administrative templates provide the primary means of administering the user environment and defining the end-user computing experience. As an administrator, you can use administrative templates to deny access to certain operating system functionality—for example, the ability to add or remove programs. Additionally, you can define settings such as the wallpaper and screensaver to use on a system, and you can rely on Windows 2000 to enforce those settings.

You need to know the following about the use of administrative templates:

- ADM files and their structure
- The Computer and User Template application

ADM Files and Their Structure

Administrative templates are stored in Windows 2000 as text files in the `\WINNT\SYSVOL\Sysvol\`*`domain`*`\Policies\`*`GUID`*`\Adm` folder. These files carry an .adm file extension. A real-world example of this directory structure is E:\WINNT\SYSVOL\Sysvol\inside-corner.com\Policies\{31B2F340-016D-11D2-945F-00C04FB984F9}\Adm, which is the directory structure on a Windows 2000 domain controller (DC) in the inside-corner.com domain.

Windows 2000 includes five administrative templates, though not all are installed by default. These files are as follows:

- **System.adm**—Installed by default in Group Policy, system.adm is used for Windows 2000 clients.
- **Inetres.adm**—Installed by default in Group Policy, inetres.adm contains Internet Explorer policies for Windows 2000 systems.
- **Windows.adm**—This template contains user interface options for Windows 9*X* systems and is used with the System Policy Editor (poledit.exe).
- **Winnt.adm**—This template contains user interface options for Windows NT 4 systems and is used with the System Policy Editor.
- **Common.adm**—This template contains user interface options common to both Windows NT 4 and Windows 9*X* systems and is used with the System Policy Editor.

You might have other administrative templates on your system as well, depending on what you have installed on your system. For example, an administrative template called conf.adm is installed with NetMeeting and contains policy settings related to that specific program.

ADM Structure

An ADM file is a text file, so it can be edited with a text editor such as Notepad. You can open any of the ADM files listed previously to view the settings, and you can even modify them if you desire. However, modifying the default administrative templates is not recommended. If necessary, you can create new administrative templates, because Windows 2000 is flexible enough to let you tailor Group Policy to your specific network environment.

The following is an edited example from the conf.adm administrative template. Following this example is a description of the file's structure and a definition of the variables you can use when creating an administrative template:

```
; NetMeeting policy settings
#if version <= 2
;;;;;;;;;;;;;;;;;;;;;;;;;;;;;;;
 CLASS USER    ;;;;;;;;;;;;;;;;
;;;;;;;;;;;;;;;;;;;;;;;;;;;;;;;
CATEGORY !!WindowsComponents
CATEGORY !!NetMeeting
```

```
          ; App Sharing
             CATEGORY !!AppSharing
             POLICY !!DisableAppSharing
             KEYNAME "Software\Policies\Microsoft\Conferencing"
             EXPLAIN !!DisableAppSharing_Help
             VALUENAME "NoAppSharing"
             END POLICY
             POLICY !!PreventSharing
             KEYNAME "Software\Policies\Microsoft\Conferencing"
             EXPLAIN !!PreventSharing_Help
             VALUENAME "NoSharing"
             END POLICY
             POLICY !!PreventGrantingControl
             KEYNAME "Software\Policies\Microsoft\Conferencing"
             EXPLAIN !!PreventGrantingControl_Help
             VALUENAME "NoAllowControl"
             END POLICY
             POLICY !!PreventSharingTrueColor
             KEYNAME "Software\Policies\Microsoft\Conferencing"
             EXPLAIN !!PreventSharingTrueColor_Help
             VALUENAME "NoTrueColorSharing"
             END POLICY
END CATEGORY ; AppSharing
[strings]
WindowsComponents="Windows Components"
NetMeeting="NetMeeting"
AppSharing="Application Sharing"
DisableAppSharing="Disable application Sharing"
DisableAppSharing_Help="Disables the application sharing feature of
NetMeeting completely.  Users will not be able to host or view shared
applications."
PreventSharing="Prevent Sharing"
PreventSharing_Help="Prevents users from sharing anything themselves.
They will still be able to view shared applications/desktops from
others."
PreventGrantingControl="Prevent Control"
PreventGrantingControl_Help="Prevents users from allowing others in a
conference to control what they have shared.  This enforces a
read-only mode; the other participants cannot change the data in the
shared application."
PreventSharingTrueColor="Prevent Application Sharing in true color"
PreventSharingTrueColor_Help="Prevents users from sharing applications
in true color. True color sharing uses more bandwidth in a conference."
```

The structure of this sample ADM file is fairly simple. The header at the top defines the purpose of the file. It is a comment, which is denoted by the semicolon at the beginning of the line. The semicolon tells Windows not to process the line when parsing the file. Following the description are sections and variables defined by keywords. Those keywords are as follows:

- **CLASS**—The first entry in the administrative template file, the `CLASS` keyword can either be `MACHINE` or `USER`, which defines whether the section includes entries in the Computer Configuration or User Configuration container in Group Policy.

- **CATEGORY**—The CATEGORY keyword is what is displayed in the Group Policy Editor as a node under Computer Configuration or User Configuration. Whether the category is located under the MACHINE or USER class determines which node it is located under. In the preceding example, the categories under the USER class define the Windows Components, NetMeeting, and Application Sharing subnodes under User Configuration.
- **POLICY**—The POLICY keyword defines the policies available for modification in the Group Policy Editor. In the administrative template, the POLICY keyword specifies a variable that is defined in the STRINGS section at the bottom of the file.
- **KEYNAME**—The KEYNAME keyword defines the Registry location for the policy the keyname is associated with.
- **EXPLAIN**—The EXPLAIN keyword is used to supply help text for a policy setting. When you view the properties of a policy in the Group Policy Editor, note the Explain tab, which contains the help text specified here. Actually, in the administrative template, the EXPLAIN keyword specifies a variable that is defined with the help text in the STRINGS section at the bottom of the file.
- **VALUENAME**—The VALUENAME keyword is also associated with the POLICY keyword, and it defines the options available within a policy. It defines the values that are located within the Registry key, specified by the KEYNAME keyword.
- **STRINGS**—The STRINGS section defines the variables used earlier in the file for the keywords POLICY and EXPLAIN.

Putting it all together, you see the results in Figure 8.1. This figure shows the Group Policy Editor with the previous administrative template as the focus of the editor. The User Configuration container is expanded to the Windows Components/NetMeeting/Application Sharing nodes, which were defined by the CATEGORY keyword. There, you find the policies defined by the POLICY keywords in the right-side window pane, such as Disable Application Sharing and Prevent Sharing.

If you double-click the first policy, Disable Application Sharing, and then click the Explain tab, you see the help text defined by the EXPLAIN keyword in the administrative template. This is illustrated in Figure 8.2.

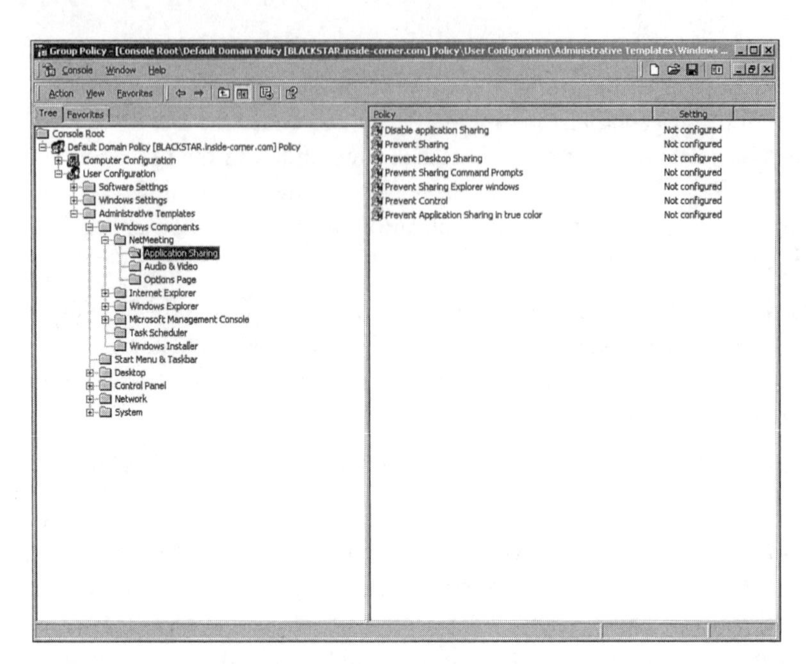

Figure 8.1 The available entries in the Group Policy Editor reflect the contents of the administrative template.

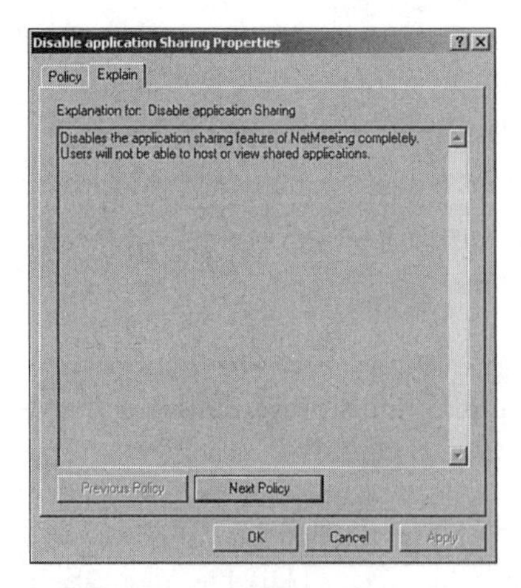

Figure 8.2 The **EXPLAIN** keyword in the administrative template provides the text that appears on the Explain tab in the policy's properties.

Creating administrative templates on your own allows you to define custom settings for your network for situations where the built-in policies are not enough. This is an easier solution than having a developer write a custom Group Policy extension with a software development kit (SDK). Windows 2000 includes everything you need to write an administrative template, which can then be added (or later removed) from a Group Policy Object (GPO), as you will see in the following section.

Adding and Removing Administrative Templates

After you've created a custom administrative template, you need to add it to the GPO in order for it to be used. Note that your custom administrative templates must be added to *each GPO* you want them to apply to.

To add or remove an administrative template, right-click the appropriate administrative templates folder in the Group Policy Editor (either under Computer Configuration or User Configuration) and select Add/Remove Templates. Figure 8.3 shows the dialog box that is presented, which displays the currently installed administrative templates. You can remove an existing one by selecting it and clicking the Remove button, or you can add an administrative template by clicking the Add button. If you click Add, the dialog box shown in Figure 8.4 appears.

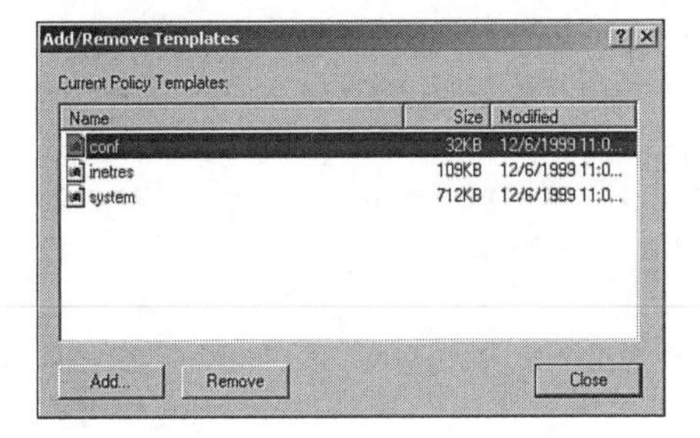

Figure 8.3 When you choose Add/Remove Templates, you first see a listing of the currently installed administrative templates.

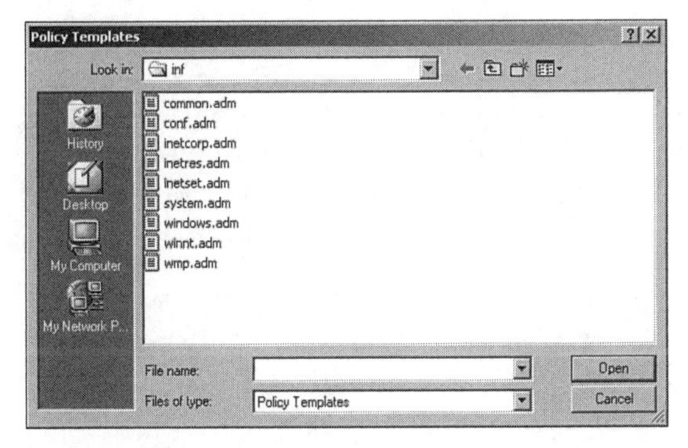

Figure 8.4 Choosing to add an administrative template allows you to browse for an ADM file to add to the current GPO.

Once you add an administrative template, the additional nodes and policies appear under the administrative templates node you added the template to. It is important to note that the template itself determines whether to install under the Computer Configuration or User Configuration container. In our example, `conf.adm` is a user template containing NetMeeting settings, so it will naturally install under the User Configuration container. Although understanding how administrative templates are constructed and how to add and remove templates is important, the majority of your experience with administrative templates will be in using them to apply policy settings.

Applying Computer and User Templates

Administrative templates allow an administrator to exert a measure of control over the user environment.

Two different administrative templates sections appear within a GPO: One is under the Computer Configuration container, and the other is under the User Configuration container. As you would expect, these separate nodes determine whether policies apply to computer accounts or user accounts. Let's look at the similarities between the two, followed by the differences, and then examine a couple of scenarios where you would use administrative templates to manage a Windows 2000 network.

Common Administrative Templates Categories

Regardless of whether the Administrative Templates container is under the Computer Configuration container or the User Configuration container, there are some common categories that create nodes:

- **Windows Components**—Contains configuration settings for common Windows components such as Internet Explorer, Task Scheduler, NetMeeting, Windows Explorer, Windows Installer, and Microsoft Management Console (MMC). The policies that exist for these categories control the behavior of the programs, from what functionality is available to the user to configuring the features of an application.

- **Network**—Contains configuration settings for network options such as Offline Folders and Network and Dial-up Connections. Different policy options are available, depending on whether you are under the Computer Configuration or User Configuration container.

- **System**—Contains configuration settings that do not really fall neatly under any other category within the administrative templates. Here, policies exist for logon/logoff, disk quotas, Windows File Protection, Group Policy, DNS (Domain Name System) clients, and general settings such as whether Registry editing is allowed or certain applications should not be allowed to run.

Differing Administrative Templates Categories

The differences between Administrative Templates under the Computer Configuration container and the User Configuration container are outlined here:

- **Computer Configuration administrative templates**—User templates are stored under the `HKEY_LOCAL_MACHINE` hive in the Registry. The administrative template that exists only under the Computer Configuration container is Printers:
  - **Printers**—The Printers category contains configuration settings for printers and their properties. Through these policies, you can control the publication of printers into Active Directory (AD), allow printer browsing, and allow Web-based printing, among other policy settings.
- **User Configuration administrative templates**—User templates are stored under the `HKEY_CURRENT_USER` hive in the Registry. Here are the administrative templates that exist only under the User Configuration container:
  - **Start Menu & Taskbar**—This template controls the appearance and behavior of the Start menu and the taskbar. Through this administrative template, you can remove functionality (such as the ability to search) or remove the Run line from the Start menu. Additionally, you can alter the default behavior of the Start menu, such as clearing the Documents folder upon exit or not allowing users to change the configuration of the Start menu.
  - **Desktop**—The Desktop policy settings complement the policy settings under the Start Menu & Taskbar category. You can configure the behavior of the Active Desktop, such as choosing the wallpaper, using filtering in AD searches, controlling the appearance of desktop icons, and indicating whether any changes specified by users are saved upon exiting Windows.
  - **Control Panel**—This template contains settings that determine what level of functionality is available to users in the Control Panel. These policies can include Add/Remove Programs, Display, Printers, Regional Options, and even whether the Control Panel is available to Windows users.

Policy Application Scenario #1

As an administrator, you will run into various circumstances that require different applications of Group Policy. To create an effective usage policy, you must first analyze your environment and determine your requirements. With that strategy in mind, let's look at a couple of scenarios and how you might approach them.

In the first scenario, you are the network administrator for a retail chain of computer superstores. Specifically, you are in charge of a customer ordering system where customers can access Windows systems to create custom computer configurations for "build-to-order" systems right in the store. These orders are fed into a database, and credit cards can be processed.

In this type of environment, you would have users who are nonemployees accessing your network. You would not want them to be able to alter the operating system or the user environment in any way. To reach that goal, you would want to use the Start Menu & Taskbar, Desktop, and Control Panel nodes in the User Configuration container to prevent changes from being made. These policies would include disabling the Control Panel, removing the Run line from the Start menu, hiding all icons on the desktop, and preventing changes from being saved upon exiting. Additionally, you would use settings under the System node in both Computer and User Configuration to disable Registry editing. This would prevent a savvy customer with malicious intent from getting around your policy settings; by disabling them in the Registry and by disabling the command prompt, you can ensure that programs cannot be executed there.

These settings essentially lock down the user environment, which is what you would want in this type of scenario. In the next scenario, however, that type of network policy would be counterproductive and inappropriate.

Policy Application Scenario #2

Consider a scenario where you are the network administrator of a medium-sized company that has a Windows 2000 network. The environment is not highly secure, nor is there a real need to limit functionality. However, three shifts of workers use the company computers. Therefore, you have three people using each computer in the company each day.

In this scenario, you would want to use Group Policy to define a common desktop for corporate use and to discard any user changes upon exiting. You could approach this goal in one of a couple ways. One way would be to create roaming profiles that follow each user wherever he or she goes. With the high number of users accessing the computers, however, simply creating a "corporate standard" and defining the desktop appearance across all computers would be preferable.

To reach this goal, you could use the Control Panel/Display policies under the User Configuration container to disable changing the wallpaper and to specify a screensaver. With the Desktop/Active Desktop policies, you would specify the wallpaper to be used. With the Start Menu & Taskbar policies, you would disable changes to the Start menu and the taskbar, disable personalized menus, and remove users' folders from the Start menu. These settings create a computing environment that has a consistent look and feel across all corporate systems while still allowing full operating system and application functionality to the users.

With Group Policy, you can also manage security configurations for Windows 2000, as you'll see next.

Managing Security Configurations

Group Policy can also be used to manage security settings on a Windows 2000 network. Under the Windows Settings node in both the Computer and User Configuration containers is a node for Security Settings. The vast majority of the settings apply to computer policies, because the only user security settings are related to Public Key Policies (which also exists under Computer Configuration). The security categories available and their purposes are as follows:

- **Account Policies**—Contains settings related to user accounts and applies them at the domain level. You can configure the password policy for a domain (minimum length, uniqueness, minimum password age, and so on), the account lockout policy (if accounts should be locked out, how many bad password attempts are allowed before lockout, and the length of time after lockout before the counter is reset), and the Kerberos policy (maximum lifetime for tickets, ticket renewal threshold, and so on).

- **Local Policies**—Contains settings for local system policies, including audit policies, user rights assignment, and security options. Auditing can be used to log the success or failure of common events, such as logging on and logging off, accessing objects, using permissions, and directory service access, among other events. User Rights Assignment allows you to control user rights for users and groups, such as the ability to log on locally, log on as a service, change the system time, shut down the system, and take ownership of objects, among other settings. Security options are numerous; as you can see from Figure 8.5, there is a wealth of policy settings you can configure for local security.

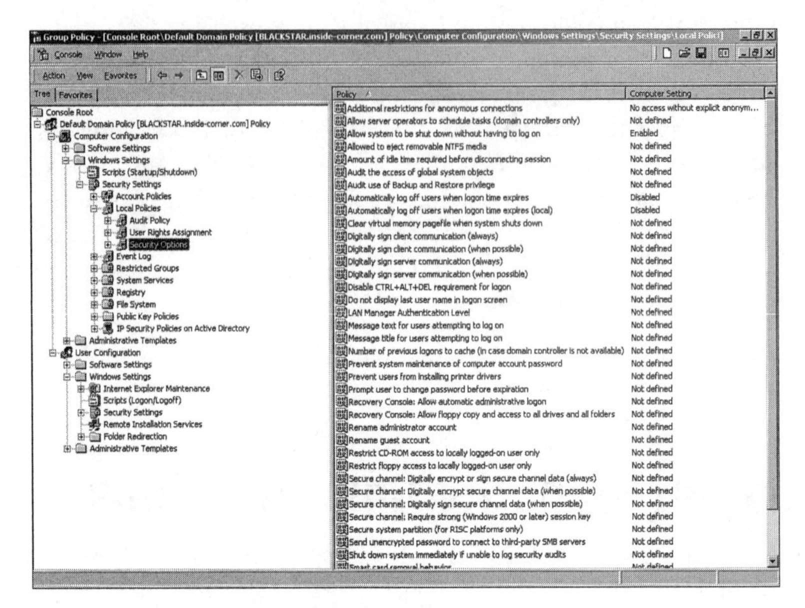

Figure 8.5 Numerous local security policy settings can be configured with Group Policy on a Windows 2000 system.

- **Event Log**—Contains policy settings that control the behavior of the application, system, and security logs on the local system. Among other settings, you can define maximum log file sizes, the retention period for log files, and whether the system should be shut down automatically when the security log is full.
- **Restricted Groups**—Allows you to add restricted groups through Group Policy, which lets you control membership in security groups. You can define who belongs in a particular group and prevent users from being added or removed from the restricted group.
- **System Services**—Contains a list of the installed Windows 2000 services on the local computer and allows you to control the behavior of these services. You can define their startup mode (disabled, manual, or automatic) and specify the level of permissions these services will have on the system. Limiting the level of permissions can prevent a hacker from exploiting a system service in an attempt to compromise system security.

- **Registry**—Allows you to audit specific Registry keys and their subkeys. You can also restrict editing of certain keys to administrators while making the same keys read-only to general users.
- **File System**—Allows you to define security settings for files and folders on the system. One use would be to ensure that only administrators could modify system files, making system files read-only to general users.
- **Public Key Policies**—Enables you to add policy settings to manage public key–related security items, such as trusted certificate authorities (CAs). You can also add additional Encrypted Data Recovery Agents if desired.
- **IP Security Policies on Active Directory**—Contains policy settings for the IPSec security protocol. These allow you to tell your server how to respond to IPSec communication requests.

As an administrator, the use of the preceding security settings allows you to provide a much tighter level of security than what is configured by default when you install Windows 2000. However, if configuring security manually seems like a daunting task, you can use one of the security templates that Windows 2000 provides.

Security Templates

The security templates in Windows 2000 comprise a set of profiles that can be imported into a GPO, and they provide a specific level of security for Windows 2000 DCs, servers, and clients. The types of security templates available in Windows 2000 are as follows:

- **Basic**—Applies the default settings that Windows 2000 is configured with during a clean installation. This policy is useful for bringing upgraded Windows NT systems into line with Windows 2000 security, because Windows 2000 has a much higher default level of security than previous versions of NT.
- **Compatible**—Increases security over the basic template to allow members of the local Users group to be able to run non–Windows 2000–compliant applications with elevated Power Users privileges. This is useful for environments where administrators do not want to require standard users to be members of the Power Users group (which grants substantial additional privileges over the Users group) and to be able to run legacy applications that will not run without Power Users permissions.

- **Secure**—Removes all members from the Power Users group and modifies security settings that pertain to the behavior of the operating system and network protocols rather than application functionality. Settings of this type include password and audit policies and Registry settings.
- **High Secure**—Goes beyond the secure template to extreme security measures. In doing so, it has no regard for functionality, performance, connectivity with non-Windows 2000 clients, or ease of use. As an example, the Secure template might warn you if you attempt to install an assigned driver. The High Secure template would simply block the installation of the unsigned driver without giving you the opportunity to override it.

To implement security templates, right-click the Security Settings folder under the Computer Configuration container (this will *not* work under the User Configuration container) and then click Import Policy. The dialog box shown in Figure 8.6 appears.

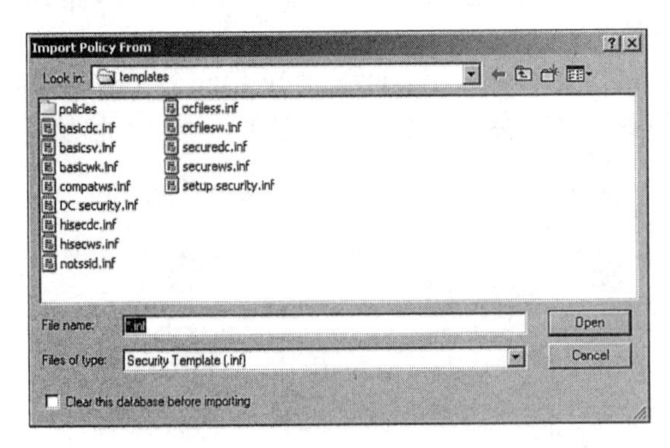

Figure 8.6 You can import Windows 2000 security templates into a GPO through the Computer Configuration container's Import Policy option.

Note the Clear This Database Before Importing check box. If you check the box, any templates currently stored in the GPO are removed. If you leave it blank (the default), any policy settings from the imported template are simply merged into the existing templates, creating a composite security policy. Table 8.1 defines the available security templates.

Table 8.1 Windows 2000 Security Templates

Template Name	Definition
basicdc.inf	Default security settings for a DC
basicsv.inf	Default security settings for a standalone (or member) server
basicwk.inf	Default security settings for a Windows 2000 Professional system
compatws.inf	Security settings that make Server or Professional backward compatible with Microsoft Windows NT 4
dc security.inf	Default settings (updated) for DCs
hisecdc.inf	High-security settings for a DC
hisecws.inf	High-security settings for a Windows 2000 Professional system
notssid.inf	Removes the Terminal Server security ID (SID) assigned to a Windows 2000 Server
ocfiless.inf	For optional component file settings on servers
ocfilesw.inf	For optional component file settings on Windows 2000 Professional
securedc.inf	Secure DC settings
securews.inf	Secure Windows 2000 Professional settings
setup security.inf	Default settings applied after installation (installation defaults)

Another way to use Group Policy to manage the user environment is through script policies, as you'll see next.

Assigning Script Policies to Users and Computers

Windows 2000 has greatly expanded the role of scripts in managing the user environment. In previous versions of Windows NT, scripts were limited to batch files that could only be run at startup. With Windows 2000, however, any or all of the following types of scripts can be run:

- **Startup**—Computer scripts that run under the Local System account and apply settings during computer startup, before the User Logon dialog box is presented.
- **Logon**—Traditional user login scripts that run when the user logs on to the system. The scripts run under the user account with which they are associated. Logon scripts are executed only after computer Startup scripts have been processed by Windows 2000.

- **Logoff**—User scripts that run when the user either chooses Start, Log Off or chooses to shut down or restart the computer. Logoff scripts are executed before computer shutdown scripts.
- **Shutdown**—Computer scripts that run when the computer is shut down. As with startup scripts, shutdown scripts run under the Local System account to apply settings at the computer level.

Additionally, Windows 2000 allows you to go beyond the limitations of DOS-based batch files into ActiveX scripting using the VBScript and JavaScript (also known as *JScript*) engines. To support these ActiveX scripting engines, Windows 2000 provides the Windows Script Host (WSH).

Windows Script Host

Windows Script Host is a scripting host that allows you to run VBScript scripts (which have a `.vbs` extension) and JavaScript scripts (which have a `.js` extension) natively on 32-bit Windows platforms. That means you can execute VBScript or JScript scripts just as you would DOS batch files. WSH is extensible, so in the future, you might be able to run third-party scripts natively as well, such as Perl or Python.

Windows 2000 ships with WSH 2. WSH 2 replaces Windows Scripting Host 1.0, which shipped with Windows 98 and was available for download as part of the NT 4 Option Pack for use on NT systems. With version 2, Microsoft changed *Scripting* to *Script* in the name. WSH 2 is fully backward compatible and is able to run any Version 1 scripts. It is beyond the scope of this book to point out the differences between Versions 1 and 2 other than to note that WSH 2 is XML based and supports many new features.

WSH comes with two executable files:

- `WScript.exe`
- `CScript.exe`

WScript

The file `WScript.exe` is the graphical version of WSH and allows you to run VBScript and JScript scripts inside of Windows by double-clicking the filename. You can also execute `WScript.exe` from the Run line in the Start menu. The syntax is as follows:

```
wscript <script name>
```

If the script is not located in a directory included in the environment variable PATH statement, you must specify the path to the script in *<script name>* for it to execute properly. WScript provides the following properties that can be configured:

- **Stop Script After Specified Number of Seconds**—This setting specifies the maximum length of time a script can run. By default, there is not a time limit placed on script execution.
- **Display Logo when Script Is Executed in a Command Console**—This setting displays a WSH banner while the script is run. This setting is turned on by default.

CScript

The file `CScript.exe` is the command-line version of WSH and is useful when you need to specify parameters at runtime. CScript is great for the computer and user scripts that are executed during startup, logon, logoff, and shutdown. The syntax of `CScript.exe` is as follows:

```
cscript <script name> <script options and parameters>
```

The definitions for the options after `cscript` are as follows:

- ***<script name>***—The full path and filename of the script to be executed by `CScript.exe`.
- ***<script options and parameters>***—Enables or disables various WSH features. Options are preceded by two forward slashes, as in `//logo`. Table 8.2 summarizes the host options.

Table 8.2 WSH Options and Their Meanings

Option	Definition
//b	Batch mode. Suppresses script errors for any user prompts that might display. The computer and user scripts discussed in this chapter typically have this option specified.
//i	Interactive mode (the opposite of Batch mode). Interactive mode is the default if neither is specified.
//logo	Displays a logo banner during script execution; this is the default setting if not explicitly specified.
//nologo	Disables the logo banner from displaying during script execution.

(continued)

Table 8.2 WSH Options and Their Meanings *(continued)*	
Option	**Definition**
//h:WScript	Changes the default script host to WScript. This is the default setting if none is explicitly specified.
//h:CScript	Changes the default script to CScript.
//e:*engine*	Specifies which engine to use in executing the script. Either the VBScript or JScript engine can be specified.
//t:nn	Timeout in seconds. This is the maximum amount of time the script is allowed to run before it is terminated by the script host.
//d	Debugger. This setting enables Active Debugging.
//x	Executes the script in the debugger.
//s	Save. This setting saves the current command-line options for this user.
//job:<*jobID*>	Runs the specified ***jobID*** from a WSH 2 Windows script file (WSF).
//u	Tells WSH to use Unicode for redirected I/O from the console.
//?	Displays the help file for syntax and options.

Assigning Scripts Through Group Policy

The hardest part about implementing scripts on a Windows 2000 network is the actual writing of the scripts. Assigning scripts through Group Policy, however, is easily accomplished.

Startup and shutdown scripts apply to computers, and logon and logoff scripts apply to users. As you know, the Group Policy Editor divides the GPO into two main nodes: Computer Configuration and User Configuration. The Scripts node is located under the Windows Settings node in each container, and parentheses indicate the type of scripts that the node supports.

To apply a script, simply click the Scripts node under the appropriate container. Double-click the desired script, such as the startup script, which brings up the dialog box shown in Figure 8.7.

In the script's properties dialog box, click the Add button to add a new script. This brings up the dialog box shown in Figure 8.8.

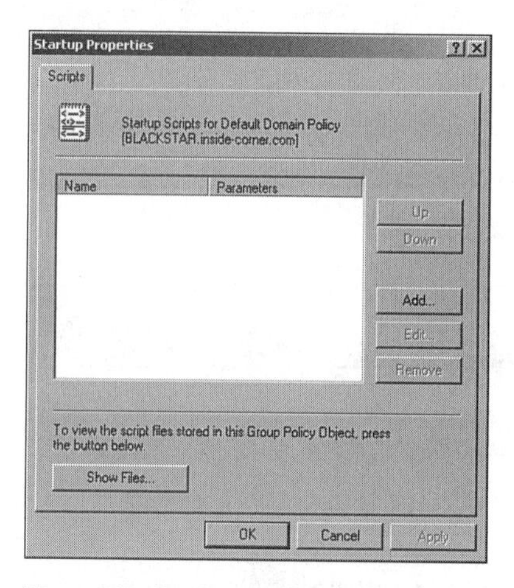

Figure 8.7 Double-clicking a script brings up a properties dialog box.

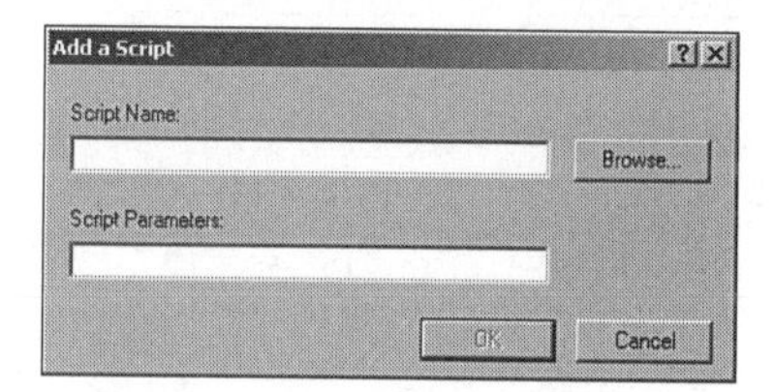

Figure 8.8 The Add a Script dialog box allows you to specify a script name and script parameters.

If you know it, you can type in the name (and path if applicable) of the script you want to use; otherwise, just click Browse. Select the script you want to use, as in Figure 8.9, and click Open. This returns you to the dialog box shown in the previous figure. Enter any parameters, such as `//Nologo`, and click OK.

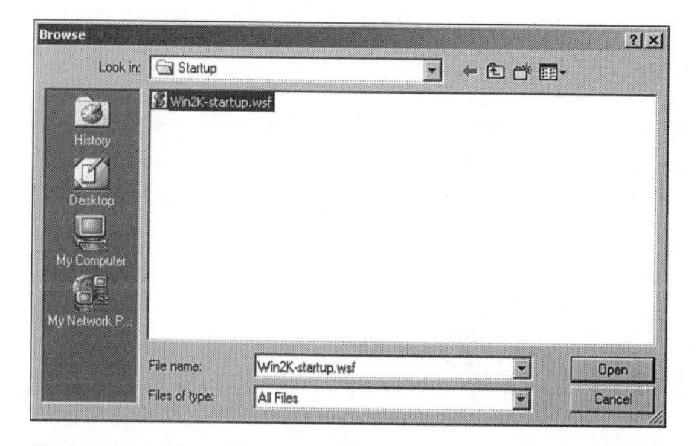

Figure 8.9 After selecting the script you want to assign, click Open.

Although it is not recommended to use locations for the storage of scripts other than the default directories, which are listed in Table 8.3, note that when you're assigning a script through Group Policy, the script can be located on any drive and folder the system can read. This is in contrast to Windows NT 4, which required login scripts to be located in the NETLOGON share, located at \winnt\system32\repl\import\scripts.

Table 8.3 The Default Directories for Windows 2000 Scripts

Script	Directory
Startup	\winnt\SYSVOL\Sysvol*domain*\Policies*GUID*\MACHINE\Scripts\Startup
Shutdown	\winnt\SYSVOL\Sysvol*domain*\Policies*GUID*\MACHINE\Scripts\Shutdown
Logon	\winnt\SYSVOLSysvol*domain*\Policies*GUID*\USER\Scripts\Logon
Logoff	\winnt\SYSVOL\Sysvol*domain*\Policies*GUID*\USER\Scripts\Logoff

In Windows NT, scripts and other files placed in the \winnt\system32\repl\export\scripts directory were replicated to the NETLOGON shares on DCs configured for replication. The File Replication Service (FRS) in Windows 2000 has replaced the NT 4 and earlier Directory Replication Service, and now replicates the entire SYSVOL directory tree across all DCs.

The exception to the recommendation about not changing the default location for scripts is if you are supporting legacy clients (Windows 9*X* and Windows NT 4) on your network. For these clients, you should copy the relevant logon scripts to the NETLOGON share, which in Windows 2000 is located under the \winnt\SYSVOL\Sysvol*domain*\scripts directory. Legacy clients cannot use the Windows 2000 features of startup, shutdown, and logoff scripts, so the NETLOGON share exists for backward compatibility with their logon script capabilities.

In addition to being able to apply settings through scripts, Windows 2000 provides a Group Policy feature called *Folder Redirection* to help administrators more effectively manage the desktop environment. We discuss this feature next.

Use of Folder Redirection

Folder redirection is the process in which Windows 2000 changes the location of certain user folders from the local hard drive to a specified network share. Only the following folders can be redirected:

- `Application Data`
- `Desktop`
- `My Documents`
- `My Pictures`
- `Start Menu`

Folder redirection is useful from an administrative standpoint for backups. In most environments, user workstations are not automatically backed up. By having folders redirected to a server share, the files are usually backed up. This provides an extra measure of protection against potential data loss.

When you right-click one of the special folders in the Group Policy Editor and choose Properties, the first dialog box you see contains the target setting. This dialog box is shown in Figure 8.10. By default, this setting is No Administrative Policy Set, but you can change it to either of the following:

- **Basic – Redirect Everyone's Folder to the Same Location**—This policy redirects all folders to the same network share. You can individualize the path by incorporating the `%username%` variable, such as specifying `\\server\share\%username%\My Documents`.
- **Advanced – Specify Locations for Various Groups**—The Advanced policy allows you to redirect folders based on security group memberships. Members of one group can have folders directed to one share, and members of another group can be redirected to a different share. Again, you can use the `%username%` variable in your path to establish individual folders for each user.

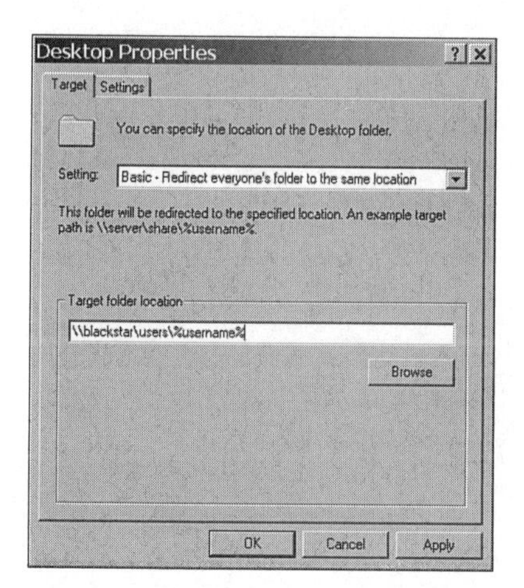

Figure 8.10 You configure Folder Redirection policies within the properties of a special folder.

Whether configuring a basic or advanced policy, you can configure the following additional settings for folder Redirection, as shown in Figure 8.11:

- **Grant the User Exclusive Rights to the Special Folder**—By default, this setting is enabled, and it gives the user and the local system account full control, and no permissions to anyone else (even administrators).
- **Move the Contents of <special folder> to the New Location**—Enabled by default, <special folder> is the name of the folder being redirected.
- **Policy Removal**—You have the option to either leave the files in the new location when the policy is removed (the default option) or have the files redirected back to their original location.

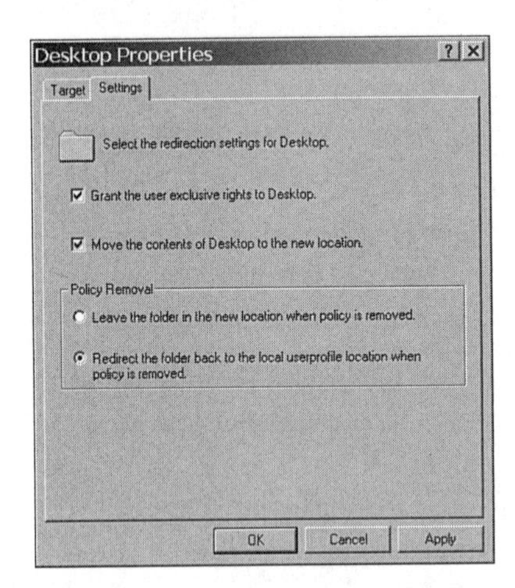

Figure 8.11 Group Policy provides additional settings for greater control over the behavior of redirected folders.

Practice Questions

Question 1

From the following list, choose the keywords that can be used in creating administrative templates and arrange the keywords in the order you would use them:

HELP

CATEGORY

EXPLAIN

VARIABLE

POLICY

CLASS

HEADER

STRINGS

REGISTRYKEY

END POLICY

NODE

The correct answer is:

```
CLASS

CATEGORY

POLICY

EXPLAIN

END POLICY

STRINGS
```

Question 2

What is the name of the executable for the command-line version of the Windows Script Host?

- ❍ a. **WScript.exe**
- ❍ b. **CScript.exe**
- ❍ c. **WSH.exe**
- ❍ d. **CMD.exe**

Answer b is correct. `CScript.exe` is the executable file for the command-line version of WSH. Answer a is incorrect because WScript is the Windows GUI version of Windows Script Host. Answer c is incorrect because WSH is merely the abbreviation for Windows Script Host, not the name of the executable. Answer d is incorrect because `CMD.exe` is the command interpreter for Windows 2000.

Question 3

Which of the following are administrative templates that are installed by default with Windows 2000? [Check all correct answers]

- ❑ a. **System.adm**
- ❑ b. **Windows.adm**
- ❑ c. **Inetres.adm**
- ❑ d. **Default.adm**
- ❑ e. **Common.adm**
- ❑ f. **Winnt.adm**
- ❑ g. **GPO.adm**

Answers a, b, c, e, and f are correct. Windows 2000 installs these five administrative templates by default. Answers d and g are incorrect because these templates would have to be created and installed by the user.

Question 4

There are two Group Policy configuration containers:

Computer Configuration

User Configuration

Identify how each of the following administrative template categories fits into these containers:

Desktop

Printers

Control Panel

Start Menu & Taskbar

The correct answer is:

Computer Configuration

- Printers

User Configuration

- Desktop
- Control Panel
- Start Menu & Taskbar

Question 5

Of the following, which are not categories of Security Settings that can be configured through the Group Policy Editor? [Check all correct answers]

- ❑ a. Account Policies
- ❑ b. Event Log
- ❑ c. Password Policies
- ❑ d. Registry
- ❑ e. File System
- ❑ f. Account Lockout
- ❑ g. Auditing

Answers c, f, and g are correct. Password Policies and Account Lockout are configured through Account Policies, and Auditing settings are configured through Local Policies. Answers a, b, d, and e are incorrect because they are security categories under Security Settings in the Computer Configuration container.

Question 6

Which of the following types of scripts are applied to computer accounts? [Check all correct answers]

- ❑ a. Startup
- ❑ b. Logon
- ❑ c. Logoff
- ❑ d. Shutdown

Answers a and d are correct. Startup and shutdown scripts are applied to computer accounts. Answers b and c are incorrect because logon and logoff scripts are applied to user accounts.

Question 7

Which of the following user folders cannot be redirected to a server location using Folder Redirection?

- ❍ a. **My Documents**
- ❍ b. **Favorites**
- ❍ c. **Application Data**
- ❍ d. **Desktop**
- ❍ e. **Start Menu**

Answer b is correct. Windows 2000 Folder Redirection cannot be used to redirect the `Favorites` folder. Answers a, c, d, and e are incorrect because these folders can be used.

Question 8

Windows 2000 includes four default security templates that can be installed. Which template would provide a security configuration that would warn a user if he or she were about to install an unsigned driver?

❍ a. Basic

❍ b. Compatible

❍ c. Secure

❍ d. High Secure

Answer c is correct. The Secure template provides a higher level of security than answers a and b, the Basic and Compatible templates, and it would not install an unsigned driver without prompting the user first with a warning. Answer d is incorrect because the High Secure template simply would not allow an unsigned driver to be installed.

Question 9

Which security template would be used to bring a system upgraded from Windows NT to Windows 2000 up to the level of security of a new Windows 2000 installation?

❍ a. Basic

❍ b. Compatible

❍ c. Secure

❍ d. High Secure

Answer a is correct. Applying the Basic template to a GPO is a great way to bring upgraded NT systems up to the Windows 2000 default security level. Answer b is incorrect because, although the Compatible template sounds like the likely answer, that security template exists to allow legacy applications to run correctly in a Windows 2000 environment. Answers c and d are incorrect because the Secure and High Secure templates are used to provide a higher level of security than what is initially set up when Windows 2000 is installed.

Question 10

Which Windows 2000 service has replaced the older Windows NT Directory Replication service? [Choose the best answer]

- ❍ a. **NETLOGON**
- ❍ b. Active Directory replication
- ❍ c. **SYSVOL**
- ❍ d. FRS

Answer d is correct. The File Replication Service (FRS) is a new Windows 2000 service that expands on the capabilities of the older Directory Replication Service. FRS replicates the entire `SYSVOL` tree between DCs (making answer c incorrect). Answer a is incorrect because `NETLOGON` is the share name for the directory that logon scripts are stored in on a DC for legacy clients. Answer b is incorrect because Active Directory replication is not the mechanism used to replicate directories.

Need to Know More?

Iseminger, David. *Active Directory Services for Windows 2000 Technical Reference*. Microsoft Press. Redmond, WA, 2000. ISBN 0-7356-0624-2.

This book is a solid reference for planning and deploying AD networks. Although coverage of Group Policy is minor, there is a strong change and configuration management section.

Microsoft Corporation. *Microsoft Windows 2000 Server Resource Kit*. Microsoft Press. Redmond, WA, 2000. ISBN 1-5723-1805-8.

The quintessential resource for Windows 2000 Server and AD, this kit has extensive coverage of AD and Group Policy in particular. If you can have only one Windows 2000 reference, this is the one to have.

Norris-Lowe, Alistair. *Windows 2000 Active Directory Service*. O'Reilly & Associates. Sebastopol, CA, 2000. ISBN 1-5659-2638-2.

Another good AD resource, this is more of a high-level technical book rather than a hands-on "how to" type of book. This is an excellent resource for learning the theory behind the technology and a great complement to the *Windows 2000 System Administration Handbook*, listed next.

Willis, Will, David Watts, and Tillman Strahan. *Windows 2000 System Administration Handbook*. Prentice-Hall Computer Books. Upper Saddle River, NJ, 2000. ISBN 0-1302-7010-5.

This book explains Windows 2000 systems administration concepts in detail, including managing user environments using Group Policy. This is a solid all-around Windows 2000 reference with good coverage of AD.

Using Group Policy in Software Deployment and Management

Terms you'll need to understand:

- ✓ IntelliMirror
- ✓ Software Installation feature
- ✓ Windows Installer
- ✓ Assigned applications
- ✓ Published applications
- ✓ Pilot program
- ✓ Package

Techniques you'll need to master:

- ✓ Configuring deployment options
- ✓ Deploying software by using Group Policy
- ✓ Maintaining software by using Group Policy
- ✓ Troubleshooting common problems that occur during software deployment

In Chapter 7, "Understanding Group Policy Implementation," and Chapter 8, "Using Group Policy in Security and Environment Control," we discussed how to implement Group Policy and how to use it to manage the desktop computing environment. In this chapter, we discuss another powerful use of Group Policy: software deployment and management. Using Group Policy, you can control what applications a user has on his or her computer. Under certain circumstances, you can even have applications repair themselves if they are missing files or settings. As you will see in a moment, software management is one of the three core functions of Microsoft's IntelliMirror initiative, which relies on Active Directory (AD) and Group Policy for implementation.

You need to have a solid understanding of how to use Group Policy to assign and publish software and how to troubleshoot when things aren't working as expected.

IntelliMirror Concepts

Many of the Group Policy concepts discussed in Chapters 7 and 8 are related to IntelliMirror, a collection of technologies that work together in Windows 2000 to reduce the total cost of ownership (TCO) by simplifying the management of Windows 2000 computers.

The features of IntelliMirror are as follows:

- **Data Management**—This feature, used to manage user data, is implemented in Windows 2000, as you have seen, through Folder Redirection. When Folder Redirection and Offline Folders are used, user data can be synchronized between a server copy and a local copy, ensuring that data files are accessible no matter where the user is and what computer he or she logs on from. Additionally, disk quotas can help track and restrict the usage of server disk space by user files.
- **Desktop Settings Management**—Desktop settings can be stored in profiles that roam with a user so that they are applied whenever a user logs in to a networked computer. Group Policy is used to control what settings should be stored and can control a user's ability to make changes to desktop settings. As we discussed in Chapter 8, Group Policy can be used to lock down desktop configurations and define a standard level of security for Windows 2000 computers.

- **Software Installation and Maintenance**—This feature of IntelliMirror (which is the focus of this chapter) allows applications to be published by an administrator for use by defined users, computers, and groups, and Windows Installer applications can even be set up to automatically replace corrupt or missing files. This reduces downtime associated with broken applications that would ordinarily require an IT staff member to go out to a workstation and manually reinstall the applications.
- **Remote Installation Services (RIS)**—RIS allows for the Windows 2000 Professional operating system to be installed remotely through preconfigured images. RIS is the focus of Chapter 15, "Remote Installation Services (RIS)."

Specifically, the following are the available Windows 2000 IntelliMirror technologies and their interdependencies:

- **AD**—This is the cornerstone of IntelliMirror, because without AD, none of the rest would be possible. AD stores the Group Policy Objects (GPOs) and other user, group, and computer information, and it provides centralized management for Windows 2000 networks.
- **Group Policy**—Through Group Policy, you can manage desktop settings and determine what to apply and where. Group Policy is dependent on AD, because it stores global policy information in the AD database. Group Policy is the primary method of managing the IntelliMirror features in the preceding list.
- **Roaming user profiles**—Roaming profiles are used to enable user settings, such as desktop wallpaper and customized Start menu settings, to follow a user to whichever computer he or she logs on from. Any changes made to the user environment while the user is logged on are saved in the profile `ntuser.dat` and stored in AD. Roaming profiles existed in Windows NT 4 and have largely been superseded by Group Policy.
- **Folder Redirection**—Folder Redirection is one of the primary components of the Data Management IntelliMirror feature discussed previously. As you learned in Chapter 8, Folder Redirection can be used to seamlessly move the contents of certain local user folders to a network location. Combined with Offline Folders, you can have much greater data protection and availability than by having files stored only on local hard drives.

- **Offline Folders**—Offline Folders is an IntelliMirror capability that allows for the synchronization of files and folders between the local hard drive and a network location. This is particularly useful for users with laptops, because you can use Offline Folders in conjunction with Folder Redirection to ensure they have full access to their files regardless of whether they are in the office on the LAN or working offline on an airplane.

The focus of this chapter is software deployment and management, so let's discuss how the technologies in the preceding list work in this context.

Software Installation and Maintenance Overview

Through IntelliMirror and specifically the Group Policy component, Microsoft has provided the Software Installation and Maintenance feature, which provides a way for administrators to deploy software so that it is always available to users and so that it repairs itself if necessary. Software Installation and Maintenance is implemented as a Group Policy extension called Software Installation. As shown in Figure 9.1, it is located under both the Computer Configuration and User Configuration containers in a GPO, beneath the Software Settings nodes.

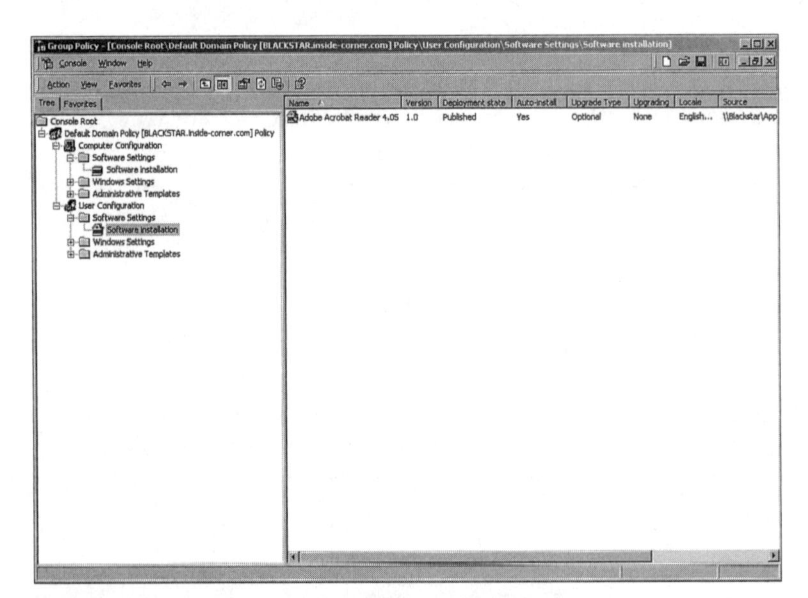

Figure 9.1 The Software Installation extension to Group Policy is located under the Software Settings node in the Computer Configuration and User Configuration containers.

Through Software Installation, you can centrally manage each of the following:

- **Deployment of applications**—You can deploy shrink-wrapped applications or custom-built, in-house applications. Almost any type of application can be deployed through Software Installation.
- **Upgrades and patches**—Through Software Installation, you can update existing software or even replace it, in the case of a product upgrade. Deploying service packs for operating systems becomes much easier as well.
- **Uninstall software**—When a product is no longer in use or supported by the IT department, you can easily remove it from users' computers without their intervention or without physically working on each computer containing the installed software.

The goal of Software Installation is to deploy applications in a way that whenever a user logs on to a computer, no matter where, that user always has his or her applications available. This technology is often referred to as *just-in-time* (JIT), because deployment occurs either during user logon or when the user goes to launch a particular application. For example, say you have assigned Microsoft Excel to Mark, a particular user. Even though Mark has not explicitly installed Microsoft Excel himself, he sees the icon for it on his desktop or in his Start menu. The first time he attempts to use the program, the system installs the application automatically, with no user intervention, and launches the program.

Likewise, if the same user attempts to use a feature of the program that is not installed by default, the application will be smart enough to automatically install the missing feature on the fly from the network and allow the user to use it. In the past, installing a missing feature has invariably meant manually running the program's setup utility and either reinstalling the entire product to add the missing feature or simply selecting the missing feature and choosing to update the installation. Either case would be an interruption to the workflow of the user and very likely would require a desk-side trip from a desktop support technician.

Requirements for Software Installation

To use the Software Installation extension, two prerequisites must first be met:

- **AD dependency**—Because Group Policy is dependent on AD, it makes sense that you cannot use the Software Installation extension unless you have deployed AD on your network. Software Installation relies on GPOs, which are stored in AD, to determine who can access managed software. As with Group Policy, Windows 9*X* and NT 4 computers cannot participate in AD.
- **Group Policy dependency**—To use the Software Installation extension, you must be using Group Policy on your network. Because Group Policy is limited to Windows 2000 computers, you can only manage software for your Windows 2000 environment. Any legacy Windows 9*X* or NT 4 clients won't be able to receive applications through Group Policy and Software Installation.

The primary function of Software Installation is to deploy software, so let's discuss that next.

Deploying Software with Group Policy and Software Installation

In this section, we explore the Software Installation extension—specifically, the following:

- Configuring Software Installation properties
- Deploying a new package
- Configuring package properties

You need to know how to deploy software using the Software Installation extension and how to configure deployment options.

These topics will allow you to deploy software—from setting up the Software Installation extension's global properties to deploying a new package—and then to configure additional properties for a deployed software package.

Configuring Software Installation Properties

To configure the global properties of the Software Installation extension, simply right-click the extension and click Properties. Keep in mind that computer and user settings are independent of each other, so making changes to the computer policy for Software Installation has no effect on the user policy, and vice versa.

The first tab you are presented with when you enter the Software Installation Properties dialog box is the General tab, as shown in Figure 9.2.

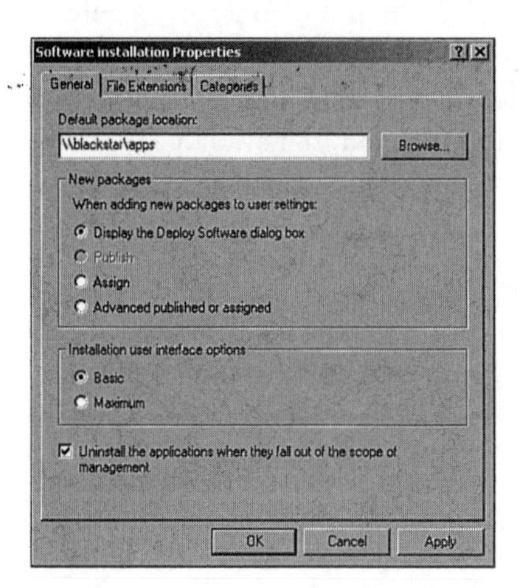

Figure 9.2 The General tab contains information about the default behavior of the Software Installation extension.

The first section on this tab's property sheet allows the administrator to define the default package location for new packages. This should be a network share rather than a local hard drive path (for example, `\\blackstar\apps` rather than `E:\apps`) and is used if you use a centralized distribution location for your software.

The General tab also contains settings that define the behavior of the extension with regard to new package creation. By default, the Deploy Software dialog box is displayed when you choose to create a new package. This dialog box contains the choice to assign or publish a package, allowing you to choose how you want Software Installation to handle packages on a package-by-package basis. Unless you strictly publish or assign applications, there is probably no need to change this default setting.

Additionally, the General tab contains the option to define how much information is presented to the user during package installation. By default, only basic information about the software installation is supplied, such as the installation progress meter. Optionally, you can specify that a maximum amount of information and options be shown to the user during installation, which includes all installation messages and dialog boxes.

Finally, the General tab has the optional setting to define whether software should automatically be uninstalled when it falls outside the scope of management. That is, if Software Installation no longer manages the software, it should no longer be available to users. By default, this option is not enabled.

After the General tab is the File Extensions tab. In many cases, you will have more than one application installed on your computer that is capable of opening a given type of file. This tab's property sheet allows you to pick a file type and set the order of precedence for applications that are capable of opening the application. If the first application listed isn't available for some reason—for instance, because it was uninstalled—the second application listed attempts to open it.

The last tab is Categories, which is an organizational option. You can create categories to help keep track of where software is deployed. By default, no categories are listed, so you must create them if you want to use this feature. You might choose to create categories for your software based on department or location or some other naming convention that makes sense for your organization.

Deploying a New Package

To deploy a new package, you must have first copied the installation files to a *distribution point*, which is simply a network share that you designate as a repository for software. Right-click the Software Installation extension and then select New, Package. The dialog box shown in Figure 9.3 appears.

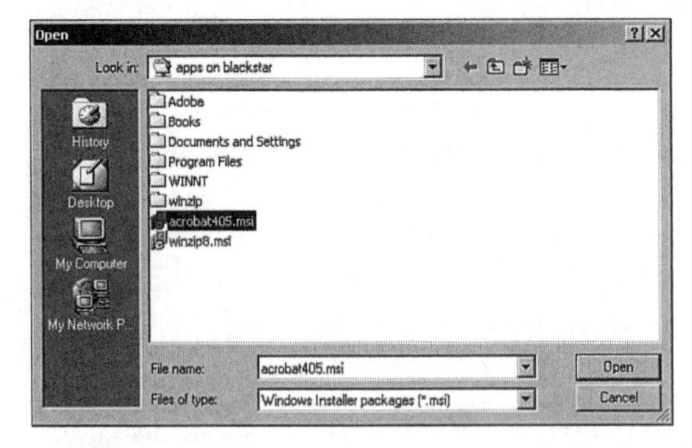

Figure 9.3 The first step in deploying a new package is to select the package that is to be deployed.

In this example, a Windows Installer package for Adobe Acrobat Reader is selected, which is located in the Apps share on the server Blackstar. This is the distribution point. When you select the file and click Open, you see the dialog box shown in Figure 9.4. You get this dialog box because the default settings in the Software Installation Properties dialog box (refer back to Figure 9.2) were not changed. If you had selected the Assign or Publish option, the action would simply be taken and you would not see this dialog box.

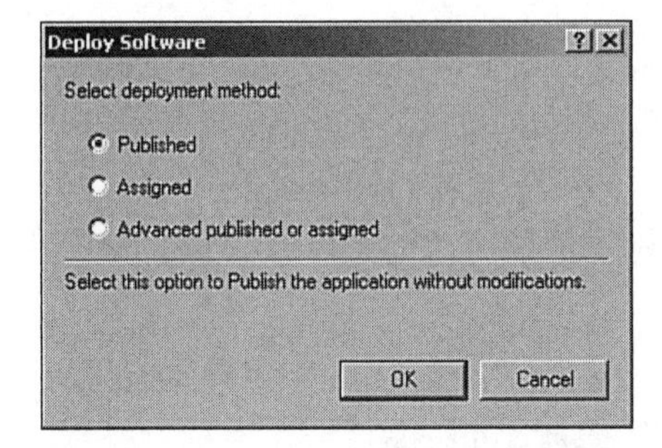

Figure 9.4 After choosing the software package to deploy, you must decide whether to publish or assign it.

Note that the Published option is available only if the package is being deployed under the User Configuration container. Software deployed to computers does not support publishing; therefore, those packages can only be assigned. When you get to the dialog box shown in Figure 9.4 and you've deployed the package under the Computer Configuration container, the Published option will be grayed out.

If you select either Published or Assigned and click OK, the package is deployed without any further prompting. If you select Advanced Published or Assigned, the package will still be deployed, but you will be prompted with a dialog box similar to the one shown in Figure 9.5. This is the same dialog box you can access later by going into the properties of a package, which is discussed next.

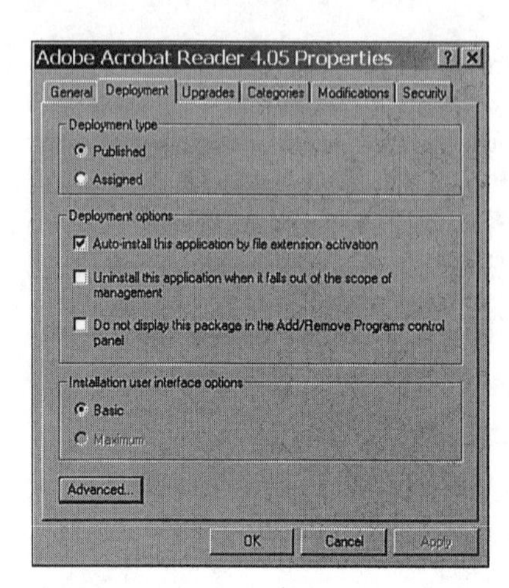

Figure 9.5 You can configure a number of advanced settings for an application once it has been deployed.

Configuring Package Properties

To access the properties of a package once you've deployed it, simply right-click the package and click Properties. You will see the same dialog box as you did previously if you selected Advanced Published or Assigned during the new package deployment. There are a number of property sheets containing settings for the package. Here is an overview:

- **General**—Contains product information, such as the name and version number, as well as contact information.
- **Deployment**—Defines the deployment type (assigned or published), which can also be changed here. In addition, this property sheet contains settings for deployment options, including whether the package should be uninstalled if it falls outside the scope of management and if it should be displayed in the Add/Remove Programs applet. Advanced deployment options determine whether the language setting should be ignored when software is installed and whether previous installations of the product should be uninstalled if the software wasn't installed through Group Policy.
- **Upgrades**—Defines the applications that are to be upgraded by this package and which packages can upgrade this package.
- **Categories**—Determines the categories that the software will be displayed under in the Add/Remove Programs applet.

- **Modifications**—Allows you to apply modifications or transforms to the package to customize the deployment.
- **Security**—Determines who has what level of access to the package. Through the Security property sheet, you control the deployment of the software to computers, users, and groups.

These are the basics of the Software Installation extension. At this point, we should take a moment to discuss assigned applications versus published applications and when to use one over the other.

Assigned Versus Published Applications

A key aspect to consider when deploying software is whether the application will be assigned directly to users or published into AD. When an application is assigned, its icons appear in the Start menu or on the desktop of the user's computer, according to criteria defined by the administrator. The first time a user attempts to launch an assigned application, the software is automatically installed without user or administrator intervention. If a user later uninstalls the application through the Add/Remove Programs applet in Control Panel, the software is still available to the user the next time he or she logs on. If a user attempts to launch a program he or she thought was uninstalled, the software simply reinstalls itself and opens. Because the software has been assigned to the user, the user cannot remove it. The advantage is that users cannot break assigned applications; rather, the software is self-healing and therefore does not require a traditional desk-side trip from an IT staff member to repair it by manually reinstalling.

On the other hand, administrators can choose to simply publish applications into the AD rather than assigning them directly to users. Assigned applications are typically used when a user needs a particular application to do his or her job. Published applications are not necessarily required by users to do their jobs but are beneficial applications that the administrator wants to make available. A published application shows up in Add/Remove Programs but must be explicitly installed by the user. No icons appear in the Start menu or on the desktop in advance to inform the user of the application's availability, and if a user uninstalls the application, it is removed from the computer just as in a traditional uninstall procedure.

Phases of Software Deployment

To ensure success, software deployment is best done through a systematic method. Managing a documented process removes many of the variables associated with deploying new software, thus reducing support costs related to troubleshooting problems.

Microsoft recommends a software deployment strategy similar to the following:

- **Preparation phase**—The preparation phase of software deployment includes analyzing the requirements of your organization to determine the needs to be filled. Some of the tasks include determining licensing requirements, whether applications will be run from a network server or local hard drives, and whether the current network infrastructure will support the deployment or you need to make modifications before deploying the new application to your users. You must also decide whether you will publish or assign applications in this phase.
- **Distribution phase**—The distribution phase includes setting up network distribution points for the new software package and copying the source installation files to your distribution points.
- **Targeting phase**—In the targeting phase, you use Group Policy to create and/or modify GPOs to effectively manage the software for users, groups, and computers. In addition, you use the Software Installation extension in Group Policy to configure deployment options for the new software package.
- **Pilot program phase**—The pilot program phase is perhaps the most important. In this phase, you deploy your software package to a select group of users, groups, and computers that is representative of the whole. By deploying to a select group and not everyone who will ultimately receive the package, you can put the application through all possible scenarios without impacting everyone if there are problems to be worked out. Once you have thoroughly tested the application under a pilot program, you are ready to deploy it to everyone.
- **Installation phase**—The installation phase is where the software is actually deployed to the desktops of all the users included in the target phase. The installation phase can involve installing new applications, installing modifications or updates to existing applications, repairing existing applications, and removing applications entirely.

Following the phases of this process gives you the best chance for a successful software deployment; however, there will probably be times when you run into difficulties. Therefore, you should know how to troubleshoot some of the common problems.

Troubleshooting Software Deployment Problems

In a perfect world, you would follow the software-deployment process outlined in the previous section and roll out an application with no difficulties whatsoever. Unfortunately, things don't always work out in the real world the way they do in a textbook. Because of this hard reality, let's discuss some of the more common problems you might run into with software deployment and what steps you might take to resolve them.

Some general guidelines to follow in troubleshooting are discussed in this section. In many cases, problems can be traced to a lack of necessary permissions. One of the first troubleshooting steps should be to ensure that an appropriate level of permissions exists to access the needed resource. Missing source files or corrupted Windows Installer packages is another potential source of trouble. As part of your troubleshooting steps, you should check to make sure the necessary files are available.

The following subsections detail some common problems and how to resolve them.

Deployment Error Messages

Unfortunately, when working with any technology in the real world, things don't seem to always work quite like they do in a textbook. Any number of variables can come into play, and troubleshooting problems often becomes the most frustrating part of being a systems engineer. With that in mind, here are some common problems related to software deployment and what to look for to fix them.

"Active Directory Will Not Allow the Package to Be Deployed" Error Message

This error is usually a result of a corrupt Windows Installer package or the inability of the Software Installation Group Policy extension to communicate properly with AD.

To resolve this problem, test for connectivity with the DNS server and DCs containing the AD database. You can use the `ping` command to establish basic connectivity and browse through My Network Places to the servers to see whether you can access the required share directories. To test for a corrupted Windows Installer package, check whether you can open the package on another similarly configured computer.

"Cannot Prepare the Package for Deployment" Error Message

This error is similar to the preceding AD error in that it can be the result of a corrupt package. However, rather than the Software Installation extension not being able to communicate with AD, in this case it cannot communicate with the `SYSVOL` share.

The troubleshooting steps are the same as with the previous error. Test for connectivity between the workstation and the `SYSVOL` share on the DCs, try from another computer if communication fails, and attempt to install the package on another system if connectivity is fine.

Installation Error Messages

A number of different error messages can appear when you install an application on a workstation. There could be a problem with the Windows Installer packages, or there could be a permissions problem where the user or computer account attempting to install the application doesn't have the necessary level of permissions to complete the installation. The permissions problem could relate to not being able to execute the particular package, not being able to access the distribution point, or not being able to install the application to the target directory on the local hard drive as defined by the package.

To troubleshoot, first determine whether you have the permission to access the distribution point. If you do, copy the package to the local hard drive and attempt to execute it from there. If the package begins installing and fails, ensure that the user account being used has Write permissions to the target directory. If the package gives an error before attempting to install, make sure the user account has Execute permissions for the package and test the package on another system to ensure its integrity (that is, make sure it is not corrupted).

"The Feature You Are Trying to Install Cannot Be Found in the Source Directory" Error Message

This type of error is most likely related to permissions or connectivity. Either the user doesn't have the necessary permissions level to access the distribution point, or the distribution point is unavailable over the network. Additionally, you should check to ensure that the source files were not accidentally deleted or moved to another location on the network.

To troubleshoot this error, first make sure the required source files exist at the distribution point. If they do, make sure the user attempting to install the feature has connectivity to the server containing the distribution point. If this checks out, check the permissions on the distribution point to see if the user has the required permissions. Most likely, one of these three sources is the cause of the error.

Shortcuts Still Appear for Removed Applications

This isn't an error message but rather a condition that might exist after uninstalling a managed application. After either the user uninstalls an application or the Software Installation extension removes the software when an administrator removes it from the applications list, the shortcuts for the applications still appear on the Start menu and/or the desktop.

To troubleshoot, determine whether the shortcuts were user-created or program-created. In many cases, users copy shortcuts from the Start menu to the desktop for convenience. The application's installation program would not be aware of this type of user-created shortcut and therefore would not be able to remove it during the application's uninstallation process.

Another cause might be that the shortcuts point to another installation of the same program. Perhaps the user belongs to multiple GPOs, and the application has been removed from only one of them. Another possibility is that there was a locally installed copy prior to the installation of the assigned or published application, and those files were not removed.

You should check to see whether the shortcuts point to valid programs. If they do, determine why the programs are installed (local install, another GPO, and so on) and if it is appropriate. If the shortcuts do not point to valid applications, simply delete them.

An Installed Application Is Uninstalled from a User Workstation

This condition almost always occurs when the software deployment option Uninstall This Application when It Falls Outside the Scope of Management is selected. However, it could result if a computer account was moved outside of the influence of the GPO managing the software.

If the computer account was not moved, determine whether a GPO that the user or computer belongs to is still managing the application.

Troubleshooting is often more of an art than a science, but if you remember to check connectivity, permissions, and the existence of source files, you'll be a long way toward troubleshooting software deployment.

Practice Questions

Question 1

From the following list, choose the correct phases of software deployment and arrange them in order.

Distribution

Installation

Preparation

Deployment

Targeting

Publishing

Pilot

The correct answer is:

Preparation

Distribution

Targeting

Pilot

Installation

Question 2

Which of the following Windows 2000 features is not considered an IntelliMirror technology?

❍ a. Group Policy

❍ b. Folder Redirection

❍ c. Terminal Services

❍ d. Offline Folders

Answer c is correct. Terminal Services is a Windows 2000 component that can provide for "thin client" solutions that can reduce total cost of ownership (TCO) for desktop systems, but it is not a part of IntelliMirror. Answers a, b, and d are incorrect because Group Policy, Folder Redirection, and Offline Folders are all IntelliMirror technologies.

Question 3

Which of the following are prerequisites to use Software Installation? [Check all correct answers]

- ❑ a. Active Directory
- ❑ b. Published applications
- ❑ c. Group Policy
- ❑ d. Roaming profiles

Answers a and c are correct. Software Installation is an extension to Group Policy, which automatically makes Group Policy a prerequisite. Because Group Policy is dependent on Active Directory, answer a is also correct. Answer b is incorrect because applications can be either published or assigned through Software Installation, and answer d is incorrect because roaming profiles are not required to use Software Installation.

Question 4

Windows 2000 supports the following two features (among others):

IntelliMirror

Software Installation

Identify which feature each of the following components falls into:

Upgrades and patches

Software Installation and Maintenance

Desktop Settings Management

Uninstall software

Data Management

Deployment of applications

The correct answer is:

IntelliMirror

- Software Installation and Maintenance
- Desktop Settings Management
- Data Management

Software Installation

- Upgrades and patches
- Deployment of applications
- Uninstall software

Question 5

Which of the following behaviors is not characteristic of an assigned application? [Choose the best answer]

- ❍ a. Installs automatically the first time a user attempts to launch a program through its shortcut.
- ❍ b. Reappears after the user logs off and logs back in, even if the user uninstalled the application through Add/Remove Programs.
- ❍ c. Is installed by the user through the Add/Remove Programs applet.
- ❍ d. Appears the next time Group Policy is refreshed.

Answer c is correct. Installing a managed application through Add/Remove Programs is characteristic of a published application, not an assigned one. Answer a is incorrect because assigned applications install themselves automatically the first time a user attempts to open them. Answers b and d are incorrect because the shortcuts appear whenever the user logs off and logs back on or whenever Group Policy refreshes. Additionally, users can remove assigned applications; however, they will reappear the next time the user logs on to the computer.

Question 6

Which of the following would most likely be the cause of software deployment problems? [Check all correct answers]

- ❑ a. Permissions
- ❑ b. The user not being logged on to network
- ❑ c. Missing or corrupt source files
- ❑ d. Network connectivity being down between the workstation and distribution point

Answers a, c, and d are correct. Permissions, missing/corrupted source files, and connectivity account for the majority of software-deployment problems. Answer b is incorrect because, although it is possible to have a Windows 2000 workstation configured to not log on to a network automatically, this is not a setting that typically would be changed if the workstation had been previously configured to log on to a domain.

Question 7

Which of the following would you check if a user complained that a formerly managed application that was uninstalled still left icons on her desktop? [Check all correct answers]

- ❑ a. Whether the shortcut pointed to a valid program
- ❑ b. Whether the user created the shortcut or it had been created by the installation program
- ❑ c. Whether the program had been reinstalled because of membership in another GPO
- ❑ d. Whether another nonmanaged copy of the program had been installed locally on the system to a different directory

Answers a, b, c, and d are correct. All these choices are valid troubleshooting steps to determine the cause of a formerly managed application still existing on a system after it has been uninstalled.

Question 8

Which Windows 2000 IntelliMirror feature synchronizes user files and folders between a network share and the local hard drive? [Choose the best answer]

- ❍ a. Offline Folders
- ❍ b. Folder Redirection
- ❍ c. My Briefcase
- ❍ d. Roaming profiles

Answer a is correct. Offline Folders provides the ability to have files and folders synchronized between server copies and local hard drive copies. This feature is used primarily by mobile users who work offline (off the network) frequently. Answer b is incorrect because Folder Redirection redirects certain local folders to a server share without any kind of synchronization. Answer c is incorrect because My Briefcase was a primitive Windows 95 attempt to synchronize files and folders. Answer d is incorrect because the roaming profiles feature does not synchronize files and folders but rather stores user environment settings (wallpaper, color schemes, and so on) on the network.

Question 9

How would you determine whether a user has an appropriate level of permissions to execute a managed application? [Choose the best answer]

❍ a. Through the Security tab in the package's properties in Software Installation

❍ b. Through the Deployment tab in the package's properties in Software Installation

❍ c. Through OU membership in Active Directory Users and Computers

❍ d. Through GPO membership in Active Directory Users and Computers

Answer a is correct. The key to this question is the permission to execute a *managed application*. Permissions for managed applications are set through the Security tab in the package's properties in the Software Installation extension. Answer b is incorrect because the Deployment tab is used to configure other package properties, such as whether it is assigned or published. Answers c and d are incorrect because Active Directory Users and Computers is used to control security group membership as a whole rather than setting permissions on a particular resource.

Question 10

In which software deployment phase would you create and/or modify GPOs? [Choose the best answer]

❍ a. Preparation

❍ b. Distribution

❍ c. Targeting

❍ d. Pilot

❍ e. Installation

Answer c is correct. The targeting phase is used to create and/or modify GPOs that will be the target of the software package. Answer a is incorrect because in the preparation phase, you determine who the target will be, but you do not actually create GPOs at that point. Answer b is incorrect because the distribution phase involves setting up the source files and placing them on distribution points you have created. Answer d is incorrect because the pilot phase involves testing the software on a limited number of users, and answer e is incorrect because the installation phase is the actual deployment.

Need to Know More?

Iseminger, David. *Active Directory Services for Windows 2000 Technical Reference*. Microsoft Press. Redmond, WA, 2000. ISBN 0735606242.

This is a solid reference for planning and deploying AD networks. Although coverage of Group Policy is minor, there is a strong change and configuration management section.

Microsoft Corporation. *Microsoft Windows 2000 Server Resource Kit*. Microsoft Press. Redmond, WA, 2000. ISBN 1572318058.

The quintessential resource for Windows 2000 Server and AD, this kit has extensive coverage of AD and Group Policy in particular.

Norris-Lowe, Alistair. *Windows 2000 Active Directory Service*. O'Reilly & Associates. Sebastopol, CA, 2000. ISBN 1565926382.

Another good AD resource, this is more of a high-level technical book than a hands-on "how to" type of book. This book discusses software deployment from a strategic perspective, which is a great help in the planning phases.

Willis, Will, David Watts, and Tillman Strahan. *Windows 2000 System Administration Handbook*. Prentice-Hall Computer Books. Upper Saddle River, NJ, 2000. ISBN 0130270105.

A solid all-around Windows 2000 reference with good coverage of AD, this handbook explains Windows 2000 systems administration concepts in detail, including managing user environments using Group Policy.

Publishing Resources Within the Active Directory

Terms you'll need to understand:

✓ Publish
✓ Active Directory (AD) Users and Computers
✓ Sharing
✓ Universal Naming Convention (UNC)
✓ **pubprn.vbs**
✓ Keywords

Techniques you'll need to master:

✓ Publishing non–Windows 2000 printers through AD Users and Computers
✓ Publishing non–Windows 2000 printers through the **pubprn.vbs** script
✓ Viewing published printers in AD Users and Computers
✓ Searching for a printer by name or location
✓ Publishing a folder within AD
✓ Establishing a description and keyword for a published folder

One of the primary purposes of a directory service is to "publish" objects so they can be easily located by users. The idea is similar to using a telephone directory service, where you call directory assistance and request a phone number. If that number is listed (published), it will be returned to you. If the number is not listed (unpublished), you will get a negative response.

Introduction to Published Resources

Within Active Directory (AD), some resources are automatically published—for example, user accounts. These are created within the AD and are immediately published. Additional objects that are published within the AD are computers and printers that are added to the AD database.

There are times, however, when resources are not automatically published to the AD—for example, printers that are available from non–Windows 2000 servers. In such cases, the administrator may need to publish these resources to the AD to help users find them. Another example is folders that are shared on the network. Folders are not published within AD by default, and they don't have to be published unless you feel it would prove useful within your organization.

Remember that printers installed on non–Windows 2000 servers and folders that have been shared on the network are not automatically published and are therefore not included within AD searches. The systems administrator must publish these on an individual basis, as necessary.

Before we discuss how to publish resources, here are several important points to remember:

- You do not have to publish resources that are published automatically through the AD.
- Published information should not change frequently because this causes excessive administrative responsibility. Instead, your goal is generally to reduce the demands placed upon you.
- Published resources enable users to find objects even if they've been moved physically, as long as you update the shortcut within the AD.

Now, let's focus on the two primary objects for publishing: non–Windows 2000 printers and shared folders.

Publishing Printers

Printers are published automatically to the AD if they have been established on a machine running Windows 2000. This makes it possible to search within a domain for printers that exist in diverse physical locations.

Imagine a global corporation with offices in every major city. On the 23rd floor of an office in the Manhattan headquarters, a document-processing member has received a job by fax from Hong Kong. The fax specifies specific edits to a document. Once the edits are completed, the document must be printed to a printer named "Apple," which is located off a server in Hong Kong. The user can know the name of the printer and still not be able to connect to that printer. However, if the printer is published to the AD, the user can search for the printer and find it. If the user has the permission to print to Apple, the job will run smoothly. If the user doesn't know where Apple is, the task becomes a lot more administrator-intensive because the administrator would need to establish a connection to Apple.

When printers are created on a Windows 2000 machine, each printer is integrated with AD by default. When printers are published, the print queue is published, and hence the AD object that is created is called a *printQueue*. When properties of the printer are modified, these modifications to the object become part of the replication procedure that automatically takes place.

Printers can be published in two ways:

- By using AD Users and Computers
- By using the `pubprn.vbs` script located within the `system32` folder on the system

Let's explore each step of both of these methods.

Steps for Publishing Printers

A printer that is installed and shared on a system that is not Windows 2000—an NT 4 server, for example—will not be published automatically within the AD. To accomplish this task, you must use the Universal Naming Convention (UNC) path.

You establish a UNC path by indicating the location of the printer (or other shared resource). First, you include the name of the server and then the official name of the shared resource. The syntax for a UNC path is ***\\server_name\share_name***. Therefore, if you had a non–Windows 2000 server called "PrintServ" and a printer shared off of that server called "HP1," the UNC path for that printer would be **\\PrintServ\HP1**.

Publishing with AD Users and Computers

To publish a printer with AD Users and Computers, follow these steps:

1. Open AD Users and Computers.
2. Find the OU to which you would like to publish the printer.
3. Right-click the OU. Click New and then Printer.
4. Enter the UNC path of the printer you wish to publish, as shown in Figure 10.1, and then click OK.

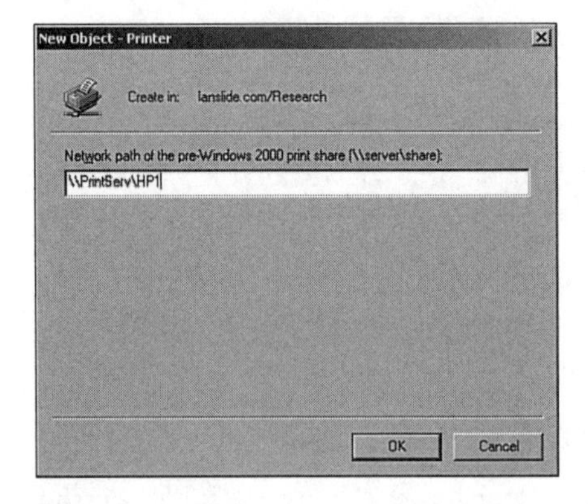

Figure 10.1 Publishing a printer with AD Users and Computers.

Publishing with the pubprn.vbs Script

The `system32` folder in Windows 2000 contains a script called `pubprn.vbs`. You can use this script to publish all printers shared off of a non–Windows 2000 server, or you can use it to publish only one printer off of a non–Windows 2000 server.

To run the script, type the following at a command prompt:

```
Cscript %systemroot%\system32\pubprn.vbs <additional options>
```

For example, let's say you have a Windows NT 4 Server hosting five shared printers that you would like published within your AD. The server's name is "SalesPrint," and you would like to publish it into an OU called "Sales" off of a domain called que.com. To accomplish this with the script, you would type the following at a command prompt:

```
Cscript %systemroot%\system32\pubprn.vbs SalesPrint "LDAP://OU=Sales,
  DC=que, DC=com"
```

In this example, %systemroot% indicates the location of the system32 partition. The name of the server can be changed to the UNC path of one specific printer, rather than publishing all printers off of the server. The LDAP path indicates the place in AD that the printers should be published to.

Viewing Published Printers

Whether you have a printer that exists on a Windows 2000 Server and is published automatically or you have a printer that you've manually published, it is certainly important to view the corresponding printer objects. To view the printer objects, you first need to enable a specific option within AD Users and Computers. You need to select View and then choose Users, Groups, and Computers as Containers. By enabling this option, you can view the published printers in the details pane after you select the computer on which the printer is located.

Once you can view the printer, you can also perform specific administrative tasks for that printer. By right-clicking the printer, you can perform the following:

- Move the printer.
- Connect to and install a printer.
- Open the print queue and perform document maintenance, such as deleting print jobs or pausing them.
- Change printer properties or print queue properties.

Searching for Printers

To search for a printer, select Start, Search and then select For Printers. The dialog box in Figure 10.2 appears.

You can search for a printer by providing a name, a location, or a model type. In addition, through the various tabs, such as Advanced, you can narrow your search further.

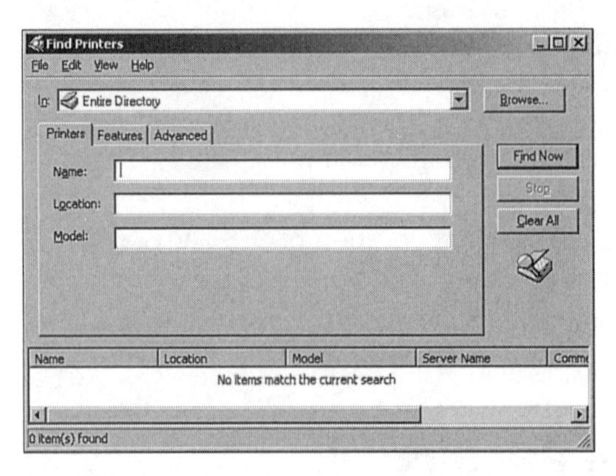

Figure 10.2 The Find Printers dialog box.

Printer Locations

One of the nice features of publishing a printer within the AD is the ability to use location definitions to assist users in their searches. When a user indicates a location, the AD search returns a list of printers at that location.

In addition, the AD search feature uses IP subnets to determine if printers are within the local proximity. If you have a network with only one subnet, the search operation will assume that all printers are in the same location. An administrator would then relate that subnet with a location naming convention. Establishing this convention would involve a certain amount of planning; for example, you can determine location based on the floor itself or based on the known department.

For additional information on this subject, select Start, Help. Then select the Index tab. In the Type in the Keyword to Find text box, type **printer location tracking**. You are then offered several helpful topics, such as Enabling Location Tracking, Naming Conventions, and Troubleshooting.

Publishing Folders

Folder sharing allows individuals with the correct permissions to use a UNC path to connect to a shared folder and explore, add to, delete, or modify its contents. Although this operation is not difficult for experienced administrators, users may not be able to comprehend UNC path mapping, or they may not know the servers' names or the share name. The solution is to publish the shared folder in the AD as an object. Once the folder is published, you can define keywords and a description to make searches easier for your users.

Steps for Publishing Folders

Publishing folders through the AD Users and Computers tool is similar to publishing printers. Before publishing the folder, you must share the folder on the network.

Once the folder is shared, perform the following steps:

1. Open AD Users and Computers.
2. Find the OU to which you want to publish the shared folder.
3. Right-click the OU. Select New and then Shared Folder.
4. Enter a name for the shared folder in the Name dialog box and indicate the UNC path for the shared folder that you are publishing within the AD. Then click OK.

Additional Search Descriptions

Once the folder is published, you can add descriptions and keywords to the folder to simplify the search process for users. The descriptions and keywords can be likened to the types of words you might include for a Web search. For instance, if you are searching the Web for some information on a Microsoft exam, you might enter **70-217** to indicate the exam covered in this book. In this case, various sites would have specified the keyword "70-217" because this would be a likely request from users.

To add search descriptions and keywords, follow these steps:

1. Open AD Users and Computers.
2. Find the OU and the published folder.
3. Right-click the published folder and select Properties.
4. In the Shared Properties dialog box that appears, as shown in Figure 10.3, enter a description and some keywords. When complete, click OK.

If a printer or folder is ever physically moved, users would not need to be aware of it; the systems administrator would just switch the UNC path. If the printer or folder remains in its physical location, but you need to switch the published resource to a different OU, you can move the object from within AD Users and Computers by right-clicking the object, selecting Move, and then supplying the destination.

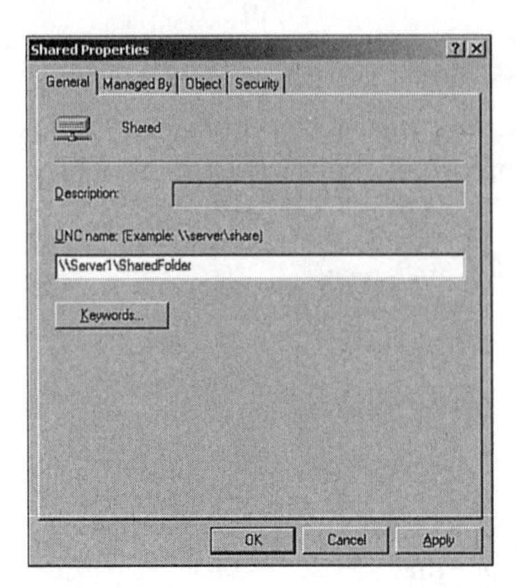

Figure 10.3 Adding search descriptions and keywords to a published folder with the AD.

Practice Questions

Question 1

You need to ensure that an Active Directory search for a non–Windows 2000 print server for the marketing department of a company called AfterShock will be successful for users within the department. As the systems administrator, what best-practice procedure should you perform?

- ❍ a. Share out the printers to members of the marketing department.
- ❍ b. Publish the printers to the AD.
- ❍ c. Upgrade the server to a Windows 2000 machine.
- ❍ d. Nothing. The search will be successful.

Answer b is correct. You must publish printers to the AD that are located off of non–Windows 2000 machines. Answer a is incorrect because this won't ensure a search; it will only ensure the possibility of connecting with those printers. Answer c is incorrect because, although this is possible, it is not considered a best practice. Answer d is incorrect because the search will, in fact, fail if you do nothing.

Question 2

Which of the following options allow you to publish printers to the Active Directory? [Check all correct answers]

- ❑ a. AD Users and Computers
- ❑ b. AD Sites and Services
- ❑ c. **pubprn.vbs**
- ❑ d. **prnpub.vbs**

Answers a and c are correct. You can use either the AD Users and Computers tool or the `pubprn.vbs` script to publish printers within Active Directory. Answer b is incorrect because this tool is used to allocate subnets into sites. Answer d is incorrect because it is an invalid script name.

Question 3

Two departments, Research and Development, are merging into one called Futures. The OUs are being deleted, and all objects are being moved into the new Futures OU. What must you do to ensure that users can still connect to published printers and folders?

- ❍ a. Change the UNC path of the published objects.
- ❍ b. Disconnect the users through Group Policy and force a reconnection.
- ❍ c. Reboot the server.
- ❍ d. Nothing.

Answer d is correct. You don't need to do anything. The users will still be able to connect. Answer a is incorrect because a UNC path change is not necessary if the physical location remains the same. Answer b is incorrect because it's an invalid solution. Answer c will only make people angry and have no effect on their connection to published resources. Therefore, it is also incorrect.

Question 4

Your company has a Hong Kong branch on the 15th, the 21st, and the 31st floors of a building. You want to find a printer in Hong Kong on the 15th floor that you can print to. You search for it and find several to choose from. What has your network administrator done to allow this type of search?

- ❍ a. The administrator has enabled searching.
- ❍ b. The administrator has enabled location tracking.
- ❍ c. The administrator has established a Hong Kong printer base.
- ❍ d. Nothing, the printer will automatically be indexed this way.

Answer b is correct. Location tracking allows searches to be made within an individual's local site or within other locations through the use of subnet and site allocation of printers within your AD. Answers a and c are incorrect because they are invalid choices. Answer d is incorrect because an administrator has to do much more than nothing to accomplish location tracking.

Question 5

When you publish folders, which of the following will make locating them easier for users?

- ❍ a. Keywords and a description.
- ❍ b. Keywords and location tracking.
- ❍ c. Location tracking and a description.
- ❍ d. Nothing. Locating folders is automatic.

Answer a is correct. Keywords and a description can be defined. Answers b and c are incorrect because these are just invalid variations of the actual answer. Answer d is incorrect because locating folders is not automatic.

Need to Know More?

Boswell, William. *Inside Windows 2000 Server*. New Riders. Indianapolis, IN, 2000. ISBN 1562059297.

This is a great resource for clear and in-depth information to strengthen your knowledge of Windows 2000 technology.

Iseminger, David. *Active Directory Services for Microsoft Windows 2000 Technical Reference*. Microsoft Press. Redmond, WA, 2000. ISBN 0735606242.

A strong resource for the structuring of AD implementation, configuration, and troubleshooting.

Scrimger, Rob, et al. *Microsoft Windows 2000 Server Unleashed*. Sams. Indianapolis, IN, 2000. ISBN 0672317397.

This is an in-depth description of Windows 2000 Server and Advanced Server.

Search the Microsoft Knowledge Base online at `http://support.microsoft.com` and consider the following two articles: Q321837 and Q234585.

Implementing Multiple Tree and Forest Structures

Terms you'll need to understand:

- ✓ Tree
- ✓ Forest
- ✓ Tree root domain
- ✓ Parent domain
- ✓ Child domain
- ✓ Transitive trusts
- ✓ Shortcut trusts
- ✓ External trusts
- ✓ Kerberos
- ✓ Global Catalog servers

Techniques you'll need to master:

- ✓ Designing multiple tree structures
- ✓ Implementing a child domain under the tree root domain
- ✓ Implementing a new domain within an existing forest structure
- ✓ Planning and creating shortcut trusts
- ✓ Creating, verifying, and removing trust relationships
- ✓ Implementing correct group configurations

The single domain tree is the recommended direction for administering an Active Directory (AD) structure. Organizational Units (OUs) remove the need to create resource domains, because you can now delegate administrative authority. However, at times, circumstances may require additional domains within a domain (called *child domains*) or additional domains that retain a separate namespace (called *forests*). Before implementing these domain structures, you should determine your organization's need for them. Doing so requires a clear understanding of what options are available to you and when you might choose to implement them.

Adding to a Tree

At times, you may need to add domain controllers (DCs) to your specific domain. These will become replica DCs for the same domain. At other times, you may need to add domains below your existing root and form trees with greater fullness. Let's consider the possible reasons for adding to your tree, keeping in mind that you should first make sure your needs cannot be met by a single domain structure:

- **Domain security settings**—Domain-level security settings are enforced throughout the entire domain. To allow for multiple domain-level security settings, it would be necessary to create additional domains that would be connected to the parent domain. For example, say the root domain (`que.com`) holds to a domain-level security policy that specifies that passwords be complex, yet a branch office in Paris would like to specify a more lax policy. The only way to accomplish this distinction is to have Paris become a separate domain within the tree (perhaps `paris.que.com`) and establish a domain security policy for that child domain.
- **Administrative control**—You may need to create multiple domains if your company has branches in different geographic locations with a qualified information technology (IT) staff that wants full administrative control over the domain. Or, you may need to separate portions of your company because of issues of sensitivity; all objects within a domain come under the supervision of the administrators of that domain, and there may be portions of your company that cannot allow for supervision from above.
- **Replication**—DCs are quite chatty. They share every little change with one another. By breaking up your organization into more than one domain under a common root, you limit replication issues to changes made in the Global Catalog (GC), the configuration, and the schema. If

you've designed your structure well, you won't be making excessive changes to these facets and your replication will be minimal between the domains.

- **Upgrading**—If you are upgrading from an NT 4 structure that contained multiple domains, you may find it easier to work with the domains and upgrade them according to the existing structure. After a migration toward Windows 2000, you may decide to continue with your domain structure, or you might decide to restructure your domains into one domain, which is the method recommended by Microsoft.

Never under any circumstances should you allow corporate politics to determine the structure of your domain. The politics within a business are a daily issue that has no place in proper domain design.

What Is a Domain Tree?

In theory, you can consider one DC as an entire tree, albeit a small one. In graphical representation, it would be a solitary triangle with any number of OUs inside. The tree holds one contiguous namespace with a common root. If you need to expand the tree in the future, you can create child domains, because they reside beneath a parent domain. These child domains continue to utilize the same contiguous name while branching out with additional naming for organizational purposes. For example, the domains `que.com` and `sales.que.com` share the same `que.com` contiguous namespace. Even `corporate.sales.que.com`, although a child further down the line, is considered part of the same tree, as shown in Figure 11.1.

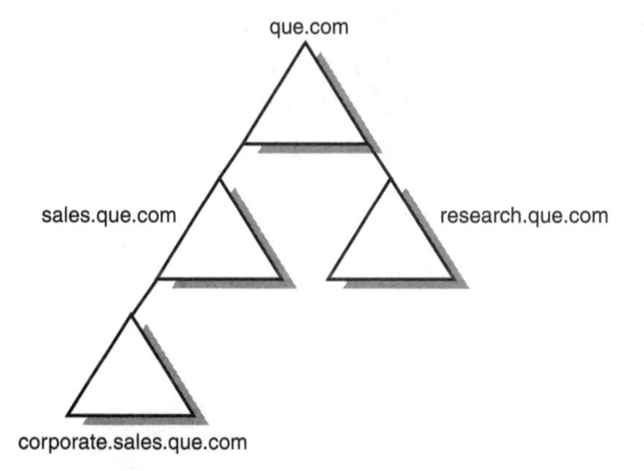

Figure 11.1 A domain tree can include child domains under a contiguous hierarchy.

A single domain tree obviously has all the features you would expect it to. It contains the unity of the AD database and a unified relationship among all DCs. When you add a child domain, you may wonder what changes in the structure and what remains the same. When you add additional domains to the tree, you continue to have a unified relationship; however, these are established through trust relationships. These relationships are automatic when the domains bond under the same name. They also must share a common schema (which means they need to utilize the same class objects and object attributes throughout the domains). In addition, they share the same site and service configuration information, as well as the GC information.

If a child domain joins a preexisting domain using the contiguous namespace, two-way transitive trusts form. *Trusts* may be a familiar concept to you if you are coming from an NT 4 background. A trust allows for one domain (the trusting domain) to utilize the user and group accounts of another domain (the trusted domain) in the establishing of permissions over resources. Thanks to a trust, users in different domains can access resources of the other domain. Trusts were originally established as one-way. A two-way trust means that both domains trust each other. The concept of *automatic two-way*, however, is definitely new. We'll discuss transitive trusts now, but keep in mind that Windows 2000 allows for other types of trusts, including shortcut trusts and external trusts, which we'll cover later in this chapter.

Transitive Trusts

Trusts allow the domains to work with the user accounts from other domains in such a way that people in one domain (which is a child domain of another domain) can share resources with others and benefit from their resources immediately, as long as the administrator provides permissions to such resources. The transitive concept enables smoother functionality. Conceptually, *transitive* means "by extension." For example, say you have two friends whom you trust, and they both trust you. Transitively, or "by extension," they might trust each other as well. Yet human relationships are complicated, whereas transitive trusts are consistent in Windows 2000.

Under Windows 2000, the trust is automatic between parents and children, and it is transitive between every other domain in the tree. In Figure 11.2, if child domain `a.corp.com` trusts `corp.com`, and `corp.com` trusts `b.corp.com`, then `a.corp.com` automatically trusts `b.corp.com`.

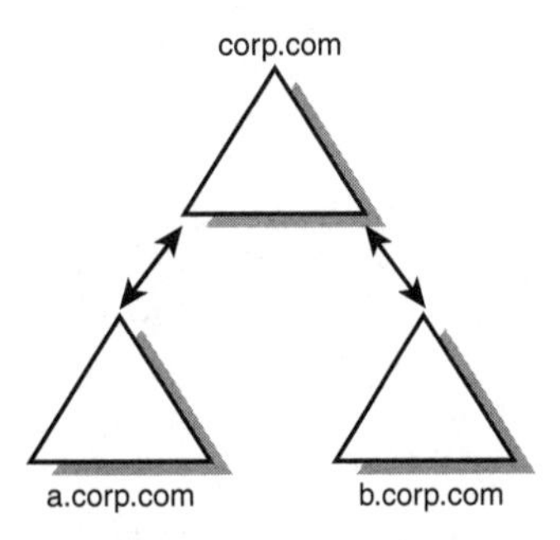

Figure 11.2 Two-way transitive trusts exist between parent and child DCs.

Transitive trusts allow users in all connected domains to be validated as domain users. Again, this trust doesn't mean unlimited access to resources for users who are part of the domain tree. In fact, one of the reasons to establish additional domains is to enhance security. Permissions are not transitive (with the exception of the Enterprise Admins group, which has administrative permissions within all domains of the forest), nor do domain administrators from various connected domains control them. This safety precaution adds an extra level of security between corporate domains.

Following are a few points to keep in mind about transitive trusts:

- They are two-way agreements that are automatically created.
- They exist between child domains and parents or the root domains of a forest.
- The trusts are transitive because the trees and forests with connecting trusts make information available with no further trust-configuration issues.
- After trusts are established, permissions must be granted to individuals and groups to allow them to access resources.

Creating a Child Domain

Chapter 4, "Windows 2000 Domains: Planning and Installation," covered the complete concept of installing a DC by implementing AD. All the necessities for AD remain true for the creation of a child domain. To create a child domain, you must start, of course, with a parent domain. Perhaps this parent domain is the forest root domain, although it could be any domain in the forest where you would choose to add child domains, as needed.

Forest Root Domains

As mentioned in Chapter 4, the forest root domain is the first domain created in the forest. As a result, it receives certain features that are implemented only once (during the creation of the first domain in the forest), and those features add unique qualities to the forest root. Some of the special features include the following:

- Holding the configuration, schema information, and GC.
- Holding two forestwide FSMO (Flexible Single Master Operations) roles—the Schema Master and the Domain Naming Master—while the RID (relative ID) Master, PDC (primary domain controller) Emulator, and the Infrastructure Master continue to be implemented in each domain in the tree or forest.
- Holding two forestwide groups: Enterprise Admins and Schema Admins. These groups are initially created under mixed mode as global groups and then switch to universal groups when the domain is changed to native mode.

The Enterprise Admins group is authorized to make changes to the entire forest, as in the case of adding child domains. The Schema Admins group can make changes that affect the entire forest as well. Changes to the schema are forestwide. The default for both groups is that the administrator of the forest root is the only account added to these two forestwide groups.

Steps for Creating a Child Domain

You begin the AD Installation Wizard from the Run box under the Start menu by typing **`dcpromo.exe`**, just as you did in Chapter 4 to create the first domain. The options are similar, with some mild changes to indicate the connection to a parent domain. Once the wizard is activated, perform the following steps:

1. Select the Domain Controller for a New Domain radio button and click Next.
2. Select Create a New Child Domain in an Existing Domain Tree (rather than starting a completely separate tree, which would lead you down the path to creating a forest; see the "Steps for Creating a Forest" section later in this chapter). Then click Next.
3. Supply the username, password, and domain name (as shown in Figure 11.3) of a user account that is a member of the Enterprise Admins group. Remember, only members of this group can create child domains. Click Next.

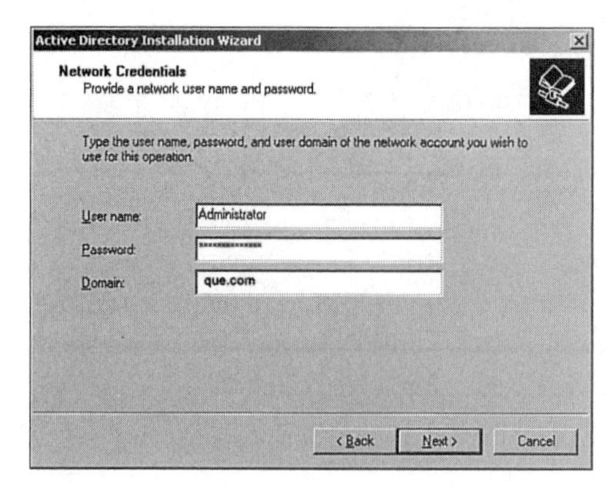

Figure 11.3 Provide an Enterprise Admins user account and the name of the domain.

4. Provide the DNS name of the parent and the name of the child domain. The wizard automatically places the two names together, as shown in Figure 11.4. Click Next.

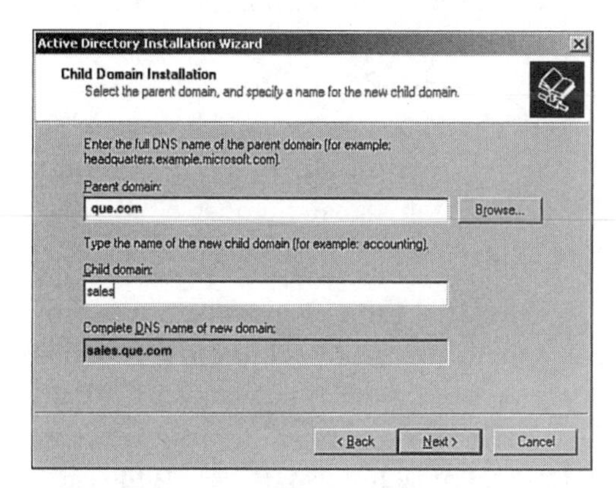

Figure 11.4 The child domain is appended to the parent DNS namespace.

5. The next wizard pages are familiar. They include the selection of database and transaction logs and then the selection of where to place your SYSVOL folder structure. Remember, for best performance, the database and transaction logs should be on separate physical disks and the SYSVOL folder must reside on an NTFS partition. Complete these pages and click Next twice to move forward.

6. The Permissions page asks whether you need pre–Windows 2000 compatibility. Select your choice and click Next.

7. Specify a password for restoration of your AD and then click Next.
8. Finally, check over your settings and complete the installation of your child domain.

Once your child domain is created, you can see the clear distinctions between your two domains. Each domain can have multiple DC replicas for fault tolerance and authentication speed, and each domain can have distinct security settings and policies. Administrative control would be somewhat segmented. There are other theories of segmented administrative control (for example, the creation of an empty root domain, discussed next).

Setting Up Empty Root Domains

You may need to decentralize the administration in an organization without creating separate root domains and forming forests (which we will discuss next). To keep security policies distinct and keep the number of administrators to a minimum, you can set up an empty root domain. The *empty root domain* does not hold OUs of its own. Unlike a normal root, which may be a headquarters for a company, it is a way of segmenting the two child domains for the purpose of administration. Each child domain can hold its own security policy and its own set of administrators, but the empty root would hold the Enterprise Admins group, which allows for a small number of administrators with full control over the organization.

One possible benefit of this setup is a true lockdown of administrative capability. Those few who are members of the Enterprise Admins group, notably a small group, can be requested to use smart card technology to verify themselves. It can even be required that a user from each child domain is necessary for the authentication to go through. One administrator holds the card; the other has the password.

If these are scenarios that still come under the tree heading, then what is a forest? We'll cover forests in the next section.

Forests

Much like a tree can be only one domain, a *forest* can be one domain tree. (Granted, this would be a very small forest.) A true forest, however, contains two or more root domains that are linked by a transitive trust, as shown in Figure 11.5. In using a forest arrangement, you have two distinct domains that do not share a common namespace. For example, `que.com` and braincore.net do not share a contiguous namespace, but they can be joined in a forest arrangement to allow sharing of resources.

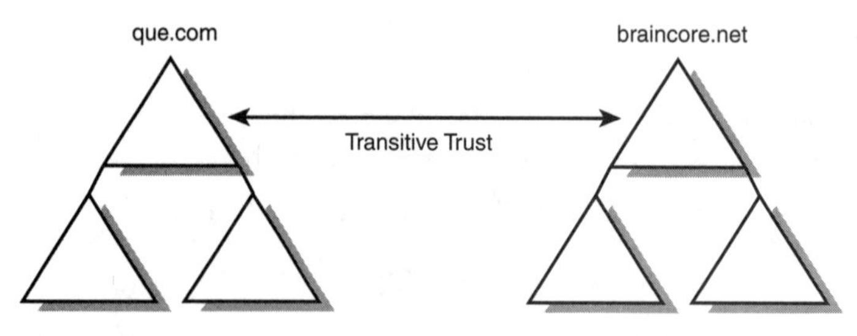

Figure 11.5 A forest contains two or more domains that are linked by a transitive trust.

The Design Decision to Create a Forest

Understanding what a forest is and what it means to your hierarchal namespace design structure is imperative. Before deciding that you must create a forest, you should establish a clear, nonpolitical reason for doing so. Following are a couple reasons why you might need to establish a forest:

- You establish a forest when two companies have a preexisting domain namespace that must be retained. The companies will probably be better left within their own spheres.
- Your company has subsidiary companies that prefer to have (for administrative control or comfortability reasons) their own namespaces.

Currently, Windows 2000 doesn't support the literal merging of two preexisting forests into one forest. These need to be established upon the installation of AD. In addition, one of the two domains must be preexisting, whereas the other would join the forest under its separate namespace.

Steps for Creating a Forest

As you did in Chapter 4 to create the first domain and to create child domains, to begin the AD Installation Wizard, select Start, Run. Then, in the Run box, type **dcpromo.exe**. The options are similar, with some minor changes to indicate the connection to a preexisting domain tree. Once the wizard is activated, follow these steps:

1. Select the Domain Controller for a New Domain radio button and click Next.
2. Select Create a New Domain Tree and then click Next.

3. Select Join an Existing Forest and then click Next.
4. Supply the username, password, and domain name of a user account that is a member of the Enterprise Admins group. Remember, only members of this group can join a preexisting forest. Click Next.
5. The next wizard pages are familiar. They concern the selection of database and transaction logs, as well as the selection of where you will place your SYSVOL folder structure. Remember, for best performance, the database and transaction logs should be on separate physical disks and the SYSVOL folder must reside on an NTFS partition. Complete these pages and click Next twice to move forward.
6. The Permissions page asks whether you need pre–Windows 2000 compatibility. Select your choice and click Next.
7. Specify a password for restoration of your AD and then click Next.
8. Finally, check over your settings and complete the installation of your child domain.

The trusts created between two domains of a forest are two-way transitive, which means, by extension, that the subsequent child domains underneath the roots that are joined are part of the trust relationships of the parent. A transitive trust relationship allows users of one domain tree to be authenticated by the other domain tree in order to share resources. The target domain—that is, the one with the resource that the user is trying to access—must verify that an account is located in the source domain, or the one in which the user resides. Keep in mind that although the transitive trust allows for authentication, this process can be a long one, depending on the levels of domains and forests that the request for authentication goes through. However, you can shorten the path for authentication by creating a shortcut trust.

Creating Shortcut Trusts

Shortcut trusts are two-way transitive trusts, but they shorten the trust path (the length of time and the number of domains that need to be pushed through for verification) that is taken for authentication, as shown in Figure 11.6. Another term used in conjunction with this type of trust is *explicit*, which can include shortcut trusts and external trusts (external trusts are covered in the "External Trusts" section later in the chapter). An *explicit trust* is defined as a trust that you create manually, as opposed to the trusts that are automatically created in Windows 2000.

Remember that explicit trusts are manually created. They include shortcut and external trusts. Shortcut trusts are used within a forest to shorten paths of verification. External trusts are used to connect with domains outside the forest to allow for the sharing of resources.

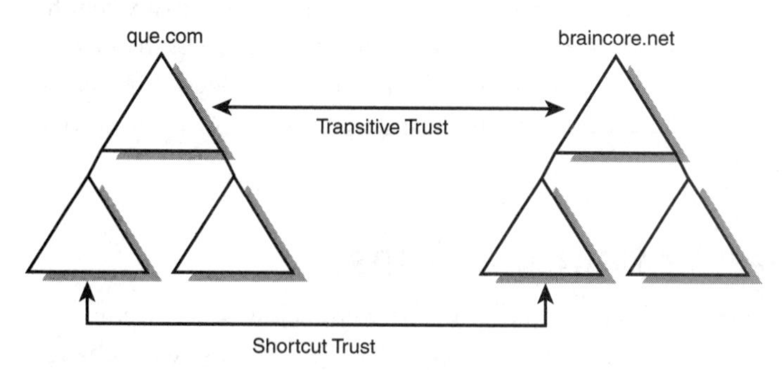

Figure 11.6 A shortcut trust shortens the trust path.

You manually create a shortcut trust from within the AD Domains and Trusts tool. Select the domain you want to involve, access the properties of that domain, and select the Trusts tab, as shown in Figure 11.7. You can specify a trust relationship in the same manner that NT 4 allowed you to create a manual trust. You can add a trusting domain or a trusted domain. You start the relationship from the trusted domain and include a password so that the trust cannot be stolen. Then, on the trusting domain, you perform the same procedure and use the password that was already specified.

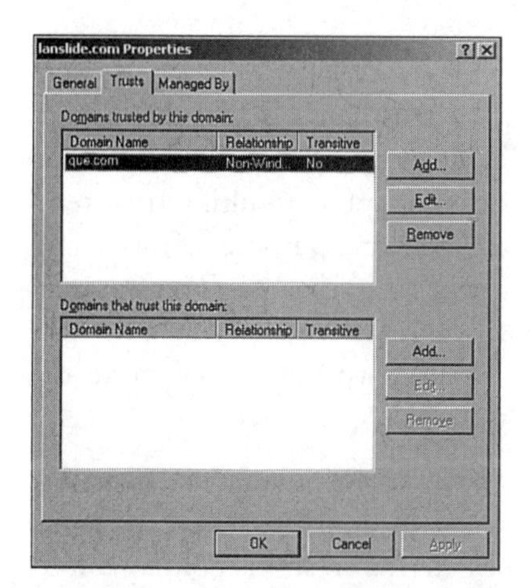

Figure 11.7 The Trusts tab is used to create additional trust possibilities.There are times, however, when a forest arrangement with transitive trusts will not completely fit the needs of the organizations involved. In that case, a forest arrangement needs to be expanded.

Multiple Forests

You may not officially start out creating multiple forests; in fact, you shouldn't even consider this a corporate plan. However, suppose you have Forest A and you have a business partnership with another company that has Forest B. You may have no intention of combining these two companies into one, but you may want to allow some authentication privileges. To accomplish this goal, you can create separate forests combined with an external trust relationship.

Why Create a Multiple Forest?

Forests hold a common schema and global directory. But what if you don't want this commonality? You know that you will need certain schema changes with additional classes and attributes in one forest that aren't necessary under the other; therefore, you might create a separate forest. Although you can synchronize the directories of two forests with the global directory, the general default rule is that there will not be a global directory.

Another reason for setting up multiple forests involves partnerships, as already stated. You may not want to mix too much business together. By using separate forests, you can separate resources between the companies and increase security by forming additional boundaries of verification before users can access certain resources that are available between forests.

External Trusts

Because the two forests have no reason to trust each other, they don't. Therefore, a manual trust relationship is needed, which would again be implemented by the AD Domains and Trusts tool. The resulting trust relationship allows users to be authenticated for the purpose of accessing resources. Permissions determine final access to a resource. This external trust relationship is one-way and nontransitive, as shown in Figure 11.8. It is possible, however, to create a second one-way trust that would make the appearance of a two-way trust (although these don't exist here).

You can see in the figure that Forest A has an arrow pointing to Forest B. This arrow indicates the direction of the trust relationship. Forest A has the actual resource—in this case, a printer. In essence, Forest A is holding out its hand to B and saying, "Here, you can use my printer if you want." That means Forest B has access to A. Forest A is the *trusting* domain (forest), and Forest B is the *trusted* domain (forest). Because the arrow only points way, Forest A cannot access anything in Forest B.

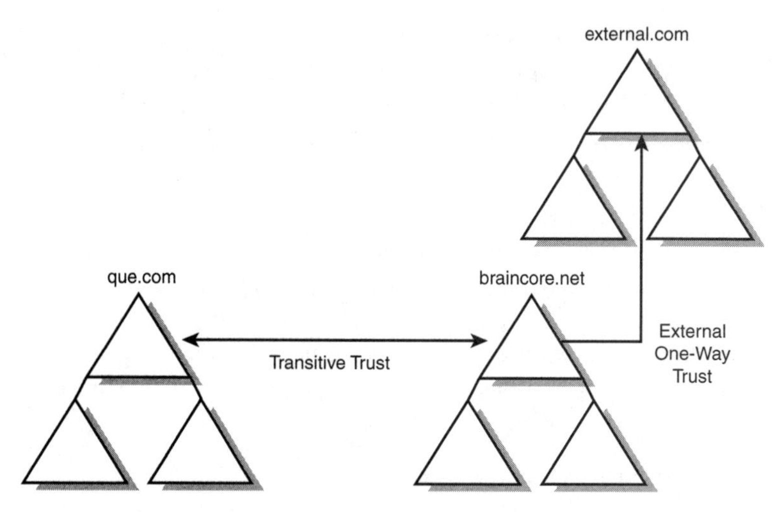

Figure 11.8 An external trust with multiple forests is often used to allow access to resources.

To further illustrate this concept, imagine you are loaning your car to someone. You may hold out the keys and say, "You can borrow my car." The person you're lending it to doesn't have to say, "Okay, and you take mine for a spin too." The person just has to take your keys.

Once this trust is established, permissions are involved. It is up to the administrators in Forest A to determine to what level that trust is going to be extended to users in Forest B. Not all users will be allowed to access resources, and even selected users will be given only so much leeway. Setting permissions allows each forest to maintain control over their forests and domains.

Creating and Verifying External Trusts

An external trust (also called a *nontransitive trust*) is a one-way trust relationship that can connect a Windows 2000 domain and one of the following:

- A Windows NT account domain
- A Windows 2000 domain under a separate forest
- A Kerberos v5 security realm

To create this nontransitive trust, you would use the AD Domains and Trusts tool and go to the properties of the domain with which you would like to establish the trust. Select Add and proceed with the steps to create the trust. The trust would, of course, need to be verified on the other end. In addition, you can use the same AD Domains and Trusts tool to verify your trust relationships by selecting the Verify/Reset option to ensure that the trust is still functional. You can also revoke the trust with the same tool by selecting the Remove button for the trust involved. Keep in mind that only nontransitive trusts are revocable. Transitive trusts that are created automatically are retained until the last DC in the domain that is trusted removes the trust.

Using Netdom

Available within the *Windows 2000 Resource Kit*, Netdom is a great command-line tool that you can use to manage domains and trust relationships. The kit includes all the various options and instructions for utilizing Netdom's many features, including the adding of trust relationships or the dissolving of trusts, the adding of workstations to a domain, and other command-line options.

Use Netdom to perform the following tasks:

- Join a Windows 2000 computer to a domain (NT 4 or Windows 2000 domains)
- Establish (one or two-way) trust relationships between domains, including trust for the following domain types: NT 4 domains, Windows 2000 domains, and Windows 2000 portions of a trust link to a Kerberos realm
- Manage trust relationships among domains
- View all trust relationships

To use Netdom, you need to open a command prompt. Then you can perform one of several options:

- To see your syntax options with Netdom, type the following:

  ```
  Netdom /?
  ```

- To verify a trust with Netdom, type the following:

  ```
  NETDOM TRUST trusting_domain /domain:trusted_domain /verify
  ```

- To revoke a trust with Netdom, type the following:

  ```
  NETDOM TRUST trusting_domain /domain:trusted_domain /remove
  ```

Kerberos v5

Developed by the a team at MIT, Kerberos is an open standard named after the three-headed dog in Greek mythology that guarded the gates of Hades. Like its mythological namesake, Kerberos has the ability to see in three directions, allowing you to view the fitting connection to a network-authentication protocol. If you are interested, MIT offers a free implementation of this protocol, although Windows 2000 contains a commercial version.

Like its Greek counterpart, there are three sides to Kerberos authentication:

- **User**—A client that has a need to access resources off a server.
- **Server**—Offers a service, but only to those that can prove their identity. That proven identity doesn't guarantee access to the service; it just proves that they even have a right to request a service.
- **Key Distribution Center (KDC)**—An intermediary between the client and the server that provides a way of vouching that the client is really who it says it is.

A Kerberos Transaction

You can read hundreds of different scenarios to explain how a Kerberos transaction works and still never absorb every last detail of it. The vocabulary is unique, and although there are many ways for the transaction to go astray, there is only one way for it to go through.

Under what circumstances is Kerberos necessary? Kerberos is needed when an individual is trying to initially log on to the network and receive an access token, as well as when an authorized user within a domain tries to access a specific resource or service on a server in the domain or forest. Several steps are involved in the process, depending on the domain levels an individual needs to flow through on his or her way to a resource.

Following is a typical Kerberos transaction. These steps correspond with Figure 11.9:

1. A user logs on to the domain by supplying a username, a password, and a domain choice. Kerberos steps in and checks the information against the DC's KDC database to verify that it knows the user.
2. If the user is valid, the user is provided a ticket-granting ticket (TGT). This means the user is preauthorized to access other resources on the domain. In future transactions, the client doesn't have to reauthenticate; rather, it presents the TGT to the KDC. This speeds up the process.
3. If you want to access a server—for example, the internal e-mail server in order to obtain your e-mail—you can now present that TGT to the

KDC ticket-granting server (TGS). This server will give you another ticket (although it doesn't take your first one because that was given to you at logon to validate you to other KDC servers in the domain). This other ticket does not grant permission to access the mail server; rather, it authenticates the client to the mail server.

4. The mail server checks to see whether you have permissions to read the email. If so, you will receive the e-mail.

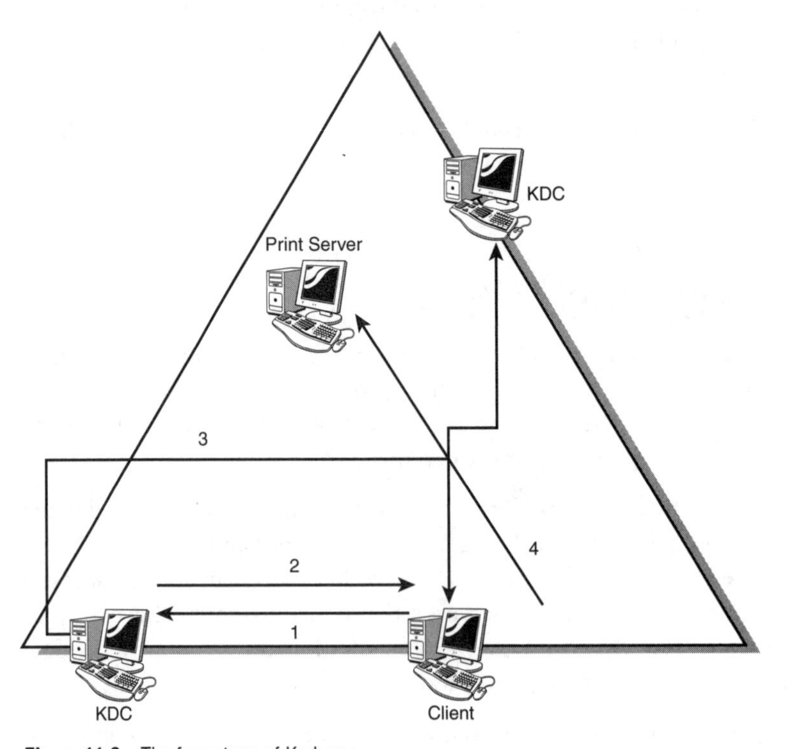

Figure 11.9 The four steps of Kerberos.

These steps provide a simple look into Kerberos under a single domain structure. Certainly, as additional domains are added to a tree and then as trees are combined into forests, the transactions become more complex.

Kerberos and Transitive Trusts

Now you understand how the Kerberos transaction works within a domain, but what happens when there are multiple domains under the same tree? By now you know that transitive trusts are established to allow authentication; however, we haven't discussed exactly how these trusts are established.

Establishing Transitive Trusts Across Multiple Domains

Let's take a look at the steps involved in establishing transitive trusts across multiple domains:

1. A user logs on to the domain (Domain `a.company.com`) by supplying a username, a password, and a domain choice. Kerberos steps in and checks the information against the DC's KDC database to verify that it knows the user.
2. If the user is valid, the user is given a TGT. This means the user is preauthorized to access other resources on the domain. In future transactions, the client doesn't have to reauthenticate, but rather, it presents the TGT to the KDC. This speeds up the process.
3. If the user wants to access a server in the root domain—for example, a print server that is sharing a printer—the user presents the TGT to the KDC within its domain and receives a session ticket that the user's client machine presents to `company.com`'s KDC.
4. The KDC in `company.com` takes the session ticket and provides another ticket that validates the user on the member server that is sharing the printer. The member server validates the request, and permissions then come into play. If the user has permissions, he or she will be able to print.

In the preceding scenario, the member server becomes what is called the *validation server*.

Establishing Transitive Trusts Across a Forest

Let's take the authentication to the next level: across a forest. Referring to Figure 11.10, notice a similar path to the path in Figure 11.9 that occurs with the Kerberos transaction. Let's take a look at the process of establishing transitive trusts across a forest step by step:

1. A user logs on to the domain (Domain `a.company.com`) by supplying a username, a password, and a domain choice. Kerberos steps in and checks the information against the DC's KDC database to verify that it knows the user.
2. If the user is valid, the user is provided a TGT. This means the user is preauthorized to access other resources on the domain. In future transactions, the client doesn't have to reauthenticate; instead, it presents the TGT to the KDC.

3. If the user wants to access a server in another domain in the forest—for example, a file server that is sharing folders with files—the user presents the TGT to the KDC within its domain and receives a session ticket that it presents to `company.com`'s KDC.

4. The KDC in `company.com` takes the session ticket and provides another ticket that validates the user on `corporation.com`.

5. The KDC in `corporation.com` provides the client with a ticket for `a.corporation.com`'s KDC.

6. The KDC in `a.corporation.com` issues a ticket that is then presented by the client to the file server. The member server that is sharing those folders accepts the ticket (if it is valid) and validates the client on that server. Then permissions determine whether the client can access the files.

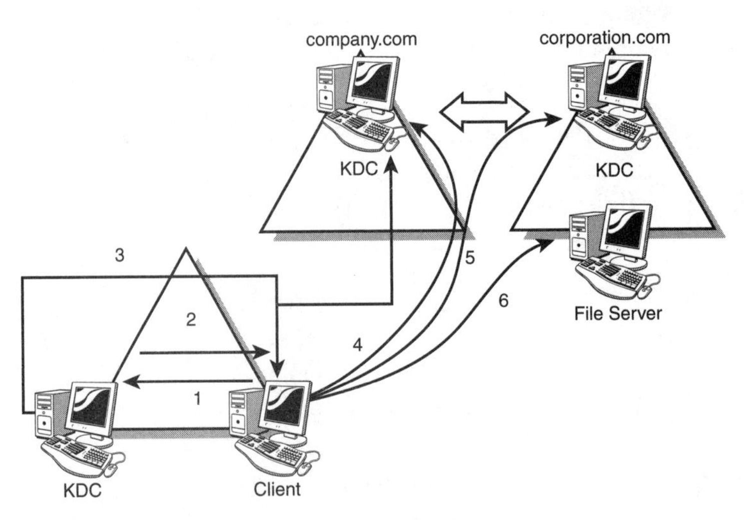

Figure 11.10 Kerberos transactions across a forest.

GC Servers

A GC contains location information for every object created, whether it was created by default upon installation or manually with the AD. It is also responsible for several other important features, such as the following:

- Logon validation of universal group membership
- User principal name logon validation through DC location
- Search capabilities for every object within an entire forest

The GC retains only frequently searched for attributes of an object. There is no need, nor would it be very practical from a replication standpoint, for the GC to retain every single detail of every single object. Then the GC would be, in fact, a DC.

There are several factors to consider with regard to the GC and how it functions to enhance logon validation under a native mode situation.

GC and Logon Validation

Universal groups (discussed in Chapter 5, "User and Group Administration") are centrally located within the GC. Which universal groups a user belongs to is quite important to the creation of an access token (discussed in Chapter 6, "Active Directory Delegation of Administrative Control"). Those access tokens are necessary for logon validation as well as resource access, so each token must include a user's universal group membership.

When a user logs on to a native mode domain (these are the only ones to include universal groups), the GC updates the DC as to the universal group information for that particular user's access token. But what if the GC is unavailable for some reason? Then the DC will use "cached credentials" to log the user on. However, those credentials would exist only if the user had logged on prior to this point. What if the user had never logged on and the GC is not available for the first logon? Then the user would not be able to log on to the domain and could either log on locally to the machine itself or wait for a GC to become available again.

Pay keen attention to the functionality of a GC. Your knowledge of GCs will enable you to determine if possible solutions will resolve defined problems.

User Principal Names and Logon Validation

Normally, an individual might log on to a domain with his or her common name and password. For example, suppose the user's common name is DonnaP and her password is bittb356. Now suppose Donna attempts to log on to system using her principal name—for example, `donna@globx.com`. If Donna is attempting to log on from a system that is in the accounting domain, the DC in `acct.globx.com` will not know her account. However, the DC will check with the GC, and that will, in turn, lead to the DC for the `globx.com` domain. The user will then be validated.

Adding GC Servers

Not all DCs are GC servers. Following are several thoughts to keep in mind:

- The first DC in a forest is a GC server.
- Any DC can be a GC server if set up to assume that function by the system administrator.
- Usually one GC is helpful in each site.
- You can create additional GCs if necessary.

To add another GC, perform the following tasks from AD Sites and Services:

1. Within the tree structure on the left pane, expand the DC that will be the new GC.
2. Right-click NTDS Settings and select Properties.
3. In the NTDS Settings Properties dialog box, under the General Tab, select the Global Catalog check box, as shown in Figure 11.11.

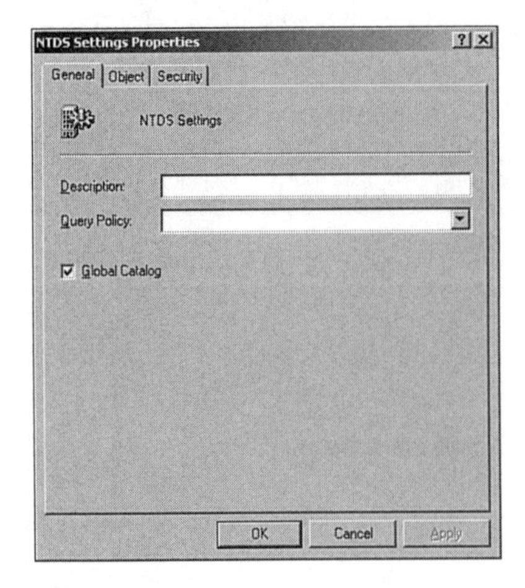

Figure 11.11 Adding a GC.

Universal Group Strategy

Chapter 5 gives a full explanation of the types of groups that Windows 2000 supports; however, we will review certain features in this chapter because Windows 2000 uses the GC to maintain universal group memberships. Because universal groups are replicated to all GCs in the entire forest, replication issues may arise. To minimize these issues, remember the following:

- Do not use universal groups unless they are necessary.
- Avoid placing individual users within a universal group. Membership information is replicated along with the group. It would be better to place members inside of another group, such as a global group, and then add the global group to the universal group. For example, if 100 users need to be part of a universal group, you should add them to a global group and then add that to the universal group. If any user information changes, that information will not affect replication of the GC.
- Make only the necessary changes to the membership of a universal group, because any change will initiate a replication of data. The entire membership list is re-replicated, rather than just an entry being changed. This could cause quite a bit of traffic.

Review of Universal Nesting

Chapter 5 provides an overview of group nesting. We'll review the information here, however, in case you have to determine the best way to implement a nesting of accounts within a universal group and then use that group to assign permissions to an object. Following is the procedure, in harmony with Figure 11.12:

1. Take user accounts and place them into a global group.
2. Take global groups and, if necessary, place them in other global groups.
3. Take global groups and nest them into universal groups.
4. Take universal groups and place them into domain local groups.
5. Finally, assign permissions for an object directory to a domain local (DL) group.

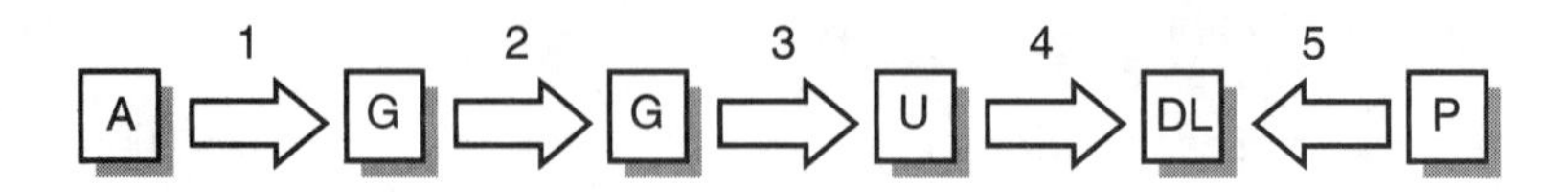

Key

A = User Accounts
G = Global Groups
U = Universal Groups
DL = Domain Local Groups
P = Permissions

Figure 11.12 Nesting accounts within groups.

Microsoft recommends this nesting method, because it prevents an unnecessary amount of replication between the GCs of universal group membership.

Practice Questions

Question 1

You are having some difficulties with a manually created trust relationship. You would like to verify that the trust exists. What tools can you use to verify the trust relationship's existence? [Check all correct answers]

- ❑ a. Active Directory Users and Computers
- ❑ b. Active Directory Domains and Trusts
- ❑ c. Secedit
- ❑ d. Netdom

Answers b and d are correct. The graphical tool to used to verify trust relationships is Active Directory Domains and Trusts, whereas the command-line utility is Netdom. Answer a is incorrect because Active Directory Users and Computers is a graphical tool that performs other tasks, including adding OUs, users, computers, and groups (security or distribution). Answer c is incorrect because Secedit is a command-line tool that provides various functions, such as the enforcement of security policy.

Question 2

You are attempting to create a universal group in a child domain. There are several child domains under a single parent domain that all have the ability to create universal groups, with the exception of this one. What would be a valid reason for such a dilemma?

- ❍ a. The domain is still residing in mixed mode.
- ❍ b. The domain is not connected by means of a shortcut trust to another child domain.
- ❍ c. The domain is still in native mode and needs to be converted.
- ❍ d. You are attempting to create the group on a backup domain controller (BDC).

Answer a is correct. If you are still residing in a mixed-mode scenario, your groups will be only domain local and global. Universal groups exist only in native mode. Answer b is incorrect because shortcut trusts speed up authentication toward resources and do not affect security groups. Answer c is incorrect because native mode is preferable to any other mode, so you would not want to convert from native mode to some other mode. Answer d is incorrect because domains in Windows 2000 do not use BDCs, nor would it matter which DC you tried to implement a security group on if the domain was not in native mode.

Question 3

Two private investment banking firms are merging together to form one company. The first currently has a Windows 2000 domain using Active Directory with special modifications to the schema to support the Exchange 2000 messaging servers that the company uses. The second company is using NT 4.0 DCs but is in the process of planning the move to Windows 2000. The second company would like to retain a separate namespace. In addition, the second company is preparing to implement a third-party messaging solution that will require for them to maintain a unique schema. Which of the following domain structures should these companies implement to share resources?

❍ a. A single domain tree

❍ b. An empty root domain with two child domains

❍ c. A forest with two domain trees

❍ d. Two distinct forests with external trust relationships

Answer d is correct. Because the request has been presented to maintain separate schemas, the only way to accomplish this task is to retain separate forests altogether. This would also require external trusts if they want to share resources. Answers a, b and c are incorrect because they all provide a solution with a single schema, whereas the request is to provide separate schemas.

Question 4

You have a parent domain called **parent.com** with three child domains: **a.parent.com**, **b.parent.com**, and **c.parent.com**. Domain A shares resources in Domain C quite frequently. What would speed up access to those resources for Domain A?

❍ a. A shortcut trust from A to C

❍ b. A private Kerberos KDC server

❍ c. A shortcut trust from C to A

❍ d. A two-way transitive trust by making **a.parent.com** a child domain of **c.parent.com**

Answer c is correct. A shortcut trust where C trusts A allows A to access C more efficiently. The Kerberos authentication still remains in effect through this new trust relationship. Answer a is incorrect because the trust is going in the wrong direction to be effective. Answer b is incorrect because Kerberos servers are functionally hidden and not above domain trust relationship boundaries without shortcut trusts. Answer d is incorrect because a child domain cannot be a child of two domains at the same time.

Question 5

What type of two-way trust relationship is created when a child domain attaches itself to a parent domain?

❍ a. Multimaster trust

❍ b. Transitive trust

❍ c. Shortcut trust

❍ d. External or nontransitive trust

Answer b is correct. Two-way transitive trusts are created in the joining of child domains or two domain trees into a forest. Answer a is incorrect because multimaster is a form of replication in Windows 2000, not a trust relationship. Answer c is incorrect because a shortcut trust is not automatically created between child/parent domains. Answer d is incorrect because these trusts are used between separate forests.

Question 6

Two companies have merged into one structure and are required by senior management to be under one contiguous namespace that retains a common schema. The network administrative departments, however, don't want one to be head over the other. What can be formed to allow for segmentation of administrative strength between each domain?

- ❍ a. Separate forests
- ❍ b. GC servers
- ❍ c. KDC servers
- ❍ d. An empty root domain

Answer d is correct. An empty root domain would allow for unique administrative control while still retaining a common schema and contiguous namespace. Answer a is incorrect because separate forests do not hold either a common schema or namespace. Answer b is incorrect because GC servers are useful for searches and logon validation but not for administrative segregation. Answer c is incorrect because KDC servers are part of the Kerberos authentication procedure, not the administrative control procedures.

Question 7

Billy is attempting to log on to a domain called **research.corp.com**, although his user account is located in **corp.com**. Billy is using his user principal name, **billy@corp.com**. What will assist Billy in logging on to the system?

- ❍ a. Organizational Units
- ❍ b. Global Catalog servers
- ❍ c. Additional domain controllers
- ❍ d. Kerberos v5

Answer b is correct. Global Catalog servers search for the domain information necessary during logon when an individual uses his or her user principal name. Answer a is incorrect because Organizational Units assist with delegation of administrative control. Answer c is incorrect because, although this will add fault tolerance, it will not assist in logon validation. Answer d is incorrect because, although Kerberos is used to verify authentication to the resources, it doesn't assist in the location of the domain controller that will validate a user.

Question 8

Danielle is the design analyst that determines the AD structure for a company called MercuryNet. The structure takes into account the physical distribution of the company, with a headquarters in Edison, NJ and three branch offices located in Italy, China, and Fiji. She determines a need to create a headquarters domain root called **mercurynet.com** with three child domains beneath. By default, how many Global Catalog servers will there be for this widely dispersed solution?

- ❍ a. One
- ❍ b. Three
- ❍ c. Four
- ❍ d. Zero

Answer a is correct. The first DC for the entire forest will contain the role of Global Catalog. By default, this is the only GC in the entire forest. It is recommended that the administrator manually create additional GCs in remote locations and do so at a time when it will be the most convenient for network traffic between the two GCs. GCs hold a copy of every object in the entire forest and a subset of attributes for each of those objects. Answers b and c are incorrect because they provide for too many. Answer d is also incorrect because there is always at least one GC for the forest.

Question 9

You want to reduce the replication between Global Catalog servers caused by universal group membership. Which of the following methods of group placement would assist in this?

- ❍ a. Place universal groups into local groups.
- ❍ b. Place global groups into universal groups.
- ❍ c. Place global groups into other global groups.
- ❍ d. Place universal groups into global groups.

Answer b is correct. By placing global groups into universal groups, you reduce the need for replication because changes made to individual users within a global group will not force replication of those changes between the GC servers. Answer a is incorrect because placing universal groups into local groups, although providing a decent method of permission allocation, would not assist with replication. Answer c is incorrect because placing global groups into other global groups will not assist in reducing replication. Answer d is incorrect because placing universal groups into global groups doesn't eliminate replication issues.

Question 10

You are dealing with two companies that need to maintain separate security boundaries as well as separate namespace domains. What type of configuration would you implement?

- ❍ a. Single domain
- ❍ b. Domain tree
- ❍ c. Empty root domain tree
- ❍ d. Forest

Answer d is correct. A forest arrangement is the only way to maintain not only separate security boundaries but separate namespace domains. Answer a is incorrect because a single domain would reside under both the same security and the same namespace. Answer b is incorrect because a single domain tree, although providing security distinction between domains, would still be under a contiguous namespace. Answer c is incorrect because an empty root domain would, again, be under a contiguous namespace.

Need to Know More?

Bersinic, Damir and Rob Scrimger. *MCSE Training Guide (70-217): Installing and Administering a Windows 2000 Directory Services Infrastructure*. Que Publishing. Indianapolis, IN, 2002. ISBN 0735709769.

Chapter 3, "Building Your Active Directory Structures," includes information on how to implement forest structures within your AD domains.

Boswell, William. *Inside Windows 2000 Server*. New Riders. Indianapolis, IN, 2000. ISBN 1562059297.

Bill Boswell is noted in the industry as being an excellent instructor, and he does a perfect job of explaining Kerberos as it relates to Windows 2000. This is a worthy resource for your shelves.

Hudson, James and Sean Fullerton. *Special Edition Using Active Directory*. Que Publishing. Indianapolis, IN, 2001. ISBN 0789724340.

Chapter 11, "Domains, Trees and Forests," goes into greater detail on the need to expand the domain arrangement to include child domains and forests.

Iseminger, David. *Active Directory Services for Microsoft Windows 2000 Technical Reference*. Microsoft Press. Redmond, WA, 2000. ISBN 0735606242.

This book is a great reference for Active Directory design issues, specifically the creation of forests and the various trusts that become a part of the verification process.

Search the Microsoft Knowledge Base online at `http://support.microsoft.com` and consider the following two articles: Q313994 and Q232179.

Active Directory Replication

Terms you'll need to understand:

- ✓ Multiple-master replication
- ✓ Loose consistency
- ✓ Originating update
- ✓ Replicated update
- ✓ Change notification process
- ✓ Globally unique stamp
- ✓ Property version number
- ✓ Propagation dampening
- ✓ Update sequence numbers
- ✓ Connection object
- ✓ Direct replication partner
- ✓ Directory partitions
- ✓ Global Catalog server
- ✓ Knowledge Consistency Checker
- ✓ Sites
- ✓ Site link bridge

Techniques you'll need to master:

- ✓ Understanding Active Directory replication
- ✓ Understanding how replication conflicts are resolved

- ✓ Knowing how to examine replication traffic
- ✓ Understanding the difference between intersite and intrasite replication

When a change, such as the creation of a group or the addition of a new user, is made on a Windows 2000 network, that change is recorded in a copy of the Active Directory (AD). A copy of AD exists on every domain controller (DC) in the domain (with a subset of data stored on every Global Catalog server in the forest). Because each copy of AD must contain the same data, a process known as *replication* takes place. Replication ensures that data recorded in one copy is disseminated to all other copies in the domain.

Because any DC in Windows can accept a change, we can say that DCs on a Windows 2000 network are *peers*. Windows 2000 uses *multiple-master* (or *multimaster*) *replication* to do its work. That is, each DC is a master for its copy of AD. The DC can accept changes and will then propagate them out to other DCs with which it is partnered. We examine this process in some detail in this chapter.

To design and control AD data, you must fully understand the process of replication. Without this knowledge, you won't be able to troubleshoot problems you may encounter or understand how to maintain your replication topology. Consistency of data is a key requirement for AD to work properly in your environment, and it should therefore be one of your prime concerns.

In simple terms, when we talk about replication, we are referring to updating information from one DC to another. This process can also be thought of as copying changed AD data. When a change is made on one DC, all DCs in the domain must be synchronized with this change. In the context of two or three DCs, this concept is easy to envision. However, when considering an enterprise network where there are hundreds of DCs dispersed throughout geographical locations that possibly cross different continents, you begin to see why knowledge of this process is so important.

Administrators do not choose which DC is updated when they make changes to AD. The process of selecting a DC to accept a change is transparent. It is then up to the replication process to replicate this event to other DCs.

Of course, replication takes time. If a change is made at a single DC in, say, Houston, it will take time for the change to appear on a DC in London. This is known as *loose* consistency. A network is not considered to be fully converged until all changes have been copied to all other DCs. In a busy network spread across the globe, it might appear that your network is never fully converged. This is to be expected.

Because no DC maintains control over the AD data, Windows 2000 is able to scale better than older network operating systems. This is because administrators can make changes to AD data on the DC that is closest to them on the network. Replication makes sure everyone else knows about the change.

There are exceptions to this rule. For instance, a set of DCs called *operations masters* have a unique task to perform in Windows 2000. We discuss operation masters in Chapter 13, "Operations Masters."

AD replication takes your network into consideration in order to optimize performance. It does this by using sites. *Sites* in Windows 2000 are groups of IP (Internet Protocol) subnets that have fast connectivity between them. IP subnets that are divided by a WAN connection (slower than 10Mbps) should be divided into multiple sites. Replication within a site (and therefore with fast connectivity) takes place automatically and assumes a fast, reliable link. Replication between different sites takes place on a schedule and is designed specifically to reduce network bandwidth usage. We'll look more closely at how sites optimize AD later in this chapter.

The Replication Process

Replication occurs when an update is made to a copy of AD. An update is not only the addition of a piece of data, such as a new user or group, but can also be the deletion of an object, the moving of an object, or a modification to a single property of an object.

Each DC must be able to accept changes from both administrators and other copies of the AD. Although replication takes place throughout an enterprise, note that at any given time, a DC can replicate its changes to only one other server. This means that AD replication occurs between two DCs at a time. Because the data is copied this way, replication conflicts may occur. All conflicts are dealt with automatically following a well-defined process. We discuss this issue in greater detail in the "Conflict Resolution" section later in this chapter.

Because the data in the AD is so important, mechanisms are required to ensure that any change it accepts is either completely committed (recorded in its entirety) or completely rejected (rejected in its entirety.) For instance, if a name is changed for a user object, the AD needs to commit either the entire name change or none of it. This prevents a DC from recording a partial change.

AD performs two types of updates:

- **Originating update**—Occurs only the first time a change is made to an AD replica
- **Replicated update**—Occurs as a result of this change

Examining a simple change to AD data allows you to easily see how these two terms are used. Imagine you have three DCs. An administrator logs on to the network and makes a change to a user object's properties. A DC is contacted, and the change is made. This change is *committed* to the AD replica at this DC. Because this is the first time this change has been made within AD, it is considered an originating update. The change must then be copied from this DC to the other DCs on the network. Replication takes care of this task. When the change is made at the other DCs, it is considered a replicated update, simply because the change did not originate at either of these DCs.

Latency and the Notification Process

Recognize that AD replication takes time, and a delay will occur before the data in the originating update is made to every DC on the network. This delay is known as *latency*. Because of how the notification process works, some level of latency will always occur.

AD uses a system—the *change notification process*—that takes care of replicating data from one DC to another. Here's how it works: When a change is committed at a DC, the replication engine kicks in and waits for a configurable period of time. By default, this period is five minutes. During this time, the replication engine collects all changes made to the replica. This is more efficient because all changes within the configurable period are replicated—rather than AD having to replicate each change as it occurs.

Once this period has expired, the DC sends a *change notification*. This notification is sent to one of the DC's replication partners. Remember what we said earlier: Each DC replicates, one at a time, with its direct partners only. AD replication does not use broadcasting to replicate data; the entire process is controlled and systematic.

A DC can have more than one direct partner. After the first partner is contacted, the DC waits a configurable period of time before letting another replication partner know about the change. By default, this is 30 seconds. After this time, the partner *pulls* the changes.

Data is never pushed from one DC to another; it is always pulled. This occurs after the DC with the change has been through the notification process.

A single DC never has a replication partner that is more than three hops away. A *hop* is a trip across a router (each router is one hop). Given this fact, you can calculate the maximum amount of time for a change to propagate from a single DC to each replication partner. Say, for example, there are three hops (or steps) from the DC with the change to a replication partner. The maximum time for a change to replicate is 15 minutes (the five-minute configurable time lapse per DC). This may or may not include the 30-second delay.

If a DC does not receive a change for a period of time (by default, an hour), it will automatically begin the replication process. This ensures that the DC gathers data even if it missed the notification.

In addition, for security-conscious data, an event called *urgent replication* occurs. For instance, an account lockout is an urgent replication, and it takes place without waiting for the configurable period. Most replication, however, takes place through the normal method.

Types of AD Conflicts

Because enterprise networks are large, busy entities where administrators are widely dispersed, replication conflicts are bound to occur. Conflict resolution takes care of this issue and maintains the integrity of the data stored within AD.

Conflicts can occur under several different circumstances. Understanding the processes that AD employs to deal with this issue helps you understand why conflicts occur.

Let's look at several types of conflicts. Then, in the next section, we'll discuss how to solve them.

Conflicting Attribute Changes

This type of conflict occurs when an attribute of an object is changed by different administrators. For instance, say your organization has a help desk ticketing system. A user calls in this morning and wants her last name attribute changed. The help desk operator enters this request into the ticketing system.

An administrator in Houston opens the help desk system and sees that a change has been requested. He pulls up the AD User and Computer snap-in and makes the change. At the same time, an administrator in London also sees the ticket. The London administrator also makes the change but accidentally mistypes the new name, transposing two characters.

Because both administrators have changed this attribute, replication will eventually find a conflict. This conflict must be resolved.

Adding/Moving Objects

Adding or moving objects can also cause a conflict to occur. In this case, an object is added to a container—for instance, a user object being added to an Organizational Unit (OU)—while the parent object is simultaneously being deleted on another DC.

When replication takes place, a conflict inevitably occurs when the user object is unable to be added to the OU on an AD replica because the parent object no longer exists. In effect, the user object is orphaned.

Duplicate Names

Because objects can be easily moved from one location in AD to another, naming conflicts may occur. Say, for example, an administrator moves an object from one parent object to another, and at the same time, another administrator moves a different object to the same location. If both objects have the same relative distinguished name, a conflict will occur.

Note that AD works differently from previous schemes Microsoft has devised for this type of replication (as seen in Microsoft Exchange 5.5). Previous models have replicated at the object level. This meant that if you changed the Description attribute of an object, every attribute of that object had to be replicated. This is far more likely to cause conflicts within the database. AD, on the other hand, replicates at the *attribute level*. This means that in the example given, only the description of the object would be replicated, thereby conserving bandwidth and reducing conflicts.

Conflict Resolution

Conflicts are easily resolved through the use of *globally unique stamps*. These stamps are recorded as part of a change to AD data and then travel with the AD data as it is replicated throughout the enterprise. If needed, these stamps can be used to resolve any conflicts in a logical and predetermined fashion.

A stamp consists of three pieces of key data, which are used one piece at a time to resolve conflicts. If the first piece of data fails to resolve the conflict,

AD uses the second piece of data. If that also fails, the third piece is used. The third piece is effectively a tiebreaker, and it will always resolve a conflict.

The three pieces of data that make up the globally unique stamp are as follows:

- **Property version number (PVN)**—The PVN is stored by every attribute. All attributes start with PVN=1. Each time an originating update takes place, this number increments by one. During replication, the property with the highest PVN prevails. For example, a PVN of 2 always overwrites a PVN of 1. Conflicts can still occur when an attribute with a PVN of 1 is changed in two different locations. In this case, the PVN of each would be 2, and a conflict would occur. If this attribute does not resolve a conflict, the second piece of data is used.
- **Timestamp**—This attribute records both the time and date the change was made. It is based on the system clock of the DC recording the originating update. In this case, the latest time prevails. So, a change made to an object's attribute at 2:15 p.m. would beat a change made at 2:05 p.m. In the unlikely event of changes being made at the same time, a third tiebreaker is employed.
- **Server GUID**—Every DC has a GUID (globally unique identifier) that allows it to differentiate itself from every other DC in the enterprise. This value is stored in the Invocation ID property of the server object. The highest server GUID always prevails.

In the case of an object's attributes being changed at two different DCs, the aforementioned globally unique stamp will resolve conflicts. In the vast majority of cases, this takes care of potential problems.

Making sure the DCs in your enterprise are time-synced is vital. Although AD is not dependent on the time set at each server, the tie-breaking mechanism can sometimes rely on it. It is common for time on a server to drift a little, or for WAN links to go down and for a time problem to occur without you knowing it. Make certain you take this into account when designing your Windows 2000 network.

One case where the globally unique stamp does not help is when objects are moved between containers. For example, say an administrator in London moves an object from the "Sales" Organizational Unit to the "Sales US" Organizational Unit. At the same time, in Houston, Texas, another administrator deletes the "Sales US" Organizational Unit. Of course, now we have a problem, because by the time the originating update made in London replicates to Houston, the Organizational Unit is not going to exist!

In this case, the object is moved to the LostAndFound container. This container is a catchall for all objects that have been orphaned. You should review this container periodically and move objects to their rightful homes or delete them as necessary. The globally unique stamp is not used in this situation.

Another instance in which the globally unique stamp alone does not remedy the situation is when two objects with the same relative distinguished name are moved to the same container. In this case, the globally unique stamp is used; however, it must be used with a GUID. The object that prevails retains the relative distinguished name. The other object is renamed in the following format:

relative distinguished name + CNF: + * + the object's GUID

The addition of the GUID ensures that this name is always unique.

Preventing Replication Loops

As explained earlier in this chapter, replication takes place between DCs automatically. On complex networks, this means that replication is unlikely to take place using the same route each time. Sometimes the route might be very direct (and therefore more efficient), whereas other times the route might be more complex. This is to be expected on complex routed networks with WAN links. Network topologies can change as routers are reset, new segments are brought online, or older segments suffer a temporary failure.

Because network topologies can change, replication can sometimes traverse the network in somewhat unpredictable ways. Therefore, a DC can receive a single update from multiple partners. Of course, receiving a single update multiple times would be inefficient, so to take care of this, Windows 2000 uses a process called *propagation dampening*. Propagation dampening is designed to prevent unnecessary data from being pulled across your network.

Propagation dampening is achieved with one piece of data: an update sequence number (USN). This data is used to record the number of updates a system has received from its replication partners. Let's look at each at update sequence numbers in more detail.

USNs

To calculate which data should be replicated and which data has already been replicated, AD uses USNs. These are stored in memory, in a table called the up-to-dateness table. This table has an entry for every DC in the domain, along with the USN at the time of the last originating update for that DC. For instance, if DC A performed an originating update to its AD replica that caused its USN to increment to a value of 130, each up-to-dateness table stored on DCs in the domain would record an entry of "A-130."

USNs can be used to prevent unnecessary data being sent across the network. As an example, say that a DC contacts a replication partner and says, in effect, "I have an originating update. When I wrote it to my replica, it made my USN increment to 130. Do you want it?" It is then a simple matter for the receiving DC to read its up-to-dateness table and see whether it already has this update. If it does, no replication is necessary. If it doesn't, it can pull the data. Remember that, as previously mentioned, replication in AD is pulled only; data is never pushed across the wire.

Topology for Replication

AD replication is tied to the physical topology of your network. In an ideal Windows 2000 network, the physical topology closely matches the topology that is used to replicate AD data. In Windows 2000, this is achieved automatically by internal mechanisms (which are defined and discussed in this section), using data provided by the system designers/system administrators.

Because replication takes place between DCs, for replication to be efficient, AD needs to take into account the proximity of DCs to each other and the amount of available bandwidth between those DCs. Once it has this information, you can let AD automatically calculate a path between DCs, and it can even determine which DCs should be allowed to talk to each other. Once this setup is in place, you have a *replication topology*.

Replication topologies can change on the fly. If AD finds that a DC has been moved or that the IP subnets on your network have changed, it automatically calculates whether changes should be made to the replication topology in your organization. You should not be worried about this; it is normal AD behavior.

DCs that swap AD data are known as *replication partners*. AD stores information in what is termed a *connection object* that defines these partners. A connection object is a one-way path between DCs, usually created in pairs to facilitate two-way communication between DCs. By having multiple connection objects, you can quickly build an entire replication infrastructure for your Windows 2000 network.

Connection objects can be created automatically or manually. Manually created connection objects override automatic connections. Of course, considerable administrative overhead is associated with creating these manually. Having them created and maintained automatically is far better. We will look at this process in the "Knowledge Consistency Checker" section later in this chapter.

Replication partners can act as both a source for AD data and as a conduit for data. In other words, a replication partner can be either a *direct replication partner* or a *transitive replication partner*. In the case of the former, the partner is acting as a source for originating updates. In the case of the latter, data is being obtained indirectly from other replication partners.

You can force replication to occur immediately by right-clicking a connection object and selecting Replicate Now. With the Replication Monitor program, you can view transitive replication partners.

Directory Partitions

The data stored within AD is actually broken out into three distinct areas called *directory partitions*. Each of these partitions records and stores a specific type of information. In addition, each can have a different replication topology, largely because not all DCs need to contain the same partitions.

The three directory partitions that exist in AD are as follows:

- **Domain partition**—Holds data regarding domain-specific objects, including users, groups, and computers
- **Schema partition**—Contains data that defines which objects can be created within AD and specifies rules regarding these objects, such as mandatory properties
- **Configuration partition**—Contains information about your AD structure, such as the domains and DCs that exist

DCs do not necessarily contain the same partitions. For instance, each DC in a forest must contain the same schema and configuration partition. However, DCs from different domains store different domain partitions. Each partition has its own replication topology—although most of the time, they end up being the same.

Global Catalog Servers

Clients on a Windows 2000 network perform searches within their local domain and outside their local domain. These include searches for users, groups, or resources such as shared folders. The data the user needs to search is stored in the domain partition. Because DCs in the user's local domain do not hold data from the domain partition of other domains, a special type of server, called a *Global Catalog (GC) server*, is needed to facilitate this function.

A GC stores data about all the domains in a forest. It is not a complete replica of the domain partition; instead, it contains a subset of data from other domains. This subset includes object names and the most commonly searched-for attributes, such as user and group names. GCs are recorded in the configuration partition of the directory so that other DCs are aware of them.

Knowledge Consistency Checker

Creating the replication topology on your own would be a daunting task. Although you can do so, this task is best left to the Knowledge Consistency Checker (KCC).

The KCC is a process that runs on each DC and is used to automatically generate the replication topology for a forest. Each time it runs, it can recalculate the efficiency of routes between DCs and configure the topology accordingly. To do this, it uses the site and subnet information that has been configured within AD. (We look at sites in more detail in the next section.) Because the KCC is constantly checking the efficiency of the connections, it can automatically detect whether a problem has occurred and can reconfigure the topology to work around DCs that are down or temporarily unavailable.

As a safeguard against possible problems, the default topology for replication is a two-way (bidirectional) ring. Also, the KCC ensures that an originating update never takes more than three hops to be replicated.

Optimizing AD Replication with Sites

Before the KCC can do its work, it requires some basic information about your network, including data on the physical aspects of the infrastructure. You supply this data by creating sites. A *site* is an object in AD that includes a list of Transmission Control Protocol/Internet Protocol (TCP/IP) subnets. Sites are parts of your network that enjoy high availability because of fast network connectivity. Once your sites have been created, you must create connection objects between them (these connection objects would imitate the physical connection of your network.) The KCC then uses this information to build the necessary replication infrastructure. By creating sites, you are effectively controlling replication on your network—albeit via an automatic process.

By adding subnets to a site, you are implying that these subnets have fast and reliable connectivity among them. You add server objects to site objects. Once a server is part of a site, the KCC can calculate a path through the network in question, with the assumption that the servers can talk to each other quickly.

The first site is created automatically when the first server is installed on your Windows 2000 network. Although this site is given the name Default-First-Site-Name, you can assign it a more meaningful name.

DCs in a site do not need to belong to the same Windows 2000 domain. The reason is that three partitions of AD are to be replicated, and although replicating the domain partition between controllers of different domains does not make sense, this connectivity could be exploited for the schema and configuration partitions.

Sites are used for many different tasks in AD. Aside from their use in AD replication, they are also used to optimize logon traffic and to select shared folders that use the Distributed File System (Dfs). They are also used for Remote Installation Services (RIS). In all cases, they are used to calculate the local server that can most efficiently provide the service. If a client contacts a server on the same subnet as itself, it is safe to assume processing time will be reduced.

Replication Within a Site and Between Sites

Although replication occurs both within a site and between sites, there are subtle differences between the two situations. Replication within a site assumes a highly available network with a lot of bandwidth. Therefore, the replicated data is sent uncompressed. Because the DC does not have to take time to compress data, there is less of a load on each DC. However, your network bandwidth suffers because a lot more data goes across the wire. The replication process is triggered by the notification process mentioned earlier in this chapter.

In contrast, replication between sites occurs on a schedule. In addition, the data is compressed before being sent. This means that the load on servers is greater, but the bandwidth requirement is reduced.

You need to be concerned about two parameters:

- **The schedule**—Defines how often replication takes place. This option allows you to configure replication to take place during off-hours or times when the most bandwidth is available.
- **The replication interval**—Defines how often DCs check for changes during periods when replication is allowed to occur.

Keep in mind that an incorrectly configured schedule and interval can prevent replication from ever occurring. For instance, if the schedule allows replication to occur only between 6:00 a.m. and 7:00 a.m., replication will only ever occur during a single hour of the day. If the interval is set for every two hours, starting at 7:00 a.m., the interval gets checked only on odd hours (7:00 a.m., 9:00 a.m., 11:00 a.m., 1:00 p.m., 3:00 p.m., and so on). Notice that there is no overlap between the schedule and the interval. In this case, the interval is not starting during the scheduled window; therefore, replication would not take place.

You must have an overlapping schedule for replication to work. In the case of multiple sites, the replication schedule may not be overlapping, but it could cause replication to be slow. For instance, suppose you have three sites—A, B, and C. If the replication schedule between A and B is 7:00 a.m. to 8:00 a.m., and the replication schedule between B and C is 2:00 p.m. to 4:00 p.m., then the updated data from A won't arrive in C until 2:00 p.m. at the earliest. This will cause it to appear that you have a replication problem.

Bridgehead Servers

Replication between sites occurs from a single point. In other words, data is exchanged between two DCs in each site and then is replicated within the site using normal mechanisms for change. These servers are known as *bridgehead servers* and are chosen automatically.

You can also select a bridgehead server or even a group of preferred servers. The process that chooses bridgehead servers is called the Intersite Topology Generator (ISTG). You simply select the servers you want to use as preferred within the site.

Protocols That Support Replication

It might sound obvious to state that DCs that want to communicate must use the same protocol. However, you should note that in terms of replication, we are referring to the protocol used specifically by AD to achieve our goal.

Two different protocols can be used:

- **Remote Procedure Call (RPC)**—This primary protocol is used exclusively for replication within a site.
- **Simple Mail Transfer Protocol (SMTP)**—This protocol has a limited implementation and is used when connections between DCs are unreliable. To use SMTP, the DCs must be in different domains and in different sites.

When replicating between sites, you can use RPC or SMTP. The preferred protocol is RPC over IP (which means the RPC calls are wrapped in IP packets for transport across the wire).

In addition to the aforementioned limitations of using SMTP, also note that SMTP cannot be used to replicate all partitions of AD. Because the domain partition has dependencies that fall outside of simply replicating AD data, such as file transfer using the File Replication Service (FRS), SMTP cannot be used for the domain partition. However, SMTP is useful when a direct connection cannot be made between DCs, because SMTP data can be stored and forwarded by mail servers. This ability can sometimes compensate for poor connections.

Site Links and Their Default Settings

Site links are used to manage replication when it occurs between sites. These settings can be used to configure site links to replicate during certain intervals and to use specific protocols. The options are as follows:

- **Transport**—The protocol you want to use for the site link.
- **Member Sites**—Two or more sites that will be part of the site link.
- **Cost**—The cost of a link is a value that is used to determine which site link is used if there are multiple site links between different sites. Cost should be based on the speed and reliability of the link. The better the speed and reliability, the lower the cost (increasing the likelihood that the link will be used). This value can be between 1 and 32,767. The default setting is 100.
- **Schedule**—This defines the window in which replication can occur. The range is one-hour increments configured over a seven-day week. The default is for the site link to be available at all times.
- **Replication Interval**—This defines how often replication happens within a window. The range is from 15 minutes to 10,080 minutes. The default is three hours.

You should familiarize yourself with the settings that can be configured when creating a site link.

Site Link Bridge

The *site link bridge* is an extension of the sites concept we covered earlier in this chapter. You use site link bridges when your physical network topology requires it. For instance, your corporate network is likely divided by a firewall. In that case, the network is not fully routed—that is, every subnet cannot communicate directly with every other subnet. For AD replication to work, AD must model the normal routing behavior of your network.

A site link bridge is a collection of site links. To create a site link bridge, you first create site links. You then add those sites to a site link bridge. For instance, let's assume you have a site link that contains both London and Houston. The cost of this link is 2. You have a second site link that contains Houston and Dallas. The cost of this link is 6. You could create a site link bridge and add both of these site links to it. This would enable London to communicate with Dallas with a cost of 8.

A site link bridge does not dictate the physical path the network packets take. This aspect of the communication cannot be controlled from within AD.

Notice that the two site links we added to the site link bridge had a site in common—Houston. This is a requirement of creating a site link bridge. If this were not the case, the site link bridge would have no way of working out the total cost of moving a message from London to Dallas.

Because site links are by default transitive, in most cases, you will not have to create site link bridges. However, by creating site link bridges and manually designating DCs that will communicate, you can alleviate some of the problems you may encounter from working on a nonrouted network.

To use site link bridges, you must turn off the Bridge All Site Links feature. Because this is an all-or-nothing affair (sites are either transitive or not), doing so increases the amount of administration you are expected to do yourself.

Note that the KCC and ISTG may become overwhelmed and be unable to build a full replication topology on a regular schedule. This happens when there are many paths on your network, and the KCC must sort through each of them to find the optimal route. In these rare cases, you could disable the Bridge All Site Links option and build site link bridges.

You can also prevent the KCC from building a site-to-site topology. However, this increases the overhead of managing your network. One of the best features of the KCC is that it runs on a regular schedule. This means it can recover from sudden changes on your network, such as a site disappearing because a router is down. If the KCC has had its feature set trimmed, you need to take care of these situations yourself. Keep in mind, however, that such situations can be difficult to detect and will take a lot of time to configure. In almost all cases, you are better off using the KCC than performing the task yourself.

Examining Replication Traffic

Although the KCC can be allowed to calculate and configure the topology for your network, you also have to use due diligence in monitoring the efficiency of your AD replication. This can be done through two utilities: Replication Monitor and the Repadmin command-line utility.

By monitoring replication, you can be alerted when you need to make changes to the topology manually. Because monitoring allows you to see replication patterns, you may then decide to step in and make changes to the topology.

Replication Monitor

Replication Monitor is a graphical utility that displays the replication topology of the computers within a site. With this utility, you can view status messages on the state of replication and the current performance of the process. Because you can also view this information at the DC level, you can determine whether a specific pair of replication partners are performing adequately. If they aren't, you might need to trigger the KCC to recalculate the replication topology.

Replication has a great deal of functionality. Some of the highlights are as follows:

- You can see which DCs are direct replication partners with other DCs. This is displayed both directly and transitively.
- You can view the USN on a particular server.
- You can view the number of failed replication attempts and the reason replication failed.

- You can set defined values that cause Windows 2000 to write to an event log or to send email should a particular condition occur.
- You can poll a server to get current statistics and save this data to a log file.
- You can view which objects have yet to replicate from a particular server.
- You can trigger replication between two DCs.
- You can trigger the KCC to regenerate the replication topology.

Replication Monitor can be run on Windows 2000 Advanced Server, whether it is installed as a DC or simply as a member server. This is one of the primary tools at your disposal when troubleshooting replication problems on your network. A typical Replication Monitor screen is shown in Figure 12.1. In this figure, you can see the names of replication partners, along with current USN values.

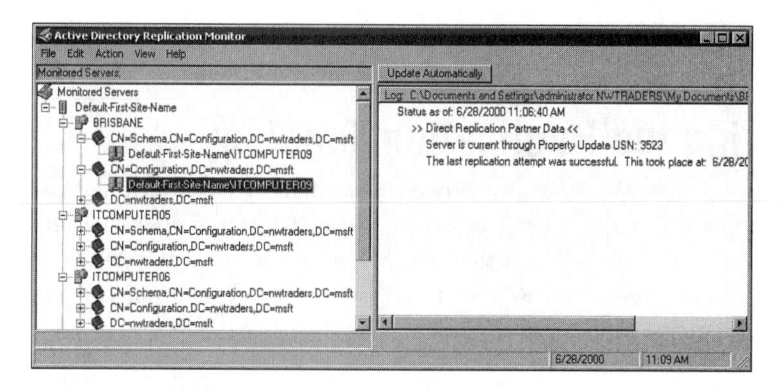

Figure 12.1 Replication Monitor.

Repadmin

Unlike Replication Monitor, the Repadmin command-line utility is non-graphical and gives data about only a particular DC. However, it also shares some crossover functionality with Replication Monitor, such as the ability to regenerate the replication topology, force events to occur, and display replication data, including the entries in the up-to-dateness table.

If you are checking many different DCs, you are better off using Replication Monitor. However, if you have easy access to a particular controller, Repadmin will likely be sufficient for anything you might need. Because Repadmin is a command-line utility, it has various command switches. These switches are shown in Figure 12.2.

```
C:\WINNT\System32\cmd.exe

C:\>repadmin /?
Usage: repadmin <cmd> <args> [/u:<domain\\user>] [/pw:<password|*>]

Supported <cmd>s & args:
     /sync <Naming Context> <Dest DSA> <Source DSA UUID> [/force] [/async]
          [/full] [/addref] [/allsources]
     /syncall <Dest DSA> [<Naming Context>] [<flags>]
     /kcc [DSA] [/async]
     /bind [DSA]
     /propcheck <Naming Context> <Originating DSA Invocation ID>
        <Originating USN> [DSA from which to enumerate host DSAs]
     /getchanges NamingContext [SourceDSA] [/cookie:<file>]
     /getchanges NamingContext [DestDSA] SourceDSAObjectGuid
         [/verbose] [/statistics]

     /showreps [Naming Context] [DSA [Source DSA objectGuid]] [/verbose]
        [/unreplicated] [/nocache]
     /showvector <Naming Context> [DSA] [/nocache]
     /showmeta <Object DN> [DSA] [/nocache]
     /showtime <DS time value>
     /showmsg <Win32 error>
     /showism [<Transport DN>] [/verbose] <must be executed locally>
     /showsig [DSA]
     /showconn [DSA] [Container DN | <DSA guid>] <default is local site>
     /showcert [DSA]

     /queue [DSA]
     /failcache [DSA]
     /showctx [DSA] [/nocache]

Note:- <Dest DSA>, <Source DSA>, <DSA> : Names of the appropriate servers
       <Naming Context> is the Distinguished Name of the root of the NC
             Example: DC=My-Domain,DC=Microsoft,DC=Com

C:\>
```

Figure 12.2 Repadmin switches.

Modifying the Replication Topology

For the most part, replication should occur automatically without intervention from the administrator. Once you have manually created your sites and site links, the KCC takes care of the rest. However, by using the AD Sites and Services tool, along with Replication Monitor and Repadmin, you can make changes to the replication topology.

On rare occasions, you might want to make a change to the replication topology that the KCC has generated. This occurs when you are not happy with the number of hops the KCC uses (as previously mentioned, by default the topology is three hops). If you want to reduce the number of hops to two or one, you have to create your own topology.

Note that there are some significant downsides to creating the topology yourself. Modifying connection objects or creating your own can prevent the KCC from completing an efficient topology by itself. In addition, it can prevent the KCC from "healing" or reconfiguring the topology should a subnet on the network fail or a DC become unavailable. With these drawbacks in mind, you should take the following into account when creating connection objects manually:

- If a DC fails to replicate with its partners, it uses the KCC to make additional connection objects, creating as many new connections as needed to achieve replication.

- The KCC cannot delete manually created connection objects.
- If a connection exists between two servers, the KCC won't generate additional connections.

Troubleshooting Replication

Replication problems may occur for many reasons and may manifest themselves in strange ways, such as user accounts that seem to disappear or data being pulled from a directory that is out of date. We'll discuss a few of these problems in this section.

Your replication topology can be quite complex, and the KCC can work only with the data you have provided. If you have not created a sufficient number of site links, the KCC may not be able to connect all sites together with connection objects. This situation can lead to some DCs never being updated. If this occurs, you should create the necessary site links and have the KCC regenerate the topology through the Replication Monitor.

If replication is slow, a scheduling problem may be occurring. As mentioned, the schedule dictates windows of opportunity for replication to occur. If the windows are too small and spread too far apart, you can end up with replication that appears to be slow or even inoperable. This might happen when the schedule for a site link is configured to occur only on Mondays. When you have a string of site links connecting DCs together, highly restrictive schedules can cause a lot of latency on your network.

If your physical infrastructure is not sufficient to support AD replication, you can also run into severe problems. For instance, if the bandwidth availability of your network has changed, replication may not be able to occur efficiently. To alleviate this problem, create a site and make sure that only DCs with fast, reliable links are members of it. Once you have done this, you can force the KCC to regenerate the replication topology.

DCs in Windows 2000 are used primarily for authentication. Slow authentication can be caused by several factors. Most likely, however, you have poorly configured sites. Clients are directed to authenticate from sites that are on the same subnet as themselves. If a site has been configured incorrectly, the client might very well be traversing slow connections to get authenticated. Once again, reconfiguring sites on your network will likely solve the problem.

Practice Questions

Question 1

A Windows 2000 network is made up of clients and servers. There are three types of servers: standalone servers (nonnetworked), member servers, and DCs. DCs authenticate users. Each DC holds a copy of AD. DCs in a Windows 2000 network are peers. They must replicate changes to AD so users can gain access to up-to-date data. What is the name of the type of replication that Windows 2000 DCs use?

- ❍ a. Single-master replication
- ❍ b. Multiple single-master replication
- ❍ c. Multiple-master replication
- ❍ d. Peer replication

Answer c is correct. In multiple-master replication, each DC (domain controller) is a peer, which means it is on equal terms with all other DCs. It can accept changes to AD (Active Directory) and will replicate the changes out to its replication partners. Answer a is incorrect because single-master replication is used in Windows NT, not Windows 2000. Answers b and d are incorrect because these are invalid replication types.

Question 2

A system administrator is sitting in a remote office and needs to make a change to AD data. He knows there is a single DC on his local network and would like to use it for these changes because it is closer to his workstation. How can the system administrator choose which DC makes the changes and takes responsibility for replicating data?

- ❍ a. He cannot choose the DC that accepts the change.
- ❍ b. He must run the administrative utility from the command line and add a switch to specify the DC he wants to use.
- ❍ c. He always connects to a local DC.
- ❍ d. Even if a remote DC receives the change first, it forwards the request to change data in AD to a DC on the same subnet as the administrator.

Answer a is correct. Although Windows 2000 will attempt to connect the administrator to a local DC (domain controller) for authentication, it does not guarantee that this will be the case. Any DC can accept a change; the local DC receives the update from normal replication. Therefore, answers b, c, and d are incorrect.

Question 3

You have three distinct subnets on your network. Two of these subnets are in the United States, and they have a 10Mbps connection between them. The third subnet is in England over a 128Kbps link. You want to make sure that replication works efficiently on your network. How many sites would you create on your network?

- ❍ a. You would create three sites: two for the United States and one for England. AD will work out an efficient replication topology.
- ❍ b. You would create a single site and add all DCs to it. AD will then configure replication.
- ❍ c. You would create two sites. One site would include a single subnet from the United States. The second site would include both England and one of the subnets from the Untied States. This allows the subnet in England to replicate with the site in the United States.
- ❍ d. You would create two sites: one in the United States that includes the two subnets there and one for the subnet in England. AD will work out the replication topology based on this data.

Answer d is correct. Sites can be defined as a group of subnets that have fast connectivity. Because the subnet in England is on the other side of a 128Kbps link, this is a slow connection and should therefore be its own site. Answers a, b, and c are all incorrect.

Question 4

There are two different types of updates to AD. One of these updates occurs when a change is recorded for the very first time. This change is then replicated to all other DCs on the network through normal replication. The other occurs when an update is accepted from a partner. What are the names of these types of updates? [Check all correct answers]

- ❑ a. Originating update
- ❑ b. Original update
- ❑ c. Replicated update
- ❑ d. Replicated secondary update

Answers a and c are correct. Answer a is correct because the first time a change is written to AD, this is known as an *originating update*. This update is then replicated to replication partners, and using the replication topology of the network, it is eventually made in all replicas. Answer c is correct because updates received from replication partners are called *replicated updates*. Answers b and d are incorrect because they are slightly skewed versions of the actual terms.

Question 5

When a DC accepts a change, it records it and then begins to replicate the change to its replication partners. This process is always a pull process—that is, a replication partner is informed that changes have occurred and that updates need to be copied. What is the name given to this process?

- ❍ a. The replication notification process
- ❍ b. The originating replication process
- ❍ c. The change notification process
- ❍ d. The replicated update process

Answer c is correct. This process is known as the *change notification process*. Once a replication partner is informed that changes have taken place at the replica belonging to its replication partner, it pulls changes from that partner. Answers a, b, and d are all invalid answers.

Question 6

The replication topology can be created automatically on a Windows 2000 network. An automatic process takes place that generates the topology. This process will even regenerate the topology should it become necessary. What is the name of the process that automatically creates the replication topology?

- ❍ a. The Replication Topology Generator
- ❍ b. The Knowledge Consistency Checker
- ❍ c. The Knowledge Constant Changer
- ❍ d. The Knowledge Replication Strategy

Answer b is correct. The automatic process is known as the *Knowledge Consistency Checker*. Although this process can be overridden, doing so is not a good idea. Most of the time, you should let the KCC make decisions about replication partners, because it requires very little configuration and can work in near real time. Answers a, c, and d are all invalid answers.

Question 7

You have two sites that need to be on different subnets. The network connection between these two sites is 128Kbps. Because the connection is slow and these sites contain DCs in different subnets, they will be connected to ensure replication. What is the name of the process that automatically decides which DCs in each of these sites will be replication partners with each other?

❍ a. The Knowledge Consistency Checker

❍ b. The Replication Topology Generator

❍ c. The Internet Site Topology Generator

❍ d. The Intersite Topology Generator

Answer d is correct. It is the job of the Intersite Topology Generator to decide which specific DCs within a site will replicate with each other. Once these two servers have replicated data, normal replication practices take place to ensure that all other DCs within a site receive the updates. Answer a is incorrect because the Knowledge Consistency Checker is the process that automatically generates the topology. Answers b and c are simply invalid answers.

Question 8

Because every DC in a Windows 2000 network is a peer, changes can be written to different replicas that might cause conflicts. Siobhan is a system administrator in Cavan, Ireland. Siobhan reads an email that was distributed to the Administrators distribution group that says a user wants his last name changed. She makes the change as soon as she reads the email. An administrator in Basildon, England, also reads the email and makes the change. However, this administrator misreads the email and makes a spelling error in the last name. As replication occurs on the network, a conflict occurs when a DC receives replicated updates for the same property. AD has a built-in mechanism to deal with such conflicts.

From the following items, create a list of only the factors that are used in conflict resolution and put them in the correct order in which they would be checked:

The date/time of the change; the later time prevails.

The status of the user; enterprise administrators override domain administrators.

The GUIDs of the DCs that made the originating update; the highest GUID prevails.

The time zone; the delegated time zone always prevails.

The site's priority; the site with the highest assigned priority prevails.

The property version number; the highest property version number prevails.

The amount of data in the update; the update with the most data always prevails.

The correct answer is:

- The version property number; the highest property version number prevails.
- The date/time of the change; the latest time prevails.
- The GUIDs of the DCs that made the originating update; the highest GUID prevails.

If the first piece of data fails to resolve the conflict, AD uses the second piece of data. If that also fails, the third piece—a tiebreaker, which will always resolve the conflict—is used.

Question 9

AD data exists in three different partitions. Two of these partitions exist on every DC within a forest. The third partition exists only on selected DCs. What is the name of the partition that does not exist on every DC in a forest?

❍ a. The configuration partition

❍ b. The schema partition

❍ c. The master partition

❍ d. The domain partition

Answer a is correct. The configuration partition contains data about the domains and configuration options set within all domains in the forest. Answer b is incorrect because the schema partition includes data regarding the objects that can exist within the directory as well as any rules that exist for that object. Answer c is incorrect because the master partition does not exist. Answer d is incorrect because the domain partition includes information that is specific for a domain, such as usernames and groups. Therefore, it does not need to exist on every DC within a forest (because a forest is made up of multiple domains).

Question 10

An administrator in Manhattan has created a new group in AD that will be used to combine user accounts from both Manhattan and Houston, Texas. Six hours after creating the group, she receives an email asking her when she is going to have time to create it. The administrator checks her server log and sees that she created the group earlier in the day. She suspects that she has a problem with replication. Which tool could she use to examine which objects are waiting to be replicated from her local DC?

❍ a. Replication Monitor

❍ a. Performance Monitor

❍ a. The Repladmin command-line utility

❍ a. The Replication Master Browser

Answer a is correct. The only option that would work in this situation is to use the Replication Monitor. Answer b is incorrect because Performance Monitor is used for checking overall system performance and does not include counters for specific object replication data. Answer c is incorrect because there is no such utility as Repladmin. (Although there is a command-line utility called Repadmin, it is used to examine a local DC.) Answer d is simply an invalid answer.

Need to Know More?

Boswell, William. *Inside Windows 2000 Server*. New Riders. Indianapolis, IN, 1999. ISBN 1-56205-929-7.

This book is highly technical and explains the details of using all facets of a Windows 200 Server, including replication.

Iseminger, David. *Active Directory Services for Microsoft Windows 2000*. Microsoft Press. Redmond, WA, 2000. ISBN 0-7356-0624-2.

This book introduces you to all aspects of working with a Windows 2000 domain, specifically dealing with AD administration.

Nielsen, Morten Strunge. *Windows 2000 Server Architecture and Planning*. The Coriolis Group, Scottsdale, AZ, 1999. ISBN 1-57610-436-2.

This book provides assistance with design and migration issues.

Search the TechNet CD (or its online version through `www.microsoft.com/technet`) and the *Windows 2000 Server Resource Kit* CD using the keywords "replication," "sites," "bridgehead," and "update sequence number."

Willis, Will, David Watts, and Tillman Strahan. *MCSE Windows 2000 Directory Services Exam Prep*. The Coriolis Group, Scottsdale, AZ, 2000. ISBN 1-57610-624-1.

Operations Masters

Terms you'll need to understand:

- ✓ Single-master replication
- ✓ Operations masters
- ✓ PDC Emulator
- ✓ RID Master
- ✓ Infrastructure Master
- ✓ Schema Master
- ✓ Domain Naming Master
- ✓ Transferring a role
- ✓ Seizing a role
- ✓ Ntdsutil

Techniques you'll need to master:

- ✓ Displaying the name of the server performing a specific role
- ✓ Transferring a role from one server to another
- ✓ Seizing a role from a server using Ntdsutil
- ✓ Assigning permissions to administer operations masters

Although it's true to say that all domain controllers (DCs) act as peers on a Windows 2000 network when we use Active Directory (AD) replication, at times the peer model does not achieve the desired result. Some functions on a network are best suited to being controlled by a single DC. These functions include implementing security measures, ensuring compatibility with down-level (Windows NT 4) servers, and ensuring that the security identifiers (SIDs) of the clients created in a domain are unique.

To this end, Microsoft has implemented *operations masters*. Operations masters have a unique role to play on your network. Management of operations masters is essential to ensuring that you have a healthy and efficient Windows 2000 network. In this chapter, we define the operations masters and what they do. We also discuss what actions you should take if an operations master fails or becomes unavailable. In addition, we talk about how the role of an operations master can be moved from one DC to another and what you should do if the original operations master comes back online.

Introducing Operations Masters

When replicating AD data, Windows 2000 uses a *multimaster* concept. This means that any DC can accept a change to AD data, and this change will then be replicated to all DCs in the domain and/or forest. Replication conflicts can, and do, occur. Chapter 12, "Active Directory Replication," discusses in detail a conflict-resolution process that deals with these issues.

Some operations that occur on a Windows 2000 network could be harmful if conflicts were to occur. In the case of these operations, Windows 2000 reverts to using single-master replication. This means that a single DC on the network takes responsibility for performing a specific task. Microsoft has coined the term *role* to describe the task that this DC performs. There are five distinct roles, collectively known as *operations master roles*. When a DC has been assigned a role, it becomes the *operations master* for that role.

Data regarding which DCs are functioning as operations masters is stored in AD. When a client needs to get in touch with an operations master, the client simply queries AD. There are no specific requirements a DC must meet to function as an operations master. This gives you flexibility in deciding which DC takes on the task. It also means that roles can be moved from one DC to another. This becomes more important when a DC acting as an operations master fails.

Although there are no requirements for which DC can act as a specific operations master, pay particular attention to the section "Recommendations for Operations Masters" at the end of this chapter. For efficiency reasons, it makes sense to assign specific roles to particular DCs.

The Five Operations Master Roles

Each of the five operations master roles that exist on your network has a scope—that is, some of the roles are specific to a domain, whereas others play a role in the entire forest. The five operations masters and their corresponding scopes are set out in Table 13.1. Your Windows 2000 network may have five servers that are acting as operations masters (this would be the case in a single-domain environment), or it could have more.

Knowing this fact becomes important when you are deciding which DC should play a specific role on your network. Once you understand each of the roles, you can decide where best to have this role placed for maximum efficiency.

Table 13.1 Operations Masters and Their Scopes

Operations Master	Scope
Schema Master	Forestwide
Domain Naming Master	Forestwide
Primary Domain Controller (PDC) Emulator	Specific to a domain
Relative Identifier (RID) Master	Specific to a domain
Infrastructure Master	Specific to a domain

Because three of the five types of operations masters are domainwide, you will have several servers in your environment playing that role. Working out the correct placement of the domainwide roles is easier than doing the same thing for the forestwide roles. This is because the forestwide roles must be placed in a location that offers administrators easy and fast access, which can be difficult on wide area networks.

All Windows 2000 installations start with a single server (if this is a migration, it is the first server upgraded). The first server installed takes on all roles. This is unlikely to be optimal for your network, and you should move the roles to other servers as they come online. (We talk about moving roles to other servers in the "Managing Operations Master Roles" section later in this chapter.) Because the first server also operates as a Global Catalog server and DC, the first server installed will be a little overloaded.

When you install a second domain into your Windows 2000 network, the first DC that joins the forest for this new domain assumes the three roles that are domain based. Once again, this may not be feasible from a performance standpoint. These default behaviors should be considered carefully when you are designing your network.

Now let's define what each role achieves. Once you fully understand why these roles exist, you can better plan their placement on your network.

Schema Master

AD is a database built up of instances of objects and objects' attributes. The types of objects and the attributes these objects can have are defined in the schema for the directory. There must be no conflicts when changes are being made to the schema. For instance, with multimaster replication, any DC can make an update to AD data. If any DC were able to make additions or deletions from the schema, you would end up with replication problems. Let's say an administrator created a new object type called Database Servers. Replication should take care of letting all other DCs know about this change. But what would happen if replication had not yet been able to replicate out this schema change to all DCs? You could end up with a situation where one DC was attempting to replicate AD data, whereas its replication partner didn't even know the object type was possible!

To go one step further, the schema is obviously a very important piece of AD. Because it defines what can exist within the directory, managing the process of updating it with new objects and attributes should be a closely monitored process. To ensure that this process is limited, there is a single read/write copy of the schema on your Windows 2000 network, stored on the Schema Master. In addition, only members of the Schema Admins group can make changes to the schema. Once a change has been made to the schema, the Schema Master then takes on the task of replicating this change to all DCs in the forest.

There is a single Schema Master per forest.

Domain Naming Master

All objects within AD must be unique. That is, you cannot create two objects in a container with the same name. To make sure this is the case, Windows 2000 must ensure that new domains added to your Windows 2000 network have unique names. This is the job of the Domain Naming Master.

The Domain Naming Master manages the addition and deletion of domains from the forest. This means that whenever you want to add a domain to your Windows 2000 network, a call must be made to the Domain Naming Master.

You will not be able to add or remove a domain if this connection cannot be made. Domains are added to Windows 2000 by running `dcpromo.exe`. This wizard contacts the Domain Naming Master on your network automatically.

Because the Domain Naming Master needs to be aware of all domains and objects available in the forest, it must also be a Global Catalog server. The Domain Naming Master queries the Global Catalog server before making additions and deletions.

There is a single Domain Naming Master per forest.

Primary Domain Controller (PDC) Emulator

The PDC Emulator plays several important roles on your Windows 2000 network. To understand these roles, remember that a Windows 2000 network can operate in two modes: mixed mode and native mode. Mixed mode means that you have Windows NT 4 servers acting as backup domain controllers (BDCs) alongside Windows 2000 DCs. You cannot change to native mode until these older servers have been eliminated from your network.

You should not change to native mode if you have older clients on your network. All clients must be compatible with AD before you change to native mode. Otherwise, these clients will be orphaned.

The PDC Emulator acts as a conduit between the newer Windows 2000 DCs and the older-style Windows NT 4 BDCs. The PDC Emulator is, in effect, the PDC for older Windows NT computers. It takes care of replicating AD data to BDCs.

The role of synchronizing older-style DCs with the newer DCs is a two-way street. For instance, if a user object is created within AD, the PDC Emulator makes sure this object is also replicated to older-style DCs. Also, if an older client—a Windows 95 client, for instance—makes a password change, the PDC Emulator accepts the change in the context of being the PDC and replicates that data to AD.

Another area of importance for the PDC Emulator has to do with *replication latency*, which is the amount of time it takes for a change made in AD to be copied to all replicas. Despite your best efforts, there is no way for this to be done in real time; it takes time for data to be processed and for packets to travel across the cable. Generally, this is not a problem, but in the case of users' passwords, it can be debilitating. For instance, say a user changes her password. This change is made at a DC in Houston. Before this DC has had a chance to replicate this password change to all other DCs, the user logs off and tries to log on again. This time, the user connects to a different DC. Because this DC does not have a copy of the new password, the logon attempt is declined.

To prevent this from happening, all password changes on a Windows 2000 network are preferentially replicated to the PDC Emulator. Before a DC rejects a logon attempt, it contacts the PDC Emulator to see if any recent changes to the password have taken place. If they have, the PDC Emulator can replicate this data immediately.

The PDC Emulator in a domain also operates as the time-synchronization master. All DCs in a Windows 2000 domain synchronize their time with the PDC Emulator. The PDC Emulator in a domain synchronizes its time with the PDC Emulator in the root domain (the first domain installed on your network). The PDC Emulator for the root domain should be synchronized with an external source.

One final area of concern is Group Policy Objects (GPOs). These objects are automatically edited on the PDC Emulator. Although this is not essential for your network, editing these objects on a single server helps eliminate any possible conflicts. This is the default action.

There is a single PDC Emulator per domain.

RID Master

AD is made up of objects known as *security principals*. A security principal is essentially something that can be assigned permissions within a Windows 2000 network. This includes users, groups, and computers. Each security principal is assigned a *security descriptor* (SID) so it can be identified. This descriptor is unique to the object and must always remain unique.

A SID is made up of two components. The first component, the *domain SID*, is common to all security principals in a domain. Because it is common to all objects within a domain, the domain SID alone does not allow objects to have a unique SID. The uniqueness comes from the addition of a second number, the *relative identifier* (RID). The RID is assigned from a pool of RIDs stored at each DC. The RIDS in this pool are assigned to each DC by the RID Master.

RIDs are assigned to each DC in blocks. Once the block of RIDs is exhausted, the DC requests another block from the RID Master. The RID Master keeps track of which RID blocks have been assigned. This ensures uniqueness.

If the RID pool on a DC is exhausted and the RID Master is not available, you will not be able to create security principals on your network. You can view the pools by using the Dcdiag utility.

The RID Master also has a role to play when objects are being moved from one domain to another. In this case, the RID Master ensures that an object is not moved to multiple domains. Further, it deletes the object from the previous domain.

There is a single RID Master per domain.

Infrastructure Master

The domain partition of AD contains data about objects that exist within the domain only. It might also contain references to objects from other domains. This occurs, for instance, when you grant permissions for users that exist in other domains to resources in your domain. Universal groups can be used for this purpose (groups are discussed in detail in Chapter 5, "User and Group Administration").

If a change is made to a referenced object, these changes need to be replicated to all domains. It is the job of the Infrastructure Master to receive these changes and to replicate them to all DCs in its domain.

Let's use an example to clarify this process. A user object named Sam Rao exists in the Asia domain, and it is referenced in the Europe domain. The Sam Rao object is then moved from the Asia domain to the Americas domain. This means the SID for the user changes. (Don't forget, the SID is made up of two components: the domain SID, which in this case will change, and the RID.) This change must be made in both the Asia and the Americas domain, and the reference in Europe must also be updated. The Infrastructure Master will make this change in Europe.

The Infrastructure Master records references to objects that it does not contain in its directory partition. In our example, this means that although it contains a reference to the user object Sam Rao, it does not contain any other object data. It is this distinction that allows the Infrastructure Master to work. If the Infrastructure Master is also a Global Catalog server (which contains a reference to all objects created in a forest), the Infrastructure Master will know about all objects in the forest, and the comparison will not work. This breaks the Infrastructure Master's operation. Therefore, the Infrastructure Master cannot also be a Global Catalog server.

Because there will be no references to external objects in a single domain, there is no need to worry about the Infrastructure Master in a single-domain environment.

There is a single Infrastructure Master per domain.

Managing Operations Master Roles

Because the first DC installed in a domain (or the forest) assumes all the roles by default, it is highly likely that you will want to change the DCs that perform some of the operations master roles.

Before you can do this, however, you must determine which servers in your environment are currently performing the role. You can then gracefully move the role from one DC to another (known as *transferring* the role), or you can *seize* the role. Seizing a role is the act of taking control away from one DC and assigning it to another without the current operations master relinquishing its role first. You would do this if the DC acting as an operations master had failed and was no longer online. Because the server is not operational, it cannot gracefully give up its role; instead, the role must be seized.

Determining Operations Masters

The tools you use to determine which server is performing a specific role depend on the scope of the role. Remember that two of the five roles are forestwide. The remaining three are domain specific. You can use a single tool to determine the domain-level roles, but you must use different tools to figure out the forestwide roles.

Domain-Level Operations Master Roles

As mentioned, the three domain-level operations master roles are PDC Emulator, RID Master, and Infrastructure Master. You can use the AD Users and Computers tool to find out which server or servers are playing this role. To do this, right-click Active Directory Users and Computers and select Operations Masters, as shown in Figure 13.1.

When you make this selection, you are presented with the Operations Master dialog box, shown in Figure 13.2. There are three domain-level operations master roles, and each is displayed on its own tab. Along with the name of the system playing the role is a Change button, which you use to change the server playing the role.

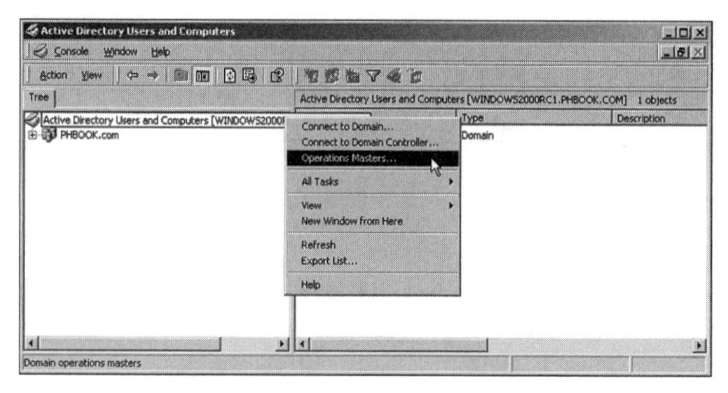

Figure 13.1 Using AD User and Computers to determine a role owner.

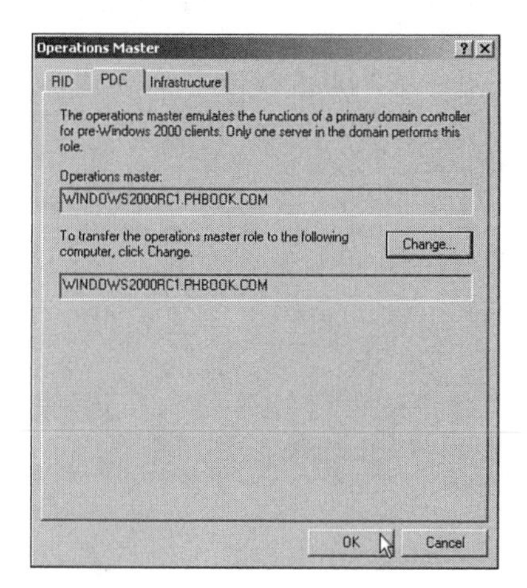

Figure 13.2 The Operations Master dialog box.

Forest-Level Operations Master Roles

As mentioned previously, two roles are forestwide: the Domain Naming Master and the Schema Master. You use two different tools to determine which DC is playing these roles. For the Domain Naming Master, you use AD Domains and Trusts. You navigate to the Change Operations Master dialog box, shown in Figure 13.3, in much the same way you reached the Operations Master dialog box in the last section. In this case, right-click Active Directory Domains and Trusts and then select Operations Master. This brings up the Change Operations Master dialog box. You can change the name of the server that plays the role by clicking the Change button.

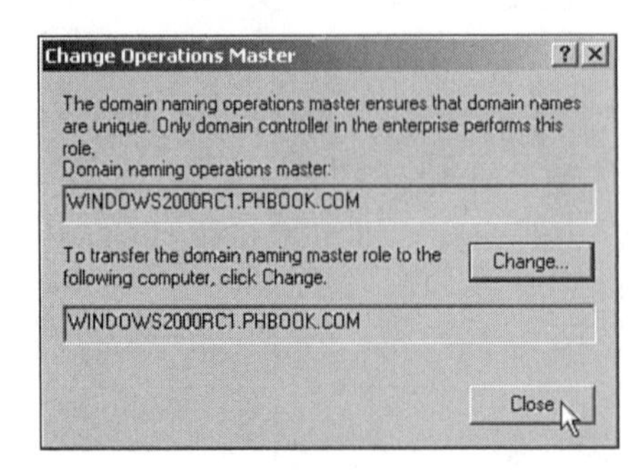

Figure 13.3 The Change Operations Master dialog box.

The Schema Master role is a little different. Editing the AD schema should be a very controlled process for several reasons. First, when a change is made to the schema, the change must be replicated to all DCs in the forest. This generates a lot of activity on those servers and consumes bandwidth. Second, you can never delete anything from the schema. You can only "deactivate" parts of the schema. That means an object can be deactivated but will still take up space within the schema definition.

To find out which server is playing the role of Schema Master, and also to change the name of the DC playing the role, you must use the AD Schema MMC snap-in. By default, this snap-in is not available. To use it, you must first register the schema dynamic link library (DLL). To do this, open a command prompt window and type the following:

```
regsvr32.exe schmmgmt.dll
```

This registers the DLL for use on your system. This command must be run on a Windows 2000 server. If the system root (usually the c:\winnt folder) is not in your path, make sure you give the full path to the schmmgmt.dll file. The path should be <systemroot>\system32.

Once you have registered the DLL, you must create a custom MMC console. Follow these steps to create a custom console:

1. Select Start, Run and type **MMC**.
2. This brings up an empty console. Click the Console menu and select Add/Remove Snap-In.
3. This brings up the Add/Remove Snap-In dialog box. Click the Add button.
4. This displays the Add Standalone Snap-In dialog box. Select Active Directory Schema and click Add. Click Close and then OK.

To display the name of the DC playing the Schema Master role, right-click Active Directory Schema in the right-side panel and select Operations Master. This displays the Change Schema Master dialog box, shown in Figure 13.4. You can change the server name by clicking the Change button.

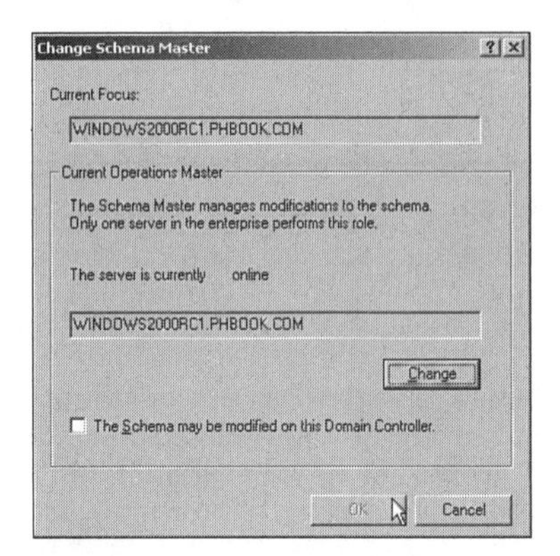

Figure 13.4 The Change Schema Master dialog box.

Each of the methods given in this "Determining Operations Masters" section includes an option to connect to an alternative DC on the context-sensitive menu from which you chose the Operations Master option. Use this option to connect to other domains and to view or change the operations master in those domains.

Permissions for Changing an Operations Master Server

Before you can move a role from one server to another, you must make sure you have sufficient permissions. Table 13.2 details what these permissions should be. Pay particular attention to the Schema Master, because this is a special group within the domain.

Table 13.2 Required Permissions for Changing an Operations Master Role

Role	Group with Permission
PDC Emulator	Domain Admins group
RID Master	Domain Admins group
Infrastructure Master	Domain Admins group
Schema Master	Schema Admins group
Domain Naming Master	Enterprise Admins group

Seizing a Role

Transferring an operations master role from one server to another using the methods outlined in the previous sections is a graceful exchange—that is, an assumption is made that both servers are functioning. With both online, normal AD replication can take care of transferring necessary data from one server to another so it can perform its new role.

This is not always the case, however. If the server playing the role of operations master fails or becomes unavailable, it may be necessary to seize control. Seizing the role forces the transfer from one system to another. It is a last resort and is not recommended.

Seizing a role is a serious matter and should be done in emergencies only. The server currently playing the role must not come back online. If it does, you will have a serious conflict on your network. If you want to reuse a server that previously played a role that has been seized, reformat the partition that contained Windows 2000 and reinstall the operating system.

The method used to seize a role depends on the operations master you are working with. If you need to seize the role for the PDC Emulator or the Infrastructure Master, you can go ahead and use the AD Users and Computers console. Use the method outlined previously when viewing and changing the current DC playing the role.

Things get more complicated if you are changing the Schema Master, Domain Naming Master, or RID Master role. For these, you must use the Ntdsutil command-line utility. This utility is a powerful tool that has many uses. The help screen displaying the various options is shown in Figure 13.5.

```
D:\WINNT\System32\cmd.exe
Microsoft Windows 2000 [Version 5.00.2195]
(C) Copyright 1985-1999 Microsoft Corp.

D:\>ntdsutil /?
Microsoft(R) Windows(TM) Directory Service Utilities Version 2.0
Copyright (C) Microsoft Corporation 1991-1999. All Rights Reserved.

NtdsUtil performs database maintenance of the Active Directory store,
management and control of the Flexible Single Master Operations (FSMO),
and cleaning up of metadata left behind by abandoned domain controllers,
those which are removed from the network without being uninstalled.

This is an interactive tool. Type "help" at the prompt for more information.


 ?                             - Print this help information
 Authoritative restore         - Authoritatively restore the DIT database
 Domain management             - Prepare for new domain creation
 Files                         - Manage NTDS database files
 Help                          - Print this help information
 IPDeny List                   - Manage LDAP IP Deny List
 LDAP policies                 - Manage LDAP protocol policies
 Metadata cleanup              - Clean up objects of decommissioned servers
 Popups %s                     - (en/dis)able popups with "on" or "off"
 Quit                          - Quit the utility
 Roles                         - Manage NTDS role owner tokens
 Security account management   - Manage Security Account Database - Duplicate SID Cleanup
 Semantic database analysis    - Semantic Checker

D:\>_
```

Figure 13.5 The help screen for the Ntdsutil utility.

As you can see, the `ntdsutil` command has a host of options. The following steps walk you through seizing a role as well as how to get help with this utility at any time by using the `help` command:

1. Select Start, Run and then type **`ntdsutil`**. Click OK.
2. At the ntdsutil prompt, type **`roles`** and press Enter. For help, type **`help`** and press Enter. Depending on the prompt displayed at the time, help information is shown.
3. At the fsmo maintenance prompt, type **`connections`** and press Enter.
4. At the server connections prompt, type **`connect to server`** followed by the fully qualified domain name (FQDN) of the DC that will be seizing the role. Press Enter.
5. At the server connections prompt, type **`quit`** and press Enter.
6. At the fsmo maintenance prompt, type one of the following commands (depending on the role you are attempting to seize):
   - seize PDC
   - seize RID master
   - seize infrastructure master
   - seize schema master
   - seize domain naming master

   Press Enter.
7. At the fsmo maintenance prompt, type **`quit`** and press Enter.
8. At the ntdsutil prompt, type **`quit`** and Press Enter.

Once you have completed the command, don't forget to verify that the role has changed by using the method outlined in the "Managing Operations Master Roles" section earlier in this chapter. Don't forget that once a role has been seized, the old server playing the role must never come online again.

Ntdsutil has a host of options. Make sure you experiment with this tool. Also, don't forget to type **help** at each prompt to see a display of available options.

Recommendations for Operations Masters

Losing an operations master does not generally have an immediate impact on your network and its users. The exception to this rule is the PDC Emulator used by down-level clients and for password changes. If the PDC Emulator goes down, you may have to seize the role fairly quickly. Protect the server playing this role as best you can.

Always transfer an operations master role rather than seizing it. Only seize a role when it is unavoidable. Make sure you have a process in place that prevents the old operations master from coming back online.

Consider network traffic when deciding which servers on your network should perform each role. For instance, the PDC Emulator is contacted by all down-level clients and by each DC when a password change takes place. This can cause a lot of traffic on an enterprise network. The PDC Emulator should be in a location that allows other servers to have easy access to it. The Infrastructure Master is dependent on the Global Catalog server. Make sure there is a Global Catalog server in the same site as the Infrastructure Master.

It's a good idea to combine the Schema Master and Domain Naming Master roles. These roles are suited to being on the same server because these tasks are usually performed by the same group within an organization.

Practice Questions

Question 1

There are five operations master roles on a Windows 2000 network. Where is the data regarding which servers are playing which roles stored?

- ❍ a. It is stored in the Registry of the server performing the role.
- ❍ b. It is stored within Active Directory.
- ❍ c. It is stored in the Registry of the clients.
- ❍ d. It is stored in a database separate from Active Directory.

Answer b is correct. This data must be in Active Directory so clients and down-level servers can query the database when an operations master is required. Answers a, c, and d are incorrect because they are not valid.

Question 2

Which of the following are the names of the operations master roles? [Check all correct answers]

- ❑ a. Schema Master
- ❑ b. Infrastructure Master
- ❑ c. SID Master
- ❑ d. Domain Naming Master

Answers a, b, and d are correct. The operations master roles that are missing are RID Master and PDC Emulator. Answer c is incorrect because there is no such role as the SID Master.

Question 3

David Aldridge is a system administrator at a large company. He is planning his Windows 2000 network with particular attention being given to the placement of the operations masters. He knows that some operations masters have particular requirements. To make his placement decision, he needs to know how many roles will operate forestwide and how many are domainwide. How many of the operations master roles are forestwide and how many are domainwide?

- ❍ a. Three of the operations master roles are forestwide and two are domainwide.
- ❍ b. Four of the operations master roles are forestwide and one is domainwide.
- ❍ c. Two of the operations master roles are forestwide and three are domainwide.
- ❍ d. Three of the operations master roles are domainwide and two are forestwide.

Answer c is correct. The Schema Master and Domain Naming Master are forestwide roles. Answers a, b, and d are incorrect because the PDC Emulator, RID Master, and Infrastructure Master are all domainwide.

Question 4

Siobhan Chamberlin is a system administrator for a large company. Siobhan has noticed that she is getting a lot of errors in the system log of Event Viewer. The errors relate to time synchronization on her network. Siobhan knows that this is related to an operations master role. Which role performs time-synchronization duties?

- ❍ a. The Infrastructure Master
- ❍ b. The Schema Master
- ❍ c. The Domain Naming Master
- ❍ d. The PDC Emulator

Answer d is correct. The PDC Emulator performs time synchronization within its domain. It, in turn, synchronizes with the PDC Emulator in the root domain. The PDC Emulator in the root domain should be synchronized with an external source. Answer a is incorrect because the Infrastructure Master is responsible for updating cross-domain references of objects. Answer b is incorrect because the Schema Master role is to operate as the single location where changes to the schema can be made. Answer c is incorrect because the Domain Naming Master is used to add or remove domains from the forest.

Question 5

Robyn Hitchcock is a member of the Domain Admins group in a Windows 2000 network. He has been asked to add a new object type to AD. However, whenever he tries to access the schema, he is denied access. A new Windows 2000 MCSE named Jaime Rodriguez says this is because of insufficient permissions. However, because Robyn is a member of the Domain Admins group, Robyn doubts this is true. Instead, Robyn thinks it is a network problem. Who is right?

❍ a. Jaime is right. Domain Admins do not have sufficient permissions to make changes to the Active Directory schema. One must be at least a Schema Admin to do this.

❍ b. Robyn is right. Domain Admins have all permissions on a Windows 2000 network; therefore, he should be able to change the schema.

❍ c. Neither is correct. Domain Admins can change a schema; therefore, Jaime is incorrect. However, receiving an "access denied message" indicates a server problem, not a network problem.

❍ d. Jaime is right. Domain Admins do not have sufficient permissions to make changes to the Active Directory schema. One must be at least an Enterprise Admin to do this.

Answer a is correct. Only members of the Schema Admin group can make changes to the schema. Therefore, answers b, c, and d are all incorrect.

Question 6

Len Watts is a system administrator. Len's company has just merged with another large organization, and so the company has reorganized the help desk. The help desk used to be dispersed in major cities; now it has been consolidated in London. Since the consolidation, Len has received complaints that some administrative operations on the network are slow. He knows one reason for the slowdown is that user accounts for the merged company are currently being added to the domain in batches but that this technique is failing. Len knows the cause of the problem is the placement of an operations master on his network, so he decides to move the role to a location with better network connectivity to the help desk. Which operations master must Len move and which tool will he use to do it?

❍ a. Len must move the Domain Naming Master. This is moved with Active Directory Domains and Trusts.

❍ b. Len must move the RID Master. This is moved with Active Directory Users and Computers.

❍ c. Len must move the Domain Naming Master. This is moved with Active Directory Sites and Services.

❍ d. Len must move the RID Master. This is moved with Active Directory Domains and Trusts.

Answer b is correct. Len must move the RID Master role, and he must use Active Directory Users and Computers to do it. You use this tool to transfer all the domain-level operations master roles, including PDC Emulator and Infrastructure Master. Therefore, answer d is incorrect. The Domain Naming Master is the incorrect role, so answers a and c are incorrect. However, Active Directory Domains and Trusts is the tool used to move all forestwide roles.

Question 7

The Domain Naming Master server has crashed. The word from the hardware techs onsite is that it will take a week to order the parts to get it back up and running. Mike DeBussey is the system administrator, and this could not have happened at a worse time. Mike was due to work all weekend creating two new domains. Mike knows that not having a functioning Domain Naming Master will prevent him from creating new domains. Therefore, Mike decides to seize the role of Domain Naming Master. Which tool will Mike use to perform this task?

- ❍ a. Mike will use the Ntdsutil command-line utility.
- ❍ b. Mike will use Active Directory Domains and Trusts to seize the role, because this is a forestwide operations master.
- ❍ c. Mike will use the Active Directory Users and Computers tool. This tool is used to seize all roles except that of the Schema Master.
- ❍ d. Mike will deactivate the current Domain Naming Master with Ntdsutil. He will then use Active Directory Domains and Trusts to assign the role to another server.

Answer a is correct. There is no need to use two tools to perform this task. Mike simply needs to use Ntdsutil, a command-line utility with many different options, to seize the role. Answer b is incorrect because Active Directory Domains and Trusts is not used to seize roles. Answer c is incorrect because one cannot use Active Directory Users and Computers to seize forestwide roles. Answer d is incorrect because Active Directory Domains and Trusts is not used to seize roles.

Question 8

Boyd Collins has just been added to the Schema Admins group, so he can make some additions to the schema of Active Directory. Boyd knows that this task is very important and that he must be careful when editing the schema. Fortunately, his development background has prepared him for the task. Boyd knows that he must create a custom MMC in order to edit the schema using the Schema MMC snap-in. However, when Boyd tries to add the snap-in, it is not available on his system. Boyd calls his help desk and asks to be added to all the necessary groups to enable this function, but the help desk tells him that it is not a permissions issue. What must Boyd do to fix this problem?

- ❍ a. Boyd must contact the help desk manager, because the help desk is incorrect; this *is* a permissions issue. One must be both a member of Schema Admins and Enterprise Admins to edit the schema.
- ❍ b. Boyd is obviously using a Windows 95 computer. The MMC does not work on a Windows 95 box. Boyd must upgrade his system to Windows 2000.
- ❍ c. Boyd must first register **schmmgmt** with the **regsvr32** command. Boyd will not be able to use the Schema MMC snap-in until this is done.
- ❍ d. Boyd should call the help desk and ask its staff to seize the role of Schema Master. The snap-in not showing on the system is indicative of the server being unavailable.

Answers c is correct. Boyd cannot use the Schema MMC snap-in until he registers `schmmgmt` with the `regsvr32` command. Answer a is incorrect because the help desk was correct; this is *not* a permissions issue. Answer b is incorrect because the MMC does work on a Windows 95 box. Answer d is incorrect because Boyd would not know that the Schema Master was not available until he tried to make a change to the schema. Because he cannot even find the snap-in, this is not the case.

Question 9

Mona Reed is performing a review of the installation plan for her new Windows 2000 network. Her staff has detailed the placement of all DCs and operations masters. The administrators are in a small building on a single subnet. There are 10 administrators. The network design team proposes that two DCs be placed in its site. Because there are only 10 people, one server would be fairly slow. A more powerful server would be a Global Catalog server and the Infrastructure Master. Mona rejects this plan and asks the network design team to reconsider. What was it about this design that Mona did not like?

- ❍ a. Although two DCs are reasonable in other circumstances, the role of the administrators is too important not to have at least three.
- ❍ b. The Infrastructure Master will not operate on a server that is functioning as a Global Catalog server. Either one of these tasks should be moved to the second DC.
- ❍ c. The Infrastructure Master role does not need to be close to the administrators. Because this role is used only for schema updates, it would be better to move this elsewhere and to replace the role with something more pertinent to the administrators' jobs.
- ❍ d. Mona wants the help desk team to be moved to another site. Having it in a separate site will cause performance issues.

Answer b is correct. Although some of the other answers sound good, only answer b has it right. Two DCs should give enough redundancy, but three would not be going overboard either. However, answer a is incorrect because not having three would not cause the plan to be rejected. Answer c is incorrect because there are other roles that could be close to the administrators, too, but depending on what type of tasks are performed most commonly, it might make sense to make the Infrastructure Master closest. Answer d is incorrect because although the administrators are in a different site, that does not necessarily mean they have a slow connection to the rest of the network. Sites are also sometimes used to manage replication. Regardless of any of this, the Infrastructure Master will not operate correctly on a server that is also a Global Catalog server.

Question 10

Darrell DeMartino is being left in charge of the network while the full-time administrator goes away for a long weekend. Darrell is confident that he can perform the tasks assigned to him, but he is concerned that in the event of a serious failure of an operations master role, he might not have sufficient permissions to do anything about it. The current administrator has added Darrell to both the Enterprise Admins groups and the Domain Admins group. Does Darrell have sufficient permissions to perform all tasks that might arise?

❍ a. No, Darrell must also be a member of the Schema Admins group in order to move the Schema Master role.

❍ b. No, Darrell must also be a member of the Schema Operation Admin group in order to move the Schema Master role.

❍ c. Yes, Darrell has all the permissions he could possibly need. The Enterprise Admins group gives him full power on his network.

❍ d. No, Darrell must also be a member of the Operations Masters group on the network. This group has permissions on all forest-level operations master servers.

Answer a is correct. A member of the Domain Admins group can move any of the domain-level operations master roles. Enterprise Admins can move the Domain Naming Master role. However, only Schema Admins can move the Schema Master role. Therefore, answers b, c, and d are all incorrect.

Need to Know More?

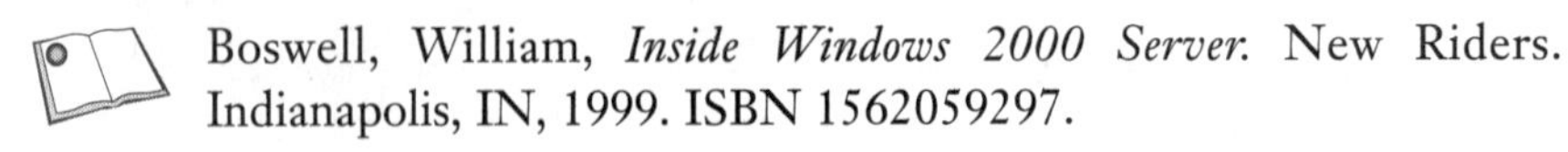

Boswell, William, *Inside Windows 2000 Server.* New Riders. Indianapolis, IN, 1999. ISBN 1562059297.

This book gives a lot of detail of the inner workings of various Windows 2000 components.

Miller, Chris and Todd Brown. *Microsoft Windows 2000 Server Unleashed*. Sams. Indianapolis, IN, 2000. ISBN 0672317397.

This book covers a lot of the administrative tasks you need to master for this exam.

Minasi, Mark, *Mastering Windows 2000 Server, 2nd Edition*. Sybex Computer Books. Berkeley, CA, 2000. ISBN 0782127746.

This book does a good job of aiming content at all levels of readers.

Watts, David, Will Willis, and Tillman Strahan. *Windows 2000 System Administration Handbook*. Prentice Hall. Upper Saddle River, NJ, 2000. ISBN 0130270105.

This book takes a day in the life of an administrator and gives examples of day-to-day tasks you will need to perform.

Active Directory Database Maintenance

Terms you'll need to understand:

- ✓ Extensible Storage Engine
- ✓ **ntds.dit**
- ✓ Active Directory (AD) log files
- ✓ Garbage collection
- ✓ Defragmentation
- ✓ Authoritative restore
- ✓ Nonauthoritative restore
- ✓ Tombstoning
- ✓ ADSIEdit
- ✓ System state data

Techniques you'll need to master:

- ✓ Performing an authoritative restore of AD data
- ✓ Using Ntdsutil to move the AD data file
- ✓ Using Ntdsutil to move the AD log files
- ✓ Using the built-in backup utility to perform a backup and restore

Active Directory (AD) is a transactional database. This means that it has built-in recovery techniques that are performed automatically should a system fail because of a hardware problem. It also means that you should know how to both back up and recover the database in the event of failure.

This chapter discusses the structure of the AD, including details of the database and log files that are used to process updates to the data. We examine how data can be backed up and restored. You will see that the AD replication process can be used to update a domain controller (DC) that has been offline for a period of time. It is also possible to force restored data to be propagated throughout the network via AD replication, even if that data is technically out of date.

Introducing AD Maintenance

Because so many areas of AD operation are automatic, you would be forgiven for thinking that there is little reason to be concerned about maintenance tasks. However, this assumption would be incorrect. Maintaining the AD database—on each DC—is an essential task that should be performed regularly. Backing up and restoring data allows you to recover lost or corrupted data.

We will look at four key tasks. Two of these tasks should be scheduled to run on a regular basis. The others should be tested periodically to make sure that you can recover from a problem and that you are enjoying optimal performance.

The tasks are as follows:

- Backing up AD data
- Restoring AD data
- Defragmenting AD data
- Moving the AD database

You can use the backup utility that ships with Windows 2000 to back up the AD database. In addition, several third-party utilities are available that can perform the same task. Whichever tool you decide to use, this task should occur on a regular schedule.

It is possible for the AD database to become corrupt or accidentally deleted. When this occurs, you must restore the database. Generally, you use the same tool you used for your backup to do this. However, some tape formats allow you to use different restore software.

There are two instances when the AD database must be moved. The first is during the defragmentation process. This ensures that the process does not corrupt the database. The second is performance related. If the hard disk that contains AD is becoming full, performance can be affected. To alleviate this problem, you could move the database.

Defragmentation increases the performance of both writing data to the database and querying the AD data. It can also be used to reduce the amount of disk space the database takes up.

Modifying AD Data

AD uses the Extensible Storage Engine (ESE), which was first pioneered in Microsoft Exchange Server. It uses the concept of *transactions* to ensure that the database does not become corrupted by partial updates and so it can recover in the case of a power failure. Each transaction is a call to modify the database. A modification can be the addition of new data or a change being made to data that is already stored.

For the transactional system to work, the AD database must have associated log files. These log files are used to store modifications before the data is written to the physical database file. We look at how this works in a moment. Before we do that, however, we must define which files are used by the database. Five files make up the AD database system:

- `ntds.dit`
- `edb*.log`
- `ebd.chk`
- `res1.log`
- `res2.log`

Each of these files has a role to play in ensuring that data can be written to the directory in a safe and recoverable fashion. You should note that these files exist on every DC in your environment. The AD database is not centralized in any way; it exists on each server that is promoted to the role of DC. Each instance must be maintained separately.

ntds.dit

This is the single file that holds all the AD data, including all objects and the schema information. This file is stored by default in the `<systemroot>\NTDS` folder, although it can be moved. The `ntds.dit` file works in conjunction with the log files. The `.dit` extension stands for "directory information tree."

edb*.log

The `edb*.log` file is the transaction log for `ntds.dit`. The file that is currently being used is called simply `edb.log`. When that file reaches a specified size (by default, 10MB), the file gets renamed to `edb*****.log`, where the asterisks are incremented from 1 upward. When the files are no longer needed, they are deleted by the system.

edb.chk

There can be two copies of changes to AD data. The first copy is kept in log files; these changes occur as data is accepted from an administrative tool. The second copy is the database file itself. This checkpoint file keeps track of which entries in the log file have been written to the database file. In the case of failure, Windows 2000 uses this file to find out which entries in the log file can safely be written out to a database file.

res1.log and res2.log

Essentially, `res1.log` and `res2.log` are two placeholders that exist to simply take up space. In the event that a DC runs out of disk space, the AD replica can become inoperable. It is far better for the DC to shut down gracefully. These two files, each 10MB in size, exist to prevent a DC from being able to write to the log files. If a DC runs out of disk space, AD can be sure that it has at least 20MB of space to write out any necessary log data.

Garbage Collection

Garbage collection is the process in which old data is purged from the AD. Because all DCs in a Windows 2000 network act as peers, deleting objects is a little more difficult than it might first appear. If an administrator wants to delete a user object from the network, he or she can simply hit the Delete key. However, how will Windows 2000 make sure that all DCs in the enterprise are aware that this deletion is taking place? If the deletion happens in real time, it can't. Hence, the use of *tombstoning*, explained next.

Data is never immediately deleted from AD. Instead, the object's attributes are deleted and the object is moved to a special container called *Deleted*

Objects. The object is then assigned a tombstone. By default, this tombstone is 60 days, although it can be changed. The tombstone means that the physical deletion of the object will occur by the configured interval. This gives AD time to replicate this change to all DCs. It also means that the deletion can take place at around the same time, no matter how distant the DCs may be.

Garbage collection also defragments the database by using the online defragmentation process. We will take a closer look at defragmentation in a moment.

To change the interval for garbage collection, you must use the ADSIEdit tool included with Windows 2000. Connect to the Configuration container and edit the **garbageCollPeriod** and **tombstoneLifetime** attributes. By default, the period is 60 days. This is displayed in ADSIEdit as **<not set>**. Be careful about setting the value too low; this can prevent your restores from working. Microsoft recommends leaving the value set at the default.

Performing Backups

A Windows 2000 DC can be backed up while it is online, thereby minimizing the disruption. It is not enough to back up only the database and log files. Instead, you must back up the system state data.

System state data is a collection of data that makes up a functioning AD infrastructure. It includes the AD database, along with other folders and files. These files collectively can be used to recover from even the most catastrophic failure. System state data includes the following:

- AD database files
- SYSVOL folder
- Registry
- System startup files
- Class Registration database
- Certificate Services database

All these may not exist on your server; for instance, the Certificate Services database is an optional component. You need all these folders because, in one way or another, they support the server.

The SYSVOL folder is a shared folder that exists on all DCs. This folder is used to replicate Group Policy Object (GPO) data and logon scripts. The

Class Registration database is composed of component services that are installed on a system.

You can back up the system state data without buying third-party utilities. To do this, simply use the built-in backup utility and follow these steps:

1. Select Start, Programs, Accessories, System Tools, Backup. When you do this, the backup utility screen shown in Figure 14.1 appears.

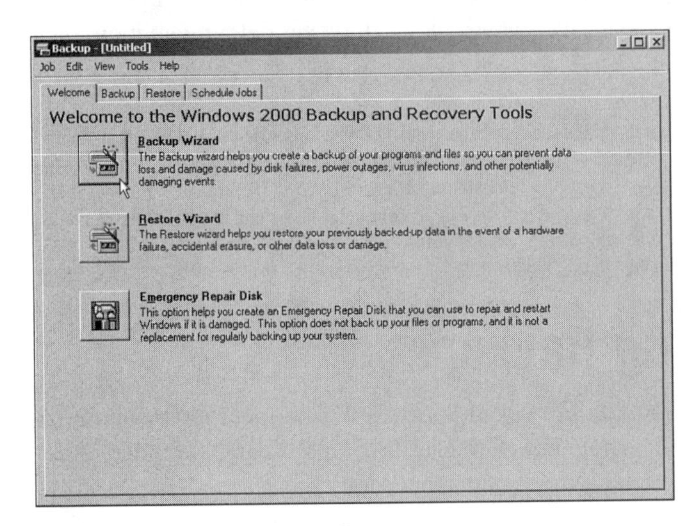

Figure 14.1 The built-in backup utility.

2. Run the Backup Wizard, which will walk you through the steps to back up your system, by clicking the Backup Wizard button.

3. Click Next on the introductory screen; doing so will bring up the What to Back Up options, which are shown in Figure 14.2.

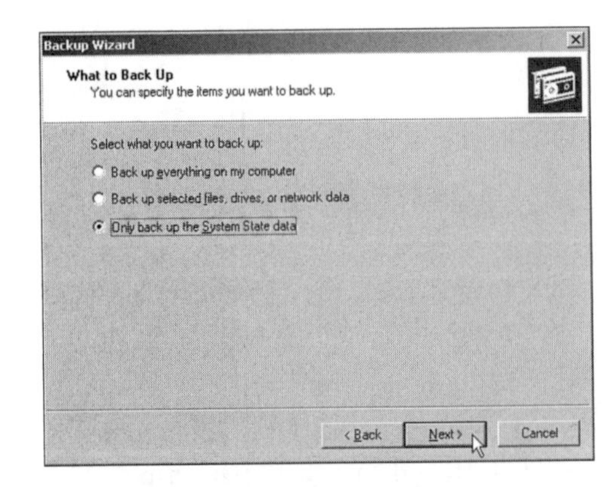

Figure 14.2 The What to Back Up options.

4. Select the third option, which is Only Back Up System State Data. Click Next.

5. You will be asked to specify a location and a type of backup. If you do not have a tape drive attached to your system, you can save the data to a file. This can be useful because the file will be backed up to tape the next time a tape backup is performed. Figure 14.3 shows a backup of system state data taking place.

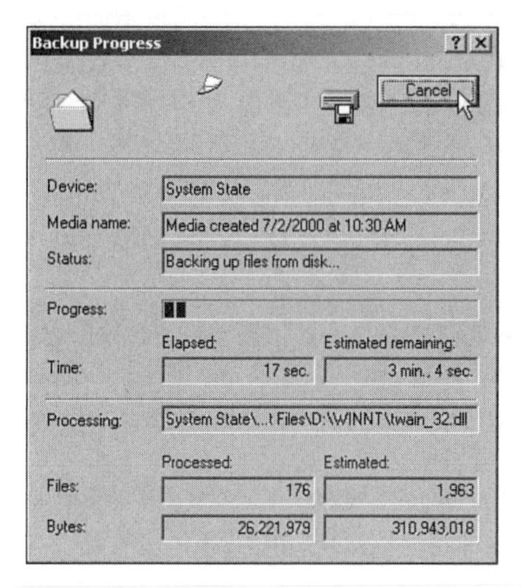

Figure 14.3 A backup taking place.

Recommendations for Backing Up Data

You can't restore a DC fully if you do not have a backup of the system state data. However, even having that data might not be enough if an entire server has been lost in, say, a flood. Make sure you are also backing up all other folders and disk drives on the server periodically. To do this, you can use the built-in backup tool or a third-party utility.

You must be a member of either the Administrators, Backup Operator, or Server Operators group before you can back up data. These are built-in groups; if you do not want to use them, you must assign permissions yourself.

The backup utility built in to Windows 2000 can only be used locally when backing up system data. This means it cannot be configured from a single server to back up system data on all DCs in your enterprise. For this reason alone, you might want to consider purchasing a utility that offers more features.

Restoring AD

Depending on the backup options you have implemented in your environment, you might have three methods to choose from when restoring a Windows 2000 DC. If you have performed a backup by following the steps outlined in the previous section, you could simply perform a restore operation with the built-in backup tool.

When you perform a restore, you have two options: You can perform an authoritative restore or a nonauthoritative restore. We will take a closer look at these two options in a moment.

Alternatively, you can simply rely on AD replication to take care of updating a new DC. In this scenario, a failed DC is simply reinstalled from scratch. Once the DC is online, it updates itself via normal replication techniques. This would occur automatically and would not require any additional administrative tasks. Because this is a simple process, we won't discuss it any further in this chapter. The AD replication process is discussed in Chapter 12, "Active Directory Replication."

Nonauthoritative Restore

The nonauthoritative restore is the simplest form of restore when you are using backup media. A *nonauthoritative restore* is simply a restore of data from backup. Because the data will probably be out of date (presumably, some changes were made to the data in AD after the last backup), normal AD replication processes make sure that the missing data elements are updated.

This would be a common practice if a hard disk failure had taken place. If a hard disk fails, the server might become inoperable. You would simply replace the failed hardware, perform a nonauthoritative restore and then wait for AD replication to bring the DC up to date. This process is faster than simply reinstalling the server and promoting it to a DC with `dcpromo.exe`, because less data will have to be replicated to the restored DC.

Performing a nonauthoritative restore is fairly simple. However, you cannot restore AD data while it is in use. For this reason, the server must be taken offline before a restore can happen. To do this, follow these steps:

1. Restart the server, pressing F8 during startup. The Advanced Startup Options are displayed.
2. Select Directory Services Restore Mode. This starts the server, but it does not start AD.
3. Log in to the server using the Administrators account. This is stored locally on each DC and can be different for each DC in your enterprise.
4. Use the backup tool to restore system state data.
5. Restart the DC.

After the server has been restarted, it is updated by its replication partners. An integrity check also takes place, and various indexes on AD data are rebuilt. This places a temporary additional load on the server during boot time.

Restore operations are highly dependent on the tombstone period discussed in the "Garbage Collection" section earlier in the chapter. If you leave the default tombstone lifetime in place (60 days), you won't be able to restore system state data from tapes that have backups on them older than 60 days. This is because data is deleted once the tombstone lifetime has expired, and introducing a DC with older data that has now been erased from other DCs will cause database inconsistencies. Be careful not to set the tombstone lifetime for too short a time.

Authoritative Restore

The *authoritative restore* can be used to restore individual pieces of AD. This is useful if an error has taken place and an object has been deleted by mistake. Let's look at an example to clarify this process. An administrator is working with the AD Users and Computers tool, and he accidentally deletes an Organizational Unit (OU). The OU contained user objects, and they are deleted as well. Because this change was accepted by a DC, it will be replicated to all AD replicas in the enterprise. Because there is no way to turn off this process, the mistake will soon be widespread on your network.

If the OU contained a small number of accounts, it might not be a problem to simply re-create it; however, if a large number of user objects were involved, it could take some time. An authoritative restore allows an administrator to restore the deleted OU from backup. When an authoritative restore takes place, the property version number (PVN) of the object is, by default, incremented by 100,000. Because the PVN is higher than the copy currently held by the DC's replication partners, the restored object is assumed to be the most up-to-date copy. This change is then forced out to all other DCs via normal AD replication processes.

It is assumed that more than 100,000 changes have not been made to the restored data since the backup took place. You can read about PVNs in Chapter 12.

The process for performing an authoritative restore is somewhat different from the process outlined for a nonauthoritative restore. Once you have restored the system state data, you must not restart the computer. Instead, perform these additional steps:

1. Open a command prompt. Type **`ntdsutil`** and press Enter.
2. Type **`authoritative restore`** and press Enter.
3. Type **`restore subtree`** ***`<distinguished name>`***, where *`<distinguished name>`* is the full path to the object. For an OU called Finance in a domain called HCSNET.COM, this would be `OU=finance,DC=HCSNET,DC=COM`.
4. Type **`quit`**. Type **`quit`** again and press Enter to exit Ntdsutil.
5. Restart the DC.

Moving the AD Database

Because AD is a transactional database, you are able to benefit from some of the standard optimization techniques employed with this type of system. One of the most common suggested techniques is to move the database file to a separate physical hard disk from the log files.

Moving the database to a different physical hard disk from the log files prevents disk contention. The log files are being written to constantly, which means the hard disk heads are fairly busy. When a query is made against the AD database, the heads have to move to read from `ntds.dit`. This contention reduces performance of the disk subsystem.

Moving **ntds.dit** does not mean you should pay less attention to the need to protect your data. Your DCs should minimally be running RAID 5. With a single RAID 5 array, you cannot ensure that the database file and log files are on different physical hard disks. If you decide to move the database file to a different disk, make sure that this disk has either RAID 1 (disk mirroring) or RAID 5 enabled.

You can move the database with the Ntdsutil command-line utility. For this to work, you must have booted your server in Directory Services Restore Mode. Remember that for most of the major database-maintenance tasks (other than performing a backup), you must have booted the server into this mode.

Following are the steps for moving the database file to another hard disk:

1. Restart the server, pressing F8 during startup. The Advanced Startup Options appear.
2. Select Directory Services Restore Mode. This starts the server, but it does not start AD.
3. Log in to the server using the Administrators account. This is stored locally on each DC and can be different for each DC in your enterprise.
4. Open a command prompt. Type **ntdsutil** and press Enter.
5. Type **files** and press Enter.
6. Type **move db to *<drive>**<folder>***, where *<drive>* and *<folder>* make up the full path to the new location. Press Enter.
7. Type **quit** and press Enter. Then type **quit** again and press Enter to exit.
8. Restart the DC.

These commands do not simply move the database file; they also update the Registry so it points to the new location. Simply moving the file will cause the DC to fail.

If you want to move the log files, enter **move logs to *<drive>**<folder>*** instead of **move db to *<drive>*/*<folder>*** in the preceding steps. This moves the log files and also updates the Registry.

Defragmenting the AD Database

Fragmentation has existed on personal computers for many years. The AD database suffers from it just like any other file. Fragmentation of the AD database occurs during the normal operation of a DC. Put simply, as database entries are made and then deleted, gaps can occur in the database file. These gaps cause subsequent records to be written randomly across the hard disk sectors, which reduces performance. Read and write operations are much faster if the database reads and writes are made to consecutive sectors of the disk. This is because the disk head moves much less if the sectors are contiguous.

Windows 2000 includes a defragmentation program that works at the file level to make sure each file is written to consecutive sectors of the disk. The defragmentation utility for AD goes one step further and reorders records *within* the database file.

Fragmentation within a database occurs in the same way that fragmentation of files occurs. As an example of how this works, imagine that an object is created within AD. This data is written to 150 consecutive sectors of the hard disk. Two properties of the object are then deleted. The properties' data was stored in sectors 50, 51, 90, and 99. New data is then written to the database. This data requires four sectors. Because it takes the first available sectors, it ends up in sectors 50, 51, 90, and 99. This data is now fragmented. It will take longer to retrieve this data than it would if the sectors that contained the data were consecutive.

AD defragmentation can occur in two modes: online mode and offline mode. These are defined in the following sections.

Online Defragmentation

Online mode means that the server remains online while the process takes place. The online defragmentation method is slower than offline defragmentation, because the DC must service requests while the defragmentation is taking place, and it offers fewer benefits than offline defragmentation.

Online defragmentation is an automatic process that kicks off, by default, every 12 hours. This method is part of the garbage-collection process discussed in the "Garbage Collection" section earlier in this chapter. Full defragmentation can take place with this method, but the size of the AD database file will never be reduced. The records in the database are moved so they exist on contiguous sectors, but even if there is a lot of empty space in the database file (for instance, after a mass deletion process), the space will not be returned to the file system.

Offline Defragmentation

Offline mode offers greater benefits, but the DC must be taken offline. Because this process is more vulnerable to being corrupted through an unexpected power failure or hardware issue, an offline defragmentation never occurs on the live database file. Instead, a copy of the database is made, and the defragmentation occurs against it. When defragmentation is complete, you must archive the current version of `ntds.dit` that is being used and move the defragmented version into its place.

Do not delete the old copy of **ntds.dit** until the DC has been rebooted and proven to work with the new defragmented file.

Offline defragmentation is the only way to return space from the database to the file system. This is useful after you have performed mass deletions in the database. By default, if you have a database that contains 50MB of data, and 50 percent of that data is deleted, the file remains at 50MB. The only way to return the 25MB to the file system is to perform an offline defragmentation.

Performing an Offline Defragmentation

You must use the Ntdsutil command-line utility to perform an offline defragmentation. For the process to run, you must reboot your server and bring it up in Directory Services Restore Mode. The steps for performing an offline defragmentation are as follows:

1. Restart the server, pressing F8 during startup. The Advanced Startup Options are displayed.
2. Select Directory Services Restore Mode. This starts the server, but it does not start AD.
3. Log in to the server using the Administrators account. This is stored locally on each DC and can be different for each DC in your enterprise.
4. Open a command prompt. Type **`ntdsutil`** and press Enter.
5. Type **`files`** and press Enter.
6. Type **`compact to`** ***`<drive>`*****`\`*****`<folder>`***, where *`<drive>`* and *`<folder>`* are the location where the compacted file will be stored. Press Enter.
7. Once the process is complete, a new `ntds.dit` will exist at this location. Type **`quit`** and press Enter. Type **`quit`** and press Enter again to exit Ntdsutil.
8. Copy the new `ntds.dit` file over the old version of `ntds.dit`.
9. Restart the DC.

Recommendations for AD Database Maintenance

The first recommendation for maintaining an AD database is to do it! Make sure that you understand which options are available to you and that they are scheduled to be performed on a regular basis. You should be especially careful of changing the default settings for tombstone lifetime. This is 60 days by default, and reducing this time frame can prevent you from being able to restore system state data that is past the tombstone lifetime. (Think of this as a sell-by date; you cannot use the backup if the sell-by date—that is, the tombstone lifetime—has expired.)

You should separate the AD database file from the log files. This prevents disk contention and increases the performance of a DC.

Keep in mind that you do not have to perform an offline defragmentation regularly. Instead, you should rely on the online defragmentation process. You should only perform an offline defragmentation if you think you can compact the database and return a significant amount of space back to the file system. This happens when mass deletions have taken place or when a server that used to be a Global Catalog server will now operate simply as a DC.

Practice Questions

Question 1

Mike Stewart is an administrator in a small branch office of 100 users. He has a single DC to speed up authentication for his users. This server is also used for applications and file and print sharing. He has noticed that disk space will get critical within the next month. He checks the server constantly because he is concerned that he will corrupt the AD database if the disk fills up. He calls the help desk, and its staff tells him that a full disk will not corrupt the database because space has already been allocated to guard against this. What are the names of the file or files that are reserving space on this DC? [Check all correct answers]

❑ a. **ntds.dit**

❑ b. **res1.log**

❑ c. **res2.log**

❑ d. **edb.log**

Answers b and c are correct. The `res1.log` and `res2.log` files are placeholders that are used to reserve space should a DC run out of disk space. If a DC runs out of space, all changes for AD can be written to these files before the server shuts down. They are 10MB each. Answer a is incorrect because `ntds.dit` is the name of the AD database file. Answer d is incorrect because `edb.log` is the log file's name.

Question 2

Kate Bush is a system administrator for a banking organization. Kate knows that she should back up her DC regularly, but she has not done it for a while because several urgent projects have been going on, and the server could not be taken offline. She places a call to Microsoft's support desk to ask for advice about protecting herself from a server failure. What did the support desk tell Kate?

- ❍ a. Kate was told that she must take the server offline to perform a backup. Suffering from the lack of a server late at night is far better than losing it completely and not being able to get it back.
- ❍ b. Kate was told that she should still perform a backup even if the server is being used. Although she won't be able to back up the log files for AD because they are in use, she can still back up the database and Registry files. This alone would be enough to get the DC functioning again.
- ❍ c. Kate was told not to worry. The database is transactional and can protect itself from failures automatically. Backing up to a file or tape is a precautionary measure that is desirable but not essential.
- ❍ d. Kate was told to go ahead and perform a backup of system state data. The DC does not have to be taken offline for this process to take place.

Answer d is correct. The built-in backup utility can be used to perform an online backup. You cannot back up remote servers using this utility; therefore, it must be run on each DC. Answer a is incorrect because it is not necessary to take the server offline to perform a backup. Answer b is incorrect because an online backup can back up log files. Answer c is incorrect because system backup is essential.

Question 3

Duncan Willis is reviewing the files and folders on his server to make sure the system is operating efficiently. When he looks in the folder that contains the AD files, he is surprised to find a group of files with similar names: **edb00001.log**, **edb00002.log**, and **edb00003.log**. Each of these files is taking up 10MB of space. Duncan is tempted to simply delete them because they are wasting space on his system, but he is concerned they might be an important part of AD. Duncan researches the situation and discovers that, indeed, these files should not be deleted. What are these files used for?

❍ a. These files are checkpoint files, and they store a pointer to the **edb.log** file. The pointer allows AD to know which entries in the log file have been written out to the database file.

❍ b. These files are placeholders that exist to prevent AD from failing when the server runs out of hard disk space.

❍ c. These files are backups of the AD database files. They are created every 60 days on each DC.

❍ d. These files are old log files. They will be deleted automatically when the system no longer needs them.

Answer d is correct. The AD log file is called `edb.log`. When this file is full, it is archived using the naming scheme `edb*****.log`, where the asterisks are replaced by a sequential number. There is no need to delete these files. Answers a, b, and c are all invalid answers.

Question 4

Zevi Mehlman is about to delete 1,000 user objects from his network. He backs up the AD database files and then deletes the records. When he checks the size of the database file to see how much space he has saved, he is disappointed to find that the file has not been reduced in size at all. Zevi decides to wait for a while to see if AD replication reduces the file size. After waiting a week, the file still has not reduced in size. Why is the file the same size it was before the deletions took place?

❍ a. At the same time Zevi is deleting records, someone else has been adding them. The space savings have been offset by the additions.

❍ b. The database will never reduce in size because of deletions.

❍ c. The database will not reduce in size until the tombstone lifetime has expired. Then the database will be compacted.

❍ d. The AD database will not be reduced until AD replication has taken place. Although this will take a variable amount of time, on average it takes 24 hours before all DCs are aware of the deletions and the size of their AD database files is reduced.

Answers b is correct. The database file size will remain static. It can grow automatically, but it does not reduce in size. Answer a is incorrect because deleting a record does not decrease the size of the database file. Answer c is incorrect because tombstoning defines the time before an object is physically deleted from the database, but even this will not physically change the database file size. Answer d is incorrect because replication will not decrease the size of the database.

Question 5

Siobhan Chamberlin has inherited a Windows 2000 network. Siobhan knows that a lot of deletions had been made from the AD database, and she would like to regain the space and have it returned to the file system. Siobhan knows that the garbage-collection process performs a defragmentation on a regular schedule (every 12 hours). She decides to wait 12 hours for the defragmentation process to take place and to regain the space. However, when Siobhan checks the next day, she finds to her disappointment that although the garbage-collection process took place, the database size has remained the same. Why didn't the defragmentation process reduce the file size?

❍ a. This is not the job of defragmentation. To recover the disk space, Siobhan must back up and restore the database file.

❍ b. The garbage-collection process performs online defragmentation. This process does not recover disk space. Siobhan must take the DC offline and perform an offline defragmentation for this to take place.

❍ c. The database file did not have any free space. Because the database file was full, it did not reduce in size.

❍ d. It is not possible to reduce the size of the database file manually. AD will do this every 60 days if necessary.

Answer b is correct. There are two kinds of defragmentation: online and offline. The garbage-collection process uses online defragmentation, and this process cannot reduce the size of the database file. Siobhan must take the DC offline and use the Ntdsutil command-line utility to perform an offline defragmentation and return the space to the file system. Answer a is incorrect because reducing the file size is indeed the job of defragmentation. Answer c is incorrect because the database file was not full. Answer d is incorrect because it is possible to reduce the size of the database file manually.

Question 6

By default, garbage collection takes place on a system every 60 days. The DCs on Leilani Evans' network have plenty of disk space. In addition, she would like to extend the usefulness of her backups. She decides to change the garbage-collection process to occur every 90 days. Which tool would Leilani use to do this?

❍ a. Leilani must use ADSIEdit to change the garbage-collection period.

❍ b. Leilani must use Ntdsutil to change the garbage-collection period.

❍ c. Leilani must use both Ntdsutil and Active Directory Domains and Trusts.

❍ d. Leilani must make the change using Active Directory Domains and Trusts.

Answer a is correct. Leilani must use ADSIEdit to do this. Answer b is incorrect because, although Ntdsutil has many uses, changing the garbage-collection interval is not one of them. Answers c and d are incorrect because Active Directory Domains and Trusts is a tool used for domain management.

Question 7

Moira Chamberlin is a system administrator for an insurance company. Moira accidentally deleted an OU and wants to get it back. Fortunately, she performed a backup of AD just one hour before the deletion. Moira starts the DC in Directory Services Restore Mode and performs a restore using the backup utility. When she is done, she restarts the server. The server comes back perfectly; however, within 30 minutes, the OU she has just restored is once again deleted. Why did this happen?

❍ a. A deleted object cannot be brought back using backup/restore because AD replication mechanisms will cause the object to be deleted.

❍ b. Moira needs to perform the restore on all of her DCs to bring them up to date. If she does not do this, AD replication will overwrite any data she restores that had previously been deleted.

❍ c. Moira forgot to check the Authoritative Restore button in the backup/restore utility. If this is not done, the restore is nonauthoritative, and the deleted data will be deleted when AD replication takes place.

❍ d. Moira cannot use the backup/restore utility alone to perform this task. After the restore is done—but before the DC is brought back online—she must run the Ntdsutil command-line utility and mark the OU as an authoritative object.

Answer d is correct. If you want to restore data and have it replicated to all other DCs in the domain, you must perform an authoritative restore. This restore operation is performed by using the backup/restore utility and Ntdsutil. Answer a is incorrect because Moira can restore deleted data. Answer b is incorrect because an authoritative restore means all the DCs do not have to be restored. Answer c is incorrect because there is no "Authoritative Restore" button.

Question 8

Pamela Young is a system administrator for a large enterprise. Pamela would like to increase the performance of AD reads ands writes. She remembers reading that to do this she should move the AD database file to a different physical disk from the log files. Her servers are all configured the same way. There is a single disk with the operating system installed on it and a RAID 5 array that includes the AD database file. Pamela decides to move the database file to single hard disk. During a conversation with her boss, however, she is told that she must not do this. Why did her boss tell her this?

- ❍ a. Her boss does not understand AD. He is wrong; the database should be moved.
- ❍ b. Although Pamela will gain some benefits from making the move, the lack of data protection in this particular instance means it is not a good idea.
- ❍ c. If performance can be gained by moving the database file, Windows 2000 will move it automatically.
- ❍ d. RAID 5 is a superior system. Disk writes on a RAID 5 system are substantially faster than any other RAID system; therefore, the file is best left where it is.

Answer b is correct. Although on the surface moving the database file to single hard disk seems like a good move, the single disk drive offers no data protection. In this case, it is best to leave the database on the RAID 5 volume. Answer a is incorrect because Pamela's boss gave good advice. Answer c is incorrect because Windows 2000 will never move the file automatically. Answer d is incorrect because writes to a RAID 5 array are actually slightly slower than writes to other types of RAID systems.

Question 9

John knows that there is a lot of space being taken up by the AD database, and he wants to return it to the file system. John realizes he must perform an offline defragmentation to achieve this goal. He boots the server into Directory Services Restore Mode and performs the defragmentation. When the defragmentation is complete, he reboots the server. Much to his surprise, the database size did not change. What is the most obvious reason for this?

❍ a. In fact, there was no free space in the database file. Although John followed the correct steps, he simply didn't gain anything.

❍ b. The defragmentation must have failed. John should check the System log on his Windows 2000 server to find out why and then run the defragmentation again.

❍ c. John forgot a step. Once the process had completed, he should have archived the old database file and copied the newly defragmented copy in its place.

❍ d. The database always keeps 25 percent of its space available. This helps in case of system failure. Although there is space in the database file, there is not enough to maintain this ratio and return space to the file system.

Answer c is correct. In the case of an offline defragmentation, a second copy of the database is made. This copy will be the compressed copy and must be copied to the AD database folder before the server is started up. Therefore, answers a, b, and d are all incorrect.

Question 10

Graham Young is a system administrator who has been diligently performing backups of his system state data every 90 days. After 85 days, a server fails because of a hard disk failure. Graham installs a new hard disk and then reinstalls Windows 2000. When this is complete, he reboots to Directory Services Restore Mode, intending to use his last backup. Graham calls a friend to refresh his mind on the steps for restoring AD, and his friend advises him that his backups are too old. Graham doesn't believe this. Who is correct?

❍ a. Graham is correct. You can use any backed up data to restore AD files.

❍ b. His friend is correct. AD has a limit of 30 days on AD restores. Data that is older than this will be replaced by the AD replication process anyway, so Windows 2000 prevents it from being restored.

❍ c. Graham is correct. Although the data is old, he can rely on the AD replication to clear up any problems he might be causing.

❍ d. His friend is correct. Because the backed up data is older than the garbage-collection process, Graham could introduce inconsistencies to his DC if he uses this backup.

Answer d is correct. You can adjust the garbage-collection process to fit in with your backup schedule. However, you should never attempt to restore data from a backup that is older that the garbage-collection process interval (the default is 60 days). Answer a is incorrect because the backups are indeed too old to be used. Answer b is incorrect because there is no 30-day limit on restores. Answer c is incorrect because replication would not fix the bad data.

Need to Know More?

Blum, Daniel J. *Understanding Active Directory Services*. Microsoft Press. Redmond, WA, 1999. ISBN 1572317213.

This resource is a guide to architecture, deployment strategies, and integration.

Iseminger, David. *Active Directory Services for Microsoft Windows 2000*. Microsoft Press. Redmond, WA, 2000. ISBN 0735606242.

This book covers all the new functionality of AD in a clear, concise manner.

Microsoft Consulting Services. *Building an Enterprise Active Directory: Notes from the Field*. Microsoft Press. Redmond, WA, 2000. ISBN 0735608601.

This book is geared toward consultants, system administrators, and other professionals charged with making big AD systems work. It contains lots of valuable database-sizing information.

Norris-Lowe, Alistair G. *Windows 2000 Active Directory*. O'Reilly & Associates. Sebastopol, CA, 2000. ISBN 1565926382.

This book covers Active Directory Services Interface (ASDI) scripting using Windows Script Host (WSH), Visual Basic, and even ASPs for browser-based administration.

Remote Installation Services (RIS)

Terms you'll need to understand:

- ✓ IntelliMirror
- ✓ Preboot execution environment (PXE)
- ✓ RISetup
- ✓ RIPrep
- ✓ Authorizing
- ✓ **RBFG.EXE**
- ✓ Prestaging

Techniques you'll need to master:

- ✓ Installing RIS on a Windows 2000 Server
- ✓ Using RISetup to create and configure a RIS server
- ✓ Using RIPrep to create RIS images for deployment
- ✓ Creating RIS boot disks
- ✓ Authorizing a RIS server
- ✓ Using Active Directory Users and Computers to configure security settings
- ✓ Understanding the implementation of prestaging

Remote Installation Services (RIS) is a Windows 2000 Server component that allows Windows 2000 Professional and Windows XP Professional to be installed remotely onto systems without requiring a support technician to set the installation options. RIS is a total desktop-management solution that combines Folder Redirection, Offline Folders, desktop settings management, roaming profiles, software installation and management, and Group Policy settings that follow a user, group, or computer. These and other technologies make up what Windows 2000 calls *IntelliMirror*. Through these technologies included in Windows 2000, an administrator can effectively deploy new PCs and even reinstall existing PCs from a central location, without having to go out to a user's office.

An Overview of RIS

With IntelliMirror, users no longer have to wait unproductively for an IT staff member to show up after they have placed a help desk call. With RIS, even the entire operating system can be reinstalled upon request, with a preconfigured operating system (OS) image applied to the computer. Users need only supply their logon information.

A very important factor of RIS to keep in mind is that the process of applying an OS image to a computer through RIS erases all existing data on the hard drive. For obvious reasons, it is therefore important to ensure that any nonreplaceable user information is backed up prior to reinstalling the OS. Because RIS erases the hard drive, it cannot be used to upgrade an existing OS, such as Windows 98 or NT Workstation 4. Furthermore, RIS can be used to install only Windows 2000 Professional. You cannot install Windows 9*X* or NT with RIS.

To automate an OS upgrade or install a non–Windows 2000 or XP Professional OS on a client PC, you need to look at a more extensive systems-management utility, such as Microsoft Systems Management Server (SMS).

A RIS Scenario

To fully realize the power of RIS and IntelliMirror, imagine a situation where the hard drive in a user's compliant PC has a hardware failure. A desktop support technician would need to go to the user's office and replace the hard drive with a new one. So far, nothing out of the ordinary. However, instead of having to be there for half a day reinstalling the OS and all the applications, the technician could activate a RIS installation and walk away.

The user would only need to type in his or her username and password, and the rest of the process of installing Windows 2000 or XP Professional would proceed automatically.

Once the OS is installed, the user would log on to the network. Group Policy would then run, and through Software Installation and Maintenance settings (assigned and published applications) and desktop settings management, the user would have access to all his or her applications. In addition, the desktop and Start menu settings would return to the state they were in prior to the hard drive crash. The user could begin productive work immediately, and all this would take place automatically, without any intervention by an administrator or desktop support technician.

RIS Functionality

RIS works by creating a *preboot execution environment (PXE)* that enables a compliant client PC to gain basic TCP/IP network connectivity. PXE (pronounced *pixie*) technology is not integrated into every network card, so you must ensure that you have a PXE-compliant adapter before you can use RIS.

Once network connectivity is established, a series of scripts can be run to bring the client to the point of installing the OS. With RIS, an administrator can choose to have a computer go through the following types of installations:

- **RISetup**—A CD-like installation of Windows 2000 Professional, as if a normal installation were taking place off a CD
- **RIPrep**—A customized installation to the point of scripting the install with an answer file so that the user isn't required to choose any options during setup

Now that you have a basic understanding of what RIS does, let's discuss the components required for RIS.

RIS Network Requirements

To function, RIS depends on a number of components already being installed and configured on a Windows 2000 network. The following components are absolutely necessary:

- Remote Installation Services (RIS) service
- Domain Name Service (DNS)

- Dynamic Host Configuration Protocol (DHCP) server
- Active Directory

RIS Service

Windows 2000 includes the RIS service as an optional component that can be installed through the Windows Components Wizard of the Add/Remove Programs applet in Control Panel. RIS runs as a service on at least one Windows 2000 Server system on the network, listening for client requests. In addition, the RIS server stores the OS images that the client computer can choose from when it invokes RIS. An administrator can use Group Policy to determine what images should be available to what users.

Domain Name Service (DNS)

DNS is the service that enables RIS clients to find RIS servers on the network. Windows 2000 RIS servers register themselves in DNS so that when a RIS client establishes network connectivity, it has the name and IP address of a RIS server to pull an image from. Microsoft DNS is not required as long as the third-party DNS server used supports RFCs 2052 (SRV RR) and 2136 (Dynamic Updates).

Dynamic Host Configuration Protocol (DHCP) Server

To establish network connectivity, a RIS client must have an IP address. Because the entire process takes place at the hardware level, it is not possible to provide a static IP address. RIS, therefore, uses dynamic addressing to obtain an IP address and connect to the network. For a RIS client to obtain a dynamic address, a DHCP server must be running on the network. This can be either a Microsoft DHCP server or a third-party DHCP server.

Active Directory

RIS depends on Active Directory (AD) to function for two reasons. First, RIS uses Group Policy, which is dependent on AD, to determine permissions for user accounts and computer accounts prior to supplying RIS image choices to the user. Second, RIS uses network configuration settings stored in AD to determine information such as what RIS server should be used in the case where multiple RIS servers exist on a network. In addition, AD information is used for tasks such as using a standard naming convention for new computers and determining what domain or Organizational Unit (OU) to place the new computer in.

Let's look at the server and client components that make up RIS.

RIS Client and Server Components

In addition to the requirement listed in the previous section, there are components at both the client and server that enable RIS to function.

Client Requirements of RIS

A client computer can meet RIS requirements in one of the following three ways:

- The client can meet the NetPC or PC98 standard.
- The client can have a compatible network adapter.
- The client can have a compliant BIOS.

In addition, there are requirements that a client computer must meet to use RIS:

- The client must meet the hardware requirements, explained in an upcoming section.
- The client must eventually invoke the Client Installation Wizard.

NetPC or PC98 Standard

One way a computer can meet the requirements of RIS is to conform to the NetPC or PC98 standard. A client computer that meets the requirements set forth by either the NetPC or PC98 standard will include PXE functionality. Compliant computers must have version 1.0b at minimum to work with RIS.

Creating a RIS boot disk is necessary if you do not have a PXE-capable network adapter or motherboard but you do have a network adapter that is supported by the RIS boot disk creation utility Remote Boot Floppy Generator (**rbfg.exe**), which we will discuss later in this chapter.

Compliant BIOS

Another way a PC can meet the requirements of RIS is to have a compliant motherboard BIOS, which will include the necessary PXE functionality for

RIS. If you don't currently have a PXE-capable motherboard, contact the manufacturer about a possible Flash upgrade, because almost all motherboards are now upgradeable.

Compatible Network Adapters

Additionally, to use RIS, a compliant client computer can simply have a compatible network adapter installed. A compliant network adapter will be PXE compliant, meaning it supports the preboot execution environment standard. Because of Plug and Play requirements, a compliant network card is also PCI based. This excludes PCMCIA (Personal Computer Memory Card International Association) network adapters typically found in laptops. Therefore, if you want to use RIS with a laptop system, you must first connect the laptop to a docking station that contains a PCI network adapter that also has PXE functionality.

If the motherboard is not compliant, the computer does not meet NetPC or PC98 standards, and you don't have a PXE-complaint network adapter, it might still be possible to use RIS. Windows 2000 includes a utility called `rbfg.exe` that allows an administrator to create a bootable floppy disk that emulates the PXE environment, although there isn't a large number of non-PXE–compliant network cards that Windows 2000 supports.

Hardware Requirements

For RIS to be used on a client computer, the client must meet the following hardware requirements:

- Pentium 166 or faster CPU
- 32MB of RAM minimum (64MB recommended)
- 800MB or larger hard drive
- DHCP PXE-based boot ROM or network adapter supported by the RIS boot floppy

Client Installation Wizard

The Client Installation Wizard is the client-side piece for RIS, which is downloaded to the client and communicates with the RIS server. A default set of screens provided by the Boot Information Negotiation Layer (BINL) server-side service is presented to the user. These screens guide the user through the Client Installation Wizard to log on and select Windows 2000 Professional installation options that have been defined by the administrator. The user invokes the Client Installation Wizard by pressing F12 once the

PC's POST (power-on self test) process has completed and before the OS starts booting.

Note that the boot process is not secure; information is sent over the network in cleartext that can be read with a packet sniffer. Therefore, you should ensure that there are only limited RIS servers on the network, and you should maintain control over who is allowed to set up and configure RIS servers in general.

Server Components of RIS

RIS servers can be either domain controllers (DCs) or member servers. The RIS services on a server are less dependent on specific hardware than client computers are, although there are some hardware requirements to consider. They are as follows:

- Pentium 166 or faster CPU. 200+ is recommended.
- 96MB to 128MB of RAM required when running AD, DNS, and DHCP services.
- 10MB Ethernet adapter. 100MB is recommended.
- Access to Windows 2000 or XP Professional installation files. This can be a CD-ROM or network share or a local directory with a copy of the files.
- 2GB hard disk for the RIS server's folder tree. Devoting an entire hard disk partition to the directory tree for RIS is recommended.
- NTFS-formatted partition for RIS images. RIS cannot be installed on Distributed File System (Dfs) or Encrypting File System (EFS) volumes.

As previously mentioned, the requirements to use RIS from the server end include AD, DNS, DHCP, and the RIS service. When RIS is installed through Add/Remove Programs (`RISetup.exe`, the program that actually installs RIS, is discussed in the "Configuring RIS with RISetup" section later in this chapter), additional services are installed on the server. These services include the following:

- **Boot Information Negotiation Layer (BINL)**—This service listens for client DHCP/PXE requests. Additionally, BINL redirects clients to the appropriate files needed for installation when using the Client Installation Wizard. It is the BINL service that verifies logon credentials with AD.
- **Trivial File Transfer Protocol daemon (TFTPD)**—RIS uses TFTP to initially download all files to a client that are necessary to begin the

Windows 2000 or XP Professional installation. Included in this download is `Startrom.com`, which is the bootstrap program that displays the message for the user to press F12 for Network Services. If the user does press F12 within three seconds, the Client Installation Wizard is downloaded through TFTP to the client computer.

- **Single Instance Store (SIS)**—The SIS service seeks to reduce disk space requirements for RIS images by combining duplicate files. The service contains an NTFS file system filter (RIS, you'll recall, can be installed only on an NTFS partition) and the service that manages images on the RIS installation partition.
- **`RIPrep.exe`**—This is another server component that is used to create RIS images. We discuss `RIPrep.exe` later in this chapter in the "Creating RIS Images" section.

Setting Up and Configuring RIS

If you perform a typical installation of Windows 2000 Server at the time you run setup, RIS will not be installed. RIS is an optional component that can either be selected in a custom setup or added later through the Windows Components Wizard of the Add/Remove Programs applet in Control Panel.

Installing RIS

The steps for installing RIS are as follows:

1. Select Start, Programs\Administrative Tools, Configure Your Server. Click Advanced, Optional Components, Start, Windows Components Wizard. Select the Remote Installation Services check box and click Next.
2. Once you click Next, the installation portion of the wizard begins configuring RIS. Windows 2000 installs RIS services, but it does not actually allow any configuration of RIS during this initial setup. Once RIS is installed, you will see the completion screen. Click Finish and restart your computer when prompted.

Configuring RIS with RISetup

Once RIS is installed and you have restarted your computer, you still need to configure RIS. `RISetup.exe` is the utility used for this purpose, and it can be invoked by selecting Start, Run and typing **risetup.exe**. The Remote Installation Services Setup Wizard, shown in Figure 15.1, prepares the server to be a RIS server.

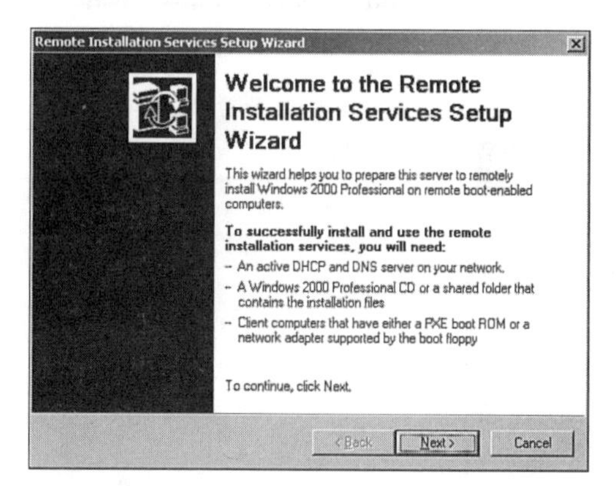

Figure 15.1 The RIS Setup Wizard is invoked through the **RISetup.exe** command.

Once the wizard is initiated, it walks you through the following steps:

1. The first option that you are presented with, shown in Figure 15.2, is the installation directory for RIS. Note that this directory must reside on an NTFS partition with sufficient disk space for your RIS images. If you attempt to install to a non-NTFS partition, the setup wizard returns an error message. Windows 2000 provides a default drive and directory, but the drive may or may not be valid (the wizard does not check the drive for file system type and disk space before offering it as a choice). Therefore, you might have to choose a different drive for your RIS installation. In most cases, however, you should not have to change the default directory name.

Be aware of the limitations on the location of your RIS default drive and directory. Not only do you need an NTFS partition, but you cannot install the remote installation folder on the same drive as the server's operating system files.

2. The next screen, shown in Figure 15.3, asks whether you want your RIS server to immediately begin servicing requests once you have completed setup. By default, RIS services do not begin immediately after setup. This is primarily a security measure, and it is best to abide by this safeguard until the server is completely configured. Because you can't use RIS anyway until you've created a RIS image, there is little sense in having the services running when, as mentioned earlier, RIS

data is sent to and from the server in cleartext. An unscrupulous individual could exploit your new RIS server if it were online before you were ready to start using it. In addition to deciding whether or not to start RIS, you can choose whether RIS should respond to unknown computers. Select your choices and then click Next.

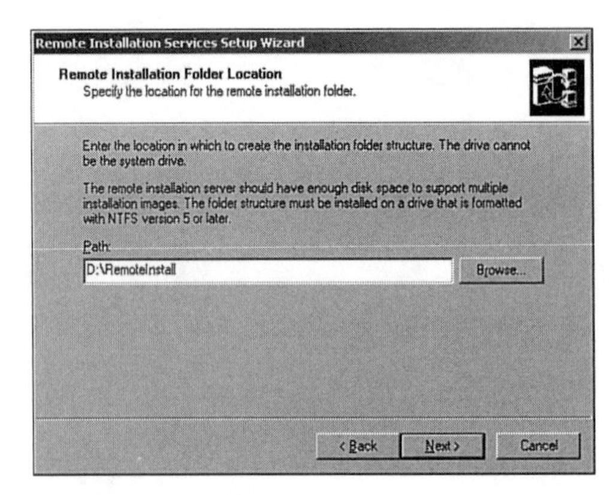

Figure 15.2 The first step in installing RIS is choosing an installation directory.

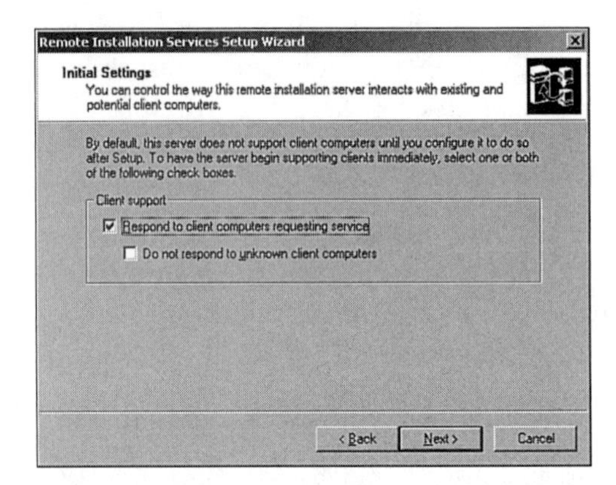

Figure 15.3 You can choose whether to start servicing RIS clients immediately and whether RIS should respond to unknown computers.

3. The next step in configuring RIS is to point the setup wizard to the installation files for Windows 2000 or XP Professional. This can be a CD or a network path. Once you define your directory, click Next.
4. Once you define your installation path, the setup wizard prompts you for the name of the folder to copy the Windows 2000 or XP Professional setup files to on the RIS server. Unless you have a specific need to change it, the default directory supplied by RIS setup should be fine. Click Next.

5. On the next screen, shown in Figure 15.4, type in a "friendly description" for your RIS image, as well as the help text that will be shown in the Client Installation Wizard when the user presses F12 to start RIS on the client. The friendly description makes it easier for users to determine what RIS image to use when they read the choices in the Client Installation Wizard. Click Next.

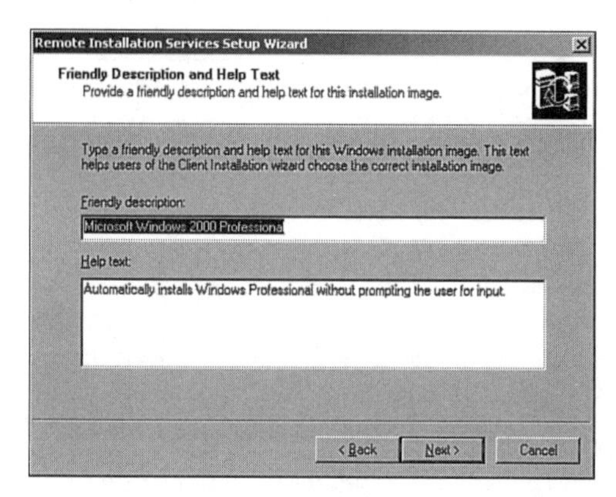

Figure 15.4 Assigning a friendly description to your RIS image.

6. Before setup actually begins, you are given the chance to review your settings and go back to change any you wish. Make a notation of the installation folder where the image will be placed. Once you click Finish, installation begins. The RIS setup then begins running through its tasks list.

7. Once you have completed configuring RIS, you can go into Windows Explorer and look at the new directory structure.

It's a good idea for RIS servers to be placed in the same site as the client computers that will be requesting RIS images. This increases performance and lowers the impact of RIS traffic across slow links to other sites.

Now that you have set up and configured RIS, let's look at how to create additional RIS images and RIS boot disks.

Creating RIS Images

As you have seen, CD-based RIS images can be created through the RISetup utility. Additionally, the `RIPrep.exe` utility allows an administrator to clone a standard corporate desktop for deployment to other systems. In this section, we examine the RIPrep utility and discuss creating RIS boot disks for compatible network adapters.

RIPrep

Unlike RISetup, which allows an administrator to deploy only a CD-based setup of Windows 2000 or XP Professional (even a network-based installation is just a copy of the files from the CD shared on a network drive), RIPrep can be used to deploy the OS, along with customized settings and even locally installed desktop applications. This process is not the true disk cloning that products such as Norton Ghost provide; it can be used only with Windows 2000 or XP Professional. Additionally, RIPrep does not support multiple hard drives or multiple partitions on the computer that the image is being created on.

Other limitations of RIPrep include the requirement that a CD-based image that is the same version and language as the RIPrep image also exist on the RIS server, and that the target system must have the same hardware abstraction layer (HAL) as the system used to create the image. By having the same HAL, an image created on a single-processor system cannot be installed onto a dual-processor system. Because Windows 2000 does not support Alpha processors like NT 4, you won't have to worry about mixing up Intel (i386) and Alpha images.

Although RIPrep has some limitations, there are advantages to using it over RISetup to create images. Most notably, RIPrep allows an administrator to create a standard desktop image and then use RIS to deploy it to new computers as they come in from an OEM (original equipment manufacturer). Additionally, reinstallation of the OS is much faster from an RIPrep image, because the image is being applied as a copy operation to the target hard drive and not running through an actual Windows 2000 installation, as would happen with a CD or network-based RISetup image.

Creating Images with RIPrep

Creating an image with RIPrep is a two-step process. First, you install and configure a computer with Windows 2000 or XP Professional and the specific applications and settings you want to include in the image. Second, you run `RIPrep.exe` from the RIS server, but it's important to remember that although the `RIPrep.exe` utility is located on the RIS server, it is *executed* from the RIS client that the image is being created on.

Here's how to execute the `RIPrep.exe` utility:

1. From the client, click Start, Run.
2. In the Run box, type the following:

   `\\RISserver_name\reminst\admin\i386\riprep.exe`

If you attempt to run `RIPrep.exe` from a non–Windows 2000 or XP Professional system, you receive an error message stating that the utility will run only on Windows 2000 Professional. When you run RIPrep from a valid system, the Remote Installation Preparation Wizard starts, as shown in Figure 15.5.

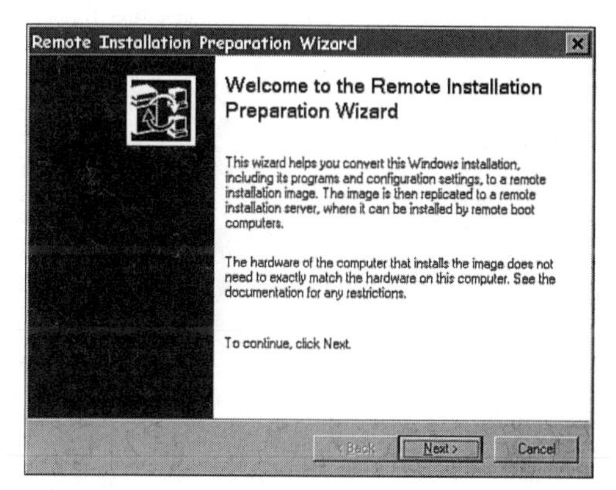

Figure 15.5 You start the Remote Installation Preparation Wizard by executing **RIPrep.exe** from a Windows 2000 Professional client computer.

Once the wizard is initiated and you have clicked Next, follow these steps to create an image with RIS:

1. Even though you ran `RIPrep.exe` from one RIS server, you do not have to necessarily copy the image you are creating to that particular server. As shown in Figure 15.6, you choose which RIS server to copy the image to. After indicating your choice, click Next.
2. Supply the name of the installation folder on the RIS server previously chosen. Typically, you would type the name of an existing folder only if you were replacing an existing image. If this new image will not be replacing an existing image, type in a new folder name, as shown in Figure 15.7, and click Next.

In this walkthrough example, the image is being created for a corporate Web developer environment. For that reason, we gave the directory a descriptive name—**webdev**—to identify the image it contains on the RIS server.

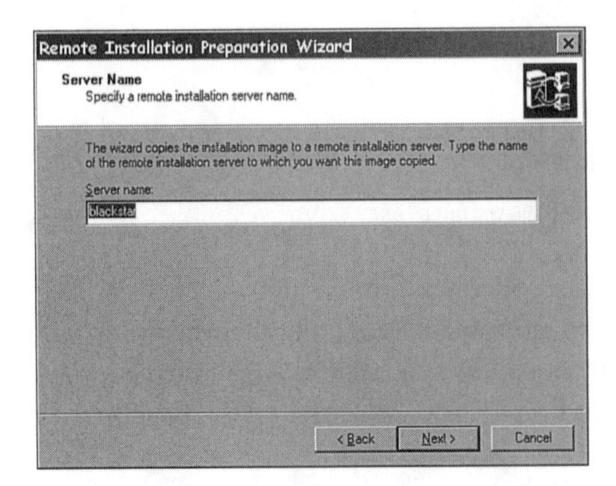

Figure 15.6 If you have multiple RIS servers on your network, you can choose which server should receive the image.

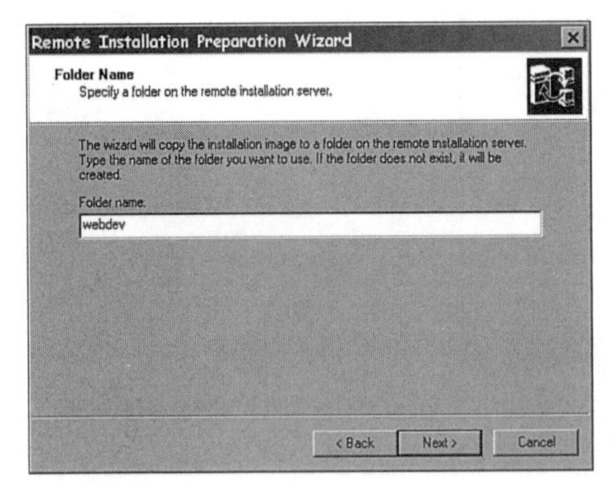

Figure 15.7 Supply a directory name on the RIS server for the Remote Installation Preparation Wizard to copy the image.

3. The next step is to assign a friendly name to the image and create the help text. The friendly name is what displays in the list of available images during the Client Installation Wizard. The help text provides an additional description to help the user identify the correct image to use when acting as a RIS client. In our sample RIS image for a Web development system, we list the applications that will be installed on the system, along with the Windows 2000 Professional OS as part of the imaging process. Click Next.

4. At this point, if you have any programs or services running that could interfere with the imaging process, Windows 2000 warns you. Figure 15.8 lists a number of programs and services that were running on the RIS image source workstation at the time this sample image was being

created. Once you have closed the programs and stopped the necessary services, click Next.

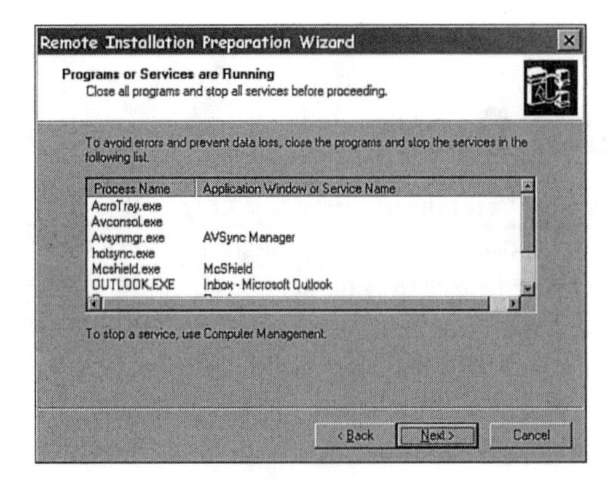

Figure 15.8 The Remote Installation Preparation Wizard prompts you to close any programs and services that might interfere with the imaging process.

5. Before beginning the actual image creation, the wizard allows you to review your choices. Once you have done so and made any necessary revisions, click Next.
6. The last step is an information dialog box from the Remote Installation Preparation Wizard that describes the process that is about to occur. Once you understand what is about to happen on your system, click Next to continue. You can watch the wizard image process taking place as various portions are completed.

Images created by the Remote Installation Preparation Wizard are stored in the same subfolder as images created during RISetup. If you did not change the default settings when we examined the RISetup Wizard earlier in this chapter in the "Configuring RIS with RISetup" section and are using an English-language version of Windows 2000 Server, your RIS directory structure will be as follows:

- `\RemoteInstall\Setup\English\Images\win2000.pro\i386\`

  This is the default image created during the RISetup Wizard earlier. There are subdirectories underneath `i386` for this CD-based installation image, for `system32`, `templates`, and `uniproc`.

- `\RemoteInstall\Setup\English\Images\webdev\i386\`

  This is the image directory we just created for our `webdev` image. A directory called `Mirror1` that appears under `i386` does not appear in the subdirectories of an RISetup-created image.

It is worth repeating that RIPrep can create images only for single-partition systems. If you want to have Windows 2000 Professional installed to a partition other than the boot partition, the RIS image process will fail.

Creating RIS Boot Disks

Creating a RIS boot disk is necessary if you do not have a PXE-capable network adapter or motherboard but you do have a network adapter that is supported by the RIS boot disk creation utility, `rbfg.exe`, which is located under `%systemroot%\system32\dllcache`. We touched briefly on the Windows 2000 Remote Boot Floppy Generator (RBFG) earlier in this chapter, but we did not discuss actually creating disks. In this section, you will experience actually creating a RIS boot disk.

There is not much to the RBFG, really. Essentially, as you can see from Figure 15.9, you have the option to view the supported adapter list or create the disk. Most of the selections are fairly self-explanatory (for example, the About selection and the possibility of using a secondary floppy). The RBFG utility erases the floppy in the drive without warning you first, so make sure you have inserted the correct disk and selected the correct drive before continuing.

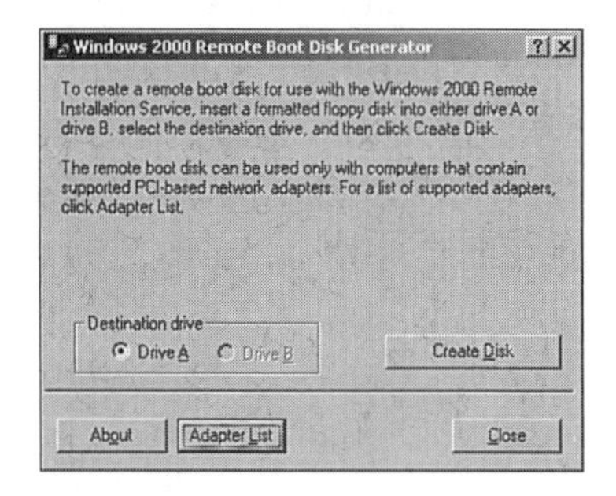

Figure 15.9 The RBFG allows you to create a network-bootable disk for supported network adapters.

To see the list of supported adapters, click the Adapter List button in the utility. The RIS boot disk emulates a PXE environment for these supported non–PXE-capable network adapters, and if you look, you will notice that, once created, the boot disk contains only a single file: `RISDISK`.

There's no file extension on `RISDISK`, and the file is only 90KB in size. However, if you have a supported network adapter, this disk is all you need to start the Client Installation Wizard.

Managing RIS Security

Security is always an important issue when discussing networking topics, and it is no different with RIS. What steps can be taken to prevent unauthorized individuals from setting RIS servers, creating images, or even gaining network connectivity through RIS and installing an image? Fortunately, RIS has some built-in safeguards that allow you to maintain some control over who is able to use RIS. Some of these security services include the following:

- Requiring RIS servers to be authorized before they can respond to RIS client requests
- Using Group Policy to manage RIS client installation options
- Editing configuration settings through the AD Users and Computers administrative tool

Authorizing a RIS Server

Before a RIS server can service client requests, it must first be authorized into AD. You can authorize a RIS server in one of the following ways:

- In the RIS Setup Wizard, you can choose to have the RIS server start responding to client requests immediately upon completion of the wizard. As discussed previously in this chapter, this is not the recommended method of authorization, and by default, the box to enable immediate authorization is not checked.
- If you install RIS onto an authorized DHCP server, you do not have to take any further steps to authorize RIS. The authorization will be passed along from DHCP to RIS because the server is already authorized in AD.
- If you install RIS onto a server that is *not* already an authorized DHCP server, you can authorize RIS through the DHCP administrator tool. In the DHCP Microsoft Management Console (MMC), right-click the DHCP root node of the tree and select Manage Authorized Servers. Click the Authorize button and type in the fully qualified domain name (FQDN) or Internet Protocol (IP) address of the RIS server. Confirm that this is the server you want to authorize, and you are set.

Similar to the requirements for RIS, Windows 2000 requires DHCP servers to be authorized in AD before they can start distributing IP addresses to clients. Because RIS is dependent on DHCP, it makes sense to use a similar authentication scheme for bringing new RIS servers into an AD network.

To authorize a RIS server, the account you are logged on with must be a member of the Enterprise Admins security group, which resides in the root domain of your organization's forest.

If a RIS server is not responding to client requests, although you have authorized it to do so, the reason might be that the changes haven't yet taken effect in AD. You can speed up the process, though, by opening a command prompt and typing the following:

```
secedit /refreshpolicy MACHINE_POLICY /enforce
```

Managing RIS Client Options with Group Policy

For an additional measure of security, Windows 2000 enables the administrator to configure options that define the behavior of the Client Installation Wizard. Specifically, the options that can be configured are the choices that are presented to the user when he or she invokes RIS through F12.

The options are configured through the RIS node of the User Configuration container in the Group Policy Editor. Because this is Group Policy, you can apply these settings at the site, domain, or OU level. You might want to use the Default Domain Policy, or you might want to configure different policy options for different OUs. No matter where you choose to apply the policy, editing it is the same. Open the Group Policy Editor and navigate to the RIS node. In the pane on the right side of the editor, right-click Choice Options and click Properties. A dialog box like that in Figure 15.10 appears, which shows the following client options:

- **Automatic Setup**—Installs by using the computer naming convention and account location already defined by the RIS server. The default setting for this option is Don't Care, which means it inherits its settings from the parent container. Eventually, through inheritance, this policy will be defined as Allow or Deny.
- **Custom Setup**—This option allows users to install custom RIPrep-created images. The default setting for this option is Deny.
- **Restart Setup**—This option allows a failed installation to restart and will not require any information that has already been provided to be reentered. The default setting for this option is Deny.

➤ **Tools**—This option allows access to maintenance and troubleshooting tools, such as disk utilities and antivirus software. An administrator might make these types of tools available for troubleshooting purposes. The default setting for this option is Deny.

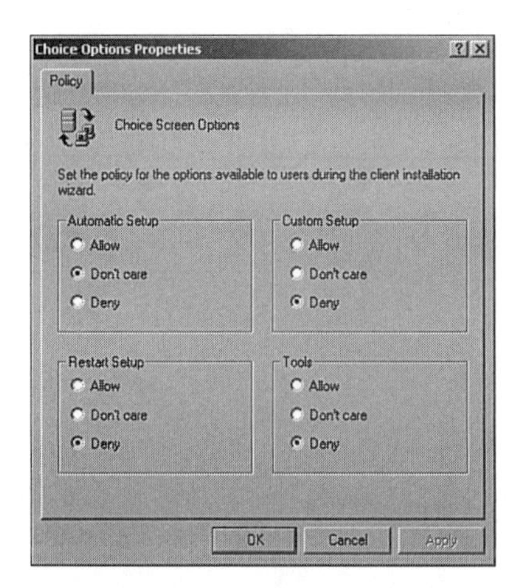

Figure 15.10 An administrator can configure client choice options for additional RIS security.

Managing RIS Settings with the AD Users and Computers Tool

The strongest security settings you can configure for RIS lie within the AD Users and Computers administrative tool. Through this utility, you can perform the following tasks as they relate to RIS:

➤ Configure client support.

➤ Define a computer-naming convention.

➤ Grant computer account creation rights.

➤ Prestage computers.

Configuring Client Support

To configure client support, which includes setting whether RIS should respond to clients and whether the RIS server should respond to unknown computers, follow these steps:

1. Open AD Users and Computers.
2. Open either the `Domain Controllers` or `Computers` folder (depending on what type of server you installed RIS on), right-click your RIS server, and click Properties.
3. Click the Remote Install tab, which brings up a property sheet like that in Figure 15.11.
4. Configure the desired settings.

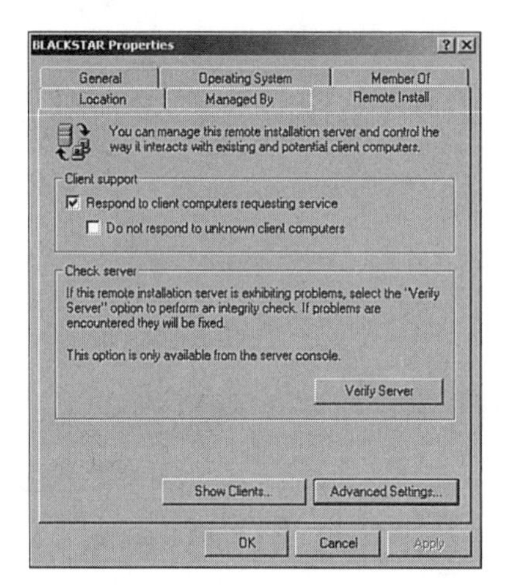

Figure 15.11 The Remote Install property sheet contains RIS server configuration settings.

Defining a Computer-Naming Convention

In addition to configuring client support on the Remote Install tab shown in Figure 15.11, you can click the Show Clients button to search the AD for known RIS client computers. For more security settings, however, click the Advanced Settings button, which brings up the property sheet shown in Figure 15.12. Through this property sheet, you can define a computer-naming convention for RIS clients. In most cases, you won't want users to come up with their own computer names when installing Windows 2000 Professional, because you would end up with a network full of irregular names, making your administrative life difficult. Through Advanced Settings, you can determine not only what the naming convention will be but also where in AD the computer account will be created.

If you choose a naming convention and an AD location for the computer accounts, the user account under which the Client Installation Wizard is run must have the necessary permissions to add computer accounts to the domain, which is described next.

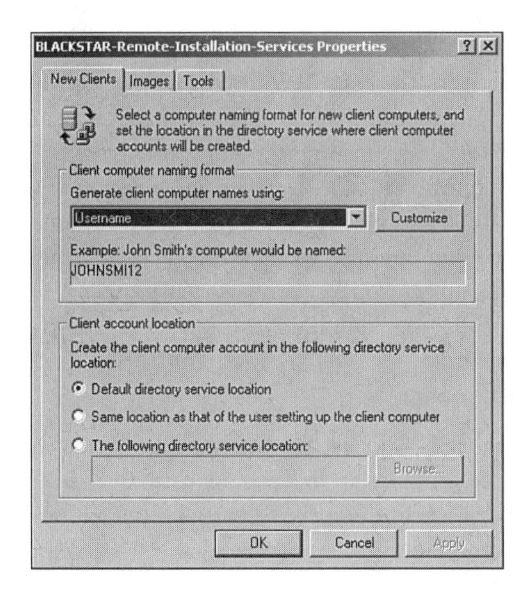

Figure 15.12 This property sheet contains additional settings to tighten RIS security.

Granting Computer Account Creation Rights

To be able to use the Client Installation Wizard to install Windows 2000 Professional into a domain, users must have Read permissions to the OU that has been defined as the AD location for the new computer account, and they must have permissions to create computer objects.

Here are the steps to follow to ensure a user has Read permissions to the required OU:

1. Click View and select Advanced Features if it is not already selected in AD Users and Computers.
2. Right-click the desired OU (such as Computers) and click Properties.
3. Click the Security tab. Highlight Authenticated Users and verify that the Read Under the Allow Column at Minimum check box is selected.

To allow a user permission to create computer objects, you need to use the Delegation of Control Wizard, which was discussed in Chapter 6, "Active Directory Delegation of Administrative Control." With this wizard, you can delegate specific control down to the creation of the computer objects themselves, and you can determine what level of permissions users and groups will have over the creation. This prevents allowing too much control in the hands of users.

Prestaging Computers

If you do not wish to delegate control for users to add their own computers to an OU, you can use a process called *prestaging* to create computer accounts in advance and to ensure that each computer name is unique. Prestaging uses the computer's globally unique identifier (GUID), which is stored in the BIOS of NetPC- or PC98-compatible computers, to identify the computer. The GUID is then stored with the computer account in AD, ensuring that the specific computer that has the correct GUID is the only computer that will use the computer account. With prestaging, an administrator doesn't have to grant computer account creation rights to users; rather, the machine's GUID will be identified by the RIS server.

In addition, by tying the computer's GUID to the computer account, an administrator can ensure that someone doesn't "borrow" a valid computer account for his or her own use, whatever it might be. That way, the administrator knows that a specific computer is using a specific computer account at all times, thus reducing a potential security risk.

Finding the GUID

To prestage a computer, you must locate the GUID, which is provided by the manufacturer. There are several ways to locate this identifier:

- Look for a label inside the computer's case or on the side of the computer.
- Check the BIOS of the client.
- Start a manual RIS installation and wait for the GUID to appear on the screen during the installation.

Practice Questions

Question 1

What type of RIS image can be created through the RIS Setup Wizard?

- ❍ a. A CD-based image
- ❍ b. A disk image containing the OS plus any desired custom settings and desktop applications
- ❍ c. A network-based image
- ❍ d. Both a and c

Answer d is correct. RISetup can be used to create both CD and network-based installation images. Answers a and c are incorrect because they are only half of the correct answer for this question. Answer b is incorrect because this describes more of an imaging solution, as opposed to a RIS solution with Group Policy.

Question 2

Which of the following is RIS dependent on to be successfully deployed on a network? [Check all correct answers]

- ❑ a. Active Directory
- ❑ b. Group Policy
- ❑ c. IntelliMirror
- ❑ d. DHCP

Answers a, b, and d are correct. Active Directory, Group Policy, and Dynamic Host Configuration Protocol (DHCP) are all necessary to have a successful deployment of RIS on a network. Answer c is incorrect because RIS is not dependent on IntelliMirror, which is simply a collection of change and configuration management utilities that complement the functionality of RIS.

Question 3

Which of the following does not fulfill the client requirements to use RIS?

- ❍ a. A PXE-compliant motherboard BIOS
- ❍ b. PC98 or NetPC compliance
- ❍ c. A PCI Plug and Play network adapter
- ❍ d. A network adapter supported by a RIS boot disk

Answer c is correct. Although a PCI Plug and Play network adapter is a requirement, that by itself does not fulfill the requirements for RIS. A compliant network adapter would still need to be PXE compliant. Answers a, b, and d are incorrect because a PXE-compliant motherboard BIOS, PC98 or NetPC compliance, and a network adapter supported by a RIS boot disk do fulfill RIS requirements.

Question 4

The IT department for Bilka Corporation has decided to utilize RIS for its deployment of desktops. The department's team leader would like to achieve the following goals:

Establish a RIS server on the network.

Create an RIPrep image of Windows 2000 Professional for the RIS server.

Create an RIPrep image of Windows 98 for the RIS server.

Deploy the image to desktop systems.

To accomplish these goals, the department begins by installing a DNS server and Active Directory within the domain. RIS is then installed on a member server of the network. Windows 98 is installed on one client machine and Windows 2000 is installed on another individual client machine. The department goes through the steps of creating images for these client machines. Deployment is attempted as the final step. Which of the following objectives have been met by the solution? [Check all correct answers]

- ❑ a. Establish a RIS server on the network.
- ❑ b. Create an RIPrep image of Windows 2000 Professional for the RIS server.
- ❑ c. Create an RIPrep image of Windows 98 for the RIS server.
- ❑ d. Deploy the image to desktop systems.

Answers a and b are correct. You can establish a RIS server on a member server within the network, so answer a is correct. Answer b is correct because in creating images, it is possible to create an RIPrep image of Windows 2000.

Answer c is incorrect because Windows 98 images are not RIS compliant; you would need a different deployment solution to deploy Windows 98. Answer d is incorrect because the RIS server will not be functional for deployment with only a DNS server and Active Directory. You still need to establish a Dynamic Host Configuration Protocol (DHCP) server and authorize the RIS server.

Question 5

Under what circumstance can you use RIPrep to create a RIS installation image?

- ❍ a. When you need to create an image that spans multiple partitions
- ❍ b. When you need to be able to support multiple system processors
- ❍ c. When you need to create an image that spans multiple physical drives
- ❍ d. When you already have a CD or network-based OS image of the same language and version on the RIS server

Answer d is correct. A requirement to use RIPrep is to first have created an RISetup CD-based image. Answers a, b, and c are incorrect because RIS does not support any of these solutions.

Question 6

You want your RIS installation to match up with specific computers in your network. Which of the following terms matches your RIS concern?

- ❍ a. RIPrep
- ❍ b. RISetup
- ❍ c. **RISDISK**
- ❍ d. Prestaging

Answer d is correct. Prestaging is the process by which an administrator ties a computer name to a specific computer's GUID in Active Directory. Answer a is incorrect because RIPrep is the utility used to create a customized installation to the point of scripting it with an answer file so that the user would be required to choose any options during setup. Answer b is incorrect because RISetup is the utility used to create a CD-like installation of Windows 2000 Professional, as if a normal installation were taking place. Answer c is incorrect because `RISDISK` is the file you would find on a RIS boot disk.

Question 7

From where would you invoke **RIPrep.exe** to create a RIS installation image?

- ❍ a. At the source client from a RIS server
- ❍ b. At the RIS server
- ❍ c. At the source client from the client
- ❍ d. From the Windows 2000 Server CD-ROM

Answer a is correct. `RIPrep.exe` is run from the RIS server at the client computer. This is done by selecting Start, Run on the RIS client and typing **`\\`*`RISserver_name`*`\reminst\admin\i386\riprep.exe`**. Answers b, c, and d do not offer the correct solution to create the image in the proper way, so they are incorrect.

Question 8

What utility do you use to authorize a RIS server?

- ❍ a. DHCP MMC
- ❍ b. DNS MMC
- ❍ c. AD Users and Computers
- ❍ d. **RISetup.exe**

Answer a is correct. You use the DHCP MMC (Dynamic Host Configuration Protocol Microsoft Management Console) to authorize a RIS server. Answers b, c, and d are incorrect because these each perform unique tasks that do not include the authorization of a RIS server. Answer b is incorrect because the DNS console allows you to administrate your DNS server, which is necessary for RIS. Answer c is incorrect because the AD (Active Directory) Users and Computers tool allows you to configure specific RIS settings for your users. Answer d is incorrect because `RISetup.exe` kicks off a RIS wizard.

Question 9

What does the Don't Care option mean when you are configuring RIS client choice options?

- ❍ a. The user invoking RIS will determine what image he or she wants to use.
- ❍ b. Permissions will be inherited from the GPO's parent container.
- ❍ c. Users will be allowed to have access because this option means that you don't care whether they have access or not.
- ❍ d. Users will not have access because permissions have not been explicitly granted.

Answer b is correct. The Don't Care setting tells Windows 2000 to use the permission settings from the parent container of the particular GPO. Answer a is incorrect because it describes the Allow option. Answer c is incorrect because the Don't Care option is not a matter of indifference. Answer d is incorrect because users' access will be determined from above; Deny would mean that users won't have access in an absolute sense.

Question 10

How does one go about installing an image on a client computer? [Check all correct answers]

- ❑ a. The RIS boot floppy automatically kicks off the installation.
- ❑ b. You must enter the BIOS and select the RIS install option.
- ❑ c. You must press F12 after the computer is turned on.
- ❑ d. You must set a jumper on the NIC card to 1-2.

Answers a and c are correct. The combination of the RIS boot floppy and pressing F12 after the computer is turned on begins the establishment of a connection with a RIS server; prompts will follow that move the user through the installation. Answer b is incorrect because the BIOS doesn't have a RIS install option. Answer d is incorrect because jumpers on NIC cards aren't used for RIS installation; rather, compatible NIC cards are required.

Need to Know More?

Boswell, William. *Inside Windows 2000 Server*. New Riders. Indianapolis, IN, 2000. ISBN 1562059297.

This is a great resource for clear and in-depth information that strengthens your knowledge of RIS technology, including RIS implementation theory as well as a complete installation and configuration section.

Iseminger, David. *Active Directory Services for Microsoft Windows 2000 Technical Reference*. Microsoft Press. Redmond, WA, 2000. ISBN 0735606242.

This book focuses on AD but does include some IntelliMirror sections.

Scrimger, Rob, et al. *Microsoft Windows 2000 Server Unleashed*. Sams. Indianapolis, IN, 2000. ISBN 0672317397.

This resource provides an in-depth description of Windows 2000 Server and Advanced Server features, including RIS services as well as installation and maintenance options.

Search the TechNet CD (or its online version through `www.microsoft.com`) using the keywords "RIS" and "IntelliMirror," along with related query items.

Search the Microsoft Knowledge Base online at `http://support.microsoft.com` and consider the following two articles: Q298750 and Q244036.

Sample Test

Question 1

You're installing Active Directory within your organization and need to determine the best approach for your DNS strategy. Currently your organization uses a Unix BIND 4.9.7 server for DNS, and this is working quite well. You would like to install Active Directory and continue to use the BIND server. In addition, you would like to allow for dynamic updates and incremental zone transfers. Which of the following statements is accurate about your considerations when installing Active Directory?

- ❍ a. Unix DNS is not compatible with Active Directory.
- ❍ b. The BIND version needs to be updated.
- ❍ c. Active Directory requires only Windows 2000 DNS.
- ❍ d. Unix uses a different protocol suite than Windows 2000.

Question 2

Your installation of Active Directory halts because the **SYSVOL** folder cannot seem to be placed where you've specified. What is the most likely cause of the problem?

- ❍ a. You've requested it go on a partition that doesn't have enough space.
- ❍ b. You've formatted the partition with NTFS.
- ❍ c. The drive letter you've specified doesn't exist.
- ❍ d. The partition you are specifying is FAT or FAT32.

Question 3

To allow for backward compatibility with NT 4 domain controllers, what mode should your domains be running in?

- ❍ a. Native mode
- ❍ b. Mixed mode
- ❍ c. RIS mode
- ❍ d. NT-compatibility mode

Question 4

Bob is looking at a diagram of the proposed AD layout for the company. It starts with a parent root of **company.com** and has several child domains, such as **miami.company.com** and **newyork.company.com**. From the following selections, what common features exist among these domains?

❑ a. Common security schemes

❑ b. A contiguous namespace

❑ c. Shortcut trusts

❑ d. A common Global Catalog

❑ e. A common schema

❑ f. Common replication schemes

Question 5

Patel is considering his use of DNS under Windows 2000 with Active Directory integrated zones. How will this impact his directory infrastructure?

❍ a. This implementation will ensure dynamic updates.

❍ b. These zones will automatically replicate to secondary servers.

❍ c. These zones will allow for secure updates through the AD.

❍ d. AD integrated zones determine the FSMO roles.

Question 6

Danielle is a domain administrator who has established a Group Policy Object (GPO), and through inheritance, the GPO's settings have flowed down toward the child OUs beneath. What can Danielle do to prevent the flow of inheritance from being blocked by lower-level objects?

❍ a. Select the Options button and then choose No Override.

❍ b. Select the Allow Inheritable Permissions from Parent to Propagate to This Object check box.

❍ c. Select the Group Policy tab for the properties of the object and choose Flow Diverted.

❍ d. Deselect the Allow Inheritable Permissions from Parent to Propagate to This Object check box.

Question 7

Daniel is logging on to a Windows 2000 domain that is in native mode. He is a member of a universal group called Managers. Which of the following will assist in the creation of Daniel's access token?

❍ a. The PDC Emulator

❍ b. Global Catalog servers

❍ c. The Kerberos transaction server

❍ d. The Infrastructure Master

Question 8

Tom is the owner of a cardboard container corporation that manufactures boxes for shipping computer products. It has a registered namespace of **stretchandshrink.com**, which it utilizes for its AD domain. Tom has just purchased an office supply company that currently has no registered namespace, nor an AD domain. In the planning discussions, it has been determined that the combination of both companies will require each to maintain a separate security configuration under a contiguous namespace. Which of the following design types should be implemented?

❍ a. Single domain

❍ b. Domain tree

❍ c. Empty root domain tree

❍ d. Forest

Question 9

Which two of the following places do GPOs that are created store their information?

❑ a. **SYSVOL** folder

❑ b. Group Policy Template (GPT)

❑ c. **Group Policy Object** folder

❑ d. Group Policy Container (GPC)

Question 10

You are working with an IT deployment team that has focused attention on the implementation of RIS within your environment. You've configured a network under DNS with AD installed and functioning. You've created quality CD-based images for your RIS server. When you go to boot from a client's machine that is PXE compliant, there is a problem locating the RIS servers images. What do you need to implement to correct this problem?

- ❍ a. A WINS server
- ❍ b. Group Policy
- ❍ c. A RIS boot disk
- ❍ d. DHCP

Question 11

Carl has formed a list of AD objects that need to be deleted. He is hoping that this will decrease the size of the database file. After his deletions, he checks the database file and is disappointed to see that the file has not reduced in size. Why is the file the same size it was before the deletions took place?

- ❍ a. These objects are not really being deleted from the database, because once an object is created, it can never be deleted.
- ❍ b. The database will never decrease in size because of deletions. Carl needs to run ntdsutil and defragment the database.
- ❍ c. The database will not decrease in size until the tombstone lifetime has expired. Then the database will be compacted.
- ❍ d. The AD database will not be reduced until AD replication has taken place. Although this will take a variable amount of time, on average it takes 24 hours before all domain controllers are aware of the deletions and reduces the size of their AD database files.

Question 12

Jaclyn is the network administrator for a global training corporation. She has created a large number of universal groups with several hundred users in each group. She has noticed that a great deal of network traffic has resulted. What is the recommended way of handling universal groups that Jaclyn should apply?

❍ a. The universal groups are established properly in the scenario; the traffic is being generated from other sources.

❍ b. Jaclyn should place the users into local groups and then place the local groups into universal groups.

❍ c. Jaclyn should place the users into global groups and then place the global groups into universal groups.

❍ d. Jaclyn should place the users into universal groups and then place the universal groups into domain local groups.

Question 13

Jenny has consistently saved the system state for the AD domain her company is running. In the process of deleting several objects, it has become necessary to bring these deleted objects back. Jenny has attempted the restore process, and the deleted objects return on the DC that she restores the directory to. However, she later notices that these objects are now deleted again. What should be done to correct this problem?

❍ a. This situation is not resolvable through a restore.

❍ b. Restore the directory on each domain controller in the domain.

❍ c. Restore the directory and then set the IsDeleted option of the object to No.

❍ d. Perform an authoritative restore.

Question 14

You are the network administrator of a single domain tree called **braincore.net** with several child domains (**ny.braincore.net**, **utah.braincore.net**, and **deleware.braincore.net**). In the NY domain there is an OU named Marketing. Inside that OU is a user named Joe User. You have implemented a number of Group Policies within the domain. They are as follows:

Site Group Policy: Wallpaper is set to Red. Task Manager is disabled.

Domain Group Policy: Display Properties tab is disabled. (No Override is set to On.)

OU1 Policy: Wallpaper is set to Blue. Display Properties tab is enabled. (Block Inheritance is set on).

OU2 Policy: Wallpaper is set to Green.

The OU policies are set in the order of OU1 being on top and OU2 on the bottom of the application order list. What is the resultant set of policies (RSOP)?

- ❍ a. Joe logs on and his wallpaper is green. Task Manager is not disabled. Display properties are disabled.
- ❍ b. Joe logs in and his wallpaper is red. Task Manager is disabled.
- ❍ c. Joe logs on and his wallpaper is blue. Task Manager is not disabled. Display properties are disabled.
- ❍ d. Joe logs in and his wallpaper is red. Task Manager is disabled. Display properties are enabled.

Question 15

The first domain controller within your domain contains all five FSMO roles. There are several domain controllers within the domain. The first domain controller fails. What allows FSMO roles to continue?

- ❍ a. FSMO roles automatically transfer when the domain controller holding those roles goes down.
- ❍ b. You need to seize the roles by using the ntdsutil tool.
- ❍ c. You can transfer the roles by using the AD Domains and Trusts tool.
- ❍ d. FSMO roles will not be able to continue.

Question 16

You are the administrator responsible for desktop settings for an OU named Legal. There are about 200 users in the Legal OU. You need to configure a custom Registry entry for each user. The entry doesn't have a preconfigured setting in Group Policy. You want to add the custom Registry entry into a Group Policy Object (GPO) with the least amount of administrative effort. What should you do?

❍ a. Configure an ADM template and use the template to create a GPO.

❍ b. Configure an INF policy and use the policy to create a GPO.

❍ c. Make the Registry changes manually on each system.

❍ d. All Registry entries are included within the Administrative Templates portion of Group Policy, so you need to simply look a little deeper for your selection.

Question 17

You have a primary name server established within your organization, and you have several secondary servers providing load balancing. You want to add another DNS server, yet you don't want to add any extra replication traffic to a network that you feel is already handling too much. What can you do?

❍ a. Add another secondary DNS server and configure it not to replicate.

❍ b. Add a caching-only server.

❍ c. Create an entirely new zone with its own set of primary and secondary zone servers.

❍ d. Install a Windows 2000 DNS server and configure it to utilize DDNS (Dynamic DNS).

Question 18

Brandon has designed and implemented a single Windows 2000 domain for his company. The company's headquarters is in Fort Lauderdale, Florida. Smaller branch locations include San Francisco, California and London, England. Each location has its own DCs and separate subnet configurations, which are connected through ISDN lines that barely support existing traffic. Brandon notices an extreme amount of replication traffic. He checks the Active Directory Sites and Services tool. What will he notice when he checks this tool?

❍ a. He will see that the replication topology is incorrectly set, and he will have to run the Knowledge Consistency Checker.

❍ b. He will see that the sites configured are missing bridgehead servers.

❍ c. He will be able to determine the performance of his ISDN traffic and see which traffic is generating the most harm.

❍ d. He will see that all DCs will be contained within the same default site, and he will need to break them up according to subnet.

Question 19

Tim is a network administrator over a Windows 2000 domain. His domain has multiple physical sites that have been broken up in Active Directory for easier replication handling. He has about 10 OUs that structure the organization easily for administrative purposes. Tim has a strange suspicion that someone is trying to break into his domain by trying different usernames and passwords. He is not sure who, though. How can Tim audit the situation to see which computer the logon failures are coming from?

❍ a. Edit the Default Domain Controllers Policy object to audit logon access failures.

❍ b. Edit the Default Domain Policy object to audit account logon failures.

❍ c. Edit the OUs to audit logon failures.

❍ d. This is not possible under AD and must be handled by third-party security software.

Question 20

Chris is a network administrator for Lockworks, Inc. He is implementing a GPO for members of a specific OU and wants the GPO to refresh every 45 minutes. How does Chris go about establishing such a policy? [Choose the best answer]

❍ a. Change the policy refresh rate to 30 minutes through the AD Policy Refresh Rate tool.

❍ b. Make no policy changes because the default will work.

❍ c. Change the policy refresh rate to 30 minutes by using the editing tool and changing the User Configuration through the Administrative Templates and the System options.

❍ d. Use the **ntdsutil.exe** command-line tool to reconfigure the default policy.

Question 21

Alexandra Jade is a senior analyst for Yeatts Global Photo. She has configured a design for site replication that takes into consideration the company's five branch offices and their 56Kbps speed connections to the headquarters in Glenn Burnie, Maryland. What further consideration should be given to site design and implementation?

❍ a. Her next consideration should be the purchase of faster links between branches.

❍ b. Her next consideration should be the establishment of one unique subnet that will work for all sites.

❍ c. Her next consideration should be designing subnets for each site where one and only one subnet per site is used.

❍ d. Her next consideration should be designing subnets for each site where one or more subnets in a site are used, without using the same subnet in different sites.

Question 22

You are a network consultant who has been brought into a company that is seeking to upgrade its existing NT domain to become a Windows 2000 domain. Which of the following steps should the company do first? [Choose two]

- ❑ a. Upgrade a BDC.
- ❑ b. Upgrade the PDC.
- ❑ c. Take a BDC offline for fault tolerance.
- ❑ d. Promote a Windows 2000 Server using DCPROMO to be the first DC for the new domain.

Question 23

Tony is attempting to set up RIS on his server. He installs RIS and then runs **RISetup.exe** from a command line. The Remote Installation Services Wizard initiates and fails immediately from the first option. What would cause a problem with the establishment of RIS images?

- ❍ a. The RIS server is not enabled to provide services.
- ❍ b. The RIS server doesn't have the path to the Windows 2000 Professional files.
- ❍ c. The RIS server doesn't have a friendly description defined for F12 selection on the client systems.
- ❍ d. The installation directory must reside on an NTFS partition, and he is trying to install it on a different one.

Question 24

Which of the following two Operations Masters are forestwide roles?

- ❑ a. Schema Master
- ❑ b. RID Master
- ❑ c. PDC Emulator
- ❑ d. Domain Naming Master
- ❑ e. Infrastructure Master

Question 25

Floren is an administrator for a storage management company called StoreVault that has its headquarters in Eatontown, NJ and five branch offices located throughout the world. He has been called in specifically to handle DNS implementation for the Windows 2000 Active Directory installation for the company. Some of the requirements that he has been asked to accomplish include the following:

Ensure fault tolerance of the zone database.

Secure the DNS traffic.

Ensure that only authorized DNS servers will update the zone information.

Ensure that clients can access DNS information from their various locations worldwide.

Floren looks over the last administrator's plans. They include the use of a DNS Active Directory integrated zone as well as the creation of a second AD DNS server at the headquarters. The plans then note a need to allow dynamic updates, but "Only Secure Updates" is mentioned. Which of the following does the previous plan cover?

- ❑ a. Ensure fault tolerance of the zone database.
- ❑ b. Secure the DNS traffic.
- ❑ c. Ensure that only authorized DNS servers will update the zone information.
- ❑ d. Ensure that clients can access DNS information from their various locations worldwide.

Question 26

Which of the following can be used to describe the data involved with an intersite replication scenario? [Check all correct answers]

- ❑ a. Data is sent uncompressed.
- ❑ b. Data is sent compressed.
- ❑ c. Data is sent through a schedule.
- ❑ d. Data is sent by default replication parameters.

Question 27

Greg has decided to implement a DNS server utilizing Windows 2000. He goes through the process of installing Windows 2000 and makes sure that the installation completes properly. What should be the next step prior to installing the DNS server?

❍ a. Begin an installation of AD by using **dcpromo.exe** and then selecting the option to install the DNS server.

❍ b. Begin DNS installation through the AD DNS Configuration utility.

❍ c. Change the default IP address that is dynamically assigned to a static IP address.

❍ d. Check his network to see whether any other DNS servers are necessary.

Question 28

You installed your Active Directory database on an NTFS volume when you promoted your server to become a domain controller. Now you notice that you are running out of disk space. You've defragmented the database and recovered some space but need to come up with another plan. You've installed a brand new drive into the system with plenty of room. What should you do next?

❍ a. Use the MOVETREE utility to move the database.

❍ b. Use the **ntfsutil.exe** utility to move the database from Directory Services Restore Mode.

❍ c. Perform a backup of the System State and then restore the Active Directory database to the new volume and delete the old volume.

❍ d. Go into Directory Services Restore Mode and copy the **ntds.dit** file to the new volume manually. Then delete the previous database file.

Question 29

Which of the following snap-in tools would you find useful to test the level of predefined security that you have established on your domain?

❍ a. ADSI Edit

❍ b. IP Security Policy Management

❍ c. Security templates

❍ d. Security Configuration and Analysis

Question 30

Dennis is the network administrator responsible for software installations. He wants to have Microsoft Word installed on all computers within his particular domain. Which of the following methods of deployment would be the best approach for Group Policy deployment of this software?

❍ a. Configure the policy to publish the software under the Computer Configuration options for a domain Group Policy.

❍ b. Configure the policy to assign the software under the Computer Configuration options for a domain Group Policy.

❍ c. Configure the policy to publish the software under the User Configuration options for a domain Group Policy.

❍ d. Configure the policy to assign the software under the User Configuration options for a domain Group Policy.

Question 31

Your organization has three office locations. One in Newark, NJ, one in New York, NY and one in Orlando, FL. Each is configured with a different subnet unique to its site. Newark and New York are connected by a T1 connection. Orlando is connected with a 56K connection. The T1 is at 92-percent bandwidth utilization, and the 56K is a dial-up connection that is only used when needed. How would you configure sites in this case?

❍ a. Establish two sites. One for Newark and New York and one for Orlando.

❍ b. Establish three sites, one for each location.

❍ c. Establish one site.

❍ d. Establish two sites. One for Orlando and Newark, and one for New York.

Question 32

The IT department for New Horizons Corporation has decided to utilize RIS for its deployment of desktops. The department's team leader would like to achieve the following goals:

Configure pre-RIS services.

Establish a RIS server on the network.

Create an RISetup image of Windows 2000 Professional for the RIS server.

Deploy the image to desktop systems.

To accomplish these goals, the department begins by installing a DNS server, DHCP, and Active Directory within the domain. RIS is then installed on a member server of the network. The Windows 2000 Professional files are copied off the CD and placed on an NTFS partition. The department goes through the steps of using RISetup to establish the direction toward these files. Deployment is attempted as the final step by booting up with a PXE boot floppy and selecting F11 to choose the RIS description.

Which of the following objectives have been met by the solution? [Check all correct answers]

- ❑ a. Configure pre-RIS services.
- ❑ b. Establish a RIS server on the network.
- ❑ c. Create an RIPrep image of Windows 2000 Professional for the RIS server.
- ❑ d. Deploy the image to desktop systems.

Question 33

Within your Windows 2000 domain you've implemented a DHCP server, but your workstations are not getting IP addresses. You check to see if a scope is defined, and everything seems fine. However, addresses still aren't being assigned. What is most likely the cause of the problem?

- ❍ a. The router is not allowing the BootP broadcasts to pass through.
- ❍ b. The DHCP service is corrupt.
- ❍ c. The DHCP server is not authorized in Active Directory.
- ❍ d. The clients don't have a PXE-compliant network card.

Question 34

When you look at your automatically configured topology through the Replication Monitor, you notice that connection paths are not established the way you would like. What can you manually do to change this?

- ❍ a. Create a manual connection object on the servers you need connected.
- ❍ b. Force the KCC to update the topology.
- ❍ c. Change the Registry to indicate the new paths you need.
- ❍ d. The KCC will not allow you to modify the replication paths. These are set in stone.

Question 35

When adding DCs to your existing domain, what should you take into consideration?

- ❍ a. Nothing. The more DCs on the domain, the better.
- ❍ b. Bandwidth usage on the network.
- ❍ c. You can only have three DCs in a domain.
- ❍ d. To promote a server to a DC, you must reinstall the operating system.

Question 36

Shannon wants to make sure that all replication takes place only during the evening hours of the day when nobody is on the network. She can do this by adjusting which portion of the site link?

- ❍ a. Frequency
- ❍ b. Cost
- ❍ c. Transport
- ❍ d. Schedule

Question 37

Which security template would show no regard for performance or functionality with non–Windows 2000 compatibility?

❍ a. Basic

❍ b. Compatible

❍ c. Secure

❍ d. High Secure

Question 38

You have an organization with three domains. Two of the domains (**root.com** and **samerica.root.com**) are connected by a high-bandwidth connection. The third domain (**spacific.root.com**) is located in Fiji and is connected to the rest of the organization by a 56Kbps connection. All three domains have 10 OUs configured. The first two domains use Group Policy for their software deployment, management, upgrades, and removal. The remote domain would like to use software deployment through Group Policy but doesn't want to run the deployment over the 56Kbps connection. What should you do to allow the third domain to have the ability to handle its software without using the bandwidth?

❍ a. Configure a Group Policy for each OU in the **spacific.root.com** domain. Configure a software package for each Group Policy that uses software installer files off a local server.

❍ b. Configure a Group Policy at the site level. Configure a software package for the Group Policy that uses software installer files off a server in the **namerica.root.com** domain.

❍ c. Configure a Group Policy for the **spacific.root.com** domain. Configure a software package for the Group Policy that uses software installer files off a local server.

❍ d. Configure a Group Policy for the **root.com** domain. Configure a software package for the Group Policy that uses software installer files off a server in Fiji.

Question 39

Your company has a Windows 2000 domain tree with three domains (**root.com**, **east.root.com**, and **west.root.com**). Your company recently purchased another organization that is using an NT domain. The domain will eventually be upgraded but currently will remain as it is. You would like for the NT domain to be able to access a printer located in the **east.root.com** domain. What type of trust relationship should configure and which way?

❍ a. A two-way transitive trust with **root.com**

❍ b. A one-way trust from **east.root.com** to the NT domain

❍ c. A one-way trust from the NT domain to **east.root.com**

❍ d. A two-way trust between **east.root.com** and the NT domain

Question 40

Maverick Corporation is a multinational company that includes several subsidiaries. It is organized into a single forest with two noncontiguous domain trees, and off one of those trees there are three child domains. What would be the total number of FSMO role servers involved?

❍ a. One Domain Naming Master, one Schema Master, one RID Master, one PDC Emulator, and one Infrastructure Master

❍ b. One Domain Naming Master, one Schema Master, five RID Masters, five PDC Emulators, and five Infrastructure Masters

❍ c. One Domain Naming Master, one Schema Master, three RID Masters, three PDC Emulators, and three Infrastructure Masters

❍ d. Three Domain Naming Masters, three Schema Masters, three RID Masters, three PDC Emulators, and three Infrastructure Masters

Question 41

Which of the following is the Operations Master role that handles interaction with NT 4 BDCs?

❍ a. Schema Master

❍ b. Infrastructure Master

❍ c. PDC Emulator

❍ d. Domain Naming Master

❍ e. RID Master

Question 42

Donna creates a Group Policy that should change the desktop settings for a test user that she is working on before her deploying the policy to an OU called Markets. She is sitting at the system and waiting for the policy to refresh, but it's taking forever. What can Donna do to force the policy?

❍ a. Run **secedit /refreshpolicy MACHINE_POLICY**.

❍ b. Run **secedit /refreshpolicy USER_POLICY**.

❍ c. Run **ntdsutil /refreshpolicy USER_POLICY**.

❍ d. Log out and log back in.

Question 43

What is the following a view of?

```
CN=Arnold Perez,OU=Research,DC=yachtgraphics,DC=COM
```

❍ a. User principal names

❍ b. Distinguished names

❍ c. LDAP names

❍ d. Common names

Question 44

Which of the following is a definition of all objects and their attributes?

❍ a. Schema

❍ b. OUs

❍ c. DNS

❍ d. Latency

Question 45

MasterWare.com has a need to implement a DNS structure before the installation of Active Directory. It has five servers to implement DNS on:

Tokyo

Los Angeles

London

Miami

New York

Three of the servers need to have secure updates, one needs to be able to accept updates, and one should not accept updates at all. The ones in Tokyo, Los Angeles, and London are domain controllers, whereas the other two, in Miami and New York, are member servers. In the DNS implementation, there is a need to place the following servers within the five locations; DNS servers can be used more than once:

AD Integrated

Secondary

Caching

Question 46

Kathy works for a worldwide organization based in the United States. Currently the organization has 50,000 employees with five different locations (Singapore, France, England, Canada, and the U.S.). The domain is a single domain tree with three configured sites: one for Singapore, one for France and England, and one for Canada and the U.S. The connection to the Singapore site is very unreliable. What can be done to configure replication better between the Singapore site and the U.S./Canada site?

❍ a. Configure a bridgehead server between the two sites.

❍ b. Change the configuration to allow Singapore into the U.S./Canada site.

❍ c. Configure IP over RPC replication to use a schedule between the two sites.

❍ d. Configure SMTP replication between the two sites.

Question 47

Meghan is responsible for IPSec implementation within her organization. Her AD domain consists of a domain tree with a parent root and four child domains. There are eight offices located throughout the nation, and sites are used to segment the replication traffic. The clients within the organization vary from Windows 2000 clients to NT 4 and 98 clients. Meghan would like to establish an IPSec policy for all clients in her site that are able to use IPSec. There are systems in the Research OU that she would like to have using a Server type of IPSec policy, but not one that would prevent access to all clients. How should she establish her policies?

❍ a. Create a site-level "Client" IPSec policy and a "Secure Server" IPSec policy for the Research OU.

❍ b. Create a domain-level "Client" IPSec policy and a "Secure Server" IPSec policy for the Research OU.

❍ c. Create a site-level "Client" IPSec policy and a "Server" IPSec policy for the Research OU.

❍ d. Create a domain-level "Client" IPSec policy and a "Server" IPSec policy for the Research OU.

Question 48

You would like to ensure that passwords within your domain are complex, and you know that this is possible to enforce through a policy. Which of the following should you perform?

❍ a. Edit the Local Security Policy on each of the DCs within your AD domain to require password complexity.

❍ b. Edit the Default Domain Security Policy to require password complexity.

❍ c. Edit the Default Domain Controller Policy to require password complexity.

❍ d. Edit the Site policy for your domain to require password complexity.

Question 49

You have three site locations for your domain **bluemoose.com**. The sites are Taiwan, Brazil, and South Africa. Replication is configured between the three sites. There is a site link between South Africa and Brazil that is close to T1 connectivity. A slower 56Kbps link connects South Africa and Taiwan. Taiwan and Brazil are connected at T1 speeds. How can you configure these sites to ensure replication between the three in the best possible way, while still providing a backup plan?

❑ a. Configure the site link for the South Africa–Brazil connection to be 100.

❑ b. Configure the site link for the South Africa–Brazil connection to be 10.

❑ c. Configure the site link for the South Africa–Taiwan connection to be 100.

❑ d. Configure the site link for the South Africa–Taiwan connection to be 10.

Question 50

There is an OU called DocProc for the document-processing department in your company, which happens to be an investment banking firm. There are two security groups in the DocProc OU—one is DocProc for the users, and one is Managers for the management staff. You have a GPO that enforces a specific wallpaper and removes the Display option changes. Managers are complaining that they do not like having this policy enforced on them. What should you do?

❍ a. Remove the Managers group from the OU.

❍ b. Select the Block Policy Inheritance option from the OU.

❍ c. Change the permissions on the policy to Deny Read and Apply Group Policy for the Managers security group.

❍ d. Remove the policy from the OU and apply it directly to the DocProc security group.

Answer Key

For asterisked items, see the textual representation of answer on the appropriate page within this chapter.

1. b
2. d
3. b
4. b, d, e
5. c
6. a
7. b
8. b
9. b, d
10. d
11. b
12. c
13. d
14. c
15. b
16. a
17. b
18. d
19. b
20. c
21. d
22. b, c
23. d
24. a, d
25. a, b

26. b, c

27. c

28. b

29. d

30. b

31. b

32. a, b, c

33. c

34. a

35. b

36. d

37. d

38. c

39. b

40. b

41. c

42. b

43. b

44. a

45. *

46. d

47. c

48. b

49. b, c

50. c

Question 1

Answer b is correct. Your BIND version needs to upgraded to at least 8.1.2 to allow support for dynamic updates and incremental zone transfers. Answer a is incorrect because Unix DNS can be compatible with an upgrade. Answer c is incorrect because Windows 2000 will work with DNS servers that support RFCs 2052 (SRV Records) and 2163 (Dynamic Updates). Answer d is incorrect because both Unix and Windows 2000 use TCP/IP as their protocol suite of choice.

Question 2

Answer d is correct. The SYSVOL folder structure must be on an NTFS partition. Answers a and c are incorrect because, although these are possible causes of the problem, the question asks for "most likely." Answer b is incorrect because putting the SYSVOL folder on an NTFS partition would have actually been a good thing.

Question 3

Answer b is correct. Mixed mode allows for backward compatibility and synchronization with the Accounts Manager. Answer a is incorrect because native mode would ensure incompatibility with NT 4 domain controllers. Answers c and d are incorrect because they are not really modes.

Question 4

Answers b, d, and e are correct. The scenario provided is an example of a growing AD tree. The common features include a contiguous namespace, Global Catalog, and schema. Answer a is incorrect because common security schemes exist within the same domain, not between domains. Answer c is incorrect because shortcut trusts must be manually established, and they can be formed only between domains you've selected. Answer f is incorrect because replication between domains is not the same type of replication within a domain. Only the schema and configuration partitions are replicated between domains. The Global Catalog information will also be replicated to GC servers that are purposely placed throughout the domain tree or forest.

Question 5

Answer c is correct. Active Directory integrated zones allow for the DNS zone files to be replicated with the directory information and also allow for secure updates to be configured. Answer a is incorrect because dynamic updates are resolved between DNS and DHCP in Windows 2000. Answer b is incorrect because AD integrated zones include replication within the Active Directory replication. Answer d is incorrect because AD integrated zones have absolutely nothing to do with FSMO roles.

Question 6

Answer a is correct. To ensure the application of the GPO to lower-level containers, Danielle must select the No Override option for the GPO. Answers b and d are incorrect because they involve selections that relate to permissions that are being accepted or denied from upper-level OUs. Answer c is also incorrect because there is no option called Flow Diverted to select in the GPO options.

Question 7

Answer b is correct. Global Catalog servers search for the domain information necessary during logon when an individual uses their user principal name. When a user logs on to a native mode domain (these are the only ones to include universal groups), the GC updates the DC as to the universal group information for that particular user's access token. Answers a and d are incorrect because PDC Emulator and Infrastructure Master are FSMO roles that are not involved with the generation of the access token. The PDC Emulator is useful in backward compatibility issues with NT 4. Answer c is incorrect because the Kerberos server is used for domain and forest user verification through tickets.

Question 8

Answer b is correct. A domain tree would include one or more domains. In this case, there is a need to maintain separate security policies, which would require two domains under one domain tree. Answer a is incorrect because a single domain would not allow for separate security policies. Answer c is incorrect because an empty root is unnecessary; no guidelines for strict separation of control have been requested. Answer d is incorrect because a forest arrangement would involve two noncontiguous namespaces.

Question 9

Answers b and d are correct. A GPO will store its information within a GPT and a GPC. Answer a is incorrect because the `SYSVOL` folder, although technically the location of GPO information, is not one of the two best answers. Answer c is incorrect because there is no such thing as a `Group Policy Object` folder.

Question 10

Answer d is correct. To implement RIS correctly, you need to have AD, DNS, and DHCP up and running. Answer a is incorrect because WINS is not a requirement for RIS and is not utilized by the RIS process. Answer b is incorrect because Group Policy, although helpful in working with RIS, would not prevent RIS from working. Answer c is incorrect because a PXE-compliant client is already mentioned, so a RIS boot floppy is not necessary.

Question 11

Answer b is correct. The database file size will remain static. It can grow automatically, but it does not reduce in size until you run ntdsutil in Directory Services Restore Mode and defragment the database. Answer a is incorrect because objects can be deleted from the database. Answer c is incorrect because tombstoning defines the time before an object is physically deleted from the database, but even this will not physically change the database file size. Answer d is incorrect because deletions are replicated within a relatively quick period of time among domain controllers.

Question 12

Answer c is correct. It is recommended that Jaclyn place the users into global groups and then place the global groups into universal groups. Because of the replication of universal group content, the user objects are being referenced and creating excess replication. It would be better to place the users into several key global groups and then place those groups into universal groups. This will reduce the replication load. Answer a is incorrect because this method actually creates tremendous amounts of replication. Answer b is incorrect because local groups would not be available for the domain. Answer d is incorrect because, although this situation is possible, the replication would not be reduced using this step.

Question 13

Answer d is correct. If Jenny wants to restore data and have it replicated to all other domain controllers in the domain, she must perform an authoritative restore. This restore operation is performed by using the backup/restore utility and ntdsutil. Answer a is incorrect because she can restore deleted items. Answer b is incorrect because she does not have to update all the DCs. Answer c is incorrect because there is no way to change the IsDeleted setting for objects.

Question 14

Answer c is correct. This is correct because the final policy blocked the site policy, so Task Manager is not disabled. The No Override on the domain policy should enforce the Display Properties tab being disabled. Because OU1 is first in the priority list and the priorities are processed from bottom to top, the OU2 wallpaper setting is ignored. Answers a, b and d provide alternative solutions but do not correctly combine the rules into a final RSOP (resultant set of policies).

Question 15

Answer b is correct. Because the server is not operational, it will be necessary to seize the roles. Answer a is incorrect because FSMO roles do not automatically transfer. Answer c is incorrect because FSMO roles are transferred smoothly with the AD Domains and Trusts tool only when the DC with those roles is still functional. Answer d is incorrect because there is a method to salvage FSMO roles.

Question 16

Answer a is correct. As the administrator, you can consider creating custom `.adm` files if the supplied template, `System.adm`, doesn't have what you're looking for. However, you should try to use the supplied template if possible. Administrative Templates propagate Registry settings to a large number of computers without requiring you to have detailed knowledge of the Registry. Therefore, answer d is incorrect. INF policies are not used with Group Policies under Windows 2000. Therefore, answer b is incorrect. Manually making the changes would work but is not the option with the least amount of administrative effort. Therefore, answer c is incorrect.

Question 17

Answer b is correct. The caching-only server doesn't generate traffic but checks in with the DNS servers when it needs help and then holds those resolutions in a TTL (time-to-live) fashion. Answer a is incorrect because although the secondary server sounds tempting, it will add replication traffic. Answer c is incorrect because adding another site with other DNS servers that replicate would certainly devour any remaining network bandwidth. Answer d is incorrect because Windows 2000 is not the cure-all for an existing DNS infrastructure, and the endeavor would be useless.

Question 18

Answer d is correct. All DCs usually go into the default site. In this scenario, it is necessary to establish multiple sites based on subnet and then set replication schedules. Answer a is incorrect because Brandon cannot use the AD Sites and Services tool to determine site topology; he would use it to manage the sites and create new sites based on his bandwidth capabilities. Answer b is incorrect because there will be no sites unless they are manually established, and there are no such components as bridgehead servers in Active Directory; they are components of Exchange Server. Answer c is incorrect because the AD Sites and Services tool is not for this purpose either.

Question 19

Answer b is correct. Auditing the domain will watch for systems throughout the domain that may be trying to log on. Then Tim will see an excessive number of logon failures and will be able to respond to those. You may have thought to choose answer a because the question speaks of logging on to the domain, which must include domain controllers, but Tim really wants to see which computer is being logged on to, because the user himself will not be apparent though a simple audit alone. Security features are handled on a domain level, so handling this at the OU level would not work. Therefore, answer c is incorrect. Answer d is incorrect because AD is very capable of auditing itself.

Question 20

Answer c is correct. By editing the GPO, Chris can configure a different setting for the refresh rate. Answer a is incorrect because there is no such tool as the AD Refresh Rate tool. Answer b is incorrect because the default refresh rate is 90 minutes. Answer d is incorrect because a command-line tool, such as `ntdsutil.exe`, is not used to change the refresh rate.

Question 21

Answer d is correct. Sites should be made up of separate subnets, but they can contain more than one subnet per site. Answer a is incorrect because it would not be part of the analyst's job to purchase faster links. Answer b is incorrect because one subnet would not create separate sites. Answer c is incorrect because there can definitely be more than one subnet per site.

Question 22

Answers b and c are correct. Microsoft recommends that you take a BDC offline (just in case) and then upgrade the PDC first. If you wanted to get a new server into the mix, you would have to install NT Server as a BDC, promote it to be the PDC, and then perform the upgrade. Therefore, answer a is incorrect. If you just take a Windows 2000 Server and use DCPROMO, you will get a new domain, but it will have no information from the NT domain. You could then migrate all the information, but this was not part of the scenario. Therefore, answer d is incorrect.

Question 23

Answer d is correct. Tony must have his RIS files on an NTFS partition; otherwise, he will receive an error message and the wizard will fail. Answer a is incorrect because it describes the second step in the process of the RIS Wizard. Answer b is incorrect because it describes the third step in the wizard's process. Answer c is incorrect because it describes the final step in the procedure.

Question 24

Answers a and d are correct. The Schema Master is the domain controller in the forest that is responsible for maintaining and distributing the schema to the rest of the forest. The Domain Naming Master is the domain controller for the forest that records the additions and deletions of domains to the forest. The Relative Identifier (RID) Master is responsible for assigning blocks of RIDs to all domain controllers in a domain. Therefore, answer b is incorrect. The Primary Domain Controller (PDC) Emulator is responsible for emulating NT 4.0 for clients that have not migrated to Windows 2000. Therefore, answer c is incorrect. The Infrastructure Master records changes made concerning objects in a domain. Therefore, answer e is incorrect.

Question 25

Answers a and b are correct. Using the current plan will certainly provide for fault tolerance of the DNS zone because it will be held within Active Directory on each DC in the domain. In addition, the updates are secured through Secure Updates Only being selected for the updates option. Answer c is not satisfied because the plan would have to indicate that the administrator go into the properties of the zone and then go to the Name Servers tab and indicate the exact servers that can update the zone. In addition, answer d is incorrect because the scenario only asks for another DNS server at the headquarters; it doesn't mention putting DNS servers closer to the users.

Question 26

Answers b and c are correct. Replication that occurs intersite requires data to be compressed and occurs under a schedule. Answer a is incorrect because uncompressed data is utilized in intrasite replication only. Answer d is incorrect because default replication parameters are used for intrasite, non–schedule-based replication, whereas intersite replication requires defined schedules.

Question 27

Answer c is correct. Windows 2000 DNS servers require static IP addresses. Answer a is incorrect because it is not necessary for Greg to implement AD with his DNS server; the two can remain separate. Answer b is incorrect because the AD DNS Configuration utility is fictitious. Answer d is incorrect because the question doesn't ask Greg to perform a search, and this is not an automatic next step.

Question 28

Answer b is correct. You use the `ntdsutil.exe` utility to move the database, defragment the database, and perform an authoritative restore of the database and a host of other things. Answer a is incorrect because the MOVETREE utility is used to move objects between domains. Answer c is incorrect because you cannot just choose to restore the AD System State to any location you'd like. Answer d is incorrect because you cannot manually move the `ntds.dit` file and expect to recover.

Question 29

Answer d is correct. The Security Configuration and Analysis tool is used to compare settings between your existing security policy and one of several predefined Microsoft security templates. Answers a, b, and c are all actual snap-in tools within the MMC, although they have different tasks. Answer a is incorrect because ADSI Edit allows you to edit your AD. Answer b is incorrect because IP Security Policy Management is used to implement IPSec policies for your VPN connections. Answer c is incorrect because security templates are static files that need to be used in conjunction with the proper tool provided.

Question 30

Answer b is correct. In this situation, Dennis wants to ensure that software is deployed to all the workstations within his domain, so it only makes sense that he establish a policy that covers the entire domain and assigns the software to the computers. Answer a is incorrect because Dennis cannot publish to computers. Answers c and d are incorrect because this would allow for some level of user involvement in the scenario, which is not requested in this case.

Question 31

Answer b is correct. Sites should be established based on the physical connectivity and subnets. It is a logical grouping of DCs to ease replication traffic. In the scenario you might think it's a good idea to create a single site between New York and Newark because of the T1 connection, but the bandwidth utilization is too high between the two locations. Answer a is incorrect because of the excessive bandwidth utilization between the two locations. Answer c is incorrect because this doesn't utilize sites correctly at all. Answer d is incorrect because the 56K connection should be kept separate altogether.

Question 32

Answers a, b, and c are correct. These options are met by the solution presented. Answer d is incorrect because the F12 key, not the F11 key, is needed to start the installation.

Question 33

Answer c is correct. The DHCP server must be authorized in Active Directory for it to be able to give out IP addresses. Answer a is incorrect because, although routers do prevent BootP broadcasts (unless configured to allow them), the question asks for the "most likely" solution. Answer b is incorrect because the DHCP service wouldn't just corrupt itself. Answer d is incorrect because PXE-compliant cards are part of RIS requirements, not DHCP.

Question 34

Answer a is correct. In this case, you can manually configure your own connection objects. The KCC manually creates a topology, but you can edit this. Answer b will most likely generate the same functioning topology, but the KCC is not able to update the topology according to what is in your mind. Answer c is incorrect because you don't update the Registry for this problem. Answer d is incorrect because the KCC does allow this.

Question 35

Answer b is correct. When you add DCs to a domain, you improve logon performance. However, the DCs will cause traffic on the domain because of the replication of data between the DCs. Therefore, the more DCs that are on the domain, the more replication that will take place. Replication will use up network bandwidth. Answer a is incorrect because the more DCs that you add, the more this will increase bandwidth usage. Answer c is incorrect because you can have more than three domain controllers in a domain. Answer d is incorrect because promoting a server to be a DC does not require a reinstallation of the operating system.

Question 36

Answer d is correct. By adjusting the schedule of the site link, Shannon can restrict or permit replication to take place at a certain time. Answer a is incorrect because replication frequency is the time interval a DC will wait before checking for changes on other DCs. Answer b is incorrect because replication cost refers to the amount of bandwidth the replication process will use. Answer c is incorrect because there is no such thing as a replication transport value.

Question 37

Answer d is correct. High Secure allows the highest level of security that the templates can provide and, in the process, can hinder performance and non–Windows 2000 compatibility, along with several other possible hindrances. Answer a is incorrect because Basic templates provide default security policy. Answer b is incorrect because Compatible, which is one level above Basic, still allows for compatibility with applications. Answer c is incorrect because Secure allows for Windows compatibility.

Question 38

The correct answer is c. To visualize the entire scenario, you need to first realize that the only way to reduce the traffic over the 56K connection is to have the software package located off a server in Fiji, which is local. The next problem is that you need to establish a Group Policy that will effect everyone in the domain. Answer a wants to use the OUs, which will work, but its much more effective to use Group Policy at the highest level possible (in this case, right at the domain level). Answer b is also incorrect because it tries to place the policy at the Site level, which is, again, too high up. Answer d tries to use the `root.com` domain, but this will not affect the users in the `spacific.root.com` domain. The flow of the policy doesn't extend that deeply.

Question 39

Answer b is correct. Remember, the trusting domain extends the trust to the trusted domain. You only need a one-way trust relationship, and it must go to the domain with the resource. Transitive trusts are only formed with Windows 2000 domains and only when the domains are part of the same tree or forest. A two-way trust between the two domains is not needed because there is no specification requesting a need for users in the Windows 2000 domains to access resources in the NT domain. Therefore, answers a, c, and d are all incorrect.

Question 40

Answer b is correct. You are allowed one Domain Naming Master and one Schema Master per forest. In addition, you need one PDC Emulator per domain, one Infrastructure Master per domain, and one RID Master per domain. In the given scenario, Maverick Corporation has two domain trees within a single forest and three child domains, for a total of five domains. Therefore, answer b is the only correct answer, and answers a, c, and d are incorrect.

Question 41

Answer c is correct. The PDC Emulator handles backward-compatibility issues. Answer a is incorrect because the Schema Master is necessary to change the schema. Answer b is incorrect because the Infrastructure Master is used to handle references to objects without them existing in the directory partitions. Answer d is incorrect because the Domain Naming Master enables all objects to be unique.

Question 42

Answer b is correct. Donna can use the `secedit.exe` command to force a policy. She can force either the machine or user policy, depending on what she needs. To refresh policies under the User Configuration node, Donna would type **`secedit /refreshpolicy USER_POLICY`** and then click OK. She would type **`secedit /refreshpolicy MACHINE_POLICY`** to refresh policies under the Computer Configuration node. Answer a is incorrect because it tries to use the machine policy, which doesn't apply in this case. Answer c is incorrect because the wrong tool is used (ntdsutil instead of secedit). Answer d is incorrect because logging in and out will not force this policy to refresh.

Question 43

Answer b is correct. This is an example of a distinguished name. Answer a is incorrect because a user principal name would be similar to `user@company.com`. Answer c is incorrect because "LDAP names" is not a true term. Answer d is incorrect because a common name would be similar to Arnold Perez.

Question 44

Answer a is correct. The schema is the definition of all objects and their attributes. Answer b is incorrect because OUs are containers for delegation of authority. Answer c is incorrect because DNS is used for name-to–IP address mappings. Answer d is incorrect because latency is the delay that exists while directory information is updated.

Question 45

The correct answer is:

Tokyo

AD Integrated

Los Angeles

AD Integrated

London

AD Integrated

Miami

Secondary

New York

Caching

Question 46

Answer d is correct. When dealing with an unreliable connection and site replication, it is better to go with SMTP because it ignores the scheduling issues and will ensure that replication occurs regardless of the connection being available at the time necessary. Answer a is incorrect because bridgehead servers are already a requirement for intersite replication. One note: If you have a proxy server that serves as a firewall, you would have to make the proxy server your bridgehead server. Answer b is incorrect because its obvious that you don't want to combine the Singapore site into a functional one. Answer c is incorrect because IP over RPC replication is better for reliable connectivity and allows scheduling to take place properly.

Question 47

Answer c is correct. The domains cross through several sites that have been created. Therefore, the domain level wouldn't suffice because the scenario requires a site policy. Using the "Secure Server" policy on the OU would prevent lower-level clients (which cannot use IPSec) from accessing those servers, and that is not requested. Answers a, b and d are incorrect because they implement the policy in the wrong location or implement the wrong policy for this scenario.

Question 48

Answer b is correct. Password requirements can only be established at the domain level, regardless of their ability to appear as if you can change them elsewhere. Answers a, c, and d are incorrect because these policies will not affect the security for the domain.

Question 49

Answers b and c are correct. The faster the connection, the lower the cost you want to establish. The slower the connection, the higher the cost you want to establish. In this case, the South Africa–Brazil connection is faster and should get a cost of 10, whereas the South Africa–Taiwan connection is slower and should get a cost of 100.

Question 50

Answer c is correct. You can prevent a Group Policy from applying to individuals (or entire groups) by altering the permissions to Deny "Read" and "Apply Group Policy" Permissions. Answer a is incorrect because, although this will work, you don't move a group to stop a policy. Answer b is incorrect because blocking inheritance will only prevent policies from above from applying; it won't stop the policy from affecting managers. Answer d is incorrect because you cannot apply a policy directly to a group, even though its called "Group Policy."

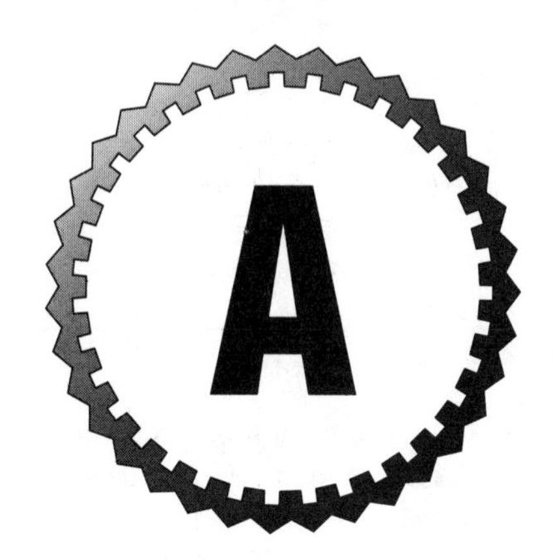

What's on the CD-ROM

This appendix is a brief rundown of what you'll find on the CD-ROM that comes with this book. For a more detailed description of the *PrepLogic Practice Tests, Preview Edition* exam simulation software, see Appendix B, "Using the *PrepLogic Practice Tests, Preview Edition* Software." In addition to the *PrepLogic Practice Tests, Preview Edition*, the CD-ROM includes the electronic version of the book in Portable Document Format (PDF), several utility and application programs, and a complete listing of test objectives and where they are covered in the book.

PrepLogic Practice Tests, Preview Edition

PrepLogic is a leading provider of certification training tools. Trusted by certification students worldwide, PrepLogic is, we believe, the best practice exam software available. In addition to providing a means of evaluating your knowledge of the Training Guide material, *PrepLogic Practice Tests, Preview Edition* features several innovations that help you to improve your mastery of the subject matter.

For example, the practice tests allow you to check your score by exam area or domain to determine which topics you need to study more. Another feature allows you to obtain immediate feedback on your responses in the form of explanations for the correct and incorrect answers.

PrepLogic Practice Tests, Preview Edition exhibits most of the full functionality of the *Premium Edition* but offers only a fraction of the total questions. To get the complete set of practice questions and exam functionality, visit PrepLogic.com and order the Premium Edition for this and other challenging exam titles.

Again, for a more detailed description of the *PrepLogic Practice Tests, Preview Edition* features, see Appendix B.

Using the *PrepLogic Practice Tests, Preview Edition* Software

This Exam Cram includes a special version of *PrepLogic Practice Tests*—a revolutionary test engine designed to give you the best in certification exam preparation. PrepLogic offers sample and practice exams for many of today's most in-demand and challenging technical certifications. This special Preview Edition is included with this book as a tool to use in assessing your knowledge of the Exam Cram material while also providing you with the experience of taking an electronic exam.

This appendix describes in detail what *PrepLogic Practice Tests, Preview Edition* is, how it works, and what it can do to help you prepare for the exam. Note that although the Preview Edition includes all the test simulation functions of the complete, retail version, it contains only a single practice test. The Premium Edition, available at PrepLogic.com, contains the complete set of challenging practice exams designed to optimize your learning experience.

Exam Simulation

One of the main functions of *PrepLogic Practice Tests, Preview Edition* is exam simulation. To prepare you to take the actual vendor certification exam, PrepLogic is designed to offer the most effective exam simulation available.

Question Quality

The questions provided in the *PrepLogic Practice Tests, Preview Edition* are written to highest standards of technical accuracy. The questions tap the content of the Training Guide chapters and help you review and assess your knowledge before you take the actual exam.

Interface Design

The *PrepLogic Practice Tests, Preview Edition* exam simulation interface provides you with the experience of taking an electronic exam. This enables you to effectively prepare for taking the actual exam by making the test experience a familiar one. Using this test simulation can help eliminate the sense of surprise or anxiety you might experience in the testing center because you will already be acquainted with computerized testing.

Effective Learning Environment

The *PrepLogic Practice Tests, Preview Edition* interface provides a learning environment that not only tests you through the computer, but also teaches the material you need to know to pass the certification exam. Each question comes with a detailed explanation of the correct answer and often provides reasons the other options are incorrect. This information helps to reinforce the knowledge you already have and also provides practical information you can us on the job.

Software Requirements

PrepLogic Practice Tests requires a computer with the following:

- Microsoft Windows 98, Windows Me, Windows NT 4.0, Windows 2000, or Windows XP
- A 166MHz or faster processor is recommended
- A minimum of 32MB of RAM
- As with any Windows application, the more memory the better your performance
- 10MB of hard drive space

Installing *PrepLogic Practice Tests, Preview Edition*

Install *PrepLogic Practice Tests, Preview Edition* by running the setup program on the *PrepLogic Practice Tests, Preview Edition* CD. Follow these instructions to install the software on your computer.

1. Insert the CD into your CD-ROM drive. The Autorun feature of Windows should launch the software. If you have Autorun disabled, click Start and select Run. Go to the root directory of the CD and select setup.exe. Click Open, and then click OK.
2. The Installation Wizard copies the *PrepLogic Practice Tests, Preview Edition* files to your hard drive; adds *PrepLogic Practice Tests, Preview Edition* to your Desktop and Program menu; and installs test engine components to the appropriate system folders.

Removing *PrepLogic Practice Tests, Preview Edition* from Your Computer

If you elect to remove the *PrepLogic Practice Tests, Preview Edition* product from your computer, an uninstall process has been included to ensure that it is removed from your system safely and completely. Follow these instructions to remove *PrepLogic Practice Tests, Preview Edition* from your computer:

1. Select Start, Settings, Control Panel.
2. Double-click the Add/Remove Programs icon.
3. You are presented with a list of software installed on your computer. Select the appropriate *PrepLogic Practice Tests, Preview Edition* title you want to remove. Click the Add/Remove button. The software is then removed from your computer.

Using *PrepLogic Practice Tests, Preview Edition*

PrepLogic is designed to be user friendly and intuitive. Because the software has a smooth learning curve, your time is maximized because you start practicing almost immediately. *PrepLogic Practice Tests, Preview Edition* has two major modes of study: Practice Test and Flash Review.

Using Practice Test mode, you can develop your test-taking abilities as well as your knowledge through the use of the Show Answer option. While you are taking the test, you can expose the answers along with a detailed explanation of why the given answers are right or wrong. This gives you the ability to better understand the material presented.

Flash Review is designed to reinforce exam topics rather than quiz you. In this mode, you will be shown a series of questions but no answer choices. Instead, you will be given a button that reveals the correct answer to the question and a full explanation for that answer.

Starting a Practice Test Mode Session

Practice Test mode enables you to control the exam experience in ways that actual certification exams do not allow:

- **Enable Show Answer Button**—Activates the Show Answer button allowing you to view the correct answer(s) and full explanation(s) for each question during the exam. When not enabled, you must wait until after your exam has been graded to view the correct answer(s) and explanation.
- **Enable Item Review Button**—Activates the Item Review button, allowing you to view your answer choices, marked questions, and to facilitate navigation between questions.
- **Randomize Choices**—Randomize answer choices from one exam session to the next. Makes memorizing question choices more difficult therefore keeping questions fresh and challenging longer.

To begin studying in Practice Test mode, click the Practice Test radio button from the main exam customization screen. This enables the options detailed in the preceding list.

To your left, you are presented with the option of selecting the preconfigured Practice Test or creating your own Custom Test. The preconfigured test has a fixed time limit and number of questions. Custom Tests allow you to configure the time limit and the number of questions in your exam.

The Preview Edition included with this book includes a single preconfigured Practice Test. Get the compete set of challenging PrepLogic Practice Tests at PrepLogic.com and make certain you're ready for the big exam.

Click the Begin Exam button to begin your exam.

Starting a Flash Review Mode Session

Flash Review mode provides you with an easy way to reinforce topics covered in the practice questions. To begin studying in Flash Review mode, click the Flash Review radio button from the main exam customization screen. Select either the preconfigured Practice Test or create your own Custom Test.

Click the Best Exam button to begin your Flash Review of the exam questions.

Standard *PrepLogic Practice Tests, Preview Edition* Options

The following list describes the function of each of the buttons you see. Depending on the options, some of the buttons will be grayed out and inaccessible or missing completely. Buttons that are appropriate are active. The buttons are as follows:

- **Exhibit**—This button is visible if an exhibit is provided to support the question. An exhibit is an image that provides supplemental information necessary to answer the question.
- **Item Review**—This button leaves the question window and opens the Item Review screen. From this screen you will see all questions, your answers, and your marked items. You will also see correct answers listed here when appropriate.
- **Show Answer**—This option displays the correct answer with an explanation of why it is correct. If you select this option, the current question is not scored.
- **Mark Item**—Check this box to tag a question you need to review further. You can view and navigate your Marked Items by clicking the Item Review button (if enabled). When grading your exam, you will be notified if you have marked items remaining.
- **Previous Item**—View the previous question.
- **Next Item**—View the next question.
- **Grade Exam**—When you have completed your exam, click to end your exam and view your detailed score report. If you have unanswered or marked items remaining you will be asked if you would like to continue taking your exam or view your exam report.

Time Remaining

If the test is timed, the time remaining is displayed on the upper-right corner of the application screen. It counts down minutes and seconds remaining to complete the test. If you run out of time, you will be asked if you want to continue taking the test or if you want to end your exam.

Your Examination Score Report

The Examination Score Report screen appears when the Practice Test mode ends—as the result of time expiration, completion of all questions, or your decision to terminate early.

This screen provides you with a graphical display of your test score with a breakdown of scores by topic domain. The graphical display at the top of the screen compares your overall score with the PrepLogic Exam Competency Score.

The PrepLogic Exam Competency Score reflects the level of subject competency required to pass this vendor's exam. Although this score does not directly translate to a passing score, consistently matching or exceeding this score does suggest you possess the knowledge to pass the actual vendor exam.

Review Your Exam

From Your Score Report screen, you can review the exam that you just completed by clicking on the View Items button. Navigate through the items, viewing the questions, your answers, the correct answers, and the explanations for those questions. You can return to your score report by clicking the View Items button.

Get More Exams

Each *PrepLogic Practice Tests, Preview Edition* that accompanies your training guide contains a single PrepLogic Practice Test. Certification students worldwide trust PrepLogic Practice Tests to help them pass their IT certification exams the first time. Purchase the Premium Edition of *PrepLogic Practice Tests* and get the entire set of all new challenging Practice Tests for this exam. PrepLogic Practice Tests—Because You Want to Pass the First Time.

Contacting PrepLogic

If you would like to contact PrepLogic for any reason including information about our extensive line of certification practice tests, we invite you to do so. Please contact us online at `www.preplogic.com`.

Customer Service

If you have a damaged product and need a replacement or refund, please call the following phone number:

800-858-7674

Product Suggestions and Comments

We value your input! Please email your suggestions and comments to the following address:

`feedback@preplogic.com`

License Agreement

YOU MUST AGREE TO THE TERMS AND CONDITIONS OUTLINED IN THE END USER LICENSE AGREEMENT ("EULA") PRESENTED TO YOU DURING THE INSTALLATION PROCESS. IF YOU DO NOT AGREE TO THESE TERMS, DO NOT INSTALL THE SOFTWARE.

Glossary

access control entry (ACE)
An entry within an access control list that grants or denies permissions to users or groups for a given resource.

access control list (ACL)
Contains a set of access control entries that define an object's permission settings. ACLs enable administrators to explicitly control access to resources.

Active Directory (AD)
The Windows 2000 directory service that replaces the antiquated Windows NT domain structure. Active Directory forms the basis for centralized network management on Windows 2000 networks, providing a hierarchical view of network resources.

Active Directory Service Interfaces (ADSI)
A directory service model implemented as a set of COM interfaces. ADSI allows Windows applications to access Active Directory, often through ActiveX interfaces such as VBScript.

Active Directory Users and Computers
The primary systems administrator utility for managing users, groups, and computers in a Windows 2000 domain, implemented as an MMC snap-in.

Address (A) record
The most basic type of resource record on a DNS server. Every client that registers with DNS has an associated A record that maps its name to its IP address.

assigned applications
Through the Software Installation utility in Group Policy, administrators can assign applications to users. Assigned applications are always available to the user, even if the user attempts to uninstall them.

asynchronous processing
Asynchronous processing occurs when one task waits until another is finished before beginning. This is typically associated with scripts, such as a user logon script not running before the computer startup script has completed. This is the default behavior in Windows 2000.

attribute
The basic unit of an object, an attribute is a single property that through its values defines the object. For example, an attribute of a standard user account is the account name.

auditing
A security process that tracks the usage of selected network resources, typically storing the results in a log file.

authentication
The process by which a user's logon credentials are validated by a server so that access to a network resource can be granted or denied.

AXFR
A DNS term that refers to a request from a primary server to one or more secondary servers for a full zone transfer.

backup domain controller (BDC)
A Windows NT 3.*x* or 4.0 server that contains a backup copy of the domain security accounts manager (user account and security information). BDCs take the load off of the primary domain controller by servicing logon requests. Periodic synchronizing ensures that data between the PDC and BDCs remains consistent.

baseline
A term associated with performance monitoring, a *baseline* is the initial result of monitoring by which all future results are measured.

bridgehead server
The contact point for the exchange of directory information between Active Directory sites.

caching
The process by which name-resolution query results are stored in order to speed up future name resolution for the same destinations.

checkpoint file
Indicates the location of the last information successfully written from the transaction logs to the database. In a data-recovery scenario, the checkpoint file indicates where the recovery or replaying of data should begin.

circular logging
When a log file fills up, it is overwritten with new data rather than having a new log file created. This conserves disk space but can result in data loss in a disaster-recovery scenario.

Computer Configuration
The portion of a Group Policy Object that allows for computer policies to be configured and applied.

container
An object in Active Directory that is capable of holding other objects. An example of a container would be the `Users` folder in Active Directory Users and Computers.

convergence
The process of stabilization after network changes occur. Often associated with routing or replication, convergence ensures each router or server contains consistent information.

counters
The metrics that are used in performance monitoring, counters are what you are actually monitoring. An example of a counter for a CPU object would be %Processing Time.

CScript
The command-line executable for Windows Script Host.

DCPROMO
The command-line utility used to promote a Windows 2000 server to a domain controller.

delegation
The process of offloading the responsibility for a given task or set or tasks to another user or group. Delegation in Windows 2000 usually involves granting permission to someone else to perform a specific administrative task such as creating computer accounts.

directory
A database that contains any number of different types of data. In Windows 2000, the Active Directory contains information about objects in the domain, such as computers, users, groups, and printers.

Directory Service (DS)
Provides the methods of storing directory data and making that data available to other directory objects.

Directory System Agent (DSA)
Makes data within Active Directory accessible to applications that want it, acting as a liaison between the directory database and the applications.

disk quota
An administrative limit set on the server storage space that can be used by any particular user.

distinguished name

The name that uniquely identifies an object, using the relative distinguished name, domain name, and the container holding the object. An example would be `CN=WWillis,CN=Inside-Corner,CN=COM`. This refers to the WWillis user account in the `inside-corner.com` domain.

Distributed File System (Dfs)

A Windows 2000 service that allows resources from multiple server locations to be presented through Active Directory as a contiguous set of files and folders, resulting in more ease of use of network resources for users.

distribution point

The network shared location for software to be stored for the purpose of making it available for installation to users.

domain

A collection of Windows 2000 computers, users, and groups that share a common directory database. Domains are defined by an administrator.

domain controller (DC)

A server that is capable of performing authentication. In Windows 2000, a domain controller holds a copy of the Active Directory database.

domain local group

A domain local group can contain other domain local groups from its own domain, as well as global groups from any domain in the forest. Domain local groups can be used to assign permissions for resources located in the same domain as the group.

Domain Name System (DNS)

A hierarchical name-resolution system that resolves host names into IP addresses, and vice versa.

Dynamic Domain Name System (DDNS)

An extension of DNS that allows Windows 2000 Professional systems to automatically register their A records with DNS at the time they obtain an IP address from a DHCP server.

Dynamic Host Configuration Protocol (DHCP)

A service that allows an administrator to specify a range of valid IP addresses to be used on a network, as well as exceptions. These addresses are automatically given out to computers configured to use DHCP as they boot up on the network, thus saving the administrator from having to configure static IP addresses on each individual network device.

Encrypting File System (EFS)

A Windows 2000 feature that allows files and folders to be encrypted on NTFS partitions, protecting them from being able to be read by other people.

Extensible Storage Engine (ESE)

The Active Directory database engine, ESE is an improved version of the older Jet database technology.

File Replication Service (FRS)

A service that provides multimaster replication between specified domain controllers within an Active Directory tree.

File Transfer Protocol (FTP)

A standard TCP/IP utility that allows for the transfer of files from an FTP server to a machine running the FTP client.

firewall

A hardware and software security system that functions to limit access to network resources across subnets. Typically a firewall is used between a private network and the Internet to prevent outsiders from accessing the private network and limiting what Internet services users of the private network can access.

flat namespace

Namespace that cannot be partitioned to produce additional domains. Windows NT 4.0 and earlier domains were examples of flat namespaces, as opposed to the Windows 2000 hierarchical namespace.

Folder Redirection

A Windows 2000 feature that allows special folders such as My Documents on local Windows 2000 Professional system hard drives to be redirected to a shared network location.

forest

A grouping of Active Directory trees that have a trust relationship between them. Forests can consist of a noncontiguous namespace and unlike domains and trees do not have to be given a specific name.

forward lookup query

A DNS name resolution process by which a host name is resolved to an IP address.

fully qualified domain name (FQDN)

A DNS domain name that unambiguously describes the location of the host within a domain tree. An example of an FQDN would be the computer `www.inside-corner.com`.

Global Catalog (GC)

Contains a partial replica of every Windows 2000 domain within the Active Directory, enabling users to find any object in the directory. The partial replica contains the most commonly used attributes of an object, as well as information on how to locate a complete replica elsewhere in the directory if needed.

Global Catalog server

The Windows 2000 server that holds the Global Catalog for the forest.

global group
A global group can contain users from the same domain as the group, and global groups can be added to domain local groups in order to control access to network resources.

globally unique identifier (GUID)
A hexadecimal number supplied by the manufacturer of a product that uniquely identifies the hardware or software. A GUID is in the form of eight characters, followed by three sets of four characters, followed by 12 characters. For example, {15DEF489-AE24-10BF-C11A-00BB844CE637} is a valid format for a GUID (braces included).

Group Policy
The Windows 2000 feature that allows for policy creation that affects domain users and computers. Policies can be anything from desktop settings to application assignment to security settings and more.

Group Policy Editor
The MMC snap-in that is used to modify the settings of a Group Policy Object.

Group Policy Object (GPO)
A collection of policies that apply to a specific target, such as the domain itself (Default Domain Policy) or an OU. GPOs are modified through the Group Policy Editor to define policy settings.

hierarchical namespace
A namespace, such as with DNS, that can be partitioned out in the form of a tree. This allows great flexibility in using a domain name because any number of subdomains can be created under a parent domain.

host ID
The portion of an IP address that defines the host, as determined by the subnet mask. For example, if a host has an IP address of 192.168.1.20 and a subnet mask of 255.255.255.0, the host ID would be 20.

HOSTS
A static file that was the primary means for TCP/IP name resolution prior to DNS, the HOSTS file contains a list of host-to–IP address mappings and had to exist on every host computer that participates on a network. It has been largely replaced by the more manageable DNS service on all but the smallest of networks.

image
The installation source for Windows 2000 Professional and any optional applications created through the RIS RIPrep utility.

inheritance
The process by which an object obtains settings information from a parent object.

IntelliMirror
A collection of Windows 2000 technologies that provide for a comprehensive change and control management system.

IXFR
A DNS process by which a primary DNS server requests an incremental zone transfer from one or more secondary servers.

JavaScript (JScript)
An active scripting language that can be used in Windows 2000 with the Windows Script Host to run more complicated scripts than what has been available in the past through batch files.

Just-In-Time (JIT)
Technology that allows software features to be updated at the time they are accessed. Whereas in the past missing application features would need to be manually installed, JIT technology allows the features to be installed on the fly as they are accessed, with no other intervention required.

Kerberos
An Internet standard security protocol that has largely replaced the older LAN Manager user-authentication mechanism from earlier Windows NT versions.

Knowledge Consistency Checker (KCC)
A Windows 2000 service that functions to ensure consistent database information is kept across all domain controllers. It attempts to ensure that replication can always take place.

latency
The delay that occurs in replication from the time a change is made to one replica and that change is applied to all other replicas in the directory.

Lightweight Directory Access Protocol (LDAP)
The Windows 2000 protocol that allows access to Active Directory. LDAP is an Internet standard for accessing directory services.

LMHOSTS
A static file used for NetBIOS name resolution. Similar to a HOSTS file, LMHOSTS needed to exist on every individual computer on a network, making it increasingly difficult to keep up to date as the size of networks grew. LMHOSTS was essentially replaced by WINS on Windows networks prior to Windows 2000.

local area network (LAN)
A network where all hosts are connected over fast connections (4MBps or greater for Token Ring; 10MBps or better for Ethernet).

Local Group Policy Objects
Objects that exist on the local Windows 2000 system and take precedence over site-, domain-, and OU-applied GPOs.

Mail Exchange (MX) record

A DNS record that defines an email server.

Microsoft Management Console (MMC)

An extensible management framework that provides a common look and feel to all Windows 2000 utilities.

mixed mode

Allows Windows NT 4.0 domain controllers to exist and function within a Windows 2000 domain. This is the default setting when Active Directory is installed, although it can be changed to native mode.

multimaster replication

A replication model in which any domain controller will replicate data to any other domain controller. This is the default behavior in Windows 2000. It contrasts with the single-master replication model of Windows NT 4.0, in which a PDC contained the master copy of everything and BDCs contained backup copies.

name resolution

The process of resolving a host name into a format that can be understood by computers. This is typically an IP address but could also be a MAC address on non-TCP/IP networks.

namespace

A collection of resources that have been defined using some common name. A DNS namespace is hierarchical and can be partitioned, whereas Windows NT 4.0 and earlier used a flat namespace.

native mode

The mode in which all domain controllers in a domain have been upgraded to Windows 2000 and there are no longer any NT 4.0 domain controllers. An administrator explicitly puts Active Directory into native mode, at which time it cannot be returned to mixed mode without removing and reinstalling Active Directory.

NetBIOS

An application programming interface (API) used on Windows NT 4.0 and earlier networks by services requesting and providing name resolution and network data management.

network ID

The portion of an IP address that defines the network, as determined by the subnet mask. For example, if a host has an IP address of 192.168.1.20 and a subnet mask of 255.255.255.0, the network ID would be 192.168.1.

network operating system (NOS)

A generic term that applies to any operating system with built-in networking capabilities. All Windows operating systems beginning with Windows 95 have been true network operating systems.

nonlocal Group Policy Objects

GPOs that are stored in Active Directory rather than on the local machine. These can be site-, domain-, or OU-level GPOs.

NSLOOKUP

A TCP/IP utility used in troubleshooting DNS name-resolution problems.

NTFS

The Windows NT/2000 file system that supports a much more robust feature set than either FAT16 or FAT32 (which is used on Windows 9*X*). It is recommended to use NTFS whenever possible on Windows 2000 systems.

object

A distinct entity represented by a series of attributes within Active Directory. An object can be a user, computer, folder, file, printer, and so on.

object identifier

A number that uniquely identifies an object class or attribute. In the United States, the American National Standards Institute (ANSI) issues object identifiers, which take the form of an x.x.x.x dotted decimal format. Microsoft, for example, was issued the root object identifier of 1.2.840.113556, from which it can create further sub-object identifiers.

Operations Master

A Windows 2000 domain controller that has been assigned one or more of the special Active Directory domain roles, such as Schema Master, Domain Naming Master, PDC Emulator Master, Infrastructure Master, and Relative ID Master.

Organizational Unit (OU)

An Active Directory container object that allows an administrator to logically group users, groups, computers, and other OUs into administrative units.

package

A collection of software compiled into a distributable form, such as a Windows Installer (`.msi`) package created with WinInstall.

parent-child trust relationship

The relationship whereby a child object trusts its parent object, and a parent object is trusted by all child objects under it. Active Directory automatically creates two-way trust relationships between parent and child objects.

patching

The process of modifying or updating software packages.

PING

A TCP/IP utility that tests for basic connectivity between the client machine running PING and any other TCP/IP host.

policy

Settings and rules that are applied to users or computers, usually Group Policy in Windows 2000 and System Policy in Windows NT 4.0.

preboot execution environment (PXE)

A set of industry standards that allow for network commands to be run on a client computer before it has booted up in a traditional manner. PXE is used with RIS in Windows 2000 to install Windows 2000 Professional images on client computers.

primary domain controller (PDC)

A Windows NT 4.0 and earlier server that contains the master copy of the domain database. PDCs authenticate user logon requests and track security-related changes within the domain.

Public Key Infrastructure (PKI)

Industry standard technology that allows for the establishment of secure communication between hosts based on a public key/private key or certificate-based system.

published applications

Through the Software Installation utility in Group Policy, administrators can publish applications to users. Published applications appear in Add/Remove Programs and can be optionally installed by the user.

Registry

A data repository on each computer that contains information about that computer's configuration. The Registry is organized into a hierarchical tree and is made up of hives, keys, and values.

relative distinguished name (RDN)

The part of a DNS name that defines the host. For example, in the FQDN `www.insidecorner.com`, www is the relative distinguished name.

Remote Installation Services (RIS)

A Windows 2000 optional component that allows for the remote installation of Windows 2000 Professional on to compatible client computers.

replica

A copy of any given Active Directory object. Each copy of an object stored on multiple domain controllers is a replica.

replication

The process of copying data from one Windows 2000 domain controller to another. Replication is a process managed by an administrator and typically occurs automatically whenever changes are made to a replica of an object.

Request for Comments (RFCs)

Official documents that specify Internet standards for the TCP/IP protocol.

resource records

Standard database record types used in DNS zone database files. Common types of resource records include Address (A), Mail Exchanger (MX), Start of Authority (SOA), and Name Server (NS), among others.

return on investment (ROI)
A business term that seeks to determine the amount of financial gain that occurs as a result of a certain expenditure. Many IT personnel today are faced with the prospect of justifying IT expenses in terms of ROI.

reverse lookup query
A DNS name-resolution process by which an IP address is resolved to a host name.

root server
A DNS server that is authoritative for the root zone of a namespace.

router
A dedicated network hardware appliance or server running routing software and multiple network cards. Routers join dissimilar network topologies (such as Ethernet to Frame Relay) or simply segment networks into multiple subnets.

scalability
Measurement (often subjective) of how well a resource such as a server can expand to accommodate growing needs.

schema
In Active Directory, a schema is a description of object classes and the attributes that the object classes must possess and can possess.

Schema Master
The Windows 2000 domain controller that has been assigned the Operations Master role to control all schema updates within a forest.

security identifier (SID)
A number that uniquely identifies a user, group, or computer account. Every account is issued when created, and if the account is later deleted and re-created with the same name, it will have a different SID. Once an SID is used in a domain, it can never be used again.

security templates
Collections of standard settings that can be applied administratively to give a consistent level of security to a system.

single-instance store (SIS)
A RIS component that combines duplicate files to reduce storage requirements on the RIS server.

single-master operations
Certain Active Directory operations that are only allowed to occur in one place at any given time (as opposed to being allowed to occur in multiple locations simultaneously). Examples of single-master operations include schema modifications, PDC elections, and infrastructure changes.

site
A well-connected TCP/IP subnet.

site link
A connection between sites, a site link is used to join multiple locations together.

slow link

A connection between sites that is not fast enough to provide full functionality in an acceptable timeframe. Site connections below 512KBps are defined as slow links in Windows 2000.

snap-in

A component that can be added or removed from an MMC console to provide specific functionality. The Windows 2000 administrative tools are implemented as snap-ins.

Software Installation

A Group Policy component that allows administrators to optionally assign or publish applications to be available to users and computers.

Start of Authority (SOA) record

The first record created on a DNS server, the SOA record defines the starting point for a zone's authority.

static IP address

Also called a *static address*, this is where a network device (such as a server) is manually configured with an IP address that doesn't change rather than obtaining an address automatically from a DHCP server.

store

Implemented using the Extensible Storage Engine, a *store* is the physical storage of each Active Directory replica.

subnet

A collection of hosts on a TCP/IP network that are not separated by any routers. A basic corporate LAN with one location would be referred to as a *subnet* when it is connected by a router to another network such as that of an Internet service provider.

subnet mask

Defines where the network ID ends and the host ID begins in an IP address. Subnet masks can result in very basic to very complex network configurations, depending on their value.

synchronous processing

Synchronous processing occurs when one task does not wait for another to complete before it begins. Rather, the two run concurrently. This is typically associated with scripts in Windows 2000, such as a user logon script running without waiting for the computer startup script to finish.

system policies

System policies are Windows NT 4.0 Registry-based policy settings, which have largely been replaced in Windows 2000 by Group Policy. System policies can still be created using `poledit.exe`, however, for backward compatibility with non–Windows 2000 clients.

Systems Management Server (SMS)

A product in Microsoft's BackOffice server line that provides more extensive software distribution, metering, inventorying, and auditing than what is capable strictly through IntelliMirror.

TCP/IP

TCP/IP (Transmission Control Protocol/Internet Protocol) is the standard protocol for communicating on the Internet and is the default protocol in Windows 2000.

Time To Live (TTL)

The amount of time a packet destined for a host will exist before it is deleted from the network. TTLs are used to prevent networks from becoming congested with packages that cannot reach their destinations.

total cost of ownership (TCO)

A change and control management concept that many IT professionals are being forced to become more aware of. TCO refers to the combined hard and soft costs (initial price and support costs) of owning a given resource.

transitive trust

An automatically created trust in Windows 2000 that exists between domain trees within a forest and domains within a tree. Transitive trusts are two-way trust relationships.

tree

A collection of Windows 2000 domains that are connected through transitive trusts and share a common Global Catalog and schema. Domains within a tree must form a contiguous namespace.

universal group

A new Windows 2000 security group that can be used anywhere within a domain tree or forest, the only caveat being that universal groups can only be used when Windows 2000 has been converted to native mode.

Update Sequence Number

A 64-bit number that keeps track of changes as they are written to copies of the Active Directory. As changes are made, this number increments by one.

user configuration

The portion of a Group Policy Object that allows for user policy settings to be configured and applied.

user profile

Contains settings that define the user environment, typically applied when the user logs on to the system.

Visual Basic Script (VBS)

An active scripting language that can be used in Windows 2000 with the Windows Script Host to run more complicated scripts than what has been available in the past through batch files. VBScript has come into the news frequently as of late due to its use in creating email viruses.

well-connected
A network that contains only fast connections between domains and hosts. The definition of "fast" is somewhat subjective and may vary from organization to organization.

wide area network (WAN)
Multiple networks connected by slow connections between routers. WAN connections are typically 1.5MBps or less.

Windows Internet Naming System (WINS)
A dynamic name resolution system that resolves NetBIOS names to IP addresses on Windows TCP/IP networks. With Windows 2000, WINS is being phased out in favor of DNS.

Windows Management Instrumentation (WMI)
A Windows 2000 management infrastructure for monitoring and controlling system resources.

Windows Script Host
Enables the running of VBScript or JavaScript scripts natively on a Windows system, offering increased power and flexibility over traditional batch files.

WinInstall
An optional utility that ships with Windows 2000 Server and can be used to create Windows Installer packages.

WScript
The Windows interface to Windows Script Host.

X.500
A set of standards developed by the International Standards Organization (ISO) that define distributed directory services.

zone
A subtree of the DNS database that can be managed as a single, separate entity from the rest of the DNS namespace.

zone file
The DNS database, traditionally stored as a text file on the primary server and replicated to secondary servers. With Windows 2000, the zone file can be optionally integrated into Active Directory.

zone transfer
The DNS process by which zone information is replicated between primary and secondary servers.

Index

A

B

C

D

H-I

J-K

L

M

N

O

P

Q-R

T

U

V

W-Z